Eppa Hunton, William Freeman Vilas

Speeches of Hon. Eppa Hunton, of Virginia, and Hon. William F. Vilas, of Wisconsin on Bill to establish the University of the United States, delivered in the Senate of the United States, December 13, 1894

Eppa Hunton, William Freeman Vilas

Speeches of Hon. Eppa Hunton, of Virginia, and Hon. William F. Vilas, of Wisconsin on Bill to establish the University of the United States, delivered in the Senate of the United States, December 13, 1894

ISBN/EAN: 9783337157333

Printed in Europe, USA, Canada, Australia, Japan

Cover: Foto ©ninafisch / pixelio.de

More available books at **www.hansebooks.com**

SPEECHES

OF

Hon. EPPA HUNTON, of Virginia,

AND

Hon. WILLIAM F. VILAS, of Wisconsin,

ON

BILL (S. NO. 1708) TO ESTABLISH THE UNIVERSITY
OF THE UNITED STATES,

DELIVERED IN THE

SENATE OF THE UNITED STATES,

DECEMBER 13, 1894.

WASHINGTON.
1894.

SPEECH
OF
HON. EPPA HUNTON.

The Senate having under consideration the bill (S. 1708) to establish a national university—

Mr. HUNTON said:

Mr PRESIDENT: I gave notice that to-day immediately after the routine business of the morning hour I would call up the bill (S. 1708) to establish a national university. I desire now to call up the bill.

The PRESIDENT pro tempore. Is there objection? The Chair hears none, and the bill is before the Senate as in Committee of the Whole. Does the Senator from Virginia desire to have the bill read at length?

Mr. HUNTON. I do not desire to have the bill read at length unless some Senator calls for its reading.

Mr. CULLOM. The bill ought to be read before we pass it.

Mr. HUNTON. Very well; then let the bill be read.

Mr. CULLOM. If the Senator from Virginia simply desires to address the Senate upon the bill called up, I do not ask for its reading. I supposed the Senator had called up the bill to put it on its passage.

Mr. HUNTON. That is my desire.

The PRESIDENT pro tempore. The bill will be read at length.

The Secretary read the bill.

Mr. HALE. Mr. President, I do not think any member of the Senate supposed, when the request was made for unanimous consent to take up this most important bill, that it was to be attempted to push it through this morning. I supposed that the Senator expected to make a speech on the subject, and so made no objection. It is very evident, however, that this measure can not pass in the morning hour, and if it is not too late, I shall object to its consideration, in order that it may go to the Calendar under Rule IX, where it can be debated in some way commensurate with its importance.

Mr. HUNTON. I gave notice that I should call up the bill after the routine business of the morning hour to-day, and I take it that it is too late now to object to taking up the bill, after it has been taken up without objection and the bill read. I hope the Senator will not object.

Mr. HALE. Does the Senator think that he can pass this most important bill in the morning hour, involving very great changes and departures from any previous course of the Government?

Mr. HUNTON. Probably not in this morning hour.

Mr. HALE. Well, I suppose the Senator is aware that if this morning hour is consumed in any way by debate the bill will go over and will not come up again without unanimous consent or a vote of the Senate.

Mr. HUNTON. I understand that, and I propose to give notice that I shall move to take up the bill to-morrow morning after the routine business.

Mr. HALE. I have no objection to the bill going over in that way, with the notice from the Senator that to-morrow morning, after the routine morning business, he will move to proceed to its consideration.

Mr. HUNTON. Unless finished to-day.

The PRESIDENT pro tempore. The bill is before the Senate as in Committee of the Whole, and the Senator from Virginia [Mr. HUNTON] is entitled to the floor.

Mr. HUNTON. Mr. President, the bill under consideration involves the question of education, and this statement of itself should commend it to the careful consideration of every Senator on the floor.

All governments are deeply interested in the intelligence of their citizens. This is especially true of our Government. It is a government "of the people, by the people, and for the people." No such government can reach its highest degree of excellence without intelligence of the people.

Much, very much has been done by the States and private enterprise to afford opportunities for common-school instruction. In each State there has been instituted a common-school system under which every person can, without cost to himself, receive its inestimable benefits. There is no excuse now for absolute illiteracy, and it is an encouraging sign of the times that the number of those who can not read or write is year by year diminishing.

In nearly all of the States, either by State legislation or by private enterprise, schools for higher education have also been established. Our country is well provided with colleges and State universities, where education of a much higher order can be obtained, and these are doing a great work in arousing the youth of the country to the necessity for still higher culture. Some of these deserve especial mention and commendation. I mention some in my own State.

William and Mary, at which many of the brightest intellects of this country in its early history were developed and where the love of liberty was carefully instilled into their minds. Patrick Henry, Thomas Jefferson, James Madison, Richard Henry Lee, and many others, the patriots and leaders of the Revolution and the fathers of the Constitution, were alumni of this college, the oldest and most venerated in this country.

The University of Virginia, founded by Thomas Jefferson, has ranked and does to-day rank with the best educational institutions of the country. Besides these are many others, and among them Washington and Lee University, the Virginia Military Institute, the Richmond College, Randolph-Macon College, and Hampden-Sydney College.

All of these and many others in and out of the State of Virginia offer to the aspiring young man the opportunity for high educational improvement. It is very gratifying to know that most of these institutions are well patronized and are doing a great work in the higher departments of educational development.

This city of Washington is fully abreast with the improvement in schools. It has a splendid free-school system. Every minor, whatever may be his conditon or color, can here obtain without price a good common-school education. Illiteracy in the city of Washington is without excuse. Nor have the higher schools been neglected here. For we find colleges of honorable rank and the beginning of universities that promise yet more. And the same is true of many other cities.

In the United States to-day, from the kindergarten to the university, whether local and independent, denominational or State, each Commonwealth is well provided with schools to fit the young man for the ordinary duties of life. But still there is an aspiration for something higher than any of these afford. The very gratification of the thirst for knowledge which these afford satisfies the ambitious and aspiring young man that there are many fields of useful knowledge still unexplored; and to meet this demand for still higher attainments, as well as for induction into the work of research and investigation, he is constrained to go to other and distant lands.

It is a fact, not willingly admitted, that European countries are a long way ahead of us in the facilities they furnish for the highest intellectual training. France, Italy, Spain, Germany, and England have each spent many millions in money to carry to the highest plane their educational institutions. This is an example well worthy of imitation. It can not be right that this country, by neglect to provide the very best facilities, should compel her sons to seek them in foreign lands.

It is eminently proper that our young men should be educated here, under the influence of our republican institutions. Abroad in early life they are apt to absorb opinions not in accord with the genius of our Government. Their teachers most likely are imbued with the love of hereditary monarchy as the best form of government, and their students bring home with them views out of harmony with a representative democracy; and yet this highest plane of culture must be reached, or we must in many respects continue to lag behind the more provident European countries. Nor is this sufficient. It is not enough that our youth should stand abreast with the world in the now actually known; they must, in all the preeminence of that word, become investigators into the larger future of human knowledge. How important, for example, it is for the physician to learn the improvements in medicine and surgery, and how still more important it is that his education should fit him to follow up and extend these improvements, till medicine, like surgery, shall become an exact science. How important that the fields of present knowledge generally should be so exhausted as to lead the explorer to enter on other and hitherto unknown fields.

How important to have at least one institution where better equipped teachers and professors may be prepared for our colleges and local universities, thus preparing them to render a better service to their students, and so on to all the lower rounds. In this way the facilities for this higher education will be multiplied and the standard be continuously raised.

But above all other considerations how important it is to have at least one institution with students from every State where the science of government is taught, and by whom the knowledge thus acquired may be diffused among the people. The questions of tariff and other questions of finance have divided the people of this country from the beginning. The people select their Representatives by whom these questions are to be decided. In theory, at least, the people settle them. How important, then, is it that the people should be helped to understand these great questions; and how much light would be shed upon them by sending forth every year men of talent, who have devoted their time to the study of these questions, not as partisans but as students, anxious to arrive at the very right of the case and to determine, without regard to party, what policy should be adopted by our Government.

How important to settle these and other great questions in such a manner that a radical change may not take place with every change in the administration of our Government. We know that when great changes in the governmental policy of the country are agitated a stagnation of business ensues; factories are idle, the monetary system of the country is deranged, failures multiply, and general distress prevails.

It may be that this country will always be divided into parties taking views radically different on these great questions. It may be that it is best for the country that there shall ever be two great parties, but it is certainly to the public interest that these questions shall be finally settled. Who can estimate the value of such a settlement if it had been made long ago?

I do not maintain that a great national university, with a department devoted especially to the study and teaching of finance, would have secured this. But I do maintain that such an institution, where partisan politics are carefully excluded, and the exact truth carefully sought without prejudice, would tend more than anything else to enlighten the people and bring them to a harmonious conclusion, which would be reflected by their representatives in both branches of the National Legislature.

These are some of the reasons that have brought me to the conclusion that a national university in this city is one of the necessities of the age.

But the founding of a national university in which not only education in all the higher departments may be obtained but where the amplest facilities for the work of research and investigation shall also be furnished—a university located right here in the Federal city of Washington—is no new idea. It is not now developed by the growing and overshadowing importance of our Government, by the wealth of the country, or the just pride our people take in the American institutions our fathers bequeathed to us.

It is an idea older than our Government and antedates the successful termination of our struggle for liberty and independence.

The idea of a national university originated with Gen. George Washington, the wisest and best of men, the patriot, hero, and leader of the Revolution, the leader in the formation of our Government, and the first President of the United States. He always had the subject of this university at heart, and never failed to press its importance on the country on all suitable occasions. We should show our appreciation of the high character of Washington for wisdom, foresight, and patriotism by carrying into effect his favorite idea of a national university, from which he believed so many blessings would flow to the Government he had in a great degree created and the people he loved so well.

Samuel Blodget, afterward author of the first formal American work on political economy, in the presence of General Washington, General Greene, and Maj. William Blodget, in Washington's military camp at Cambridge, in October, 1775, said in answer to remarks upon the damage the militia were doing to the colleges in which they were quartered:

> Well, to make amends for these injuries, I hope after our war we shall erect a noble national university, at which the youth of all the world may be proud to receive instructions.

General Washington, in response to the foregoing, replied:

> Young man, you are a prophet, inspired to speak what I am confident will one day be realized.

Yet more memorable was the remark of Washington after the Revolutionary war, the permanent location of the national capital, and a most careful consideration of the university interest, to wit:

> While the work of establishing a national university may be properly deferred until Congress is comfortably accommodated and the city has so far grown as to be prepared for it, the enterprise must not be forgotten; and I trust that I have not omitted to take such measures as will at all events secure the entire object in time.

In his letter to the commissioner of the District of Columbia of January 28, 1795, Washington says:

> A plan for the establishment of a university in the Federal city has frequently been the subject of conversation. * * *
>
> It has always been a source of serious reflection and sincere regret with me that the youth of the United States should be sent to foreign countries for the purpose of education. Although there are doubtless many, under these circumstances, who escape the danger of contracting principles unfavorable to republican government, yet we ought to deprecate the hazard attending ardent and susceptible minds from being too strongly and too easily prepossessed in favor of other political systems before they are capable of appreciating their own.
>
> For this reason I have greatly wished to see a plan adopted by which the arts, sciences, and belles-lettres could be taught in their fullest extent, thereby embracing all the advantages of European tuition with the means of acquiring the liberal knowledge which is necessary to qualify our citizens for the exigencies of public as well as private life, and (which with me is a consideration of great magnitude) by assembling the youth from the different parts of this rising Republic, contributing from their intercourse an interchange of information to the removal of prejudices which might perhaps sometimes arise from local circumstances.
>
> The Federal city, from its centrality and the advantages which in other respects it must have over any other place in the United States, ought to be preferred as a proper site for such a university. And if a plan can be adopted upon a scale as extensive as I have described, and the execution of it should commence under favorable auspices in a reasonable time with a fair prospect of success, I will grant in perpetuity fifty shares in the navigation of the Potomac River toward the endowment of it.
>
> What annuity will arise from these shares when the navigation is in full operation can at this time be only conjectured, and those who are acquainted with it can form as good a judgment as myself.
>
> As the design of this university has assumed no form with which I am acquainted, and as I am equally ignorant who the persons are who have taken or are disposed to take the maturing of the plan upon themselves, I have been at a loss to whom I should make the communication of my intentions. If the commissioners of the Federal city have any particular agency in bringing the matter forward, then the information which I now give to them is in proper course. If, on the other hand, they have no more to do in it than others who may be desirous of seeing so important a measure carried into effect, they will be so good as to excuse my using them as the medium for disclosing these my intentions; because it appears necessary that the funds for the establishment and support of the institution should be known to the promoters of it, and I see no mode more eligible for announcing my purpose. For these reasons I give you the trouble of this address, and the assurance of being, etc.

In his letter to Governor Brooke, of Virginia, of March 16, 1795, he repeats his indorsement of a national university, as follows:

> It is with indescribable regret that I have seen the youth of the United States migrating to foreign countries in order to acquire the higher branches of erudition and to obtain a knowledge of the sciences. Although it would be injustice to many to pronounce the certainty of their imbibing maxims

not congenial to republicanism, it must nevertheless be admitted that a serious danger is encountered by sending abroad among other political systems those who have not well learned the value of their own.

The time is therefore come when a plan of universal education ought to be adopted in the United States. Not only do the exigencies of public and private life demand it, but if it should ever be apprehended that prejudice would be entertained in one part of the Union against the other, an efficacious remedy will be to assemble the youth of every part under such circumstances as will, by freedom of intercourse and collision of sentiment, give to their minds the direction of truth, philanthropy, and mutual conciliation.

In his message to Congress (the eighth) of December 7, 1796, he said:

> I have heretofore proposed to the consideration of Congress the expediency of establishing a national university and also a military academy. The desirableness of both these institutions has so constantly increased with every new view I have taken on the subject that I can not omit the opportunity of once for all recalling your attention to them. The assembly to which I address myself is too enlightened not to be fully sensible how much a flourishing state of the arts and sciences contributes to material prosperity and reputation. True it is that our country, much to its honor, contains many seminaries of learning highly respectable and useful; but the funds upon which they rest are too narrow to command the ablest professors, in the different departments of liberal knowledge, for the institution contemplated, though they would be excellent auxiliaries. Among the motives to such an institution, the assimilation of the principles, opinions, and manners of our countrymen, by the common education of a portion of our youth from every quarter, will deserve attention. The more homogeneous our citizens can be made in these particulars, the greater will be our prospect of permanent union; and a primary object of such a national institution should be the education of our youth in the science of government. In a republic what species of knowledge can be equally important, and what duty more pressing on its legislature than to patronize a plan for communicating it to those who are to be the guardians of the future liberties of the country?

The proposition was unanimously approved by the Senate of the United States, in its address of December 10, 1796, to President Washington, as follows:

> A national university may be converted to the most useful purposes; the science of legislation being so essentially dependent on the endowments of the mind, the public interests must receive effectual aid from the general diffusion of knowledge; and the United States will assume a more dignified station among the nations of the earth by the successful cultivation of the higher branches of learning.

Washington, as set out in the first part of his letter to Governor Brooke, of Virginia, above referred to, had certain shares in a company for the navigation of the Potomac River which he was authorized to dispose of. In his last will and testament he gives them to the founding of this national university in the following language:

> It has always been a source of serious regret with me to see the youth of these United States sent to foreign countries for the purpose of education, often before their minds were formed, or they had imbibed any adequate ideas of the happiness of their own; contracting too frequently principles unfriendly to republican government and to the true and genuine liberties of mankind; which, thereafter, are rarely overcome. For these reasons it has been my ardent wish to see a plan devised on a liberal scale, which would have a tendency to spread systematic ideas through all the parts of this rising empire, thereby to do away local attachments and State prejudices, so far as the nature of things would, or indeed ought, to admit, from our national councils. Looking anxiously forward to the accomplishment of so desirable an object as this is (in my estimation), my mind has not been able to contemplate any plan more likely to effect the measure than the establishment of a university in a central part of the United States, to which the youths of fortune and talents from all parts thereof might be sent for the completion of their education in all the branches of polite literature; in arts and sciences, in acquiring knowledge in the principles of politics and good government, and (as a matter of infinite importance, in my judgment) by associating with each other, and forming friendships in juvenile years, be enabled to free themselves in a proper degree from those local prejudices and habitual jealousies which have just been mentioned, and which, when

carried to excess, are never failing sources of disquietude to the public mind, and pregnant of mischievous consequences to this country; under these impressions, so fully dilated, * * *

I give and bequeath in perpetuity the fifty shares (value $500 each) which I hold in the Potomac Company (under the aforesaid acts of the legislature of Virginia) toward the endowment of a university to be established in the District of Columbia under the auspices of the General Government, if that Government should incline to extend a fostering hand toward it; and until such a seminary is established and the funds arising on these shares shall be required for its support, my further desire is that the profit accruing therefrom shall, whenever dividends are made, be laid out in purchasing stock in the Bank of Columbia, or some other bank at the discretion of my executors, or by the Treasurer of the United States for the time being, under the direction of Congress; and the dividends proceeding from the purchase of such stock is to be invested in more stock, and so on until a sum adequate to the accomplishment of this object is attained.

It will be seen that this was a matter dear to the heart of the great and good Washington. The idea was conceived and first expressed in the midst of war and before there was a Government to be benefited by it. It was made prominent all through two terms of his Presidency, and remembered substantially in his last will and testament.

These words of Washington should have a controlling effect upon the people of this great Government that he founded, and cause the blush of shame to mantle the cheek of those who have lived after him, because for one hundred years his most earnest wish has been disregarded, his most emphatic recommendations have been neglected, and the funds he bequeathed to help carry out his wishes have been squandered.

John Adams, the second President, was deeply interested in a national university. This is shown by his voting with Madison, Pickering, and others to insert in the Constitution a provision for it. He made no effort during his Administration to bring this matter before Congress, discouraged, it may be, by the unsuccessful efforts of Washington.

Thomas Jefferson was from the beginning in favor of what was so near the heart of Washington. In his message to Congress, December 2, 1806, he said:

Education is here placed among the articles of public care; not that it would be proposed to take its ordinary branches out of the hands of private enterprise, which manages so much better all the concerns to which it is equal, but a public institution can alone supply those sciences which, though rarely called for, are yet necessary to complete the circle, all the parts of which contribute to the improvement of the country, and some of them to its preservation. * * * The present consideration of a national establishment for education particularly is rendered proper by this circumstance also, that if Congress, approving the proposition, shall yet think it more eligible to found it on a donation of lands, they have it now in their power to endow it with those which will be among the earliest to produce the necessary income. This foundation would have the advantage of being independent in war, which may suspend other improvements by requiring for its own purposes the resources destined for them.

Jefferson was very earnest about higher education, and founded the University of Virginia, which is one of the very best State universities on this continent, and stands to-day the proudest and most lasting monument to the genius and patriotism of our beloved philosopher and statesman.

James Madison, the father of the Constitution, the historian of the convention that framed it, and fourth President of the United States, was one of the earnest and most constant friends and advocates of a national university. He wanted the express power to establish it inserted in the Constitution, as will appear from the following proceedings of the convention as recorded by himself:

1698

May 29, 1787.—Mr. Charles Pickering laid before the House the draft of a Federal Government, which he had prepared, to be agreed upon between the free and independent States of America:
The legislature shall have power * * *

* * * * * * *

To establish and provide for a national university at the seat of government of the United States.

* * * * * * *

August 18, 1787.—In convention Mr. Madison submitted, in order to be referred to the committee of detail, the following powers proposed to be added to those of the general legislature:
* * * To establish a university.

* * * * * * *

September 14, 1787.—Mr. Madison and Mr. Pickering moved to insert in the list of powers voted in August a power to establish a university in which no preference or distinction should be allowed on account of religion.

Mr. Wilson and others supported the motion, but Gouverneur Morris strongly insisted that such addition to the Constitution would be a superfluity, since "the exclusive power at the seat of government would reach the object." This view was shared by enough members to defeat the proposition; Pennsylvania, Virginia, North Carolina, South Carolina, and Mr. Johnson, of Connecticut, voting for it as a means of making the university more sure, and Massachusetts, New Hampshire, New Jersey, Delaware, Maryland, Georgia, and Mr. Sherman, of Connecticut, voting in the negative. Not one word appears to have been said against the desirability of the proposed university.

President Madison, in his message of December 5, 1810, again urged its establishment in the following language:

While it is universally admitted that a well-instructed people alone can be permanently a free people, and while it is evident that the means of diffusing and improving useful knowledge from so small a proportion of the expenditures for national purposes, I can not presume it to be unreasonable to invite your attention to the advantages of superadding to the means of education provided by the several States a seminary of learning instituted by the national legislature within the limits of their exclusive jurisdiction, the expense of which might be defrayed or reimbursed out of the vacant grounds which have accrued to the nation within these limits. Such an institution, though local in its legal character, would be universal in its beneficial effects.

By enlightening the opinions, by expanding the patriotism, and by assimilating the principles, the interests, and the manners of those who might resort to this temple of science, to be redistributed in due time through every portion of the community, sources of jealousy and prejudice would be diminished, the features of national character would be multiplied and greater extent given to social harmony. But above all a well-constituted seminary in the center of the nation is recommended by the consideration that the additional instruction emanating from it would contribute not less to strengthen the foundations than to adorn the structure of our free and happy system of government.

In his seventh annual message, December 15, 1815, he again strongly commended it to Congress; and in his last message, December 3, 1816, when he was about to retire from the Presidential chair which he had filled so splendidly, he yet again urged action on this proposition in the following words:

The importance which I have attached to the establishment of a university within this District on a scale and for objects worthy of the American nation induces me to renew my recommendation of it to the favorable consideration of Congress.

The efforts of President Monroe, whose sympathy with the plans of Washington were often expressed, and who was glad to believe that Columbian College would in time become a national university, as appears from his letter of March 28, 1820, in which he says:

The establishment of the institution within the Federal district, in the presence of Congress and of all the departments of the Government, will secure to those who may be educated in it many important advantages, among which are the opportunity to hear the debates in Congress and in the Supreme Court. * * * If it receives hereafter the proper encouragement, it can not fail to be eminently useful to the nation.

President John Quincy Adams was no less a friend to the establishment by the Federal Government of a university. In his first message, in 1825, he makes an eloquent reference to the efforts and wishes of Washington in its behalf, and says:

> Among the first, perhaps the very first, instruments for the improvement of the condition of men is knowledge; and to the acquisition of much of the knowledge adapted to the wants, the comforts, and enjoyments of human life, public institutions and seminaries of learning are useful. So convinced of this was the first of my predecessors in this office, now first in the memory, as he was first in the hearts, of his countrymen, that once and again, in his addresses to the Congresses with whom he cooperated in the public service, he earnestly recommended the establishment of seminaries of learning, to prepare for all the emergencies of peace and war, a national university, and a military academy. With respect to the latter, had he lived to the present day, in turning his eyes to the institution at West Point, he would have enjoyed the gratification of his most earnest wishes. But in surveying the city which has been honored with his name, he would have seen the spot of earth which he had destined and bequeathed to the use and benefit of his country as the site for a university still bare and barren.

President Grant, in his message to Congress in December, 1873, soon after the country had emerged from a long war, which left a huge debt upon the Government, urged the establishment of this university as follows:

> I would suggest to Congress the propriety of promoting the establishment in this District of an institution of learning or university of the highest class by donation of lands. There is no place better suited for such an institution than the national capital. There is no other place in which every citizen is so directly interested.

President Hayes in his message, December, 1878, indorses "the enactment of an appropriate measure by Congress for the purpose of supplementing with national aid the local system of education in the several States."

It is believed that our present able and patriotic President, Grover Cleveland, has always favored this proposition, while seeing but little in the past history of Congressional neglect to encourage a direct recommendation. In his first Administration, L. Q. C. Lamar, Secretary of the Interior, and one of the ablest of his Cabinet, in his report for the fiscal year ending in 1885, indorsed a national university, and urged it upon the Congress and country in the following words:

> Eighty years ago President Jefferson, then in the fullest tide of his authority as a party chief, told Congress that to complete the circle of Democratic policy a national university was a necessity and should at once be created. In this he followed the recommendations of his predecessors, Washington and Adams, the former of whom ten years before declared that the desirableness of a national university had so constantly increased with every new view he had taken of the subject that he could not omit the opportunity of recalling the attention of Congress to its importance. Mr. Madison, in 1810, renewed the recommendation, with the declaration that such an institution would contribute not less to strengthen the foundations than to adorn the structure of our free and happy system of government, and that it would be universal in its beneficial effects.
>
> This national institution which Washington, Adams, Jefferson, and Madison thought so necessary has never been established; and in these later years the idea of a national university constitutes no part of the plans of statesmen and seems to have been lost sight of by the people.
>
> In the meantime scientific bureaus have grown up one by one under the Government, with observatories, laboratories, museums, and libraries, until the whole range of physical science is represented by national institutions established by the Government for the purpose of prosecuting researches embracing astronomy, meteorology, geography of land and sea, geology, chemistry, statistics, mechanical inventions, etc. If the various commissions, bureaus, and divisions of the Executive Departments at Washington which

have for their object the prosecution of scientific research could be combined as integral parts of one scientific institution, such an institution would be of greater proportions and more comprehensive than any other in the world; and should a university be erected thereon, with a superstructure commensurate with the foundation, it would be without a rival in any country.

The common-school system, designed to furnish every citizen with an education which ought to be a strict necessity for his daily work of life, constitutes the foundation of our democracy. But this is not enough to satisfy its instincts. In the history of nations democracies have been the cradles of pure thought and art. The same cause which operated in them exists in American society, and whether through a national university or in fragmentary institutions in the several States, sooner or later a higher education, higher than the common school or the academy or the college can furnish, will alone realize and express the higher aspirations of American democracy.

Mr. Lamar was himself a learned professor in a college, had a high appreciation of the advantages of higher education, and rounded up his brilliant life by adorning a seat on the bench of the Supreme Court of the United States.

It is thus shown that the founders of our Government thought the establishment of a national university of the greatest importance to our country; that eight Presidents have strongly indorsed and recommended it to Congress, and that another, through Secretary Lamar, argued for it in strong and eloquent language.

It was never a partisan recommendation, but was alike indorsed by all shades of politics represented by the nine Presidents. They felt it to be a pressing want of the country which rose above the din of partisan politics. They represented the best thought of the country, without regard to party, and we in a like spirit should approach this great subject with no thought of party politics in our minds.

But earnest advocacy of this university was not confined to Presidents and Cabinets. It was widespread among the statesmen and patriots, the scholars and scientists of the country. The great want of a higher, a complete education in our own country has been the all-pervading thought of our best minds. Mr. Samuel Blodget, called a prophet by Washington, petitioned Congress for the university in 1803 and again in 1805. And in 1810 Hon. R. H. Wilde, from the Committee of the House of Representatives, to whom was referred the message of President Madison, made the following report:

The committee of the House of Representatives, to whom was referred so much of the President's message as relates to the subject of a national university, report to the House, as the result of their deliberations, a bill for the erection and endowment of such an institution.

The committee, pursuant to usual forms, might, perhaps, without impropriety, regard this a sufficient performance of their duty, and after presenting the bill without comment, have left it to find its appropriate place among others, and to receive or be denied consideration, according to the opinion entertained of its consequence and urgency.

But the number of communications relative to the subject which, though they have received attention, seem to have escaped it because they have not been definitely acted on may possibly expose the House to a censure more serious than that of merely neglecting the successive recommendations of several successive chief magistrates—a censure as injurious as unjust, yet not unbecoming that body to prevent by making as soon as possible some disposition of a question that ought to be determined on account of its frequent occurrence, even though it should not otherwise be thought particularly interesting. * * *

Your committee therefore have ventured to suggest some of the reasons which recommend the present as a favorable time for investigating and perhaps also adopting the plan they have proposed.

Among these, the prosperous state of our finances, leaving a large unappropriated surplus, the probability of a long-continued peace, the flourishing condition of our capital, and the facility with which a portion of the public property within it might now be advantageously disposed of, so as at once to increase the convenience of the city and support the proposed institution, may fairly be enumerated.

Besides, the information heretofore collected has enabled the committee to report at an early period, and it is believed that the present session, though inevitably a short one, will not present so many objects of great difficulty or deep interest as entirely to exclude others of a more tranquil and less obtrusive character to which it is possible a portion of time might be profitably devoted.

The acquisition of a scientific and literary reputation not unworthy of their naval and military renown can never be beneath the ambition of a people, since the most durable of all glory is that of exalted intellect. The world is still a willing captive to the spells of ancient genius, and the rivalry of modern empires will be perpetuated by their arts and their learning—the preservers of that fame which arms alone may indeed win, but can never keep.

Any measure which contributes, however scantily, to give American literature and science a rank and name among mankind can not, therefore, be regarded with indifference by our citizens, and every effort toward that end must be witnessed at the present moment with universal satisfaction, since it will present the interesting spectacle of a young nation bending its whole strength to the pursuit of true greatness and anxious to emulate all that is amiable in peace as well as all that is noble in war.

That the institution contemplated will have a happy influence on the harmony and welfare of our country and the unity of our national character has been often supposed, and your committee feel inclined to anticipate effects no less happy from its operation on the genius of our people. If America's invention, unassisted as it has been, already excites the astonishment of Europe, what may not be expected from it when aided and encouraged? And why should not aid and encouragement be yielded by institutions like the present, founded and endowed by the munificence of the state? In our own day we have seen them work wonders in physical science, even when directed by a stern, jealous, and exacting Government, which, while training the mind to be quick, dextrous, and daring, darkened its vision and circumscribed its flight. Is it here alone they would be impotent, where no depth could be hidden from its glance, no height forbidden to its wing?

But your committee, fearful of exhausting your patience, forbear to extend this report by arguments which it is easier to multiply than to withhold. For the same reason they refrain from answering objections which could be stated without injury, since in replying to them force and perspicuity must be sacrificed to conciseness. Nor can such a course be required when it is intended merely to present a general result, not the particular process of reasoning by which that result has been attained. Your committee, however, desire it to be understood that they have not declined examining any objection which occurred to them; and though some have been found which, it must be confessed, are not without difficulty, all are thought capable of a satisfactory answer.

Under a conviction, therefore, that the means are ample, the end desirable, the object fairly within the legislative powers of Congress, and the time a favorable one, your committee recommend the establishment of a national university, and have directed their chairman to submit a bill and estimates for that purpose.

Estimates of the value of lots and squares belonging to the United States, as furnished by communications from the superintendent of the city.

Four thousand building lots of 5,205 square feet each, and about 2,000-foot front on the waters of the Potomac River, Eastern Branch, valued at	$750,000
Squares 1 to 6, proposed to be laid off into building lots, containing in the whole 816,000 square feet, or 155 standard lots, valued at	200,000
But the latter amount is the only one which it is supposed could be speedily utilized.	
Estimate of the expense of buildings for the national university, on a plan susceptible of extension, but calculated for the present to answer for 160 persons	200,000

Mr. Wilde's committee also presented a bill for the establishment of a national university, as follows:

Be it enacted, etc., That the President of the United States be, and he is hereby, authorized and required to cause to be surveyed and laid off into building lots such part as he shall think proper of the ground reserved of the United States in the city of Washington, and to cause the same to be sold at such times and places and in such proportions and under such regulations as he shall prescribe; and the proceeds thereof, after defraying the charges of survey and sale, to be invested in such stocks or public securities as shall by him be deemed advisable; and the same, when so invested, and the dividends thereon arising, shall constitute a fund for the support of a national university.

SEC. 2. *And be it further enacted*, That the President of the United States be, and he is hereby, authorized to cause to be erected, on such site within the District of Columbia as he shall elect, the buildings necessary for a national university; and for defraying the expense thereof the sum of —— dollars is hereby appropriated, to be paid out of any money in the Treasury of the United States not otherwise appropriated by law.

SEC. 3. *And be it further enacted,* That the President of the United States be, and he is hereby, required to cause to be prepared and laid before Congress at its next session a plan for the regulation and government of said university.

Following these, there were noteworthy efforts all through the first half of the century and to a later date; as by Hon. Charles H. Atherton, of New Hampshire; by Drs. Josiah Meigs, Cuthbert, Sewall, Law, McWilliams, and Judge Cranch, in 1819 and 1825; by Hon. Mark L. Hill, of Massachusetts, and Mr. Robbins, of Rhode Island, from 1819 to 1825; by President Holley, of Transylvania University, Kentucky, and Dr. Charles Caldwell, professor, from 1820 to 1828; by Professors Agassiz, Peirce, Guyot, Hall, Mitchell, and Dana, in 1851; by Samuel B. Ruggles, Prof. Joseph Henry, Bishop Alonzo Potter, and others, in 1852; by Hon. Edward Everett, Charles Dudley, Dr. Bache, of the Coast Survey, Benjamin Peirce, Benjamin Apthorp Gould, and other scientists, in 1855 and 1856; and so on, until the beginning of systematic effort by Hon. John W. Hoyt; first, by his tour of university inspection in both the Old and the New World, under commission of the United States Government, in 1867 and 1868, with reports thereon, and secondly, by his appeals to the National Educational Association for organized work, in an address before that body at Trenton, N. J., in 1869.

It was at this meeting and after this address that the following resolution was unanimously adopted by the National Association, the Hon. E. E. White, of Ohio, presiding:

Resolved, That in the opinion of this association a great American university is a leading want of American education, and that, in order to contribute to the early establishment of such an institution, the president of this association, acting in concert with the president of the National Superintendents' Association, is hereby requested to appoint a committee, consisting of one member from each of the States, and of which Dr. J. W. Hoyt, of Wisconsin, shall be chairman, to take the whole matter under consideration, and to make such report thereon at the next annual convention of said association as shall seem to be demanded by the interests of the country.

This was followed by the appointment of a national committee, composed of Dr. John W. Hoyt, Madison, Wis., chairman; Hon. N. B. Cloud, Montgomery, Ala.; Hon. Thomas Smith, Little Rock, Ark.; Prof. W. P. Blake, San Francisco, Cal.; Hon. B. G. Northrup, New Haven, Conn.; Prof. L. Coleman, Wilmington, Del.; Hon. T. C. Chase, Tallahassee, Fla.; Hon. Newton Bateman, Springfield, Ill.; Hon. B. C. Hobbs, Indianapolis, Ind.; Hon. S. S. Kissell, Des Moines, Iowa; Hon. P. McVicker, Topeka, Kans.; Hon. Z. T. Smith, Frankfort, Ky.; Hon. T. W. Conway, New Orleans, La.; Hon. Warren Johnson, Augusta, Me.; Hon. M. A. Newell, Baltimore, Md.; Hon. Joseph White, Boston, Mass.; Hon. O. Hosford, Lansing, Mich.; Prof. W. F. Phelps, Winona, Minn.; President Daniel Reed, Columbia, Mo.; Prof. J. M. McKinsey, Peru, Nebr.; Hon. A. N. Fisher, Carson City, Nev.; Hon. Thomas Hardy, Concord, N. H.; Hon. C. S. Apgar, Trenton, N. J.; Hon. J. W. Bulkley, Brooklyn, N. Y.; Hon. S. S. Ashley, Raleigh, N. C.; Prof. A. J. Rickoff, Cleveland, Ohio; Rev. George H. Atkinson, Portland, Oreg.; Hon. J. P. Wickersham, Harrisburg, Pa.; Hon. T. W. Bicknell, Providence, R. I.; Hon. J. K. Jillson, Charleston, S. C.; Rev. C. T. P. Bancroft, Lookout Mountain, Tenn.; Hon. J. S. Adams, Montpelier, Vt.; Hon. W. H. Ruffin, Richmond, Va.; Prof. Z. Richards, Washington, D. C.

Action was repeated by the National Association at its meeting at Cleveland, Ohio, in August, 1870, and yet later at St. Louis with reports on the principles that should govern in planning the institution, and finally by the appointment of a permanent committee to be charged with the duty of further conducting the enterprise to a successful issue; the said committee, consisting of Dr. John W. Hoyt, of Wisconsin, chairman; ex-President Thomas Hill, Massachusetts; Mr. E. L. Godkin, New York; Hon. W. P. Wickersham, state superintendent of public instruction, Pennsylvania; Dr. Barnas Sears, Virginia; Col. D. F. Boyd, president University of Louisiana; Dr. Daniel Read, president University of Missouri; Dr. W. F. Phelps, president State Normal School, Winona, Minn.; ex-Governor A. C. Gibbs, Oregon; Hon. Newton Bateman, State superintendent of public instruction, Illinois; with the following ex officio members: The president of the National Educational Association; the National Commissioner of Education; the president of the National Academy of Sciences; the president of the National Association for the Advancement of Science, and the president of the American Social Science Association.

It was this committee, aided by Senators Lamar, Sumner, Howe, Patterson, Ingalls, Garland, Carpenter, and others, as well as by Profs. Joseph Henry, Spencer F. Baird, and Louis Agassiz, that prepared the bill of 1872, which was unanimously reported by the House Committee on Education and Labor in 1873, and with which the bill now before the Senate is substantially identical.

Unhappily, the report of the House committee was made too late in the session for action, and, for reasons which need not be set forth, further Congressional action was not had until the introduction and reference of the bill offered by Senator George F. Edmunds, which appears not to have been reported.

In October, 1891, the Pan-Republic Congress, during its session at Philadelphia, very emphatically indorsed the university proposition by its unanimous adoption of the following preamble and resolution, offered by John W. Hoyt:

Whereas this general committee, formed for the purpose of advancing the cause of peace and liberal government throughout the world by means a succession of congresses of the representatives of all civilized lands, could yet further contribute to these great ends by encouraging such organizations and enterprises as look to the increase of knowledge and of liberal thought among men; and

Whereas it is manifest that a truly national university established at the seat of government of the United States, and aiming, first, to crown the present incomplete system of American education; secondly, to promote the advancement of knowledge by means of the researches and investigations of its members, as well as by its influence upon the science and learning of other lands; and, finally, to encourage a finer intellectual intercourse and community of feeling among the leading minds of the world, would at once prove conservative of our own free institutions, strengthen the bonds of fraternity among all peoples, and contribute to the betterment of governmental institutions everywhere; and

Whereas it appears from the records of history not only that on this very spot, sacred to liberty and independence the importance, of such a university was urged by the framers of the American Constitution, but that several of the Presidents, including George Washington, John Adams, Thomas Jefferson, James Madison, James Monroe, John Quincy Adams, Ulysses S. Grant, and Rutherford B. Hayes, pressed its early establishment as a patriotic duty; that President Washington even remembered it with a liberal gift in his dying bequest; * * * that the proposition to establish it has been sanctioned by other leading statesmen throughout the period of our national history, and, finally, that such proposition has been thrice unanimously indorsed by that great body of American educators, the National Educational Association; therefore,

Resolved, That in order to aid in the founding of such an institution the chairman of this general committee is hereby requested to appoint a special committee, consisting of one or more members from each of the States and

Territories, whose duty it shall be to adopt and carry forward such measures to this end as to them shall seem proper, reporting to this committee in their discretion, or as required from time to time, and in particular at the time and place of the Pan-Republic Congress to be held in the year 1893.

The committee found under this resolution includes men of eminence in many departments of intellectual activity, with ex-Governor John W. Hoyt as chairman, of whom it is but just to say that throughout this whole period of a quarter of a century he has not only never lost sight of the great end in view, but has labored assiduously and sacrificed much for its realization. He has exhausted the subject in his memorial to the Fifty-second Congress, to which highly interesting and valuable document I am greatly indebted for the historical references herein contained; and which, besides its systematic array of arguments unanswerable and persuasive, also presents the affirmative action of learned bodies, as you have seen, together with historic proofs of the earnest sympathy of a long line of the most illustrious citizens our country has produced. He has also urged the matter upon public attention in numerous addresses. Indeed, the great cardinal reasons for the establishment of the university are nowhere more cogently stated than in his address before the National Association at Detroit, 1874, to the following passages from which I ask special attention:

Certainly no American will deny that self-reliance is an essential element of individual manhood, as well as of a noble national character. It is precisely for this reason, among others, that we urge the duty of the Government to care for the highest practical education of the whole people. For there is no dependence so abject as that of a profoundly ignorant man or nation; no self-reliance so complete and royal as that which comes of intelligence. Ignorance is slavery; knowledge is power and independence. * * *

As I understand it, the Government of this country is nothing very different from a trusteeship or agency, established by the whole people for the public convenience and for permanent as well as present advantage. The Constitution is a binding agreement of the people as to the purpose and organization of this agency, the kind of agents to be employed, the manner of their choosing, and the nature and scope of the duties they are to perform.

Cherishing the theory of self-reliance, the people have not usually deemed it duty or wisdom to take of their common substance and give to the individual citizen or the individual State, even when such giving would promote a necessary public object, unless it has seemed very clear that such object could not, or pretty certainly would not, be attained without the national aid. But who will say that the people, acting through this agency—the Government—are not both competent and in duty bound to lend the public aid to all such enterprises not in conflict with expressed provisions of the Constitution, and in acknowledged harmony with its whole spirit and purpose, as are by them, the people, deemed essential to the general welfare, and as are either not possible of accomplishment without that aid or, being possible, are in great danger of being too long delayed?

Admitting, for the sake of the argument, the full force of the doctrine of some, that government is not to do a public good, even, unless that good be otherwise unattainable, the argument is still good for nothing against the object we seek to accomplish; since it is a public good otherwise unattainable. Primary schools there would be without public aid, but they would be scattering in location, irregular and inefficient in their work, and, worst of all, utterly wanting in many cases where most needed. Colleges there would be, as anyone may see who looks abroad, but except here and there, when particularly favored with the accumulations of generations or the princely gift of a noble man, they must of necessity have a sickly life and do a feeble work. While of a great university, with its vast auxiliary establishments, its multitude of learned professors, and its requisite annual income of a million and more, it is hardly necessary to say the hope of such an institution on any merely private, denominational, or even State foundation must be long deferred.

Last of all, if the question of means were not involved there is one broad reason why this public good, the schools the country needs, including the university, are otherwise unattainable, this, namely, that if established and maintained in sufficient number, and of every class and rank, by private means, they would still not be public schools, wholly free from the warping influence of private or denominational aims of whatever sort, institutions equally open to all qualified candidates, as well as purely concentrated to the culture of the people, and to the advancement of science and learning among men. * * *

The Government can not now repudiate or reverse its beneficent educational policy. The logic of facts and of reason will not permit it to stop short of the most complete provision for every department of American education. The people are growing in their realization of the necessity there is for insuring the best possible education of the masses. The variety and vastness of the national resources and the rapid progress of other nations are making a strong and growing demand upon the industrial arts which they are powerless to meet without the help of the best technical schools; while the conspicuous place we hold among the great nations of the earth, the nature of our Government, and the genius and aspirations of our people are reasons deep and urgent for a high and thorough culture that must early move the nation to adopt measures that will give to the United States a true university. * * *

Nor have the efforts of this patriotic chairman of committees ceased. He is still the earnest advocate of the great measure so long before the country, having, as heretofore, the hearty cooperation of a great number of our most distinguished scholars, jurists, and statesmen—men such as the honorable Chief Justice of the United States, ex-Senator George F. Edmunds, and Hon. Andrew D. White, the officers of the Smithsonian Institution, the president of the American Association for the Advancement of Science, the president of the American Academy of Political and Social Science, the president of the National Educational Association, the president of the National Geographical Society, the heads and members of Government bureaus, libraries, and museums, the presidents of leading colleges and universities in all sections of the country, and the State superintendents of public instruction in nearly all the States.

A considerable number of these have recently written earnest letters in expression of their views, and many others have given notice of their purpose to do so at an early day, which letters already received I shall wish to have printed as an appendix to my speech.

All these distinguished representatives of the best scholarship, scientific culture, and statesmanship of the country, in common with the multitude of illustrious men of the past who have championed the same great cause, plainly see that, while we have already gained a certain acknowledged superiority among the nations by reason of the vastness of our material resources and by the general intelligence and inventive genius of a people living under free institutions, we have not yet reached that higher eminence which pertains to the profoundest culture in letters, science, and philosophy. And they also see that in order to attain such eminence the Government itself should plant and foster, at this national capital, a great and true university, so endowed as to enable it to become not only a supreme leader in the work of the highest instruction for our own people, but also foremost among the universities of the world in the yet grander work of advancing the boundaries of human knowledge.

Why, then, should Congress hesitate to adopt a measure so earnestly advocated by the foremost of our citizens from the very foundation of the Government? Can any reason be given why Congress should not at once enter upon the great work?

Will the proposed University of the United States interfere with the colleges and so-called universities? On the contrary, it will tend to increase their prosperity by newly kindling a love of learning throughout the land and by adding to the number of their students, since only through study in these can they become candidates for the honors to be conferred by the coming national university. That such would be the result is conclusively demonstrated by the support the proposition has received from the eminent heads and professors of so many of our principal colleges and State universities.

Can not the country spare the money to establish it? Our best men in the beginning of the Government wanted it established. If it was possible to do this out of the poor resources of an infant country, just emerged from the throes of a revolutionary struggle, what must be said of our ability to do it now that we have grown from three to sixty-five millions of people, and from thirteen original States along the Atlantic coast to nearly fifty States, extending from the Atlantic to the Pacific Ocean?

Can it be said that there are more pressing demands for our expenditures? Surely none are so pressing as this. The best men in all periods of our Government have urged this expenditure. The Government has given its aid to all classes of education except this by donation of millions of acres of land. It has with a lavish hand extended its aid to schools and colleges, and these very schools and colleges are now crying aloud for this university in order to complete the circle of education and to carry to the highest point the work so well begun by them.

Is the location at the national capital objectionable? Surely not, for the many reasons given by eminent men in quotations already made. This of all others is the spot, and in my opinion the only spot, where a national university can be constitutionally established by the Federal Government. Anywhere else in the States the constitutional power of Congress would be wanting. Here Congress has the same relation to the District of Columbia as the several legislatures have to their respective States. It will not be contended that legislatures have no power to establish and endow universities in their several States.

The extract from the proceedings of the convention heretofore made shows that this was considered so important that Mr. Madison proposed to insert in the list of powers conferred upon Congress the power to establish a university. It was not adopted because it was deemed a superfluity, but no word was uttered against the propriety of such an establishment. It was voted to be a superfluity because of the following provision:

Article I, section 8, seventeenth clause: The Congress shall exercise exclusive legislation in all cases whatsoever over such district (not exceeding 10 miles square) as may by cession of particular States and the acceptance of Congress become the seat of government of the United States.

They gave to Congress all the powers in the District of Columbia which inhered in the legislatures over their States respectively. The Congress is the legislature for the District of Columbia, and has sovereign power as such unless abridged by the Constitution.

But it can not be necessary to discuss its constitutionality when Washington, Jefferson, and Madison, all prominent framers of that sacred instrument, have been so earnestly in favor of it. They all favored it earnestly without a suggestion of the want of power in Congress. This must satisfy the most skeptical.

There can be no valid objection to a national university, but everything to commend it.

The committee has taken great pains to provide for a university that will fill the expectation of the illustrious men who have so earnestly advocated it.

It is called in the bill reported "The University of the United States," because there is already founded here by private effort an institution named the "National University."

The board of regents (the governing power of this university) is to be appointed by the President, by and with the advice and consent of the Senate, and shall consist of eight members so appointed, no two of whom shall be from the same State; and the President, Vice-President, Speaker of the House of Representatives, the Chief Justice of the United States, the Commissioner of Education, the secretary of the Smithsonian Institution, and the president of the university shall be ex-officio members of the board of regents. This secures the institution from sectional bias and denominational influence, and gives as its governors thirteen of the best men of the land. Five of these shall be designated by the board as an executive committee, charged with such duties as the board shall entrust to them. This board shall also choose a president, charged with general supervision, etc.

Section 6 provides for a council of faculties, which shall consist of the president and deans of faculties, and this council shall plan and direct the instruction and discipline of the different departments.

Section 8 provides that no chair for instruction sectarian in religion or partisan in politics shall be established.

Section 9 provides that the facilities of the university shall be open to all who are competent to use them, under rules prescribed by the executive committee, and that degrees shall only be conferred upon such as shall have received degrees from existing colleges and universities. This not only insures a higher degree of education than State institutions can afford, but greatly increases their students by the requirements so made.

Section 10 gives to all the States and Territories at least one free scholarship for each Representative or Delegate in the House and two for each Senator, and confides the power of withholding scholarships, or any other privileges, to the board of regents alone, the highest power of the university.

Section 11 provides for fellowships under the regulation of the board of regents, and section 12 provides for admission or appointment, making competency the sole test. Section 13 donates the University or Observatory Square in this city as the seat of the university—the property selected and appropriated by President Washington.

Section 14 appropriates and sets apart for the establishment and support of this university one-third of the net proceeds of the sale of public lands for ten years, to be held by the Treasurer of the United States; one-half of which shall be used for securing and improving grounds, for the necessary buildings and equipments, and for conducting the institution after its opening. The other half shall remain as a permanent fund, bearing 5 per cent interest, which interest is to be used for conducting the university. This money can only be drawn according to law on the requisition of the president and secretary of the board of regents, under its order. The money to support it is thus secured beyond the possibility of loss.

It is sincerely hoped that the most economical member of Congress will not object to this appropriation of one-third of the public lands for ten years. Ten times this amount has been given to railroads, and a larger quantity given to education in the States. If this scheme be worthy of the earnest solicitude of Washington and his successors, the statesmen and patriots of the Revolution, and of the sages, philosophers, and educators of all periods of our Government, then surely it is worth all that is here given, and much more.

The aggregate wealth of this country is perhaps as great as that of any other, and this small sum could not be better spent. The very fact that the Government has taken it in hand will draw to it benefactions of the rich, who will take a patriotic pride in identifying themselves with an institution that will be world-wide in its reputation and confer countless blessings upon the country and the world.

The bequest of Washington, if properly secured and properly managed, would now amount to a large sum (as shown by calculation, to over $4,000,000) and form the nucleus for a great university fund.

Mr. HOAR. May I ask the Senator from Virginia a question at this point, if it will not interrupt him? Perhaps he stated what the fact is while my attention was drawn away. What has become of the proceeds of the bequest of Washington?

Mr. HUNTON. I have not stated it, but I will do so with pleasure. By the neglect of Congress to take care of it the shares in the navigation company became worthless, so that nothing was realized from that source.

Mr. HOAR. Where is the ownership of the shares at this moment—in the Government?

Mr. HUNTON. I suppose the title really vested in the executors and their successors under the will of Washington.

Mr. HOAR. Is the company in existence?

Mr. HUNTON. No, sir.

Mr. HOAR. The reason why I asked the question is because a very distinguished historical investigator wrote and asked me some time ago if I could give him the information. He said he had been unable in his researches to discover what had become of that bequest, and he wanted to know if I had the means of informing him.

Mr. HUNTON. By the neglect of Congress to take hold of and accept the bequest, it was allowed to stand without being utilized. The company failed, and the stock became worthless.

Looking to the reception of gifts, devises, and bequests to this institution, the fifteenth section provides that all such may be received by the board of regents and the money deposited with the Treasurer of the United States at 5 per cent interest.

According to the eighth section no chair for instruction sectarian in religion or partisan in politics shall be permitted in any form.

Section 16 gives to the members of this university well-regulated access to the numerous institutions and collections now held by the Government here in Washington City, and brings the bureau heads, whose work is of a sort to justify it, into proper advisory and cooperative relations with the heads of corresponding departments of the university.

What a field of scientific study is here laid before the young man ambitious of attainments of the highest order. See what is thus laid before him that he may choose in what particular branch of science he may pursue and perfect his studies. They embrace almost every branch of scientific work, and are presided over by men already familiar with their respective departments, and who, it may be added, most fully realize how great is the loss that results from allowing the opportunities here offered to run waste.

Examine for yourselves, Senators, the inventory of them:

In the Treasury Department of the United States—
　The Office of the Coast and Geodetic Survey.
　The Office of the Life-Saving Service.
　The Marine-Hospital Service.
　The Bureau of Statistics.
　The Bureau of Engraving and Printing.
In the War Department—
　The several military bureaus.
In the Navy Department—
　The Naval Observatory.
　The Office of the Nautical Almanac.
　The Hydrographic Office.
　The Bureau of Navigation.
　The Bureau of Yards and Docks.
　The Bureau of Ordnance.
　The Bureau of Construction and Repair.
　The Bureau of Steam Engineering.
　The Museum of Hygiene.
　The Bureau of Medicine and Surgery.
　The Dispensary.
In the Department of the Interior—
　The Patent Office.
　The Bureau of Education.
　The Office of the Geological Survey.
　The Census Office.
In the Department of Agriculture—
　The Botanical Division, with the gardens and grounds.
　The Division of Vegetable Pathology.
　The Pomological Division.
　The Microscopical Division.
　The Chemical Division.
　The Ornithological Division.
　The Forestry Division.
　The Entomological Division.
　The Silk Section.
　The Experimental Stations.
　The Office of Statistics.
　The Bureau of Animal Industry.
　The Weather Bureau.
　The Agricultural Museum.
Of establishments not under departmental control—
　The Smithsonian Institution.
　The National Museum, with its twenty-two departments.
　The Medical Museum.
　The Medical Library.
　The Bureau of Ethnology.
　The Light-House Board.
　The Commission of Fish and Fisheries.
　The Arsenal.
　The Congressional Library.
　The United States Botanic Garden.
　The Zoological Garden (in preparation).
　The Government Printing Office.
　The Soldiers' Home.
　Office of the National Board of Health.
　Government Hospital for the Insane.
　The National Deaf-Mute College.
　Courts, district, circuit, and Supreme.

What opportunities for the earnest student of science, and how eagerly would they be accepted!

The seventeenth and last section provides for an annual report to Congress of the operation and condition of the university, and for scattering broadcast in the country the information contained. This places the institution under the very eye and control of Congress, and it can not stray away from its ends and objects except by the utter neglect of that body. These reports will tend to further awaken and deepen the thirst for higher learning and direct the attention of the benevolent rich to the best of objects for their bounty.

The committee in charge of this bill have given to it very great care, and some of its members have devoted much time to the earnest consideration of this important subject.

It is believed that the bill, as amended and reported, will result in a short time in the formation and endowment of the greatest institution of learning in the world. It will afford to the youth of this country thirsting for the highest attainments in knowledge and intellectual power the opportunity to satisfy their demands at the fountain provided at home. It will spread abroad in our land the desire for the highest education, and inform the ambitious student in our colleges that when he shall have mastered all that is taught there new and higher opportunities still lie before him and within his reach. It will tend to educate large numbers of young men in the science of government, who in turn will educate the people, the real governors in this country.

It will keep at home the young men who can not at present here gratify all their intellectual cravings. It will draw students from foreign lands as soon as it is known that this institution carries education to a higher plane and is better equipped for the work of investigation than any other; and the love of democratic government imbibed here will be carried back and instilled into the minds of their own people. It will elevate, energize, and enlarge the minds of our own people, and especially of those who by the cultivation of their powers may hope for a conspicuous part in conducting our governmental affairs and in defending the Constitution itself.

It is in the power of no man to properly estimate the benefits bestowed upon our country by the million of college graduates heretofore distributed to all parts of it by the institutions already established—young men who with the helps thus afforded have become our leading mechanicians, architects, engineers, experts in every field of science, teachers, physicians, lawyers, and lawmakers, who have infused into the minds of the people a thirst for knowledge, a love of country, and a patriotic desire to preserve this Government as the fathers made it. Neither is it in the power of any man to estimate the possibilities of such an institution as is now proposed—an institution that shall crown and complete the now incomplete system of American education; that shall become a mighty uplifting force in its influence upon all classes of institutions below it; that shall furnish the facilities for which our aspiring young men now visit the Old World by thousands: that shall draw to us men of genius from all other lands, and that shall early become the leading university of the world.

I think I have not overstated the benefits to flow from a national university. If not, who can doubt that we should make haste to establish it and thus wipe out the shame of the long neglect of the wishes and earnest advice of the Father of his Country, so often repeated by his successors in the high office of President, so ably reenforced by the appeals of our foremost educators and statesmen, and so in harmony with the ardent aspirations of the wise and patriotic in all periods of our country's history?

APPENDIX A.

Recent letters concerning the National University proposition from distinguished public men, scholars, and scientists, and from college and university presidents.

PHILADELPHIA, *November 27, 1894.*

DEAR SIR: The project of establishing a national university at Washington has interested me for years, but I never saw any plan proposed that did not have serious objections or manifest shortcomings. I examined, therefore, your Memorial, expecting to find that its scheme, too, would be open to like unfavorable criticism; and was agreeably surprised to perceive that you had avoided the objectionable features visible in others and present a practical, beneficent, and truly liberal outline, which if filled in and carried out in the same spirit will endow our land with an institution which will prove an advantage and a glory to it for indefinite generations. Wishing your effort every success, I remain,

Very truly, yours,

D. G. BRINTON
(President of the American Association, for the Advancement of Science, etc).

Hon. JOHN W. HOYT.

AMERICAN ACADEMY OF POLITICAL AND SOCIAL SCIENCE,
Philadelphia, December 3, 1894.

DEAR SIR: I am much interested in the work of the committee on the National University, of which you are chairman. I hope that you will send me whatever information you may have about the great enterprise.

Very truly yours,

EDMUND J. JAMES
(President, etc.).

Hon. JOHN W. HOYT, *Washington, D. C.*

No. 1507 SPRUCE STREET, *Philadelphia, December 8, 1894.*

MY DEAR SIR: Yours of the 5th instant has just reached me here. The health of my family deprives me of the opportunity of being active in respect to the university, but all I can do I will with pleasure. I am glad the prospects appear so favorable.

In haste.

Yours, very truly,

GEO. F. EDMUNDS.

Hon. JOHN W. HOYT, *Washington, D. C.*

LITTLE ROCK, ARK., *January 15, 1894.*

DEAR SIR: Most decidedly you may count me among the friends of the National University proposition.

Very truly, yours,

J. C. BRANNER *(State Geologist).*

Hon. JOHN W. HOYT, *Washington.*

CHICAGO, *November 3, 1894.*

MY DEAR SIR: I sincerely hope that the effort to secure the establishment by Congress of a National Post-graduate University at Washington may be crowned with speedy success. Such a university will be the noble and worthy representative of the nation in the republic of letters and in the growing empire of science. It will give a new luster to our national capital and a new glory to our national name. I believe that it will stimulate investigation and heighten scholarship and quicken educational interest and enthusiasm throughout the country.

With much regard, I remain, yours cordially,

JOHN H. BARROWS
(President Late Parliament of Religions).

Hon. JOHN W. HOYT.

PHILADELPHIA, PA., *November 29, 1894.*

MY DEAR SIR: Accept my sincere thanks for your thoughtful kindness in sending me your memorial in behalf of a National University at Washington. I read it with the deepest interest, alike for its rich retrospect and for its bright outlook. I regard it as being, in many respects, the most valuable document of its kind in the world.

When I come to Washington again I shall be most glad to confer with you on this momentous matter.

Believe me to be, with great respect,

Faithfully, yours,

GEO. D. BOARDMAN.

Hon. JOHN W. HOYT, *Washington, D. C.*

OFFICE OF CUSTODIAN OF AMERICAN HISTORY,
2302 Spruce Street, Philadelphia, Pa., October 20, 1891.

DEAR DOCTOR: If Washington left in his will the sum of £5,000 to found a national university, why is not that institution now established? I have met with some men who are deeply interested in the subject of the erection of a national university at Washington, and the organizing of a distinctly national system of education that would be the natural outcome of such an institution.

If a national university is established one of the most important schools to be erected would be that of "Americana." The study of civics has been largely omitted in our schools and colleges, and where political economy has entered into the curriculum it has been generally considered not from a purely American standpoint, but usually from the rulings and ideas of Europe, which are more monarchical than republican. Then, too, the teaching has been for the aid of the ruler while it ought to be for the instruction of the voter first, leaving the study of governmental and diplomatic service as secondary. We have a distinctly American political economy, and it is yet to be fully developed. American history is but little known. The schools learn something of English history and the English constitution, but practically, American history and American constitutional law are known by few who have made these studies a specialty. We have a vast country and our post-office reaches to every nook and corner, but the boy of 12 is supposed to have learned all the geography there is for him to know. It seems to me that our countrymen ought to be informed respecting all the various parts of our land, its minerals, its productions, its facilities for transportation, and all the other various things that make the United States one of the richest, if not the richest, lands of the earth. We have an interstate commerce, and we will soon have a reciprocal interchange of commodities with the other remaining American States that are not of our Union. The student of "Americana" ought to be instructed in all the matters relating to our own and our neighbors' public affairs, and be thoroughly informed respecting everything that relates in any way to the American continent, its business, its social life, its history, its geography, its productions, and its laws. Our country needs such a school and a class of men that such a school will graduate.

HENRY BALDWIN
(Custodian of American History).

Dr. G. Brown Goode,
   Smithsonian Institute.

THE CONCORD, *Washington, D. C., December 5, 1894.*

MY DEAR SIR: Careful observation of educational thought in this country for a quarter of a century convinces me that its natural outcome is to be found in the realization of the idea of a National University sustained by Government patronage at the capital of the nation, outranking all others in the land, so earnestly urged by Washington and his compeers. Many have feared the injurious effects of a political capital upon a seat of learning located near it. This fear led some to oppose the establishment of the University of Berlin; but experience has proved that the university was not injured, and the capital was benefited.

Intelligence and virtue joined must indeed be the corner stone of our free institutions, and their influence must pervade them from foundation to capstone. The more their influence is concentrated upon the management of public affairs, the greater the safeguards against ignorance and corruption, and the more likely the improvement of the public service. The greatest republic has need of, and should have at command, the conditions favorable to the highest learning.

The selection of Washington as the seat for great universities under private control points to a growing appreciation of the fact that nowhere else are such favorable conditions possible. The Senate bill does not antagonize them, but would crown them with higher opportunities. Besides, the most remote district school needs, and would be benefited by, the University proposed, and the maintenance at Washington of the grandest university of the world would serve to answer the legitimate demand of the aspiring peoples of the earth that our institutions of learning should afford opportunities for research and instruction not excelled under any other form of government.

Very respectfully, yours, etc.,
JOHN EATON
(Ex-President Marietta College, Former United States Commissioner of Education).

Hon. JOHN W. HOYT:

HARTFORD, CONN., *August 25, 1894.*

MY DEAR GOVERNOR: Accept, I pray you, my sincere thanks for your kindness in sending me a copy of your admirable Memorial, with the Report of the Senate Committee on the National University. I have read again with renewed interest your able and exhaustive exposition of the great scheme you have so long had at heart. That scheme will one day find realization. Perhaps it will come soon; and whenever it shall come * * *

On the two days following Thanksgiving Day the College Association for all the Middle States will hold its annual session at Baltimore, under the hospitalities and auspices of the Johns Hopkins University. What do you think of holding a conference then and there?

Ever yours,
JAMES C. WELLING
(Late President Columbian University).

Hon. JOHN W. HOYT,
   Chairman National University Committee.

PENNSYLVANIA STATE COLLEGE,
Center County, Pa., November 23, 1894.

DEAR SIR: The establishment at Washington of a national university of the broadest scope, and supported by ample income, is in my judgment one of the most important projects now before Congress. It is a measure worthy of the most earnest efforts of the highest statesmanship. Not only could such a university contribute immensely to the growth of a sound and vigorous citizenship, but there is in our present conditions a peculiar reason why it would be of incalculable service to the cause of public education throughout the United States. It is the peculiarity of all institutions in a free country that they spring up and grow spontaneously, and to some extent irregularly, so that they often fail of proper correlation and mutual support.

That has been true of the growth of our systems of public education, higher and lower. We have as many different systems as there are States and Territories. It is only within recent years, and in only a portion of the States, that an effort has been made to bring institutions of primary, secondary, and higher education into such mutual relations as would give to each the strength and support of all. Unless I greatly mistake, however, the tendency in that direction is now one of the most powerful in the educational world and in the public mind generally. But that movement is at present necessarily confined within State or Territorial limits. There is no bond of connection (except that which is supplied by purely voluntary associations) among the systems of the different States.

Now, Congress has already taken two or three steps of immense importance and of rapidly growing influence in this direction. In providing for the establishment of what are known as the land-grant colleges in every State in the Union, and in supplementing the original act by the laws of 1887 and 1890 (known as the Hatch act and the Morrill act, respectively), it has helped to create a great group of institutions which already hold the leadership in many States and are rapidly approaching it in others. These institutions would find their common head in a great National University.

They are naturally bound together already through their common relationship to the Federal Government, and they closely touch the life of their respective States through their relations to the several State governments. The graduates of these State colleges and State universities would naturally pass on to the National University, and it would seem natural and proper that special inducements to do so should be offered primarily to them. We have, therefore, all the elements of a magnificent system leading up to one institution which should crown and dignify and inspire the whole. The only suitable place for such an institution is the city of Washington, the capital of the nation, and the movement for its establishment has my most earnest and ardent "God-speed."

Faithfully yours,

GEO. W. ATHERTON *(President).*

The Hon. JOHN W. HOYT, *Washington, D. C.*

OHIO STATE UNIVERSITY, *Columbus, Ohio, November 26, 1894.*

MY DEAR SIR: It will give me pleasure to comply with your request for cooperation in securing the passage of the bill for the establishment of a National University. Will you kindly send me a copy of the bill?

One set of the documents that you have already sent me will be placed in the university library, as you suggested.

Truly yours,

W. H. SCOTT *(President).*

Dr. JOHN W. HOYT, *Washington, D. C.*

THE UNIVERSITY OF THE SOUTH,
Sewanee, Tenn., November 22, 1894.

MY DEAR SIR: I am very much interested in the establishment of a National University for post-graduate instruction, and I desire to urge upon Congress the importance of taking immediate and favorable action in the matter. It gives me pleasure to indorse the reasons which have been so admirably set forth by prominent educators throughout the Union. The establishment of such a university would do more for the upbuilding of this great nation than anything else.

With assurances of sympathy in your laudable undertaking, I am,

Yours, very faithfully,

B. L. WIGGINS *(Vice-Chancellor).*

Hon. JOHN W. HOYT,
Chairman National University Committee, Washington, D. C.

GIRARD COLLEGE, *Philadelphia, November 13, 1894.*

DEAR SIR: I most cheerfully give my indorsement to the scheme for the establishment of a National University in the city of Washington. Our Government and people need such a seat of learning, where the first scholars and the most eminent scientists of the nation or of the world may be gathered, and who, by their learning and attainments, may draw around them the best and brightest young men of the land.

The National University should have its standard so high as not to be the rival of any institution already existing. Its equipment should be thorough and complete and its endowment ample. Such an institution would inspire not only the young men but also all other colleges and universities to higher aims and greater efforts.

I shall write to our Senators and Representatives, urging their support of the measure.

Yours, very truly,

A. H. FETTEROLF (*President.*)

Hon. JOHN W. HOYT, *Washington, D. C.*

UNIVERSITY OF MICHIGAN, *Ann Arbor, November 29, 1894.*

DEAR SIR: Washington has large facilities to aid in carrying on the work of a genuine university. The libraries, museums, and laboratories, which are in the main under the control of the Government, and the large number of learned men employed in them, could be made of service in such an institution.

The purpose to take up Washington's idea of establishing a great National University at our capital, on a plan comparable to that of the German Universities, appeals to our patriotism and our pride, and must commend itself to many if it can be made clear that it will be adequately supported and will be unembarrassed by the interference of political partisans. The plan, before adoption, should be carefully matured and thoughtfully guarded against perils by the conference of able statesmen and men experienced in university administration.

Yours, very truly,

JAMES B. ANGELL
(*President University of Michigan*).

Hon. JOHN W. HOYT.

SWARTHMORE COLLEGE, *Swarthmore, Pa., December 4, 1894.*

FRATERNAL FRIEND: I was glad of our interview at Baltimore. * * * If our country could have a university truly worthy of that great name it would be a blessing indeed to the cause of education from the highest to the lowest grade. * * *

EDWD. H. NAGILL
(*Late President*).

Hon. JOHN W. HOYT.

WEST VIRGINIA UNIVERSITY,
Morgantown, November 13, 1894.

DEAR SIR: I have your letter and "Memorial Concerning a National University." From such information as I have about the matter, and from such attention as I have been able to give to it, I am decidedly of the opinion that the project to establish such a national university as proposed is entirely feasible, and that the expenditure necessary to create and maintain such an institution could be devoted to no purpose that would bring more benefit to the country or more honor to the authorities founding it. I shall be ready to contribute whatever I can to the success of the enterprise, and sincerely hope the efforts of yourself and others in its behalf may be successful.

Yours, very respectfully,

P. B. REYNOLDS
(*President West Virginia University*).

Hon. JNO. W. HOYT,
Chairman National University Committee, Washington, D. C.

UNITED STATES DEPARTMENT OF AGRICULTURE,
OFFICE OF ASSISTANT SECRETARY,
Washington, D. C., August 25, 1894.

MY DEAR SIR: It gives me pleasure to acknowledge the receipt of your valued favor of the 20th instant, forwarded to me here from the University of Tennessee. I am very glad to hear from you upon such a subject, for I am favorable to the scheme for a National Post-graduate University.

I am at present, and have been since the 1st of January, presiding over this office, where I shall be glad to see you at any time.

With warm personal regards,

Very truly, yours,

CHAS. W. DABNEY, JR.
(*President University of Tennessee*).

JOHN W. HOYT, *Washington, D. C.*

UNIVERSITY OF CALIFORNIA, *Berkely,*
November 12, 1894.

DEAR SIR: I have not time at present to argue the matter of the National University, which of course has its very attractive aspects. * * * If there is to be a national university, it should (as you intimate) bear to the existing universities and collegiate institutions a relation such as a university bears to the secondary schools. That is, it must be above them and far superior to them. * * *

Yours truly,

MARTIN KELLOGG (*President*).

Hon. JOHN W. HOYT.

NEWPORT, R. I., *September 11, 1894.*

My DEAR GOVERNOR HOYT: If by the united efforts of all the friends of the movement the present bill can be passed and become law, it will doubtless be an easy matter, in future years, to secure any amendment found desirable. You may depend upon it that I will cordially and loyally cooperate with you and others. The more rigidly the operations of the proposed university are limited to the field of post-graduate instruction the better. I will await at all times whatever suggestions you may desire to send me, and will always be ready to do all in my power.

Yours, very truly,

WILLIAM PEPPER
(*Late President University of Pennsylvania*).

Hon. JOHN W. HOYT, *Washington, D. C.*

PRESIDENT'S ROOMS, CORNELL UNIVERSITY,
Ithaca, N. Y., October 23, 1894.

DEAR SIR: I am heartily in favor of the project of establishing a National University at the Federal capital, to be maintained by the Federal Government and controlled by a board which it shall appoint. Such an institution would not interfere with or rival any existing educational agencies. It would be an institution not for undergraduates, but for graduates; an institution not for instruction, but for the conduct of original research and investigation and for the expansion of the boundaries of human knowledge.

I need not dwell upon the vast and valuable equipment which the Federal Government already possesses for such an institution in the city of Washington. There we have $30,000,000 worth of books, specimens, apparatus, and other appliances either belonging to the Government or under its control, and the Government is spending annually $4,000,000 to maintain and enlarge these collections. The scientific bureaus; the Agricultural Bureau, with its meteorological, zoological, and other divisions; the Navy Department, with its engineering appliances; the Congressional Library, the largest on the continent; the great National Museum, the Smithsonian Institution, the various astronomical appliances and equipments—these all only await organization to supply the equipment which a university devoted to research and investigation absolutely needs.

While it will be admitted that we have the facilities, it will be asked whether it is our national duty to establish such a university. Replying to this question, I take the highest moral ground and assert that it is our duty to minister to our civilization and to increase those intellectual and ideal goods which constitute its imperishable essence. I am unwilling to say that this great free Republic has no other mission than to accumulate wealth and to add to the material comforts and conveniences of the race. The glory of a nation is not its wealth or its territory, but rather its knowledge and its virtue. Virtue the state can not directly undertake to produce or to increase. But knowledge the Republic can increase by organizing facilities which already exist in the city of Washington.

The greatest of our statesmen from Washington down have favored the scheme of establishing a national university. The Father of his Country left a portion of his property as a partial endowment of such an institution; Jefferson and Madison and the two Adamses recommended it. This idea has run through our history from the beginning till now; furthermore, the reasons given by Washington remain substantially sound, even to this day. He did not, it is true, insist on the duty of a great nation to enlarge the stock of existing knowledge and contribute its share to the civilization of the race, but he did insist on the importance of the maintenance of higher learning amongst us; he did feel, with his successors, that if the new Republic was to take a prominent place among the nations of the world it could be only by "exalted intellect," to use the phrase which occurs in a report made by a committee of Congress on this subject. President Washington pointed out that such a university would also tend to allay sectional feeling and promote a sense of harmony and solidarity throughout our great Republic. Though railways and telegraphs have been perhaps a more effectual agency in bringing about this ond than even the establishment of a national university would have been, yet all will admit that the presence in a Federal capital of scholars and scientists who are drawn from all parts of the country, and are afterwards to be leaders in their own spheres, would have a most potent influence in developing this sense of harmony and solidarity on which Washington, after the importance of learning, laid the greatest stress.

Think of the effect of such an institution in kindling patriotism and loyalty and awakening public spirit among educated men and through them among all classes of the community. I recall the glorious description which Thucydides gives of Athens at the time of the Peloponnesian war. He explains why the Athenians have shown such spirit, why they are so proud of their country and are sacrificing their lives to support her. Foremost of all the incentives to patriotism he places the ideal goods of art and science and literature and philosophy which Greece, and Athens especially, had contributed to the world. I hope this Republic of ours, the largest the world has yet seen, will some day equal the smallest in its service to higher civilization. Animated by this sense of national vocation, I believe most heartily in the establishment at Washington, under the auspices and with the support of the Federal Government, of a National University devoted, not to the teaching of undergraduates, but, first, to the guidance of graduates in research and investigation, and, secondly, to the enlargement of learning and scholarship, the progress of art, science, and philosophy, the elevation of professional and industrial pursuits, and, in a word, the promotion of civilization and the best interests of humanity.

Truly yours,
J. G. SCHUEMAN (*President*).

Hon. JOHN W. HOYT.
Chairman National University Committee, Washington, D. C.

UNIVERSITY OF NEBRASKA, EXECUTIVE OFFICE,
Lincoln, October 23, 1894.

DEAR SIR: I recall receiving and reading with interest the printed matter you sent me during the summer, but do not recall any request for an expression of my opinion in this matter.

We are still in the midst of settling the university for the year, and it is a great task because of the enormous and unexpected increase in numbers without a corresponding increase in revenues. It is therefore quite impossible for me to say more than that I heartily favor the general plan of a National University for post-graduate work. It should stand in exactly the same relations to the great and public free school systems of each State as the State university now occupies with regard to the separate State systems. It would give a great stimulus to higher education in every direction, and would add a desirable uniformity (by which I do not mean absolute identity) to all school work.

I am sorry I can not say more, but I certainly would not be content to say less.

Cordially yours,
JAMES H. CANFIELD (*Chancellor*).

Mr. JOHN W. HOYT, *Washington, D. C.*

ALABAMA POLYTECHNIC INSTITUTE, A. & M. COLLEGE,
Auburn, Ala., Oct. 26, 1894.

DEAR SIR: The subject is one in which for years I have been interested and strongly approved, provided it could be made free from political influences. I would be glad to receive the memorial, etc., now, and will with pleasure write you my views.

Yours, respectfully,
WM. LEROY BROUN (*President*).

Dr. JOHN W. HOYT,
Chairman National University Committee, Washington, D. C.

KENTUCKY UNIVERSITY, *Lexington, Ky., October 31, 1894.*

DEAR SIR: The documents you sent me some weeks ago, I think, in the main, so far as I can judge, set forth the right conception of the object in view.

You are advocating a good cause, which I hope will ere long succeed. I trust in the midst of so many other interests just now or at any time engaging the attention of Congress, this noble enterprise will not fail of sufficient friends in and out of that body to give it the support necessary to carry it to victory.

As ever, your friend,
CHAS. LOUIS LOOS (*President*).

JOHNS HOPKINS UNIVERSITY, OFFICE OF THE PRESIDENT,
Baltimore, January 4, 1893.

DEAR SIR: I thank you for allowing me to see the draft of the bill for a National University, which I return immediately in accordance with your request. * * *

The bill appears to me to be drawn with great care and to avoid most of the difficulties which are inherent in a project of such magnitude. * * * The real province of the university, as it seems to me, should be to provide special facilities for study and work to properly qualified persons, whatever may be their academic standing, especially in connection with the great foundations now gathered and likely to be increased in the national capital.

Yours, very truly,

D. C. GILMAN.

UNIVERSITY OF THE STATE OF MISSOURI,
Columbia, October 26, 1894.

DEAR SIR: I received some time ago a copy of your Memorial concerning a "National University," and I have been intending to write you a letter on this subject; but the coveted opportunity for doing so has not yet appeared.

I am heartily in favor of the establishment of a National University, provided that it be built on the right lines and be adequately supported. It [inoq] not but post graduate work, and much care should be exercised on this point. It should also sustain certain relations to the State universities in the different States. This last point I hold to be of much importance. It carries out in education the general idea of our system of government.

The management of the National University should be separated from politics in every way. Too great care can not be exercised on this point. Another point of less importance, but worth mentioning, is that the management of the university should involve but few persons ex officio. But it is impossible to say more now than that I am very heartily in favor of establishing a national university separate from politics, to be built on proper lines for post-graduate work only, and to be adequately supported by the National Government.

With kind wishes, I am, very truly, yours,

R. H. JESSE (*President*).

Hon. JOHN W. HOYT, *Washington, D. C.*

ELMIRA COLLEGE. *Elmira, N. Y., November 1, 1894.*

DEAR SIR: Replying to your card of recent date, would say that I failed to receive anything from you during the month of August. This was due, possibly, to my absence from home during the summer. I trust your efforts for the establishment of a National University will meet with the success they deserve.

Cordially, yours,

RUFUS S. GREEN (*President*).

Mr. JOHN W. HOYT, *Washington, D. C.*

THE UNIVERSITY OF MINNESOTA,
Minneapolis, November 2, 1894.

DEAR SIR: I have been absent from home for three weeks. I take the first opportunity to acknowledge the receipt of yours of October and the memorial in regard to a National University. I need not attempt to formulate the reasons why a national university at Washington, supported by the General Government for the benefit of the whole country, is desirable. These reasons have been clearly stated by others again and again. I can only say that in the interest of the highest education, it seems to me that such an institution ought to be established at the national capital. It ought to take up work where other universities in the country practically leave off. For this work of original investigation and study no place is better than Washington, and no university in the world ought to be better than ours at Washington.

Very truly, yours,

CYRUS NORTHROP (*President*).

Hon. JOHN W. HOYT.

WASHINGTON AND LEE UNIVERSITY,
Lexington, Va., November 7, 1894.

DEAR SIR: The president of this institution (G. W. C. Lee), who is but just recovering from severe illness, desires me to say, in answer to your letter of the 5th instant, that he is hardly yet able to do much; but will carry out your wishes as soon as he can do so.

Respectfully,

THOS. E. MARSHALL, JR.
(*Private Secretary.*)

Hon. JOHN W. HOYT,
*Chairman National University Committee,
Washington, D. C.*

MARIETTA COLLEGE, *Marietta, Ohio, November 7, 1894.*

MY DEAR SIR: I am glad to learn of the movement for the establishment of a post-graduate university to be located at Washington. I can see decided advantages in such an institution located in that city. The movement is one in which I am greatly interested, and which I should like to see carried out to a successful completion. I hope the committee will be strongly supported, and that your efforts may be crowned with large success.

Very truly, yours,

JOHN W. SIMPSON (*President*).

Hon. JOHN W. HOYT,
 Washington, D. C.

COLUMBIA COLLEGE, IN THE CITY OF NEW YORK,
PRESIDENT'S ROOM, *November 8, 1894.*

MY DEAR SIR: Your letter of November 6 reached me in due course, and later the pamphlet to which you allude. If I get time I shall be glad to look into the matter, as you request, but I am under such heavy pressure that it is quite impossible to say when I shall be able to do so. There is undoubtedly very much to be said in favor of a National University at Washington. Something, perhaps, would depend upon its organization and its relation to other institutions of the higher learning; but of this, of course, I can not hope to speak without much more study and reflection than I have given to the subject.

Yours, faithfully,

SETH LOW
(*President*).

Mr. JOHN W. HOYT,
 Chairman, Washington, D. C.

OHIO STATE UNIVERSITY, OFFICE OF THE PRESIDENT,
Columbus, Ohio, November 8, 1894.

MY DEAR SIR: Your letters and the documents which you kindly sent me have been received. I am interested in the object which you propose, but have not been able as yet to examine the details of the plan. I hope soon to give it some attention, and if it is what I hope I shall be glad to cooperate to the extent of my ability in securing favorable action by Congress.

Yours, truly,

W. H. SCOTT (*President*).

Dr. JOHN W. HOYT, *Washington, D. C.*

WESTERN UNIVERSITY OF PENNSYLVANIA,
Pittsburg, November 10, 1894.

DEAR SIR: I owe you an apology for not having replied before this to your esteemed letters of recent date. I have been too busy to give the matter that attention which the magnitude and importance of the undertaking merits until to-day. Having just completed the reading of the documents you have kindly sent me, I desire now to say that it is impossible for me to add by any words of mine to the presentation of the merits of the cause you have espoused and which has already so long and so ably been advocated by those who possess far more influence, knowledge, and eloquence than I can claim.

The plan set forth in the papers before me is most noble, most feasible, most necessary. The best gift of man to man is an education, using that word in its broadest sense, as involving the development alike of the intellect and moral faculties. The American people are awake to the general necessity of providing an elementary education for the children of the Republic. The older institutions of learning and many of those more recently established have received princely gifts, reflecting alike the wisdom and the generosity of those who have made them, but it remains for the people to set a crown upon all the splendid efforts of the past by establishing through those who are the representatives of the people in the highest sense such an institution as that which it is proposed to bring into being at the national capital.

You have my best wishes for entire success in your truly enlightened efforts, and any help which I can give in forwarding the design I shall be most happy to render.

I have the honor to be, very faithfully, yours,

W. J. HOLLAND
(*Chancellor of the Western University of Pennsylvania*).

Hon. JOHN W. HOYT,
 Chairman National University Committee.

WESTERN UNIVERSITY OF PENNSYLVANIA,
Allegheny, Pa., December 6, 1894.

MY DEAR GOVERNOR: The more I reflect upon the proposition embodied in the proposed legislation the more I like it. It is plain to me, as it already is to you, that the establishment of such an institution will prove a mighty stimulus to the other institutions throughout the land, and could not fail to do a vast amount of practical good.

I am yours, very truly,

W. J. HOLLAND,
Chancellor of the Western University of Pennsylvania.

Hon. JOHN W. HOYT,
Washington, D. C.

UNIVERSITY OF SOUTH DAKOTA,
Vermillion, S. Dak., November 7, 1894.

SIR: I heartily thank you for your letter of August 20, the card of October 22, and the two documents referred to. Though amid extraordinary perplexities, I could not, consistently with any sense of gratitude for your persistent and patriotic endeavors, do less than examine in detail what you sent. This I have done to-day with sincere and growing interest.

It would be a piece of the wisest business economy for the Federal Government to found the proposed university as a means to the fullest fruition of enormous grants heretofore made to many independent schools for primary and secondary education. Schools so aided have their own widely differing standards, and are working in the particular interest of the several States by whose appropriations they are in part maintained. Their services are of necessity largely local, and their instruction upon questions of national application is exposed to such local influences as dominant political views, the temper of legislatures as to appropriations, and the like. If they resist tendencies to sectionalism—one of the gravest tendencies in national affairs—it is in spite of our so-called system of education. The greater the number of such schools the greater the need of a National University.

Can the General Government afford to thus spend millions without adding a reasonable amount for a university which shall fix a standard of excellence, which shall carry that standard, through its graduates, down to the lower schools already receiving Government aid; which shall bring the young from all parts of the land, and correct their sectional bias by contact with associates of different views, with the National Legislature, Administration, and courts? A university so located could do far more than any other agency in the correction of extreme and harmful sectional tendencies and passions, and in imparting that broader view of national questions which can not be gained outside of Washington.

From the educational standpoint it is a shame that so great a people do not have one University. The word "University" as a misnomer is so common that the majority of graduates of American institutions have no intelligent conception of the proper function and scope of a University. It is not surprising that public men are slow to appreciate the fact so palpable to educators that we have not a single university proper in this broad land. So far from interfering with existing institutions, the one you propose would be of incalculable benefit to all.

If there were not other and greater reasons, patriotism and national pride should supply this want for the sole purpose of avoiding the humiliating spectacle of thousands going abroad for the higher education, a standing confession of weakness of their own country, imbibing foreign ideas, expending American wealth upon an education which often requires no more time to acquire than is necessary to adjust it to the needs of their native land. A National University of their own would have none of these disadvantages and would instill a patriotism akin to that which so conspicuously marks the student of West Point or Annapolis.

Partisan plaudits may reward one who supports measures which are repeatedly changed by mutations of partisan control. Those who found the proposed university will enjoy the lasting credit of favoring an enterprise about which, once established, there will be no question in the future aside from extent of support.

Very respectfully, yours,

JOSEPH W. MAUCK (*President*).

Governor JOHN W. HOYT, *Washington.*

OFFICE OF THE PRESIDENT,
LELAND STANFORD JUNIOR UNIVERSITY,
Palo Alto, Cal., October 21, 1894.

DEAR SIR: I am most heartily in favor of the establishment of a genuine National University in the city of Washington. Such an institution should not be a school for ordinary collegiate instruction, but a place for advanced research in all departments of science and liberal learning. The development of research is the essential work of the university. To this end the National Capital, with its wealth of libraries and museums, offers advantages never to be found elsewhere in our country. These great advantages have never been in any high degree utilized. They can not be utilized except by placing them at the disposal of a body of investigators of various grades such as should compose the faculty and student body of a true university.

Of the multitude of schools called colleges and universities in America only a few are properly equipped for even the elementary work of the grade called collegiate. Not one is prepared to carry on advanced investigations of the character contemplated in the proposed National University. All schools which are capable of really good work are now carrying all that the limits of their endowments permit. The establishment of a National University would mean the setting of higher standards and more worthy ideals in all branches of higher education. It could enter into no rivalry with existing schools. Even should it do so, no harm would be done, for every improvement in aim or methods in one institution helps raise the plane of all others. A genuine university tends to make higher education respectable. Only the narrowest view of education would wish to hold students in existing institutions by preventing the existence of a better one.

The most valuable advance which the American people could take to mark the beginning of the new century would be the establishment of a National University.

Very truly, yours,
DAVID S. JORDAN *(President)*.
Hon. JOHN W. HOYT, *Washington, D. C.*

B.

Letters from State Superindendents of Public Instruction.

DEPARTMENT OF PUBLIC INSTRUCTION,
Frankfort, Ky., November 12, 1894.

DEAR SIR: I am so pressed by my official work that I can not command my time, and I have, therefore, been somewhat tardy in expressing myself as to the National University.

At length, however, I have concluded my examination of all the documents submitted to me; and so important did the matter seem to me from the first that my astonishment has grown with every step of the investigation that the recommendation of the fathers of the Republic was not long ago carried out.

There is no tenable ground for a valid argument against the university, while the reasons for its establishment are many and cogent. It would be not only "the crown and culmination of our whole series" of public schools, but the crowning glory of the practical statesmanship of the century now drawing to its close.

Yours, truly,
ED. PORTER THOMPSON,
Superintendent of Public Instruction.
JOHN W. HOYT, Esq., *Washington, D. C.*

STATE OF MISSOURI, DEPARTMENT OF EDUCATION,
City of Jefferson, December 6, 1894.

MY DEAR SIR: Having read the report of the committee to establish the University of the United States, I hereby heartily endorse this great institution for pushing investigation beyond the present limits of human knowledge. The original investigator needs greater competence and freedom from class drudgery than are afforded in the average State university.

Yours, very truly,
L. E. WOLFE
(State Superintendent, etc.).
Hon. JOHN W. HOYT, *Washington, D. C.*

COMMONWEALTH OF PENNSYLVANIA,
DEPARTMENT OF PUBLIC INSTRUCTION,
Harrisburg, October 22, 1894.

DEAR SIR: I have not had time to give the subject of a national university the attention which it deserves, and do not feel prepared to say anything for or against the movement. In a general way I am heartily in favor of any forward movement in the cause of higher education.

Yours, truly,
N. C. SCHAEFFER
(State Superintendent Public Instruction).
Mr. JOHN W. HOYT.

STATE OF CONNECTICUT, OFFICE OF BOARD OF EDUCATION,
Hartford, November 3, 1894.

DEAR SIR: The pamphlet and bill were duly received. The subject of a national university has never come pointedly to my attention. I certainly see no objections to the plan.

Yours, truly,
CHARLES D. HINE
Mr. JOHN W. HOYT,
937 K Street, Washington, D. C.

STATE OF RHODE ISLAND,
OFFICE COMMISSIONER OF PUBLIC SCHOOLS,
Providence, October 23, 1894.

MY DEAR SIR: Your postal, received a day or two since, reminded me of my neglected duty, and I at once exhumed the documents received last summer from where they were lying covered by the accumulation of the past few months.

I have read over the sketch of the bill which has been prepared, and, so far as I can judge therefrom, I am heartily in favor of its passage. I have long felt that the facilities afforded by our Government for the highest education were very defective; that we should never attain to the position in the world of science and letters to which we are really entitled until the National Government made definite and adequate provision for the support of our best scholars while engaged in the highest realm of knowledge.

It is impossible for one engaged in work of this highest order to either make it yield him a livelihood or to turn aside therefrom and earn it. These upper walks allow no subordinate subject to divert the mind.

Such a scheme as that proposed would, it seems to me, tend to correlate and unify the work of our institutions of learning throughout the country and offer an incentive to bright, active, vigorous young men in every State to push their studies to the highest attainable point.

I am confident it would raise the general scholarship of the whole country. I shall hope to see the measure carried through during the next session of Congress. Wishing you the fullest success, I have the honor to be,

Yours, very sincerely,
THOS. P. STOCKWELL (*Commissioner*).

Hon. JOHN W. HOYT.

STATE OF NORTH DAKOTA,
DEPARTMENT OF PUBLIC INSTRUCTION,
Bismarck, September 6, 1894.

DEAR SIR: Yours of the 25th ultimo and a copy of your Memorial in regard to the National University at hand. I have examined into the subject carefully. I am heartily in sympathy with the movement, and trust that you may be able to secure the passage of some reasonable bill establishing the University in such a manner as will take it wholly out of competition with existing institutions of this country and make it of universal value to the nation.

I believe that the time is fully ripe for the establishment of such an institution. More, I believe that the condition of our country financially and politically demands such an institution. The Northwest is educationally wide awake and ready to aid in raising the standard of our national educational character, and will heartily join hands with the West, South, and East in aiding toward the proposed University.

Wishing you success,
Fraternally yours,
LAURA J. EISENHUTH
(*State Superintendent*).

Mr. JOHN W. HOYT,
1234 Massachusetts avenue, Washington, D. C.

OFFICE OF SUPERINTENDENT OF PUBLIC INSTRUCTION,
STATE OF WASHINGTON,
Olympia, Wash., September 15, 1894.

MY DEAR SIR: I have long felt a deep interest in the proposition to found a National University at our Federal capital, as suggested by Washington and since urged by many of our distinguished statesmen and scholars, and have at times grown almost impatient with the delay in consummating this grand and patriotic conception. Such a university should stand for all that is modern and scholarly throughout the world; but it should especially emphasize what is distinctively American and should afford foreign students the opportunity of studying American institutions on their native soil.

I should hardly urge it from the standpoint of the economist as a means of keeping our students at home and offering them all the opportunities available at foreign universities, for I believe it is wise for the student to go abroad; but I urge it most earnestly as a competitor of the best foreign universities for the patronage of students from every nation. It should be the common opinion in all foreign countries within the next fifty years that their scholars could lay no claim to an adequate knowlede of American institutions unless they have studied in the "University of the United States." The fostering of such a sentiment at home and abroad is necessary to the greatness of American scholarship and American institutions.

Very truly, yours,
C. W. BEAN
(*Superintendent Public Instruction.*)

JOHN W. HOYT,
1234 Massachusetts Avenue, Washington, D. C.

OFFICE OF SUPERINTENDENT OF PUBLIC INSTRUCTION,
Raleigh, October 22, 1894.

MY DEAR SIR: Yours, dated October, 1894, is before me. I had received your Senate "Memorial concerning a National University (wholly post-graduate)," with "Senate committee's unanimous report on the pending bill," but have been too busy in the field lifting up my voice to our people in the "byways and hedges," in the woods and fields, in the swamps and on the hills, in the valleys and on the mountains for better support of our public free schools and for longer terms of the schools of the people to give much attention to a great post-graduate national university. If the Congress of the United States shall see fit to establish such a university, with proper safeguards thrown around it, "Barkis is willin'."

Very truly, yours,
JOHN C. SCARBOROUGH,
(State Superintendent Public Instruction for North Carolina.)
JOHN W. HOYT, Esq.,
Chairman National University Committee, Washington, D. C.

NEW HAMPSHIRE DEPARTMENT OF PUBLIC INSTRUCTION,
Concord, October 23, 1894.

MY DEAR SIR: My attention is just called to your communications. Before making any reply it will be necessary for me to study carefully the scheme for a national university, and this I can not do at present, but I may later.

Yours, truly,
FRED GORRING
(State Superintendent Public Instruction).
Hon. JOHN W. HOYT, *Washington, D. C.*

SUPERINTENDENT OF EDUCATION, STATE OF VERMONT,
Montpelier, September, 1894.

DEAR SIR: During my absence in August the "Memorial" was misplaced, and was not discovered till last week, or I should have replied earlier. I mean while had been waiting for the document, thinking you had not sent it.

It is a magnificent undertaking, and I heartily hope it will go through.

Very sincerely,
MASON S. STONE *(Superintendent).*
Mr. HOYT.

SUPERINTENDENT OF EDUCATION, STATE OF VERMONT,
Montpelier, October 6, 1894.

DEAR SIR: Your communication asking my opinion concerning the establishment of a national university at Washington is received, and I take pleasure in giving my unqualified and hearty indorsement of the project.

Such an institution would meet a national want and form a fitting capsheaf to our educational system.

It would be a means for the perpetuation of those ideas distinctly American and furnish an opportunity and stimulation to such as desire to pursue post-graduate work here in America.

A progressive nation like our own can not afford to have it said that its young men must go to Europe to complete their education.

We have resources sufficient to support such a university, the advancement of learning demands such, and our reputation among the nations of the earth can be enhanced in no better way.

Hoping that the present Congress will be wise in the nation's highest educational interests, I remain,

Very sincerely, yours,
MASON S. STONE,
(Superintendent of Education State of Vermont.)
Hon. JOHN W. HOYT, *Washington, D. C.*

OFFICE STATE SUPERINTENDENT OF PUBLIC EDUCATION,
Jackson, Miss., January 2, 1892.

MY DEAR SIR: I beg to state that I favor the establishment of a national university at Washington.

Yours, truly,
J. R. PRESTON *(State Superintendent).*
J. W. HOLCOMBE.

IN THE SERVICE OF THE COMMONWEALTH,
STATE BOARD OF EDUCATION,
State House, Boston, October 24, 1894.

DEAR SIR: I beg your indulgence for not acknowledging at an earlier date the receipt of your exhaustive and convincing "Memorial concerning a national university."

I assure you of my very deep interest in the plan. I see in particular fine possibilities for the exertion of a potent and beneficent influence upon all our institutions of learning. Why, for instance, may not some of the work that is now done under the auspices of the National Educational Association toward securing the proper coordination of subjects of study be done more thoroughly and with greater authority by the proposed university?

I should like to write at greater length upon this particular point, but can not do so at present. Meanwhile I content myself with expressions of deep interest in the plan and earnest hopes for its ultimate realization.

Very truly, yours,
FRANK A. HILL (*Secretary*).
Mr. JOHN W. HOYT, *Washington, D. C.*

STATE OF SOUTH DAKOTA,
DEPARTMENT OF PUBLIC INSTRUCTION,
Pierre, October 23, 1894.

DEAR SIR: I sincerely hope that Congress may soon be brought to see the importance of a National University, one that will in time compare favorably with the European universities, and one which, like them, will attract and call together the educational leaders of the country.

I am watching the movement with much interest.

Yours, very truly,
CORTEZ SALMON (*Superintendent*).
Dr. JOHN W. HOYT, *Washington, D. C.*

STATE OF IOWA,
OFFICE OF SUPERINTENDENT PUBLIC INSTRUCTION,
Des Moines, October 24, 1894.

MY DEAR SIR: I have not had time to give your letter and circulars the attention which they deserve. The press of official duties has been very great and will continue so until after New Year's. Upon the general point concerning which you write, I fully agree with you in the desirability of establishing a strong National University at Washington. If established under national auspices for post-graduate work, having the support of the General Government, it could in a short time be made to exert an immense influence upon the cause of education throughout the nation. It should be a university, however, worthy the name and worthy the nation which founds it. It should be made the leading university in the Union. How this can be done is a matter of great moment, but it can better be discussed by others who are more conversant with the conditions and circumstances than I am.

Yours, very cordially,
HENRY SABIN
(*Superintendent Public Instruction*).
Hon. JOHN W. HOYT, *Washington, D. C.*

OFFICE STATE SUPERINTENDENT OF PUBLIC INSTRUCTION,
St. Paul, Minn., September 12, 1894.

DEAR SIR: Answering yours of the 27th ultmo, I will say that the plan for establishing a post-graduate university at Washington meets my hearty approval. Let it once be admitted that such an institution would serve any useful purpose whatever, that its influence would be felt for good in the slightest degree throughout the country, and the question is settled. No argument worthy of a moment's consideration can be brought against it. The expense, when distributed among the 70,000,000 inhabitants of the United States, would not be of a feather's weight.

Every movement toward a higher culture and a nobler civilization originated at the head of the column gradually extends to the rear. The educational forces are drawn forward by the magnetism of those in advance, not pushed along by pike poles in the hands of the hindmost. Our colleges, by demanding more and better preparation of students applying for admission year by year, are constantly elevating the standards of the high schools, which in their turn require more and better work in the grammar grades, and this can be accomplished only by a similar movement in the primary schools. So an advance is scored along the whole line. A great post-graduate university at Washington would, if rightly managed, stimulate every college in the land to higher achievements, and the circle thus begun would go on broadening till the most sequestered rural schools would feel the new-born impulse, and even Sleepy Hollow might rub its eyes and ask "What time is it?"

This is not all. The graduates of this grand University of the United States would be in the army of progress as leaders, with influence wider than the continent and lasting as humanity.

One Horace Mann in a community is worth more than a thousand easy-going citizens whose sympathies and aims, so far as they have any, run in the same channels with his, but who are satisfied with simply being "right on all the great moral questions of the day."

Then let us have the University; let it be begun at once, and when done let it be a beacon light for the nations.
Very truly,
W. W. PENDERGAST
(Superintendent Public Instruction).
Hon. JOHN W. HOYT, *Washington, D. C.*

OFFICE OF SUPERINTENDENT OF PUBLIC INSTRUCTION,
STATE OF WASHINGTON,
Olympia, Wash., October 26, 1894.

MY DEAR SIR: I have the honor to acknowledge the receipt of your postal card of a recent date, which seems to indicate that you did not hear from me in response to your letter of last summer, asking for an indorsement of the proposition to found a national university at Washington, D. C.

I inclose herewith a copy of the letter which I wrote you on the 15th of September in regard to the matter, assuming that you did not receive it.

With best wishes for the success of the plan, and assuring you of my assistance to the extent of my ability and opportunity, I am,
Very truly, yours,
C. W. BEAN
(State Superintendent).
JOHN W. HOYT, *Washington, D. C.*

DEPARTMENT OF PUBLIC INSTRUCTION,
STATE OF NEW JERSEY.
Trenton, October 31, 1894.

DEAR SIR: If you will kindly send me a copy of Senate memorial concerning a National University, I shall take pleasure in looking it over and will write you a strong commendation of the general proposition.
Very truly yours,
A. B. POLAND *(State Superintendent).*
Hon. JOHN W. HOYT,
Chairman National University Committee, Washington, D. C.

STATE OF ARKANSAS, DEPARTMENT OF EDUCATION,
Little Rock, October 10, 1894.

DEAR SIR: I am in full sympathy with the measure to establish in the United States a National University. I have always agreed with the first and greatest of our Presidents upon this question, and have always been proud of the men who, since his day, have given their abilities to the consummation of the idea.

As I see it, such an institution has become a public necessity. We have hundreds of aspiring institutions that would like to be universities. A national institution comprehensively established would level these and contribute to their real power. It would also exercise a disciplinary as well as an elevating power upon the thousands of colleges and preparatory schools that, with varying standards, not only oppose each other, but lower the real value of education.

Besides this the needs of public elementary education press eloquently for such a school. Systems, city and State, are everywhere. Each of them has a dimly defined end, and this in turn is reached through the slow stages of experience and experiment. These systems need an inspiring central light—such as can come from a great national school.

I join with you cheerfully in the request that the National Congress give to the United States a National University as the great capstone to our educational development. I trust that the bill now before the Senate will pass.
Respectfully,
JOSIAH H. SHINN
(Superintendent Public Instruction).
HON. JOHN W. HOYT, *Washington, D. C.*

STATE OF CALIFORNIA,
DEPARTMENT OF PUBLIC INSTRUCTION,
Sacramento, October 30, 1894.

DEAR SIR: A copy of your Senate Memorial relative to the establishment of a National University came to hand in due season, but in consequence of the demand upon my time and labor in the discharge of my official duties, I have put off the consideration thereof to "a more convenient season."

Adverting to the matter now, permit me to say that I am in hearty accord with you in your efforts to accomplish an enterprise that should have been begun and carried to completion many years ago. I fully believe that the organization of such an institution will accomplish more for the great cause of public education and for the inculcation of a higher and purer patriotism than any other agency can hope to accomplish. If instituted upon the broad basis proposed, such a university will be of inestimable benefit in the new and powerful impetus which it will give to our different State universities, to our colleges, and to the cause of education throughout the entire land. That such a university is a leading want of our times and of our nation no lover of our noble institution of free American government can gainsay.

I most fully indorse all that has been said in reference to this important matter, and I sincerely wish for you most abundant success in your efforts to accomplish the object for which you have so earnestly and so disinterestedly labored. It will be my pleasure, as it is my duty, to contribute my mite of influence in aid of an enterprise so abundantly fraught with benefit to the people and to the institutions of our country.

Very truly, yours,

J. W. ANDERSON
(Superintendent Public Instruction.)

Hon. JOHN W. HOYT,
Chairman National University Committee,
Washington, D. C.

DEPARTMENT OF EDUCATION,
Austin, Texas, November 2, 1894.

DEAR SIR: I certainly wish you much success with your efforts for the establishment of a National University. I regret that I have not the time to give the matter a more careful investigation at this time.

Most respectfully,

J. M. CARLISLE *(State Superintendent).*

Mr. JOHN W. HOYT, *Washington, D. C.*

STATE OF MARYLAND, EDUCATION DEPARTMENT,
Baltimore, November 2, 1894.

DEAR SIR: Referring to your postal of October, 1894, I beg to state that it will give me great pleasure to add anything in my power to the efforts to establish a National University in Washington.

I was absent from home during the summer, and my correspondence was somewhat interrupted. I regret to state that I can not now find the copy of your Senate Memorial. Will you kindly send me another copy?

Very respectfully,

E. B. PRETTYMAN
(State Superintendent Public Instruction).

Hon. JOHN W. HOYT,
Chairman National University Committee.

STATE OF MARYLAND, EDUCATION DEPARTMENT,
Baltimore, December 11, 1894.

DEAR SIR: I beg to state that I am most heartily in favor of the establishment of a national post-graduate university in Washington City. This is essential to complete the systems of public education, already established by the different States, and to give to American youths the opportunity for full development amidst the best possible surroundings at the capital of their own country. The free intercourse of our best and brightest young men from all parts of the country at the period of character molding, mental development, and the establishment of fixed opinions, would tend to curb egotism, provincialism, bigotry, and sectionalism. Such university training certainly has for our youth great advantages over that of any foreign universities, and would confirm patriotism and strengthen the union among our people.

Very respectfully,

E. B. PRETTYMAN
(State Superintendent, etc.).

Hon. JOHN W. HOYT, *Washington, D. C.*

DEPARTMENT OF PUBLIC INSTRUCTION, MICHIGAN,
OFFICE OF SUPERINTENDENT,
Lansing, November 5, 1894.

DEAR SIR: Absence from home and press of public business have caused the delay in replying to your Memorial concerning a National University. The memorial is mislaid, so I do not know exactly what you wish me to do concerning it, but I would state here that I am most heartily in favor of a post-graduate university in Washington. It would certainly be a fitting climax to the great educational systems of our States. I wish you hearty success in your enterprise.

Yours, very truly,

HENRY R. PATTENGILL
(Superintendent Public Instruction).

Hon. JOHN W. HOYT, *Washington, D. C.*

STATE OF ILLINOIS, PUBLIC INSTRUCTION,
Springfield, November 7, 1894.

DEAR SIR: I have no doubt that a post-graduate university, such as is described in the Memorial you kindly sent me, would be the keystone of the educational system of the country. I hope every effort will be put forth to secure the passage of the bill now before Congress, and any assistance I may be able to render by conferring with Senators or Members of the House from Illinois will be cheerfuly given.

Very truly, yours,

HENRY RAAB
(State Superintendent Public Instruction).

Hon. JOHN W. HOYT, *Washington, D. C.*

STATE OF KANSAS, EXECUTIVE DEPARTMENT,
OFFICE OF SUPERINTENDENT OF PUBLIC INSTRUCTION,
Topeka, Kans., December 6, 1894.

DEAR SIR: Your card of recent date is before me, and in reply will say that the 13,000 teachers of Kansas heartily indorse the establishment of a National University. Personally, I have long felt that such an institution should be established. I trust that you will succeed at this session.

Respectfully,

H. N. GAINES
(State Superintendent Public Instruction).

Dr. JOHN W. HOYT, *Washington, D. C.*

STATE OF NEBRASKA,
DEPARTMENT OF PUBLIC INSTRUCTION,
Lincoln, September 18, 1894.

DEAR SIR: It affords me pleasure to reply to your favor of August 25 in regard to the establishment in the city of Washington of a great National University.

It may be assumed that in the Memorial, the receipt of which I have the honor to acknowledge, the term university means university, the culminating and crowning educational institution of the nation.

Such an institution, to subserve its highest purpose, should be, must be, in proximity to the sources of information; its students making original research must be in the fields to be searched.

These conditions are present in the national capital in the form of museums, libraries, laboratories, art collections; in the form of departments and bureaus of the National Government; in the form of local institutions; in the form of learned associations; and these are side by side with the hundreds of experts in many branches of the Government service.

While all this is true it concerns the location only of such an institution.

We should have such an institution, because in this way only can we meet the demands made upon our nation by learning; because it would afford an enormous incentive to research and consequent scholarship; because it would be a powerful factor in crystallizing, or, better, organizing our many educational systems into one system; because it would offer to students at home and abroad an opportunity for the study of our governmental, our economic, and our social systems, and thus open the way for the correction of errors, as well as for the dissemination among the peoples of the earth of the excellencies that exist in a "government of the people, for the people, and by the people."

Yours, truly,

A. K. GOUDY
(Superintendent Public Instruction).

Hon. JOHN W. HOYT, *Washington, D. C.*

SPEECH

OF

HON. WM. F. VILAS.

The Senate, as in the Committee of the Whole, resumed the consideration of the bill (S. 1708) to establish a national university—

Mr. VILAS said:

Mr. PRESIDENT, I desire to address a few observations to the Senate in reference to this bill, which I think can be easily submitted by 2 o'clock.

I regard it a privilege to contribute voice and vote to this measure. After more than a century's waiting there are embodied in it the patriotic dreams, the generous hopes of the noblest of them who laid the foundations of this nation. Regardless of all dividing opinions, on this project were united the chief spirits who gave form to the liberty and constitutional order of America. Washington and Franklin, Adams and Jefferson, Madison and Monroe, Wilson, Pickering, Rutledge, Randolph, all whose words are saved, no voice dissenting, shared with paternal wisdom and affection in the conception of this institution as the crowning ornament of the Republic.

In the convocation of sages that wrote the Constitution special grant of power, in explicit terms, to establish the university was omitted only because after debate it was found to be unnecessary, and no word should be superfluous in that grandest instrument written by man. By his last will and testament Washington bequeathed a sum for its foundation to be accumulated at interest, which if husbanded and compounded until to-day would have been near $5,000,000. Nor ever from the hour when he first meditated the noble project did his confidence fail that his countrymen would rise to its execution.

Sir, I think we may share that generous ardor, the thrill of his inspiration touch us, as we shall join hands to upraise the structure which so moved his heart and the spirit of the fathers.

The bill before us I find especially satisfactory, because it carries the aims and purposes peculiarly befitting the place of such an institution in our Federal system. Three leading objects ought to govern its work. First and foremost, to advance by research and discovery the sum of human learning. Next, to gather in store and assure the safe preservation of every part and circumstance of it. And thirdly, to teach so as to lead the mind to the highest reaches of its power.

The university of the United States has no place to occupy as a competitor in the instruction of youth. It ought to enter no field held by the educational systems of the States or institutions of private benevolence, which ought to be, and are or will be, amply equipped and competent for such uses. But beyond and above these, standing upon and supported by them, the Federal establishment should rise for advancement and accumulation of learning—the crown, the head, the center, the illuminating sun of all.

In the service of society the prime value and usefulness of the educational agencies already on foot—the common schools, academies, colleges, and universities—are tuition, to impart knowledge to and train the minds of successive generations of youth in preparation for the tasks and duties of life in every art and vocation. But there is a higher range of perfection in scholarship which few are given the ability to grasp, and fewer yet are willing to consecrate their lives to acquire, with the common or too frequent doom of accompanying poverty. Yet these are especially the men whom the nation ought to reach out to raise up to the highest intellectual strength. Not in mere benefaction to them; that is but an incidental benefit in the pursuit of the aims of such a university. The greater end is to establish a pioneer corps to push the way of knowledge, and a garrison for its storehouse, as well as to provide constant recruitment of both these forces.

For, as I said, the supreme purpose of a national university ought to be the discovery, deduction, and acquisition of truth lying beyond the utmost confines of the known; the ambition of inquiry, insatiable curiosity, its ruling passion. The stock of learning grows, like the oak, in successive layers, slowly gathered from the elements of nature; and the power of the human mind finds increase only as it gathers more and more the secrets of her laws.

What is it, sir, that has brought to us the marvelous comforts and delights of our civilization of which we daily boast? Surely no one will contest the answer. Scientific knowledge expanding and applied in the air and light of liberty.

I doubt if any instructed man will say that the human mind holds greater faculties now than in ages past. In what were the native powers of the Chaldean sages, the wise men of the East, the philosophers of classic days, the subtle brains of the Middle Ages, inferior to our modern thinkers? Is not the only advantage of the latter in the since-discovered wealth of facts and deductions showing so much of the composition, nature, and operative laws of the earth we live on, the heavens it rolls and swings among? The measure of our modern superiority is not vertical, but lateral. We climb no higher peaks, although vastly more in number, as our modern thought has swept far wider ranges. Had the great men of ancient Rome enjoyed the sciences and liberty of to-day what might have been our state and condition? Projecting from the base of our attainments, who can picture or limit the marvels that await the generations to succeed us? Where, sir, should research end until man's knowledge and nature's laws are coextensive?

Sir, in better hands this argument might be amplified, I think, with attractive force. I will do no more than to assert the wisdom, as it seems to me, of making this a national purpose incorporate in a national university. Let it be the vanguard, the forlorn hope of science, abundantly equipped to lead the quest for knowledge, with a power never before gathered to such an end. The United States of America in Congress assembled, all the power of man, can establish no nobler project; nay, nor one which, in the shrewd wit of a good bargain, will return greater dividends, reckoning them only in the dollars of wealth to be so distributed to the nation.

Happily the site proposed in this bill, and at our service again, is the very one chosen by Washington himself for the seat of this institution. Adorned and beautified as this city already is, full of features of interest and patriotic pride, and still more as it shall be, not many years will pass before its most cherished object and the warmest boast of the pride of Americans would be the university of the United States. I trust, sir, that we may share the honor of decreeing its establishment.

I shall not now occupy more time. There may be points of discussion which will elicit further debate in the future, although I have no desire to prolong the consideration of the measure. I trust the Senate will not fail to pursue its consideration to an end.

During the delivery of Mr. VILAS's remarks—

The PRESIDENT pro tempore. The hour of 2 o'clock having arrived, it is the duty of the Chair to lay before the Senate the unfinished business, which will be stated.

The SECRETARY. A bill (S. 1481) to amend an act entitled "An act to incorporate the Maritime Canal Company of Nicaragua," approved February 20, 1889.

Mr. MORGAN. Without displacing the unfinished business, I ask unanimous consent that the Senator who is now occupying the floor may be allowed to proceed with his remarks.

The PRESIDENT pro tempore. Is there objection to the request?

Mr. MILLS. What is the request?

The PRESIDENT pro tempore. That the Senator from Wisconsin be permitted to conclude his remarks upon the university bill.

Mr. HALE. Then the Nicaragua bill will come up and occupy the rest of the day?

Mr. MORGAN. I stated that the request was to be without prejudice to that bill.

The PRESIDENT pro tempore. The request is that the unfinished business be passed over informally in order that the Senator from Wisconsin may conclude his remarks.

Mr. HALE. So that the university bill, if it comes up again, must come up by vote of the Senate.

The PRESIDENT pro tempore. The university bill will necessarily go to the Calendar when the Senate resumes the consideration of the Nicaraguan Canal bill. The Chair hears no objection, and the Senator from Wisconsin will proceed.

After the conclusion of Mr. VILAS's remarks,

Mr. HUNTON said: By the consent of the Senator from Alabama I have the floor to give notice that to-morrow, after the routine business is completed, I shall move to take up the university bill during the morning hour.

National University Bill.

"The Capstone of our Educational System."

SPEECH

OF

HON. JAS. H. KYLE,

OF SOUTH DAKOTA.

IN THE SENATE OF THE UNITED STATES,

Tuesday, December 18, 1894.

The Senate, as in the Committee of the Whole, resumed the consideration of the bill (S. 1708) to establish a national university—

Mr. KYLE said:

Mr. PRESIDENT: The question has arisen thousands of times in many minds why we have no great national university under the support and care of the General Government. The failure to establish such an institution can not be laid to poverty, for we are one of the richest nations of the earth. We cannot say that the people do not want it, for it has been the dream of scholars and statesmen for a hundred years. We can explain our failure to provide it only by the fact that our minds have been wrapped up in the material welfare of a new and rapidly growing nation. A nation is a human family upon a larger scale, and it must necessarily struggle first with the problem of subsistence and development of the material home, leaving the questions of culture and higher education for later years.

But withal we can say with pride that the United States stand second to none in point of general education and intelligence. Our public schools, extending to every hamlet and precinct of the most remote districts, crowned with our State universities, are open alike to rich and poor, and the percentage of illiteracy is reduced to a minimum in the United States. In the United States nearly 90 per cent of our white population can read and write, which is remarkable, considering the fact that twenty-five years have brought to our shores nearly 11,000,000 foreigners, the majority of whom could not be expected to learn to read and write our language. Our farmers and the laborers in our factories and mines, through the advantages derived from our village high schools, are fitted to transact their business affairs and to fill acceptably positions under the civil government.

Our national policy is education for the masses. It was Webster, I think, who said, "We must educate, or short will be our race from the cradle to the grave." Ignorance and barbarism are closely related. The superstitions and oppressions of the masses in past history are attributable to their ignorance. With intelligence human rights are respected, proper laws are framed for the protection of the weak against the strong, and society is established on a broader moral foundation. Education disseminates new ideas, broadens the views of men, enlarges the possibilities, creates new and higher aspirations, beautifies the individual and the home, conduces to morality, produces greater independence of thought and action, and in every way raises men and the nation to a higher plane. It is penny wise and pound foolish to tighten the purse strings when considering questions of public education.

A glance at our roster of splendid State institutions and our vast expenditure in the public-school system, over $170,000,000 annually, shows that we have not acted niggardly. But in order to the greater efficiency of those minor institutions we must not forget the crown—the capstone of our educational system—the national university. Such an institution will not only produce a highly beneficial reflex influence upon the whole system, but will create the possibilities for highest research in literature, philosophy, and the arts, and will infuse as nothing else will an ambition and inspiration into the great body of American youth to reach the highest attainments in culture.

It was the dream of the founders of the Republic to establish seats of learning second to none in the world. They realized the necessity of beginning at once, as great universities do not grow in a day. Like individuals, they are born, but must mature slowly. The character of an institution is a process of growth which years of patient toil alone can produce. They saw as clearly as we see to-day the nation mapped out in great independent commonwealths, with teeming millions of population; that in wealth and power the United States would ultimately lead the world, and that it was fitting that we should contribute accordingly to the progress of knowledge by the highest research and investigation.

They realized the necessity of educating their sons and daughters in the atmosphere of American institutions. In fact, jealousy of British influence and system of government and the desire to promote patriotism in the minds of American youth were probably the occasion of the first discussion in regard to the national university.

President Washington, in a letter March 16, 1795, to Governor Brooke, of Virginia, writing concerning university endowment, used the following language:

It is with indescribable regret that I have seen the youth of the United States migrating to foreign countries in order to acquire the higher branches of erudition and to obtain a knowledge of the sciences. Although it would be injustice to many to pronounce the certainty of their imbibing maxims not congenial to republicanism, it must nevertheless be admitted that a serious danger is encountered by sending abroad among other political systems those who have not well learned the value of their own.

It may be a question to-day whether our youth do not inculcate some foreign ideas detrimental to true Americanism. We need to-day an education in Americanism. We go abroad for our music, our painting, our literature, art, science, and philosophy. We look to Europe for guidance in all things. Our youth bow the knee to foreign culture and the aristocracy of blood. It seems to me our national pride should impel us to exalt our American institutions, and herald to the world that America leads and no longer follows.

It was the earnest desire of Washington in the latter years of his life to found in this city a national university for the higher education. He wrote to many influential men in regard to it, devoted much of his public addresses to it, and provided generously for it in his will. As early as January 8, 1790, in his address to Congress, President Washington said:

> Nor am I less persuaded that you will agree with me in the opinion that there is nothing which can better deserve your patronage than the promotion of science and literature. Knowledge is, in every country, the surest basis of happiness. In one in which the measures of government receive their impressions so immediately from the sense of the community as in ours it is proportionably essential. To the security of a free constitution it contributes in various ways—by convincing those who are interested with the public administration that every valvable end of government is best answered by the enlightened confidence of the people and by teaching the people themselves to know and to value their own rights; to discern and provide against invations of them; to distinguish between oppression and the necessary exercise of lawful authority, between brethren, proceeding from a disregard to their convenience, and those resulting from the inevitable exigencies of society; to discriminate the spirit of liberty from that of licentiousness, cherishing the first and avoiding the last; and uniting a speedy but temperate vigilance against encroachments with an inviolable respect for the laws. Whether this desirable object will be best promoted by affording aids to seminaries of learning already established, by the institution of a national university, or by any other expedients, will be worthy of a place in the deliberations of the Legislature.

Again, in his eighth annual message, his last to Congress, he uses the following language, December 7, 1796:

> I have heretofore proposed to the consideration of Congress the expediency of establishing a national university and also a military academy. The desirableness of both these institutions has so constantly increased with every new view I have taken on the subject that I can not omit the opportunity of once for all recalling your attention to them. The assembly to which I address myself is too enlightened not to be fully sensible how much a flourishing state of the arts and sciences contributes to material prosperity and reputation. True it is that our country, much to its honor, contains many seminaries of learning highly respectable and useful; but the funds upon which they rest are too narrow to command the ablest professors, in the different departments of liberal knowledge, for the institution contemplated, though they would be excellent auxiliaries. Among the motives to such an institution, the assimilation of the principles, opinions, and manners of our countrymen, by the common education of a portion of our youth from every quarter, will deserve attention. The more homogeneous our citizens can be made in these particulars the greater will be our prospect of permanent union; and a primary object of such a national institution should be the education of our youth in the science of government. In a republic what species of knowledge can be equally important and what duty more pressing on its legislature than to patronize a plan for communicating it to those who are to be the guardians of the future liberties of the country?

I would call special attention to the will of this great man, July 9, 1799—just before his death—in which he provided, as he thought, for the neucleus of this great institution. As the fiduciary of this great trust we are called upon to report to the people of our country what steps were taken to carry out the provisions of this last will and testament, and whether we can not yet discharge the duty imposed upon us.

The will reads as follows:

> It has always been a source of serious regret with me to see the youth of these United States sent to foreign countries for the purpose of education, often before their minds were formed, or they had imbibed any adequate ideas of the happiness of their own; contracting too frequently principles unfriendly to republican government and to the true and genuine liberties of mankind; which, thereafter, are rarely overcome. For these reasons it has been my ardent wish to see a plan devised on a liberal scale, which would have a tendency to spread systematic ideas through all the parts of this rising empire, thereby to do away with local attachments and State prejudices, so far as the nature of things would, or indeed ought to, admit, from our national councils. Looking anxiously forward to the accomplishment of so desirable an object as this is (in my estimation), my mind has not been able to contem-

plate any plan more likely to effect the measure, than the establishment of a university in a central part of the United States, to which the youths of fortune and talents from all parts thereof might be sent for the completion of their education in all the branches of polite literature, in arts and sciences, in acquiring knowledge in the principles of politics and good government, and (as a matter of infinite importance, in my judgment) by associating with each other, and forming friendships in juvenile years, be enabled to free themselves in a proper degree from those local prejudices and habitual jealousies which have just been mentioned, and which, when carried to excess, are never failing sources of disquietude to the public mind, and pregnant of mischievous consequences to this country; under these impressions, so fully dilated. * * *

I give and bequeath in perpetuity the fifty shares (value, $500 each) which I hold in the Potomac Company (under the aforesaid acts of the legislature of Virginia) toward the endowment of a university to be established in the District of Columbia under the auspices of the General Government, if that Government should incline to extend a fostering hand toward it; and until such a seminary is established and the funds arising on these shares shall be required for its support, my further desire is that the profit accruing therefrom shall, whenever dividends are made, be laid out in purchasing stock in the Bank of Columbia, or some other bank at the discretion of my executors, or by the Treasurer of the United States for the time being, under the direction of Congress; and the dividends proceeding from the purchase of such stock is to be invested in more stock, and so on until a sum adequate to the accomplishment of this object is obtained.

I need not quote further on this subject except to say that the establishment of the university was publicly and favorably discussed by the great periodicals of the day, and was championed by such men as Thomas Jefferson, Samuel Blodgett, John Barlow, Col. John P. Van Ness, President James Madison at three different times in his annual messages to Congress, President James Monroe, and President John Quincy Adams, besides other distinguished statesmen and scholars down to the present time. The last public reference by a President was, I believe, by President Grant in his message to Congress December 1, 1873. He used these words:

I would suggest to Congress the propriety of promoting the establishment in this District of an institution of learning or university of the highest class, by donation of lands. There is no place better suited for such an institution than the national capital. There is no other place in which every citizen is so directly interested.

But, Mr. President, the question most important now is, do we need a national university supported from the public funds? Have we not now ample opportunities for higher educational work in our sectarian colleges and State universities? The same question might have been put with equal propriety when the founders of the Republic were discussing this subject. The population of the United States was then but 5,000,000, scattered over a very few States, and yet Harvard College, founded in 1636; Yale College, founded in 1701; Princeton College, founded in 1746; Dartmouth College, founded in 1769; Columbia, 1754; Washington and Lee, 1749; William and Mary, 1649; Georgetown College, 1788, besides many others, were well-established institutions, and were second to no undergraduate colleges.

To-day we have the above institutions with a hundred years of added prosperity, together with scores of newer colleges and universities in every State of the Union. But our population and our progress have gone beyond our educational facilities. The times demand not only more but better universities; and it would be just as logical to argue that having the high schools of the country we need no colleges as to argue that having the undergraduate colleges we need no higher institutions.

Our undergraduate colleges to-day matriculate boys and young men; and their curriculum of studies, limited to four years, must necessarily comprise but a mere smattering of science and philosophy, with only a fair foundation in mathematics and the languages. We need institutions, or at least one institution, where those young men who have shown a talent for certain lines of study can go, and where as men they can be encouraged to devote their lives to the advancement of learning. One hundred years, fifty years even, have witnessed a revolution of methods and opened fields of investigation heretofore unknown. Philology, geology, chemistry, are not old sciences. Electricity is in its infancy; scientists are theorizing about it, and men like Edison and Tesla are forging ahead, revealing wonders to the world. Psychology is known only so far as the faculties and laws of the human mind are concerned.

The phenomena of the occult sciences are but the outcroppings of laws yet unknown or little known. Biology, bacteriology, ethnology, astronomy, the science of medicine, the histories of religions, and many other fields are practically new fields for research. And while America can boast with pride of her accomplishments—of her Agassiz, Dana, Bancroft, Whitney, Longfellow, and a few others who have pursued special lines of investigation, or have arrived at some distinction in letters—we are yet a nation of amateurs. England points to Milton and Bacon, Mills, Spencer, Macaulay, Gibbon, Hume, Smith, Tyndall, and scores of like men; Germany to Fichte, Schelling, Hegel, Schleiermacher, Neander, Kant, Uhland, Schiller, Goethe, and others. France points to long lists of statesmen, scientists, and philosophers who are the product of the University of France or institutions of like grade.

Our small colleges, dependent upon the generosity of those benevolently disposed, can not hope to equip themselves to compete with Government institutions. In Austria-Hungary they have eleven universities aided by the General Government. Each has the four faculties of law, theology, medicine, and philosophy. The University of Vienna had (in 1892) 374 professors and 4,919 students; Prague, 304 professors and 4,602 students; Innsbruck, 105 professors and 849 students; Graf, 135 professors and 1,323 students; Cracow, 122 professors and 1,196 students; Lemberg, 73 professors and 1,193 students; Cznernowitz, 37 professors and 301 students, or a total in Austria of 1,150 professors and 13,383 students.

Hungary has universities at Budapest, Klausenburg, and Agram, with a total of 296 professors in the year 1891 and 4,498 students. These do not include forty-five theological colleges. There are also seven Government technical schools, with 428 professors and 2,502 students. I do not include amongst these the minor schools, of which there are thousands, nor the undergraduate colleges.

In France the budget of 1890 carried 162,681,000 francs for primary instruction and 11,600,370 francs were set aside for the support of the university faculties. France supports her universities liberally. They are called "faculties de l'état" and are known as faculties of literature, faculties of science, of theology, medicine, law, etc.

Germany compels all children from 6 to 14 years of age to attend school, and requires all teachers to hold Government certificates. A system of public schools, colleges, and universities is supported by the Government. There are 21 high class universities, the most important of which are Berlin, Erlangen, Frieburg, Gottengen, Halle, Heidelberg, Jena, Königsberg, Leipzig, Munich, Strausburg, and Tübingen. These were manned (1892-93) with 2,431 professors, and in the four departments of theology, jurisprudence, medicine, and philosophy there was a total of 28,500 students. This does not include 2,985 nonmatriculated students at the University of Berlin.

Italy maintains her universities from the public treasury. The total sum granted by the state for public instruction in 1891-'92 was 41,711,985 lire. There are 21 universities, with a total of 966 professors and 16,518 students.

Switzerland maintains a system of compulsory education, and supports her universities at public expense. There are five of them, located at Basle, Zurich, Berne, Geneva, Lausanne, and two academic institutions at Frobourg and Neuchatel. The faculty (1893) consists of 431 professors, and the total number of students was 2,758.

In the United States, 1891-'92, there were 442 colleges and universities, with 9,326 professors and 135,582 students; 158 female seminaries, with 2,185 teachers and 24,611 students. There were also professional schools (theology, law, and medicine) to the number of 309, with 4,215 professors and 30,392 students. Nearly all these institutions are supported from private benevolence. Michigan University probably approaches most nearly to the European idea of a State institution.

By comparing our population it will be seen that the United States is not behind in the number of her colleges. But in the list of foreign institutions I have not enumerated the undergraduate colleges. Europe has these and has taken a step in advance. Europe has long since reached the climax of material development, and has devoted herself to culture, and has advanced by specializing her institutions and chairs. It is time for the United States to act. We should establish one institution at least which would compel the admiration and elicit the praise of the world's scholars. But at the present time our people look abroad for scholarship, and point with pride to their doctors of law, medicine, science or philosophy or theology, and say our men have had superior advantages. Colleges and churches even are proud to say that their teachers and pastors took their Ph. D. or D. D. or M. D., or whatever it may be, in Germany. It should make patriotic citizens blush and ask why we can not produce these leaders of thought.

I do not wish to be understood as underrating the standing of such institutions as Johns Hopkins or Harvard or Yale or others that are doing excellent post-graduate work. The aim is to plant a university which shall be different from the ordinary American institution. It will begin where the others leave off, and will be in no sense a competitor. It will rather add to their usefulness by providing possibilities for the undergraduates and stimulating the ambition of those gifted with special talent. In the words of another:

An institution broader in its scope, more complete in its organization, more philosophic and practical in its internal regulations, with the highest possible educational standards and aims; an institution above and beyond the best of the colleges, with their loosely attached professional schools, and on its own higher plane existing for the extension and diffusion of all branches of useful knowledge; an institution where the love of knowledge * * * shall be fostered and developed; where advanced students, devoted to any branch of knowledge, whether science, language. literature, or philosophy, or to any of the combinations of these constituting the numerous professional courses of instruction, shall intermingle and enjoy friendly intercourse as peers of the same realm; where the professors, chosen from among the ablest and best scholars of the world, with absolute freedom of conscience and of speech, shall be not teachers of the known merely, but also earnest searchers after the unknown and capable, by their genius, enthusiasm, and moral power, of infusing their own lofty ambition into the minds of all who wait upon their instruction; a university not barely complying with the demands of the age, but one that shall create, develop, and satisfy new demands and aspirations, that shall have power to fashion and mold the age unto its own ideal and which through every change and every real advance of the world shall still be at the front, driving back from their fastnesses the powers of darkness, opening up new continents of truth to the grand army of progress, so leading the nation forward and helping to elevate the whole human race.

The bill before us in section 3 provides that there shall be a board of regents consisting of eight persons, appointed by the President; and section 5 provides that these shall choose a president, who shall be the chief officer of the university. Section 6 provides for a council of faculties, each of which is to be presided over by a dean, who shall occupy the same relation to his department as the ordinary college president. Each faculty shall have chairs filled by the most expert students of the age, who shall prosecute the most advanced lines of research; and no person shall be admitted as a student or pupil who shall not have taken a bachelor's or some equivalent degree.

With such an institution the United States would at once take rank in facilities for higher education with the most advanced nations. We should have a university with the wealth of the nation behind it, and the beneficent gifts of a patriotic people. One hundred years ago the question arose as it arises now, shall we establish a national university, or shall we aid the institutions already established. Upon this people will differ. A large class are advocates of the sectarian institution; but the majority of the people, while not willing to divorce education from religion, are unwilling to yoke education and sectarianism. It is no use to argue the question. The feeling exists, and we can not overcome it.

It is a wise provision, therefore, of section 8 of this bill that "no chair for instruction sectarian in religion, etc., shall be permitted in any form."

This measure, Mr. President, has the support of the leading educators of the day. The college presidents of note in the United States, with very few exceptions, have given it their approval. Letters recently received urging Congress to act are now in the hands of the committee. The National Educational Association has been almost unanimous in advocating the national university. At the annual meeting at St. Louis, in 1871, the committee reported in the following words:

Your committee are also gratified to be able to report a general concurrence on the part of the many eminent men who have expressed their views upon the subject in those large and liberal ideas of university education which only are adequate to the growing and already pressing demands of our country and times.

It was not deemed important in submitting our first report, nor is it necessary in this, to mark the details of what the institution should be. * * * It may be proper, however, to state in general terms:

"1. That it should be broad enough to embrace every department of science, literature, and the arts, and every real profession.

"2. That it should be high enough to supplement the highest existing institutions of the country, and to embrace within its field of instruction the utmost limits of human knowledge.

"3. That, in the interest of truth and justice, it should guarantee equal privileges to all duly qualified applicants for admission to the courses of instruction, and equal rights, as well as the largest freedom, to all earnest investigators in that vast domain which lies outside the limits of acknowledged science.

"4. That it should be so constituted and established as to command the hearty support of the American people, regardless of section, party, or creed.

"5. That its material resources should be vast enough to enable it not only to furnish, and that either freely or at nominal cost, the best instruction the world can afford, but also to provide the best-known facilities for the work of scientific investigation, together with endowed fellowships and honorary fellowships, open respectively to the most meritorious graduates and to such investigators, whether native or foreign, as, being candidates therefor, shall have distinguished themselves most in the advancement of knowledge.

"6. That it should be so coordinated in plan with the other institutions of the country as not only in no way to conflict with them, but, on the contrary, to become at once a potent agency for their improvement and the means of creating a complete, harmonious, and efficient system of American education. * * *

"The idea of a national university, then, is as old as the nation; has had the fullest sanction of the wisest and best men of succeeding generations, and is in perfect harmony with the policy and practice of the Government."

There can certainly be no valid objection to establishing a national university. The only real difficulty that confronts us is that of providing funds. But a little generosity and foresight will enable us to see that one-third the proceeds derived from the sale of our public lands could not be used to a better purpose. Our whole public school system is supported in part by a generous donation of public lands. To support a national university by this method will be right in line with our policy. From the Government reports we discover that the lands available for settlement are rapidly going, and that the fund derived from their sale is rapidly diminishing. In 1892 the sum total received from sale of these lands was $4,387,670.27; in 1893, $4,191,465.29, and in 1894, $2,674,285.79.

One-third of the sum for 1894 amounts to $891,428. This sum decreasing at the same rate would amount to—for 1895, about $650,000; for 1896, $450,000; for 1897, $250,000; for 1898, $150,000; and for 1899, $100,000; or a total endowment of $2,491,428.

This, as all know, is far from extravagance. It is a very small endowment. But with additional appropriations from time to time, and with large bequests from private fortunes, which can surely be counted upon, and with the score of bureaus, art collections, laboratories, departments of governments, collegiate institutions already established here and which would be accessible to the student, an ample endowment and equipment would soon be realized.

Such an institution, Mr. President, would be an honor to our country, and it seems strange that we should differ among ourselves in the face of so great educational possibilities. With patriotic pride the five hundred young men who now go abroad annually for these advantages would turn their steps to Washington. In this city would be congregated the greatest scientists and philosophers of the world. In a generation we should have in this country hundreds of specialists where now we have but few, and our country would contribute her share to the advanced thought of the age.

The structure of our educational system, Mr. President, is to-day incomplete. We have built well from the kindergarten to the State university; but the capstone—the national university—is yet needed to complete the structure. Let us do honor to the nation and to ourselves by finishing the work inaugurated one hundred years ago.

| 54TH CONGRESS, | SENATE. | REPORT 429, |
| 1st Session. | | Part 3. |

IN THE SENATE OF THE UNITED STATES.

JUNE 4, 1896.—Ordered to be printed.

Mr. KYLE, chairman, from the Committee to Establish the University of the United States, submitted the following

REPLY TO VIEWS OF THE MINORITY

BY THE CHAIRMAN OF THE NATIONAL UNIVERSITY COMMITTEE OF ONE HUNDRED:

[To accompany S. 1202.]

To the Honorable the Senate Committee to Establish the University of the United States:

The report of the Senate Committee to Establish the University of the United States, submitted by its chairman on March 10, is certainly very complete, embracing, as it does, not only the views of the present committee, with leading portions of the former unanimous reports submitted in its behalf by Senators Proctor, of Vermont, and Hunton, of Virginia, in 1893 and 1894, respectively, but also the affirmative arguments before the Senate and House committees by ex-Senator George F. Edmunds, ex-Provost Dr. William Pepper, Dr. Simon Newcomb, Gen. John Eaton, President Gardiner G. Hubbard, ex-United States Ministers Andrew D. White and John A. Kasson, and ex-Governor John Lee Carroll, president of Sons of the Revolution, a review of the objections offered by representatives of the so-called "American University" and others, a list of members of the National University committee of one hundred, and some 350 letters from approving jurists, statesmen, college presidents, State superintendents, heads of scientific organizations, and numerous other men of distinction in various departments of life.

Both on account of its weight of argument and because of the great number of eminent men most competent to express an opinion in such a matter whose communications are embraced, said report is in fact so convincing that no further discussion could be thought necessary but for the minority report finally submitted, whose erroneous statements, fallacies, and half-supporting views of certain university presidents, seem to challenge some attention by way of review, to the end that the nature and weakness of the opposition may be made yet more conspicuous.

I also have pleasure in transmitting for the committee's use a number of additional communications from college presidents and others in support of the national university proposition.

For convenience of reference, I shall deal with the contents of the minority report in the order of their occurrence:

"ATTEMPTS TO FOUND A NATIONAL UNIVERSITY."

Of the minority's quotations under this head, from some anonymous writer, it is proper to say that a number of them are grossly incorrect historically, while as a whole they give such evidence of an unfriendly bias as to invalidate their claims to confidence.

For example, it is not true that Washington's plan for a national university was ever "rejected;" it was simply *neglected;* nor is it true that a committee of Congress, reporting unfavorably upon the plan submitted in 1810, deemed it "unconstitutional for the Government to found, endow, and control" such an institution. What the committee did say is this:

> The Constitution does not warrant the creation of such a corporation *by any express provision.* But it immediately occurred that, under the right to legislate exclusively over the District, wherein the United States have fixed their seat of Government, Congress may erect a university at any place within the 10 miles square ceded by Maryland and Virginia. *This can not be doubted.* (Annals, Eleventh Congress, second session, p. 975.)

True, there have been those who questioned the authority of Congress in this regard because of the absence of any express provision in the Constitution, but they were most emphatically in the minority at the beginning of the Government, and constitutional objection has long since ceased to be urged by statesmen. Indeed, to-day there is probably not a constitutional lawyer in the country who would risk his reputation by denying that the exclusive jurisdiction of Congress in the District of Columbia furnishes the amplest authority for the founding here of any institution which, in its judgment, the public welfare may demand.

Again, the minority are less than just in the declaration that "there is no effort to conceal the fact that the Government is to provide the necessary funds [*i. e.*, all the funds] to secure the establishment and maintenance of the university, involving, it is believed, an outlay of an immense amount of money." On the contrary, provision is made in section 14 of the pending bill for receiving gifts and bequests and for their investment in bonds of the United States; and there is a reasonable expectation that such gifts and bequests, made after the example of Washington, will become very common and very great, the university offering, as it would, opportunities not only for a most judicious as well as patriotic use of funds, but also for making such gifts in the face of the whole world and with a certainty of corresponding distinction for the giver. The minority should know that the friends of the national university proposition, from Washington down, have never for one moment contemplated the endowment of it by the Government alone. In the nature of things, it would become a powerful magnet for the munificence of private fortune. The minority's reference to "an addition to burdens of taxation or to the further issue of bonds" is therefore entirely without warrant.

"IS THERE A NECESSITY FOR A NATIONAL UNIVERSITY?"

After a page of history setting forth the beginnings and slow progress of the older institutions, the minority report concludes the discussion under this head with sundry statements concerning the facilities already furnished by the more than four hundred colleges and universities of the country, with "their one hundred and fifty millions in productive funds and their aggregate annual income of some twenty millions," saying, last of all, "It would seem there is no longer any necessity for our young men going abroad for college training."

No; not for *college* training, surely. But that there is need of their going abroad for *university* facilities is clearly shown by the important fact that they do actually go by the thousand, and that, too, not unfrequently at a very great sacrifice.

Finally, the minority declare, most surprisingly, that "here in Washington, besides other institutions of high rank which are supported by private means and endowment, we have a grand university representing the Catholic faith, and the American University, representing the Protestant faith, will soon commence the erection of its buildings;" and, finally, that "present and future demands at the capital, it is believed, will be met by institutions existing and projected, embracing all branches of learning and research."

One regrets to speak of such declarations as they deserve. Surely these Senators know what constitutes a university, and it is therefore quite incomprehensible that they should have thought to dispose of so important a matter in such a manner. Have they not, rather, in the pressure of many measures, trusted too implicitly the contributions of one whose high position has secured for him a large measure of confidence? They certainly know that the friends of a national university are not concerning themselves especially with "demands *at the capital*," but rather with the demands of the whole country, and that, as compared with even the foremost universities of Europe, still less with any ideal standard, there is not as yet a single *university* in America—an institution, I mean, wholly above the college and embracing the whole vast field of higher learning, with the best and highest possible training in every field of original work.

Upon further reflection they must realize that if the Catholic, Methodist, and Baptist institutions at Washington *were* universities in even the German sense, they could not, either one or all of them, meet the demands of this great people of seventy millions, embracing citizens of every sect and of no sect. If themselves satisfied that every university should bear some denominational stamp, do they not see that an institution under the most absolute Methodist rule could not meet the demands of all the other denominations? They also understand full well that in their own higher realm letters, science, and philosophy, as well as original work of every kind, are of right free from denominational and party trammels of every name and nature. They must know—what is of vital importance to American education—that neither a Catholic, nor Methodist, nor Baptist, nor any other denominational university could so relate itself to the now incomplete public-school system of the country as to supplement and complete it and thus become a potential agency for the coordination and perfection of the whole series. Nor can they fail to realize that a national university at the seat of the Government, gathering unto itself a multitude of able and aspiring college graduates from every section of the country for yet higher and the highest possible university culture, and again distributing them for a supreme service in every department of intellectual and industrial activity, would become a powerful means of national progress and of national concord. And hence it is confidently believed that, upon further consideration, they also will clearly see how well grounded is the conviction of the great body of those most in touch with these matters that such a University of the United States as the Government and people are abundantly able, and therefore in duty bound, to set up would greatly advance the dignity and honor of the Republic; promoting its material prosperity, while so greatly contributing to its intellectual and moral ascendency among the nations of the earth.

"IS A NATIONAL UNIVERSITY DESIRABLE?"

This question has been more than answered already by showing that a crowning and purely post-graduate university is even *necessary* to the efficiency of existing institutions of learning, to the public welfare, and to the honor of the United States.

But "there are many practical difficulties in the way," say the minority. Of course. There are always difficulties in the way of every great cause, the failure to view it comprehensively, clearly, and without prejudice being chief. But the difficulties alluded to in the report of the minority are nothing more nor less than fictitious ones, primarily conjured up and urgently offered by one intent, as it would seem, upon gaining and holding as exclusively as possible this great field of the national capital, made rich by its millions' worth of resources at the public cost, for his own denominational institution. The "difficulties" suggested—partisan, ethical, religious—every one of them, lie as truly in the way of the State universities, one and all (if not, indeed, in greater measure), as against the proposed university of the United States. They are "difficulties" such as the great University of Michigan and other State universities have already shown to be purely imaginary.

With such as make no proper distinction between religion and denominationalism there may be questionings as to the spirit that would pervade a national university; but what reasonable man can doubt that the University of the United States would, in the nature of the case, be characterized by that love of truth and righteousness and that profound reverence which not only create an atmosphere favorable to purity and nobleness of living, but which are, indeed, the very essence of religion itself? Who believes it could not and would not, in the nature of the case, deal with history, ethics, social and political economy, constitutional and international law in the broadest manner possible, presenting all the differing views of recognized authorities with a breadth, thoroughness, and completeness wholly impossible in any local or denominational university? Who will question that, because of its chief function of leadership in the vast fields of historical research and of ethical, social, economical, and general scientific investigation, it would *of necessity* be characterized by a supremely careful, liberal, and truth-loving spirit and practice? Who believes that a university of the United States, with its many departments under command of the foremost men of the times, could be other than loyal to truth and virtue, nay, religious in the best sense of that term—the sense in which we are and must remain a religious people, the sure and faithful guardians of interests so at once universal and vital?

It is an encouraging sign of progress in the study of this subject that the old-time question of "political interference" has not been seriously revived either by the minority of the Senate committee or by Bishop Hurst and his followers. It is more than a sign of progress; it is evidence, indeed, that, with men willing to give attention to the subject, such presupposed interference is no longer a ground of anxiety. Such men have noted the history and present status of the Smithsonian Institution, of the scientific and educational bureaus of the Government (no one of which is ever tampered with politically), and of the present State universities.

Like President Eliot, they have seen the progress of civil-service reform and the rapid decay of "political influence." They have also seen how carefully the pending university bill guards against the possibility of it by associating with the nine regents of Presidential appointment, for the choice of all officers of instruction and for the internal management of the university, six non-political members, to wit, the Chief Justice of the United States, the Commissioner of Education, the secretary of the Smithsonian Institution, the president of the National Academy of Sciences, the president of the National Educational Association, and the president of the university, together with twelve other citizens of the United States to be appointed by the regents from among eminent educators connected with leading institutions of learning in as many States.

Moreover, it is beyond question that the higher the rank and work of an institution or bureau, the less the danger of political meddling; and hence that the proposed university of the United States, with its work of instruction and research quite beyond the range and familiar acquaintance of the great public, would, in the nature of the case, be free from this sort of embarrassment.

It is confidently believed, therefore, that a careful and unprejudiced weighing of all these facts and considerations will put a final end to this ancient query among the sincere friends of science and learning throughout the country.

Having spoken thus freely of the minority's views on these several subjects, let us turn briefly to what is said on another head, though not touched by the pending bill:

"PUBLIC LANDS."

If it shall be proposed [say they] to resort to the public lands for this purpose [of endowment], an objection which would seem to be decisive is that this can not be done without a reversal of the settled policy of the Government to devote these lands liberally to educational purposes *in the States*, to aid in the support of both common schools and colleges, so that the immediate benefits, so far as possible, may reach all the people. This policy seems to find full justification in the consideration that these lands, the property of the people, should, so far as devoted to educational purposes, be applied as much as practicable for the benefit of the *people in general*, and not to a purpose which, directly at least, would benefit but a *limited class*.

Could there be anything more illogical and unreasonable? When the Government of the United States began the creation of its educational, scientific, and industrial bureaus and departments, was it a "reversal of the settled policy of the Government," or only a *grand step forward?*

As a champion of the Morrill bill for the endowment of colleges of agriculture and the mechanic arts, the writer of this review recalls the cry of similar import against that beneficent measure. That, too, was "class legislation," and "an unjustifiable use of public lands that should be educationally used for the support of common schools alone."

But for the printed text before me it would be deemed incredible that any citizen of the United States should frame such an argument against the founding of an institution whose important functions it must be (1) to strengthen our public-school system, from kindergarten to State university, by the elevation and unification of standards and by insuring a supply of better-equipped instructors and professors; (2) to increase and satisfy in our own country the demand of aspiring college graduates for the very best facilities for advance study the world can furnish, thus securing to the United States a new dignity in the world of science and learning; (3) whose chief, and yet more difficult, task is to be that of advancing the world's knowledge by means of original investigations and by the systematic induction of qualified persons into the methods by which such investigations are made, with the largest prospect of important results—whose work, therefore, from beginning to end, is to be done, not in the interest of a given locality or "class," much less in the special interest of any particular religious organization, but in the common interest of the whole American people; of a country whose high mission it should be to lead the world in civilization.

"Limited class!" What benefactions are more universal than those of scientific discovery? And what surer way to promote discovery than by creating an institution one of whose leading offices it shall be to qualify discoverers?

Is it not beyond question that the higher the work the more universal its influence in the promotion of human welfare?

The argument of the minority, if logically and practically enforced, would put an end to every expenditure by the State and National Governments in the interest of higher education, much more to appropriations for our great libraries, museums, laboratories, observatories, and scientific expeditions. But, happily, there is no danger of this, nor could the minority themselves, after due reflection, desire to see it applied at so great a cost to our people and to the standing of our country among the great nations. It savors of a doctrine once held by good and able men, but which has long since given way to the more rational view, that the *people* are sovereign in the United States and competent to do whatsoever, being without constitutional prohibition, will clearly advance the public welfare.

Surely the American people, in their capacity as a nation, having given millions of acres of the public domain in aid of public schools, local and State, as a potent means of strengthening all these for an increase of knowledge, for the advancement of the State and local industries, and for the general furtherance, may now, without question from any intelligent source, devote yet other lands, if they will, to the universal good and for the honor of the American name.

LETTERS ACCOMPANYING "VIEWS OF THE MINORITY."

Of the nine communications from college men which accompany the minority report, it may be said in general terms that but four of them are deserving of consideration, namely, those from the presidents of Pennsylvania, Columbia, Yale, and Harvard universities. Of the remaining five, two are to be found in no published list of which the writer has knowledge, and the other three give unmistakable evidence of both a very marked prejudice and a singular ignorance of what constitutes a university.

Moreover, the opposition of the four really important institutions first mentioned is in good part neutralized by its very nature; that of Yale lying against Government appropriations in aid of higher institutions generally—past, present, and future; that of Columbia being rather a dissent from the scope and extent of the proposed national university and from details of the bill than from the advantage of a national university, duly planned and administered; that of Pennsylvania expressing a desire for some means of utilizing "the vast collections of the

United States Government in Washington for purposes of study," but distrusting the proposed form of control; and that of Harvard's president ignoring, as heretofore, the exclusively post-graduate and national character of the proposed institution, as well as the vastness of the facilities already here, mildly questioning whether there would be due freedom for students in certain departments, and making irrelevant allusions to the meeting of all local needs of the District of Columbia by the institutions already here and in prospect. Only this and nothing more. *Not one of these objectors touches the great motives which have prompted the national university movement!*

In answer it is proper to say, in general terms, that the bill in question is not of cast iron. As now before Congress, it represents the final judgment of the dozen or more distinguished scholars and statesmen who had part in framing it and of the great number of prominent educators whose opinions were solicited in correspondence. It is, of course, open to amendment—indeed, has been modified somewhat by the Senate Committee to Establish the University of the United States.

The objections raised by President Low, of Columbia, can all be satisfied but one, that which would deny to the university the powers of a "teaching organization." His objection to free tuition has already been met by the committee by the substitution of the word *open* for the word "free," in the second line of section 9; and yet other changes suggested by him are likely to be made, perhaps all the others save that which, upon further consideration, he will himself see can not be made, namely, the denial to the institution its vital function of guidance for students in their post-graduate work in the several departments to be embraced; which guidance is nothing other than *instruction*. It can not be that so able a man as he could think of turning loose some hundreds, perhaps thousands, of earnest seekers after the ultimate known and the unknown to grope their way alone in the vast fields to be opened to their inquiry; nor would he deny to the distinguished corps of guides to be furnished them the privilege of dealing with them in groups and by means of lectures, instead of with each one alone. Having conceded so much as this, he will have yielded the whole ground—all that is asked.

As for President Eliot, of Harvard, it is highly gratifying, in view of his sweeping objections of a quarter of a century ago, to find him conceding that the present measure has been made "more acceptable" than former ones, and that, since the progress of civil service reform, one may now hope that the proposed university would be at least in good measure "exempted from the operations of the spoils system"— a system which every day becomes more and more a thing of the past, which never had and never can have any disturbing influence in the high realms of science and learning. For the remaining part, being notably a conservative educator, the Doctor unduly takes counsel of his fears.

After all his concessions, and in view of the fact that he stands for the oldest, if not the greatest, of American collegiate institutions, with a natural pride of supremacy, and has been taught to cherish something of a prejudice against public education, it is not difficult to pardon his failure to recognize all such high claims of our movement as rest upon the place the National University would hold in the American system, and upon the nationalizing and harmonizing influence it could not fail to exert upon the country.

It is much less difficult than to understand the boldness with which the minority have at so great length republished adverse arguments of more than twenty years ago, made by him before the National Educational Association, although so completely answered, first at Elmira and then at Detroit, by such men as Presidents Daniel Read, of Missouri; George P. Hays, of Pennsylvania; James McCosh, of Princeton, and Andrew D. White, of Cornell; by Dr. W. T. Harris, present United States Commissioner of Education; Superintendent John Hancock, and others—so completely that the resolutions in support of the national university proposition were finally carried by that great body of educators without one dissenting voice.

The suggestions made by Provost Harrison, of the University of Pennsylvania, have evidently come, in like manner, from a misapprehension of the real intent of the framers of the pending bill. He doubtless had in mind a series of fixed and unvarying courses of study, after the manner of annual classes in the existing institutions, rather than that free and varying work of guidance of which mention has been made, and which it would be the business of those in charge to make as valuable as possible in each individual case; which entire great work would also be conducted with due reference to the interests of all other institutions, especially those to any considerable extent similarly engaged, as provided in section 10 of the pending bill, which reads as follows:

SEC. 10. That the university shall have authority to establish, with other institutions of learning in this and other countries, such cooperative relations as shall be deemed advantageous.

Provost Harrison wisely says:

If some arrangement could be made by which advanced students should have the benefit of the vast collections of the United States Government at Washington for purposes of study, that would be an excellent arrangement.

And we simply add that such benefit could only come in due measure from the very kind of assistance proposed—from the help to be given by men of genius, masters, each, in their several fields of inquiry.

As for the communication of Bishop Hurst, chancellor of the so-called "American University," it is a singular mixture, demanding a large amount of charity from both the national and the ethical points of view.

Plainly cherishing prejudices against public education, and having succeeded, with the help of a usurped title and liberal assurances, in gaining important advantage at Washington, he resumes his true rôle of sectarist, mingling with his adverse declarations such expression of sympathy with "the interests of higher education" and such pretension to reasons therefor as are very surprising.

How truly "American" said institution would be—in other words, with what singleness of purpose "the interests of higher education in this country" would be guarded and advanced—if left to Bishop Hurst and the institution to be managed by him may be inferred, first, from the terms of a charter requiring not only that "at all times at least two-thirds of the trustees and also the chancellor of the said university shall be members of the aforesaid Methodist Episcopal Church," but that "all trustees elected after the 1st day of December, A. D. 1891, shall be submitted to the General Conference of such church for its approval;" secondly, from the spirit of the man most conspicuous in the founding of it; and, third, from the avowed aims of some of his ecclesiastical coadjutors, as set forth in their addresses before the General Conference in 1892 (pages 106–108 of Senate Memorial), from which the following brief quotations are made:

From the address of Rev. Dr. Payne:

> Methodism is building for a vast future and for uncounted millions. Let us build this glorious temple of Methodism [the "American University"] with its marble front toward the future; build for the coming generations; build for all the years of time and eternity.

From the address of Bishop Fowler:

> This American University, located at the heart of the nation, not far from the most distant home, with vast accumulations of appliances [by the Government], and to offer the utmost possible advantages, can not long wait for any good thing. * * * If we fail to see our day of opportunity, we shall drop into the rear and cease to do our part for the evangelization of this land and the world, and that sad voice from the broken-hearted watcher of Olivet will come to us, saying, "O, Methodism, Methodism, if thou hadst known, even thou, at least in this thy day, the things which belong to thy peace!"

From the address of Rev. Dr. (now Bishop) McCabe:

> If the past is prophetic of the future, this American University will have much to do with the cause of missions. The name of a university professor is a household word in Methodism, because it is connected with that all-conquering theology which is believable and preachable and which is destined to take the world—James Arminius, of the University of Leyden.

From the address of Bishop Newman:

> Providence ordains the times and seasons according to an infinite wisdom, and raises up men to accomplish the exalted purposes of Jehovah. * * * It comes to us more and more that in the roll of the centuries, in the ordering of time, God Almighty, the God of our fathers, has selected Bishop Hurst to lay the foundation of the American University for American Methodism.

Had these things been said of a Methodist university of America, criticism would not be in order, for denominational institutions have rights that should be scrupulously regarded, even as the people through their agencies, the State and National Governments, may of right establish and maintain public schools and higher institutions that shall be wholly free from denominational influence. But no institution has the moral right to hang out a false banner, whether for the sake of larger endowments or as a means of securing increased patronage, much less as a means of forestalling and preventing the establishment of an institution for which there is clearly an important demand by the country, without regard to section. And how do the charter provisions and public expressions above quoted tally with the high claims of "Protestant," "nonsectarian"—nay, "American?" How far do they illustrate and confirm the claim of Bishop Hurst to a supreme solicitude for the "interests of higher education?"

Again can anyone believe that in the coming national university he sees "only danger to our educational system?"

What "educational system?" Our only educational *system* is the *public* educational system, in which he does not believe; to which, apparently, he only yields assent for policy sake, or, rather, because it is established and he can not abolish it—a system still incomplete and sadly needing the very national university in question as the only means of providing it with the necessary coordinating, stimulating, and inspiring head.

And *what danger?* He prudently omits to point it out.

Confusing matters somewhat, the Bishop may have substituted his own denominational university for our entire "educational system." But even then his fears can have only a conditional foundation. For while a truly national university of the highest type would undoubtedly embarrass any man's ambitious plans for a grand, overshadowing, all-absorbing, and all-excluding sectarian university, it would, on the other hand, render most important service to such an institution as his charter provides for, and to all other like institutions of the country. In the language of the eminent astronomer of Cambridge, Dr. Benjamin Apthorp Gould—

> There is no one of them but would develop to new strength and beauty under its genial emanations; none so highly favored or so great that its resources and powers would not expand; none too lowly to imbibe the vitalizing, animating influences which it would diffuse like perfume.

Tolerating the common schools and State universities, which he is constrained to name as the first two elements of our American system, for a third and final member of the series he adds: "The postgraduate and professional schools to be left to the voluntary benevolence of the individual citizen."

Why? It would probably trouble the Bishop as much to answer this question as to account for his misrepresentation of the university purposes of George Washington (see majority report of Senate committee, March 10, 1896, pp. 44 and 45) in his argument of February 21. There are many reasons why the higher education should *not* be left to the chances of individual and denominational provision and control; but we challenge this ecclesiastical objector to give one valid reason for his singular proposition. If compelled to divulge his thought it would doubtless be found to have a sectarian cast; else why should he have even dreamed of calling upon the Church to prevent the establishment of the National University? And yet what inconsistency does this involve. For, having consented (on paper) to the training of American youth in the public schools during their tender years and to their higher education in "the State universities and colleges," during the period of adolescence—the formative periods, when, if ever, they should have religious guardianship—why such profound anxiety for their moral and spiritual welfare after they have attained to the years of manhood and entered upon such postgraduate study as directly takes hold on the business of life?

And what does the Bishop mean by "ministerial and other associations" in such connection? Is he really planning to "rally the Christian Church," as he has ventured to intimate, against the effort of patriotic citizens to complete the American system of public education? Does he think his own spirit of intolerance so universal that all the 143 religious sects in the United States stand ready to array themselves under his leadership for such a crusade? How great a mistake! Not one of them will enlist in so unpatriotic, absurd, not to say wicked, a war. Already he finds one great religious organization (and that the one from which he would fain protect the people) quite competent to teach him worthy lessons, not only in patriotism, but also in religious toleration, as will appear by the following communication from that broad-minded and distinguished leader in many fields of beneficent work, the learned rector of the Catholic University of America:

THE CATHOLIC UNIVERSITY OF AMERICA,
Washington, D. C., April 16, 1896.

MY DEAR GOVERNOR HOYT: Accept my thanks for your kindness in sending me Congressional documents connected with the proposed national university. Accept also my thanks for your very kind estimate of my attitude toward the project. We will do the best we can here to give the very highest and best education, but we will do nothing to hinder others from doing as well, or better, if they can.

Very truly, yours,
JOHN J. KEANE, *Rector (per Sec.).*
Hon. JOHN W. HOYT,
4 Iowa Circle, Washington, D. C.

It can not be doubted that all the great leaders in the other churches will be governed by like rational and Christian principles, since not a few such from the several greater organizations have even pledged themselves to the most earnest cooperation with the National University Committee of One Hundred.

Nor can it be questioned that the Methodist Episcopal Church, whose work in the cause of education has been important, and whose patriotism has hitherto been equal to every test, will acquit itself in a like worthy manner, building up its own institutions and leaving the Government and people to the work of rearing and maintaining a crowning university for the good of the whole country and for the progress of science and learning in the world. For if Bishop Newman did, in the fervor of an extemporaneous speech, confuse matters a little, making Methodism next to synonymous with country, he also used these words:

> As I said, great thoughts never die. So it is true in regard to this. A hundred years have passed, but during that century the thought of an American university has been conspicuous in the teachings of the great jurists and statesmen of the past and has been the dominant thought of those master minds, Jay and Kent and Marshall, and in our days of the scholarly Sumner and that great jurist of Vermont, Edmunds.

We commend these words to Bishop Hurst, who may delay, but can not prevent, the early realization of the cherished hopes of Washington and his immortal compatriots.

Last of all, the Bishop asks, "Why should the State undertake to do what the citizen is ready and glad to do?"

What the citizen has *not* done and *can not* do is our answer. The citizen may create a very worthy and quite important private institution, like some of those which may be named; but no citizen, however great his fortune, and no single Commonwealth, much less any sectarian organization, or any combination of these, can create an institution that shall be wholly free from bias of any and every sort—that shall complete our public educational system; that shall exert so nationalizing and harmonizing an influence upon all portions of our great country; that shall be always ready to meet the demands of the Government for service in whatsoever field, and that shall at the same time secure to the United States an acknowledged ascendency in the ever-widening field of intellectual activity.

Should this not wholly satisfy, the Bishop is respectfully referred to the yet fuller answer, in anticipation of such queries, to be found on page 7 of the unanimous report of the Senate committee, submitted on May 24, 1894, which says:

> And so of the possible question whether, with the efforts of princely givers and of powerful religious denominational bodies aiming at universities, the wants of our people are not likely to be met without the help of the nation, the answer is simple. If we should wholly ignore the insufficiency of their endowments, even the richest of them, and that denominational bias which they can not escape if they would—which, indeed, was and is and will remain the mainspring of their great endeavors—the answer must still, and necessarily, be a most emphatic negative.
>
> No institution, whatever its name or aim, that is local, or that rests on either a private or a denominational foundation; no institution with partial aims, however worthy as viewed from a local or a partisan standpoint; no institution with aims less than national and universal, and on this account able to command the confidence, active sympathy, and moral as well as material support of the whole people; no institution not so related to the public-school system of the United States, with its primary, secondary, academic, and university gradations, as to furnish the crown and culmination of the whole series, and so become to them a mighty coordinating

and uplifting force; no institution resting on a foundation less broad, ample, and unfailing than that which is furnished by the geographic empire and boundless resources of the American Union; no institution with less of dignity, or less loftiness of purpose than with absolute impartiality to meet all the intellectual and ethical aims of a great people, and to secure for that people an acknowledged leadership among the nations in all things that make for the progress and highest welfare of the human race; no institution less than equal to all these exalted ends can satisfy the needs and demands of such a people as dwell under the flag of the American Republic.

Having here in an important sense a great university already, in the form of libraries, museums, laboratories, and observatories, with many leaders in many fields of science, shall not the people, through their agency, the Congress of the United States, provide for its organization without further delay, making now, in this time of financial embarrassment, only such appropriations as shall render that organization possible, and confidently looking to the better future for such joint efforts of Government and citizen as shall in time insure to the United States the foremost university of the world?

Very respectfully,

JOHN WESLEY HOYT,
Chairman of the National University Committee of One Hundred.

4 IOWA CIRCLE, WASHINGTON, D. C.,
May 30, 1896.

ADDITIONAL COMMUNICATIONS

FROM

COLLEGE PRESIDENTS AND OTHER EMINENT CITIZENS IN SUPPORT OF THE UNIVERSITY MEASURE.

[Additional to the more than three hundred and fifty included in the Senate committee's report of March 10, 1896.]

[The following important communication from Hon. William Wirt Henry, LL. D., President of the Virginia Society of Sons of the American Revolution, etc., having been omitted by mistake from the numerous papers transmitted to the chairman of the Senate committee in March last, is offered with pleasure in the present connection:]

WASHINGTON, *January 1, 189—*.

DEAR SIR: In answer to your letter of recent date concerning the proposed national university, I inclose herewith the concluding portion of a paper lately read at a meeting of Sons of the American Revolution, from which you can extract what you wish.

Very truly, yours, W. W. HENRY.

[Accordingly, the following extracts are made:]

In concluding this paper I would call the attention of the association and of the country to one of Washington's earnest recommendations, having the creation of a distinctive American character in view. It ises the tablishment of a grand national university at the Federal capital. His views upon this important subject will be best shown by extracts from his will, by which he dedicated to this object 50 shares of the Potomac Company, put at his disposal by the State of Virginia.

The establishment of such an university he urged in his speech to Congress December 7, 1796, at the same time that he advised the establishment of a national military school. Had his well-matured views been then acted upon in establishing such a liberal national school, the result might have been a check to that passionate sectionalism which made inevitable the great civil strife of 1861-1865. But it is not now too late to act upon the dying request of the Father of his Country. Indeed, the lapse of a century seems to bring with it the fullness of time for the realization of Washington's great conception.

The subject has been ably discussed by our accomplished secretary, Dr. Herbert B. Adams, in his most valuable monograph upon William and Mary College, issued in 1887 by the Bureau of Education, who traces Washington's proposal to his connection with that college.

Among other most important results which might be accomplished by such an institution, he points out the education of youth from all parts of the Union in the special branches required to be learned for the proper conduct of our civil service, and he most justly remarks that "there is in these times as great need of special knowledge in civil service as in military or naval science. A civil academy for the training of representative American youth would be as great a boon to the American people as the Military and Naval academies have already proved."

Such a national university need not excite the jealousy of our many admirable institutions of higher learning, but should be made the capstone of the American educational system.

It is a hopeful sign of the interest which is awakening on this subject to find among the committees of the United States Senate one appointed to consider the subject of a national university. Let us hope the day is not far distant when an additional memorial will be erected to Washington, the most suitable of all, in the establishment of a grand national school of universal learning, into which not only American youth may proudly enter, but to which will be attracted the youth of other lands, eagerly seeking to imbibe American ideas with which to infuse new life into the older governments of the world.

[In like manner omitted by oversight from the collection of letters published in March, 1896:]

PORTLAND, OREG., *October 23, 1895.*

MY DEAR SIR: I am in receipt of your favor of the 16th instant. As you know, I have been relegated to private life, and I fear I am unable to aid much in the national university enterprise. I have not lost my interest, however, in the matter, and my sympathies and best wishes are with you.

I think favorably of the plan outlined by you of a committee and "executive council."

Sincerely, yours, J. N. DOLPH.
(*Ex-United States Senator, etc.*)

[From Benj. Apthorp Gould, LL. D., the eminent astronomer, who ever since his eloquent oration of 1856 (quoted on pages 60 to 62 of Senate Memorial of 1892) has stanchly stood for a central post-graduate university:]

CAMBRIDGE, MASS., *March, 1896.*

MY DEAR GOVERNOR: * * * My faith and confidence have been suffering in recent years by reason of the scattering of the energies which ought to have been concentrated long ago upon this great work.

The Johns Hopkins University has done much in what seems to be the right direction. But in general my apprehensions have been excited by the manifest indications that people suppose money only to be needed for the desired end, and by the fear that the essential need of men is left out of sight, even at present.

We have not the leaders in scholarship, science, and art in sufficient numbers to supply the demand already existing.

So-called universities, to supply increasing local (and denominational) ambitions, are continually springing up, and the one essential of an adequate number of men competent to guide seems to be growing less and less understood.

The *Americanism* needed has to be sacrificed by an overwhelming importation of foreign teachers.

A central post-graduate university, equal if not superior to any in the world, would at once establish truer standards and provide experts for guidance in every field. It would help us to reach a level from which it could be distinctly seen that money and numbers are but means, rather than ends to be attained; and having gained this right understanding we shall have made the greatest step toward the attainment of our hopes that could be desired.

Again I wish you all possible success.

Very sincerely, yours, B. A. GOULD.

BROOKLYN, N. Y., *June 2, 1896.*

DEAR SIR: I am in full sympathy with the desire and purpose of the university committee to promote the establishment of a "University of the United States" at

Washington, and my name may be added by you to the list of members, if you desire. * * *

Very truly, yours,
RICHARD S. STORRS.

[Rev. Richard S. Storrs, D. D., LL. D., is president of the Long Island and of the American Historical societies.]

WAR DEPARTMENT,
OFFICE OF THE JUDGE-ADVOCATE-GENERAL,
Washington, June 1, 1896.

DEAR SIR: I am just in receipt of your note with reference to the projected national university, and beg to say in reply that I shall be glad to have you place my name among those of the friends of this noble undertaking. It has, I can assure you, my heartiest interest.

Yours, truly,
G. NORMAN LIEBER.
(*Judge-Advocate-General.*)

BISHOP'S HOUSE,
Davenport, Iowa, April 19, 1896.

DEAR SIR: I heartily approve of the scheme of a national university for postgraduate study, at Washington, as outlined by President Washington, and now urged upon the attention of Congress.

WILLIAM STEVENS PERRY.
(*Bishop of Iowa, late President of Hobart College, Geneva, N. Y., Chap. Gen. Soc. Cincinnati.*)

BUREAU OF AMERICAN REPUBLICS,
Washington, May 26, 1896.

DEAR SIR: I have the honor to acknowledge the receipt of yours of the 25th instant, and take great pleasure in cordially indorsing the project in which you are engaged, and pledge to you whatever support I may be able to render you. I believe that the establishment and maintenance of a university such as you propose at the national capital is of great importance under existing conditions.

Yours, very truly,
CLINTON FURBISH, *Director.*

WASHINGTON, D. C., *April 14, 1896.*

MY DEAR SIR: I assure you I appreciate the benefit that it would be to this city to have a national university located here, and I shall do all in my power to advance its interests whether I am connected with it or not. I think if Congress were carefully to consider the subject, in the course of a year or two some legislation could be procured which would be of decided advantage to the university and to the city.

Yours, very truly,
B. H. WARNER
(*Ex-President Washington Board of Trade*).

SMITHSONIAN INSTITUTION,
BUREAU OF AMERICAN ETHNOLOGY,
Washington, May 28, 1896.

MY DEAR SIR: Returning to the city after an absence of a few days I find your note of the 25th instant, and am moved to thank you for the opportunity for giving expression to sentiments concerning a national university, but the time seems so far spent as to render it needless to write formally or to do more than assure you of my sympathy and of such aid as it may lie in my power to afford.

With great respect, yours, cordially,

W. J. McGEE, *Ethnologist in Charge.*

SUPERINTENDENT'S OFFICE,
UNITED STATES NAVAL ACADEMY,
Annapolis, Md., April 9, 1896.

DEAR SIR: The receipt of your note reminds me that a former communication was not acknowledged, probably from a press of business, and partially for the reason that I may have thought that my name would not add greatly to the distinguished list of names found on the pages of your committee.

I am heartily in sympathy with the object sought, both through patriotism and the undoubted wisdom of establishing a great central university.

Yours, sincerely,

P. H. COOPER,
Captain, U. S. N. (Superintendent).

BROOKLYN, N. Y., *June 3, 1896.*

DEAR SIR: I am in hearty sympathy with the project of establishing a great national university at the capital of the American nation; not that it might rival the old and famous colleges of the land, but that it might cooperate with them in diffusing among the people a love of letters and science.

I am in full accord with this noble undertaking and wish all the success it deserves.

Very truly, yours,

CHARLES E. WEST
(*President of American Ethnological Society*).

---

177 WEST END AVENUE, NEW YORK, *June 6, 1896.*

DEAR SIR: I have read with attention the "Outline of the Memorial" which accompanied your letter and am of the opinion that the plan is feasible; that there is scope for such an institution, and that if established it will greatly promote the interests of higher education in our country.

I shall therefore be happy to have my name included in the noteworthy and illustrious list which your circular contains.

With sincere respect I am, very truly, yours,

ROBERT R. BOOTH.

[Rev. Robert R. Booth, D. D., LL. D., is moderator General Assembly of the Presbyterian Church in the United States of America, 1895–96.]

OFFICE OF THE CHIEF OF ENGINEERS, UNITED STATES ARMY,
Washington, D. C., June 9, 1896.

DEAR SIR: Your note of May 30 received, and I have read with real interest the leaflets therein.

There is no longer need for arguing the question of the propriety and the advantage to all the people of the foundation of a great national university. The time for that is past. It is now the plain duty of all to work zealously for the attainment of the result desired.

Any aid I can properly give in that direction you may confidently expect.

Respectfully, yours,

W. P. CRAIGHILL
(*Chief of Engineers, U. S. A.*).

THE UNIVERSITY OF VERMONT,
Burlington, Vt., April 21, 1896.

DEAR SIR: When Senator Edmunds was interesting himself in the establishment of a national university at Washington I had some correspondence with him in relation to the project, and expressed my approval of it under certain conditions, which are not infeasible. I am willing to express again the same hearty, though qualified, approval.

Yours, truly, M. H. BUCKHAM, *President.*

PENNSYLVANIA COLLEGE,
Gettysburg, Pa., April 11, 1896.

DEAR SIR: Am I mistaken in the impression that a considerable time since I gave my indorsement to the movement to establish "the University of the United States?" I cordially approve of it, but suggest that its sphere should be strictly limited to post-graduate work. [The projectors have never had any other thought.]

Very truly, yours,
H. W. MCKNIGHT, *President.*

FRANKLIN COLLEGE,
Franklin, Ind., April 20, 1896.

DEAR SIR: I am not crystal clear on this matter. But so far as I have canvassed it, I incline to favor the movement.

You may use my name. I have lost or misplaced the petition.

Most truly,
W. S. STOTT,
President Franklin College.

EUREKA COLLEGE,
Eureka, Ill., April 10, 1896.

DEAR SIR: Your letter to President Johann has just been received. I regret that he is not here to reply. He is in San Domingo just now, and will visit Europe before his return home; but I feel assured that he would approve of the proposed national university.

Yours, truly, MRS. C. JOHANN.

BUCHTEL COLLEGE, *Akron, Ohio, April 10, 1896.*

DEAR SIR: I am in hearty sympathy with the grand conception of a national university, and should be glad to do anything in my power to further its realization.

Yours, truly,
O. CONE, *President.*

GUILFORD COLLEGE, N. C., *April 11, 1896.*

DEAR SIR: I shall be glad to do all in my power to promote the founding of a national university having in view the purposes outlined in your circulars just received.

Very respectfully, yours, L. L. HOBBS, *President.*

ROSE POLYTECHNIC INSTITUTE,
Terre Haute, Ind., April 24, 1896.

DEAR SIR: The establishment of a national university I consider desirable, if wisely and properly organized. The problems presenting themselves in this connection are, however, very difficult.

If I can in any manner aid in bringing about the desired end I shall certainly be ready to do so. Any specific action you wish on my part will be carefully considered and, if possible, promptly taken.

Yours, sincerely,

C. LEO MEES, *President.*

AMITY COLLEGE,
College Springs, Iowa, April 22, 1896.

DEAR SIR: Your favor of April 8 to hand. I wrote you some months ago but evidently you have not received it.

I very carefully considered the papers you sent me some time ago. I very heartily indorse the movement in favor of a national university. Since coming to the United States seven years ago I have studied very carefully the educational system, especially the university and college system of the United States. I have often expressed my surprise that the Legislature of the United States and the State legislature should take so little interest in education, leaving it entirely or almost entirely to voluntary efforts. Educated as I was in the European schools, and conversant with the European State control and endowment of university education, I appreciate the effort to inaugurate this national university and to make such a university the national educational home of scholars. It has always seemed to me that education suffered largely from the disintegrating influences in the United States arising from the entire isolation of college from college.

I rejoice that you have, in a measure, been successful in giving realization to the hopes of the early scholars of this united nation, and that there is the prospect in the near future of a national university, which is essential, as I view it, to the efficiency and perfection of the university system of education. I trust that this university will be a bond of union among the already historic colleges of the United States, and that while preserving the traditions of these colleges, all of them will delight to form an integral part of the one great university of the United States.

I will be very much delighted to do anything or say anything when occasion demands in behalf of this grand and glorious object.

Yours, very truly,

J. MARTIN LITTLEJOHN, Ph. D., LL. D.,
President of Amity College, Iowa.

COTNER UNIVERSITY,
Bethany, Nebr., April 22, 1896.

DEAR SIR: * * * I heartily approve the effort to establish a national university, and shall be delighted to render the enterprise any assistance in my power.

Very truly, yours,

D. R. DUNGAN,
Chancellor Cotner University.

MARYVILLE COLLEGE,
Maryville, Tenn., March 28, 1896.

DEAR SIR: I have always thought it a great pity that the American people did not second the earnest recommendation of Washington, that a central national university should be established at the seat of the National Government. If a strong institution had been early established for the education of youth from all parts of the Union, no one can say what vast influences might have emanated from it favorable to patriotism, union, and liberty. Possibly the war of 1861-1865 might have been avoided. You are at liberty to use my name as favoring a national university, if it can be of any service, in any way you may choose.

Sincerely, yours,

SAM'L W. BOARDMAN, *President.*

MARYVILLE COLLEGE,
Maryville, Tenn., April 11, 1896.

Hon. JAMES H. KYLE, *Senator, etc.*

DEAR SIR: I received some time ago a printed list of college presidents favoring the university of the United States, including my own name and that of this college of 450 students, and inquiring if I would allow the use of my name in that way. I wrote a cordial assent, with a statement of my long-cherished conviction that a very great mistake had been made by the country in not complying with the earnest desire of President Washington for the early establishment of such an institution. It was a real disappointment to me to find, on receiving the report (Fifty-fourth Congress, first session, No. 429), that my name and that of this Southern college had been omitted. I would be glad, if you would think proper, to have you communicate this note to the compiler and to have our approval and desire associated with those of so many others in any future similar publications. Though a very slight participation, yet I would not wish to be left out of a movement which we regard with very great interest and hopefulness.

Very sincerely, yours, SAMUEL W. BOARDMAN.

CALIFORNIA COLLEGE,
Highland Park, Oakland, Cal., April 14, 1896.

DEAR SIR. I shall be glad if by the use of my name on the committee of one hundred or by any other means I can further the early founding of a national university at Washington.

Most fraternally, yours, SAMUEL B. MORSE, *President.*

WESTERN RESERVE UNIVERSITY, ADELBERT COLLEGE,
Clereland, Ohio, April 16, 1896.

MY DEAR MR. HOYT: The pamphlet which I have just received relating to the progress of the endeavor to establish the university seems to me of great value. The argument founded on the facts is sound and has great strength.

I am, with great regard, very truly, yours,

CHAS. F. THWING, *President.*

URSINUS COLLEGE,
Collegeville, Pa., April 16, 1896.

MY DEAR SIR: The organization of a national university is justified by educational experience. Such an institution is necessary to the highest development of the national spirit, as well as to the uplifting of the educational activity of the country as a whole. In education progress must come from above.

Very truly, yours, HENRY T. SPANGLER, *President.*

MISSOURI VALLEY COLLEGE,
Marshall, Mo., April 14, 1896.

DEAR SIR: You must pardon me for not examining into the merits of the University of the United States sooner. I can only plead lack of information and therefore of interest.

I now write to approve the idea and to bid the plan Godspeed.

Yours, truly, WILLIAM H. BLACK, *President.*

TABOR COLLEGE,
Tabor, Iowa, April 14, 1896.

DEAR SIR: Replying to your communication of the 8th, I beg leave to say that I heartily approve of the proposition to establish a national university of the United States, to be located at Washington, D. C.

I see no reason why we may not have advantages here (in time) equal to any in the world.

Respectfully, yours,
WM. M. BROOKS, *President.*

ST. OLAF COLLEGE,
Northfield, Minn., April 13, 1896.

DEAR SIR: Your communication in regard to the establishment of a national university is at hand. It is the first information I have received from you in regard to the matter.

I shall work for the establishment of such a university with all the honorable means at my command, as far as time and opportunity permit.

Awaiting your further orders,
I remain, very truly, yours,
TH. N. MOHR, *President.*

ILLINOIS COLLEGE,
Jacksonville, Ill., April 11, 1896.

DEAR SIR: Your circular letter of April 8 is at hand. Your previous letter seems to have escaped my attention. I am heartily in favor of a national university, and hope the movement for its establishment will continue to gather strength. You may, if you wish, add my name to the committee to promote its establishment.

Very truly, yours,
JOHN E. BRADLEY, *President.*

ROLLINS COLLEGE,
Winter Park, Fla., April 14, 1896.

DEAR SIR: I am most earnestly in favor of a national university at Washington.
Very truly, yours,
J. H. FORD, *Acting President.*

OTTAWA UNIVERSITY,
Ottawa, Kans., April 11, 1896.

DEAR SIR: Your circulars addressed to President Colegrove are before me. For some two months President C. has been incapacitated for work, and is now absent from the State. However, I am quite confident he is in hearty sympathy with your movement.

It seems to me that a national university at Washington would be the crowning glory of our nation. Washington, with the best museums, libraries, and the personnel of the Army and Navy, all organized as a university and at the service of students, would be the Mecca of our youth. What we can do, even though it be but little, is at your service.

Yours,
M. L. WARD, *Chairman Faculty.*

OTTERBEIN UNIVERSITY,
Westerville, Ohio, April 1, 1896.

DEAR SIR: Your communication regarding the founding of a national university is received.

You may put me down as heartily in favor of such an institution as you propose. I would like to see the United States lead the world in higher education. I thought I had sent in my name long ago.

Sincerely, yours,
T. J. SANDERS, *President.*

KNOX COLLEGE, *Salisbury, Ill., April 10, 1896.*

MY DEAR SIR: I have your note of April 8. I beg to say in answer that weeks if not months ago I wrote you most heartily indorsing the plan for the establishment of a national university. I shall be very glad to have you add my name to your already long list if it will help in promoting the object of your efforts. I beg to add my best wishes for the success of this great enterprise.

I have the honor to be, yours, very truly,

JOHN H. FINLEY,
President of Knox College.

NORTHERN ILLINOIS COLLEGE,
Fulton, Ill., April 13, 1896.

DEAR SIR: In answer to your note concerning the proposed university of the United States, I beg to say that you have my hearty approval of the enterprise. Pardon haste, and believe me,

Fraternally, yours,

J. H. BREESE, *President.*

IOWA STATE COLLEGE, AGRICULTURE AND MECHANIC ARTS,
Ames, Iowa, April 13, 1896.

DEAR SIR: Your letter of April 8 is duly received. I replied favorably from the start, but I presume it missed you in some way. Inclosed you will find excerpt from an address of mine as president of the Iowa State Teachers' Association one year ago last December, in which favorable mention is made of the project. I am heartily in favor of such an enterprise and would be pleased to have you include me among its friends.

Sincerely,

W. M. BEARDSHEAR, *President.*

EXCERPT—THE UNIVERSITY OF THE UNITED STATES.

There is now pending in our national Congress a bill whose object is the crowning of our educational system by the establishment of a university for the United States, under the patronage of the National Government—a university to take rank with any in the world. The name, "The University of the United States," has magic in it, and is full of statesmanlike purpose and patriotic devotion to our country's institutions. Such a plan lay near the patriotic heart of the great Washington. In 1795 he said: "It is with inexpressible regret that I have seen the youth of the United States migrating to foreign countries in order to acquire the higher branches of erudition, and to obtain a knowledge of the sciences." Among the motives of such an institution he conceived the assimilation of principles and manners of our countrymen by a common education of a portion of our youth from every quarter, and especially the study of the science of government in the light of our own national needs and destinies.

The very first spirit to bring the new South to the sympathy and fellowship of a reunited country, after our civil war, was the common ties and kindred learning of the alumni of a number of our Northern institutions whose interests and aims were in the South, but whose education had verified the philosophy of Washington by associating themselves and forming friendships in juvenile years that enabled them to free themselves from local prejudices and habitual jealousies which had been carried to excess, and demonstrated his very language of provincialisms, being "a never failing source of disquietude to the public mind, and pregnant with mischievous consequences to this country."

The most catholic and touching alumnal meetings I ever observed were when the southern alumni of Yale University first began to come back after the war. Both wings fought most valiantly as enemies in war, and as lovers of learning and their alma mater became brothers again. We should lead the world in learning as well as in government and philanthropy. Austria has eleven universities supported by the general Government, embracing most generous provision of professors and facilities for education. Germany has an educational system under governmental support, including twenty-one higher class universities. You are familiar with the fact that these universities lead the world. In the catalogue of faculties in our American institutions, the degree of Ph. D., M. D., and others credited to German universities, give first rank in the estimation of the scholarly world.

America ought to afford at least one university broad enough to embrace the field of learning, science, and art, employing in its faculty the most capable specialists in the world, having in its equipment the completest educational facilities known to the teaching profession, all pervaded with a spirit of investigation and research that would be in brotherly touch with the learned nations, and the worthy pride of every intelligent and patriotic American. Yea, more! As the environment of every country is imparted to the culture of its institutions, a University of the United States ought to send out a new leaven of broad culture that would gratify the lawful pride of American scholarship and wholesomely vie with the knowledge and philosophy of the world's best thinkers. Some years ago Japan, by governmental sanction, selected a number of her choicest young men and young women and sent them to be educated in American colleges and universities. Prominent in the new national spirit of Japan that has brought it almost within a day to the primal rank of Eastern Empires and Governments have been these same young men, now educated and alive to larger and better things for their own country.

The wife of the commander in chief of the Japanese armies, that have made such inroads upon the century-deep conservatism and Chinese wall power of the Celestials, is a graduate of Vassar College. So that the power of educated womenhood played no small part in the most admirable marshaling of armies and the remarkable triumph at Port Arthur. American education is making wondrous progress in incarnating the best there is for Japan. If our private and public institutions, hampered by limited resources and burdened with overwork, can bring such speedy returns for the elevation of one nation, what could not a university education do under the unity and freedom of the Stars and Stripes, pervaded by the patriotic devotion of Washington, Jefferson, Madison, Monroe, John Quincy Adams, and the world-hearted Grant, all advocates, as Presidents, of such a measure, portraying the sanctified ambition and ideal of our best scholars from the time of Washington to the present, bearing the seal of the advocacy of the National Educational Association as early as the meeting in St. Louis in 1871, embodying in it the catholicity and man-wide toleration that brought the world's congress of education and religion, at the Columbian Exposition, in which peoples of all Governments and creeds, fellowshipped in the fatherhood of God and the brotherhood of man, culminating in the University of the United States of America, upheld by the gold and silver of our thousand hills and mountains and the hearts of a liberty-loving and knowledge-aspiring people. I hope the Iowa teachers will be among the first State associations to pass a resolution in favor of such a national university.

IN THE SENATE OF THE UNITED STATES.

UNIVERSITY

OF

THE UNITED STATES.

MARCH 10, 1896.—Submitted by Mr. KYLE, from the Committee to Establish the University of the United States, and ordered to be printed.

[To accompany S. 1202.]

WASHINGTON:
GOVERNMENT PRINTING OFFICE,
1896.

REPORT OF COMMITTEE.

The Committee to Establish the University of the United States, to whom was referred the bill (S. 1202) to establish the University of the United States, have had the same under careful consideration for several sessions, and have heard advocates both for and against the measure.

To those giving a thought to the unparalleled progress of nations in this close of the nineteenth century there would seem to be no question as to the need of such an institution in the United States as is contemplated in this bill. The spirit of the age calls for deeper penetration into the sciences and arts, and demands better equipped men. Why should not the United States, the cradle of liberty and the leader of enlightened Christendom, contribute her share to the advancement of mankind? Why should we borrow modern educational methods from Europe, and patronize foreign institutions? Why should we not build here an institution which would stir the pride and patriotism of American students, and furnish facilities unequaled in the world for the extension of knowledge?

The more we know of Washington the broader appears to have been his conception of a great nation and great institutions. Besides giving us a wise Constitution and laws, he planned a beautiful city, with wide streets and avenues, with parks and boulevards, rivaling the finest cities of Europe. He saw here the seat of government of a mighty nation, equipped with political and scientific departments and to utilize these in the promotion of advanced learning he conceived the proposed national university. He talked and wrote about it for years, and at his death bequeathed $25,000 as a first endowment, placing the institution in effect under the fostering care of Congress. Opponents have sought to belittle Washington's idea of a university, contending that he thought of nothing but an institution for political science, or at most but an ordinary undergraduate college. His thoughts were higher than this. His published words are clear and unmistakable. Harvard College, founded almost a hundred years before he was born, Yale College, founded early in the century, and other colleges, South and North, were doing splendid work when this university was proposed.

Washington spoke of them as seminaries of learning, and to this end endowed the University of Virginia. But in discussing the question of a national university he stated in the address to Congress, 1790, in a letter to the Commissioners of the District of Columbia, 1791, and in his letters to Thomas Jefferson, Governor Brooke, and Alexander Hamilton, that his proposed university should be for the higher branches of learning, that "the youth of all parts of the United States might receive the polish of erudition in the arts, sciences, and belles-lettres," and should be open for those who had already passed beyond the seminary training. His fellow-statesmen, who had labored side by side with him in the formation of the Constitution, were possessed of the same ideas. Presidents John Adams and Thomas Jefferson and others united with such distinguished scholars as Dr. Benjamin Rush in declaring for a Federal university, "into which the youth of the United States shall be received after they have finished their studies and taken their degrees in their respective States." At no time was it contemplated to establish a rival of the undergraduate colleges. The vision of these men is worthy the most advanced thinkers of to-day.

There can be no need for an undergraduate university at Washington supported at national expense. Sectarian colleges have already covered this field. This bill contemplates an institution for men, not for boys subject to class-room drill and control; for men seeking wide fields for scientific and philosophic research, and with the world's best equipments at hand; " an institution broader in its scope, more complete in its organization, more philosophic and practical in its internal regulations, with the highest possible educational standards and aims; an institution above and beyond the best of the colleges, with their loosely attached professional schools, and on its own higher plane existing for the extension and diffusion of all branches of useful knowledge; an institution where the love of knowledge * . * * shall be fostered and developed; where advanced students, devoted to any branch of knowledge, whether science, language, literature, or philosophy, or to any of the combinations of these constituting the numerous professional courses of instruction, shall intermingle and enjoy friendly intercourse as peers of the same realm; where the professors, chosen from among the ablest and best scholars of the world, with absolute freedom of conscience and of speech, shall be not teachers of the known merely, but also earnest searchers after the unknown, and capable, by their genius, enthusiasm, and moral power, of infusing their own lofty ambition into the minds of all who wait upon their instruction; a university not barely complying with the demands of the age, but one that shall create, develop, and satisfy new demands and aspirations, that shall have power to fashion and mold the age unto its own ideal, and which through every change and every real advance of the world shall still be at the front, driving back from their fastnesses the powers of darkness, opening up new continents of truth to the grand army of progress, so leading the nation forward and helping to elevate the whole human race."

We have no such institution in the United States or on the Western Hemisphere to-day. Between 2,000 and 3,000 American students are abroad each year for post-graduate work in European universities; a confession that American institutions do not fully equip men for special lines of work. It is understood that many prominent American educators, representing our best universities, are at the present time petitioning the universities of France to open their doors to American students for special work—a confession that European universities have facilities that we have not.

The need of a national university and the interest taken in its establishment by the founders of our Government are set forth in a clear manner in the reports submitted for this committee by Chairman Proctor, of Vermont, during the Fifty-second Congress, and in like manner by Chairman Hunton, of Virginia, during the Fifty-third Congress; selections from which reports the committee incorporate as part of this report.

From the report submitted by Chairman Proctor, March 3, 1893:

"The value of knowledge is recognized in all civilized countries; but in no country does it deserve higher recognition than in our own, for our Government is founded upon it, and we need it everywhere, and all forms of it, for our highest development. Hitherto there has been practical recognition of this in the United States in providing for State universities, for schools of agriculture and the mechanic arts, for military and naval schools, for the Department of Agriculture and the different surveys, and for great libraries. It is the purpose of this bill to make such organization more complete and more worthy of a great and progressive people by creating at the capital of the nation one supreme institution that (1) shall complete the system of American education by supplying the crowning and true university it lacks, both as a means of furnishing upon American soil every possible facility for the highest available culture, and of exciting a stimulating and elevating influence upon all classes of schools of lower rank; (2) that shall bring together in friendly as well as high intellectual intercourse a large number of the most gifted and aspiring representatives of all the States for the pursuit of the highest knowledge in all departments of learning; thus supplying in endless succession the best-trained thinkers and workers for every field of intellectual activity, with broader views of men and things, as well as increased love of country and a juster regard for the citizens thereof, irrespective of locality, and more certainly assuring to the United States their proper place in the forefront of advancing nations.

"That there has ever been in the past a deep realization of our deficiencies in this field is manifest:

"First. From the great number of ambitious young men of the country who, from the beginning, have been accustomed to go abroad for opportunities they could not find at home.

"Second. From the zealous and repeated efforts of many of the foremost scholars, scientists, and statesmen to have in this country at least one post-graduate university of the highest possible grade.

"Third. From the many honorable, but still inadequate, efforts of existing institutions, and of large-minded, philanthropic men to meet this demand by increase of endowments devoted to proper university work.

"Fourth. From the strong declarations repeatedly made by individual citizens and organized bodies of men most competent to judge, that when all shall have been done that can be through individual and denominational agencies, it will still be the high duty and interest of the nation itself to establish and liberally endow an institution of such rank as is proposed by this bill.

"Such an institution only could in any proper sense complete the now incomplete system of American education, most wisely direct all worthy efforts in the field of original research, and utilize the facilities for it so rapidly accumulating at Washington.

"Such an institution only could possibly become the long-deferred realization of the aspirations and official appeals of those profoundly wise founders of the Republic, some of whom not only outlined the principles upon which it should be established and the relations it should sustain to the Government and people, but also devised for it sources of revenue, and set apart lands of the District of Columbia deemed suitable for the location of its buildings.

"The proposed bill is intended to represent and give fruition to the plans and desires of Washington, Jefferson, Madison, and other Presidents, together with a multitude of citizens in other high stations. It was prepared with the concurrence of citizens most competent to advise in such matters; and not only the ends sought to be attained, but also the means and agencies to be employed have received the sanction of many of the foremost scholars and statesmen of all portions of the country.

"It provides for the establishment of a university of the highest type, resting upon the State universities and other institutions of collegiate rank as they rest upon the high schools and academies—a university whose facilities shall be open to all who are competent to use them, but whose degrees shall be conferred upon such only as have already received a degree from some institution recognized by the university authorities; whose opportunities are to be open without price to qualified representatives from every State and Congressional district of the United States; whose several departments shall have endowed fellowships, open to persons of genius from whatever quarter of the world, for the advancement of knowledge by means of original researches; to whose professors, fellows, and students all Government collections, literary, scientific, and practical, are to be freely open without detriment to the public service, and whose several heads of departments are to have advisory and cooperative relations with the heads of Government bureaus for the mutual advantage of the Government itself and the cause of universal science.

* * * * * * *

"Your committee are of the opinion that the cause of American learning demands such an institution as this bill provides for; that the highest dignity and welfare of the nation demand it; that it should be established at the capital of the country; and that after a delay of one hundred years since it was first proposed and sought to be established by the founders of the Government it would be unworthy of so great a people to wait longer for a more favorable time in which to meet all these high demands.

"The committee, therefore, unanimously approve the bill and recommend its passage."

From the unanimous report of the committee under the chairmanship of Senator Hunton, of Virginia, submitted May 24, 1894:

"In the opinion of your committee such an institution should be deemed necessary, first of all, on account of the supreme work it would do in every division of the purely educational field—work at present but very partially and scatteringly done at those few institutions so fortunate as to have a concurrence of competent men with the means requisite to the support of systematic courses of post-graduate instruction.

"(2) It would powerfully contribute to the improvement of the whole series of schools of the country, from the kindergarten to the university.

"(3) It would correlate, broaden, elevate, and strengthen the entire circle of the so-called professions, not only furnishing but indirectly elsewhere compelling better preparation for professional studies, with higher standards of professional attainment, and hence broader and more thorough courses of instruction.

"(4) It would prove a most important means of supplying to a multitude of industrial occupations the scientific principles requisite to their highest success; thus dignifying labor and building up many new professions.

"(5) It would enlarge the field of human knowledge by means of the original researches and investigations of its members, while at the same time inducting students of genius into the art of investigation; thus helping mankind to an earlier mastery over the hidden forces of nature.

"(6) Such an institution would prove a powerful defender as well as discoverer and teacher of truth.

"'Among its members there would always be moral heroes as superior to the menaces of power as to the insidious arts of the most skillful and corrupt devotees of false gods—men able to unmask error and bold to stand for the right at all hazards. The sacredness of truth, freedom of thought, and freedom of speech will be the inscription upon its portals.'

"(7) The proposed university is also a patriotic necessity. It would secure to us as a great people the independence we need in things intellectual. It would strengthen our love of country, and so prove a new and powerful safeguard of free institutions. It would gather to its seat not only persons of genius and of lofty aspirations from all portions of the Union, but from all parts of the civilized world; thus at once stopping the present exodus to foreign institutions for advantages we do not here furnish, and turning the tide of superior learning to our own shores. It would help the United States to a commanding influence as a beneficent power among the nations; to a practical leadership in the march of civilization.

"For these important reasons the establishment of such an institution as the one now proposed has been in the minds of the foremost scholars and statesmen of our country from a period anterior to the adoption of the American Constitution.

"We find that Gen. George Washington considered the subject and predicted the establishment of a national university when in his military camp at Cambridge in 1775; that James Madison, John Adams, Charles C. Pinckney, Benjamin Franklin, William Samuel Johnson, James Rutledge, and others, realizing its importance and being unwilling to trust to the chances of future legislation, strongly favored provision for it in the Constitution itself; that upon the failure of this proposition in the convention,[1] solely because a majority deemed it an unnecessary encumbrance of that instrument, Dr. Benjamin Rush, signer of the Declaration of Independence and the leading American scientist of his time, eloquently pressed the subject upon the country in an address to the people of the United States, saying:

"Let one of the first acts of the new Congress be to establish within the district to be allotted them a Federal university, into which the youth of the United States shall be received after they have finished their studies and taken their degrees in their respective States. * * *

"Let it not be said, this is not the time for such a literary and political establishment. Let us first restore our public credit. * * * Let us regulate our militia, let us build our navy, and let us protect and extend our commerce. * * * This is false reasoning. We shall never restore public credit, regulate our militia, build a navy, and revive our commerce until we remove the ignorance and prejudices and change the habits of our citizens.

"It was in this great interest that Thomas Jefferson, afterwards its supporter as President, while yet Vice-President (in 1795) even went so far as to propose the importation of a learned faculty from Geneva as a means of beginning the work of such a university.

"It was because of his continued and ever-deepening interest in the early founding of the institution that President Washington, having

---

[1] Madison Papers, II, 740; III, 1354, 1577.

consulted with James Madison and Edmund Randolph, announced to the Commissioners of this District, in 1795, his purpose to contribute a considerable sum, in stocks of the Potomac Company, toward the founding of a university peculiarly American in character, saying:

"For this reason I have greatly wished to see a plan adopted by which the arts, sciences, and belles-lettres could be taught in their fullest extent, thereby embracing all the advantages of European tuition with the means of acquiring the liberal knowledge which is necessary to qualify our citizens for the exigencies of public as well as private life, and (which with me is a consideration of great magnitude) by assembling the youth from the different parts of this rising Republic, contributing from their intercourse an interchange of information to the removal of prejudices which might sometimes arise from local circumstances.

"It is known that he actually did contribute a sum which, had the purposes of the giver been carried out, would now have amounted to over four millions of dollars; that in the preparation of his farewell address, in 1796, he set apart the 19 acres of land long known as 'University Square' as a site for that institution; and that in his final message to Congress he said, among other things, on this head:

"'I have heretofore proposed to the consideration of Congress the expediency of establishing a national university and also a military academy. The desirableness of both these institutions has so constantly increased with every new view I have taken on the subject that I can not omit the opportunity of once for all recalling your attention to them. The assembly to which I address myself is too enlightened not to be fully sensible how much a flourishing state of the arts and sciences contributes to material prosperity and reputation. True it is that our country, much to its honor, contains many seminaries of learning, highly respectable and useful, but the funds upon which they rest are too narrow to command the ablest professors in the different departments of liberal knowledge for the institution contemplated, though they would be excellent auxiliaries. Among the motives to such an institution, the assimilation of the principles, opinions, and manners of our countrymen by the common education of a portion of our youth from every quarter will deserve attention. The more homogeneous our people can be made in these particulars the greater will be our prospect of permanent union; and the primary object of such a national institution should be the education of our youth in the science of government. In a republic what species of knowledge can be equally important, and what duty more pressing on its legislature, than to patronize a plan for communicating it to those who are to be the guardians of the future liberties of the country?

"We also find that, immediately after this last appeal of Washington, the commissioners appointed under the act to establish the temporary and permanent seat of the Government of the United States presented to Congress a memorial in this same behalf, urging the importance of the project, and especially saying:

"'We flatter ourselves it is only necessary to bring this subject within the view of the Federal Legislature. We think you will eagerly seize the occasion to extend to it your patronage, to give birth to an institution which may perpetuate and endear your names to the latest posterity.

"It is also a matter of history that Presidents John Adams and Thomas Jefferson favored the university proposition throughout their terms of office, repeatedly urging its importance upon Congress.

"For example, in his sixth annual message, President Jefferson, having already predicted favorable action by Congress and discussed the use of the Treasury surplus for a national endowment, said:

"Education is here placed among the articles of public care; not that it would be proposed to take its ordinary branches out of the hands of private enterprise, which manages so much better all the concerns to which it is equal, but a public institution can alone supply those sciences which, though rarely called for, are necessary to complete the circle, all the parts of which contribute to the improvement of the country, and some to its preservation. * * * The present consideration of a national establishment for education particularly is rendered proper by this circumstance also, that if Congress, approving the proposition, shall yet think it more eligible to found it on a donation of lands, they have it now in their power to endow it with those which will be among the earliest to produce the necessary income.

"The utterances of President Madison are so emphatic and important that we quote briefly from a number of them.

"From his second message these words:

"By enlightening the opinions, by expanding the patriotism and by assimilating the principles, the interests, and the manners of those who might resort to this temple of science, to be redistributed in due time through every portion of the community, sources of jealousy and prejudice would be diminished, the features of national character would be multiplied, and greater extent given to social harmony. But, above all, a well-constituted seminary in the center of the nation is recommended by the consideration that the additional instruction emanating from it would contribute not less to strengthen the foundations than to broaden the structure of our free and happy system of government.

"From his seventh message:

"Such an institution claims the patronage of Congress as a monument of that solicitude for the advancement of knowledge without which the blessings of liberty can not be fully enjoyed or long preserved; as a model of instruction in the formation of other seminaries; as a nursery of enlightened preceptors; as a central resort of youth and genius from every part of the country, diffusing on their return examples of those national feelings, those liberal sentiments, and those congenial manners which contribute to cement our Union and add strength to the political fabric of which that is the foundation.

"In his final message he further said:

"The importance which I have attached to the establishment of a university within this District on a scale and for objects worthy the attention of the American nation induces me to renew my recommendation of it to the favorable consideration of Congress.

"The university proposition also received the support of President James Monroe, whose sympathies with the desires and plans of Washington found expression at many times, and who fondly hoped that Columbian College, which did at different times later receive aid from Congress, would somehow grow into the desired institution. On the 28th of March, 1820, he said:

"The establishment of the institution within the Federal District in the presence of Congress and of all the Departments of the Government will secure to those who may be educated in it many important advantages. * * * If it receives hereafter the proper encouragement, it can not fail to be eminently useful to the nation.

"The same, and more, may be said of John Quincy Adams, who often urged it, even before he came to the Presidency, and who in his first message referred to it with a touching eloquence in these terms:

"Among the first, perhaps the very first, instruments for the improvement of the condition of men is knowledge, and to the acquisition of much of the knowledge adapted to the wants, the comforts, and the enjoyments of human life public institutions and seminaries of learning are useful. So convinced of this was the first of my predecessors in this office, now first in the memory as he was first in the hearts of his countrymen, that once and again, in his addresses to the Congresses with which he cooperated in the public service, he earnestly recommended the establishment of seminaries of learning to prepare for all the emergencies of peace and war—a national university and a military academy. With respect to the latter, had he lived to the present day, in turning his eyes to the institution at West Point, he would have enjoyed the gratification of his most earnest wishes, but in surveying the city which has been honored with his name he would have seen the spot of earth which he had destined and bequeathed to the use and benefit of his country as the site for a university still bare and barren.

"Again, it was President Jackson who, in 1832, approved the appropriation of $25,000 to Columbian College on account of the generally acknowledged 'utility of a central literary establishment,' and of his hope that said institution was to realize the dreams and aspirations of the long line of his illustrious predecessors.

"Disheartened, as it would seem, by continued disregard of all these earnest appeals of their predecessors, but two of the more recent Presidents have ventured to urge the subject upon the attention of Congress, although several of them are known to have favored the founding of a central university as the crown and completement of the public educational system of the country. Of such as have done so, honorable mention may be made, first, of President Grant, who, in his annual message of 1873, said:

"'I would suggest to Congress the propriety of promoting the establishment in this District of an institution of learning or university of the highest class by donations of lands. There is no place better suited for such an institution than the national capital. There is no other place in which every citizen is so directly interested.

"So fully convinced was he of the importance of such an institution, that he half believed that had it been founded in the time of Washington for the higher education of influential representatives of all sections the late unhappy conflict might never have come. So impressed was he with the wisdom of appropriating lands as a broad and sure foundation, and finally, so confident of early action by Congress, that he thought chiefly of the concurrence of all friends of the proposition upon Washington as the seat of the institution.

"It is well known that similar views were cherished by President Hayes, of whose recommendations that of 1877 is especially worthy of note:

"The wisdom of legislation upon the part of Congress in aid of the States for the education of the whole people in those branches of study which are taught in the common schools of the country is no longer a question. The intelligent judgment of the country goes still further, regarding it as also both constitutional and expedient for the General Government to extend to technical and higher education such aid as is deemed essential to the general welfare and to our due prominence among the enlightened and cultivated nations of the world. * * * I shall be glad to give my approval to any appropriate measure which may be enacted by Congress for the purpose of supplementing with national aid the local systems of education in * * * all the States; and having already invited your attention to the needs of the District of Columbia with respect to its public-school system, I here add that I believe it desirable, not with reference to the local wants of the District, but to the great and lasting benefit of the whole country, that this system should be crowned with a university in all respects in keeping with the national capital, and thereby realize the cherished hopes of Washington on this subject.

"We further note the agitation of the national-university question from that time forward, with special activity at intervals, by leading scholars, scientists, and statesmen of every portion of the country; its support by the presidents and professors of nearly, if not every, State university, as well as by those of the denominational schools and universities of every section, and even by the heads of the great and new universities founded upon those munificent bequests of distinguished private citizens which have gained for them the admiration and gratitude of all friends of education throughout the world; also the earnest and systematic support of the proposition by duly-authorized committees of various national educational, scientific, and patriotic organizations; and finally, its cordial approval by that great body of eminent men who constitute the managing and working force of scholars and scientists in the many divisions, educational, industrial, and scientific, of the Federal Government, notable examples from the distinguished class last named being found in the successive superintendents of the Coast and Geodetic Survey, of the Naval Observatory, of the bureaus of Navigation, Hydrography, Medicine and Surgery, Anthropology, Ethnology, and Education; the National Museum, Museum of Hygiene, Government libraries, etc., together with those scientific and other organizations, having more or less connection with the Government, which are so honorably represented by the Smithsonian Institution.

"As is shown in the memorial of John W. Hoyt, recently published by order of the Senate, and of which liberal use has been made in the preparation of this report, a very considerable number of the army of learned men and officials have at various times advocated the university measure in published papers, public addresses, and official reports—so great a number, indeed, that the proper limits of this report will not justify more than the mention of the fact, unless we venture this final quotation from a very able report of Hon. L. Q. C. Lamar, Secretary of the Interior in 1885, wherein he said:

"Eighty years ago President Jefferson, then in the fullest tide of his authority as a party chief, told Congress that to complete the circle of Democratic policy a national university was a necessity and should be created. In this he followed the recommendations of his predecessors, Washington and Adams, the former of whom ten years before declared that the desirableness of a national university had so constantly increased with every new view he had taken of the subject that he could not omit the opportunity of recalling the attention of Congress to its importance. Mr. Madison, in 1810, renewed the recommendation, with the declaration that such an institution would contribute not less to strengthen the foundations than to adorn the structure of our free and happy system of government, and that it would be universal in its beneficial effects.

"This national institution which Washington, Adams, Jefferson, and Madison thought so necessary has never been established, and in these later years the idea of a national university constitutes no part of the plans of statesmen and seems to have been lost sight of by the people.

"In the meantime, scientific bureaus have grown up one by one under the Government, with observatories, laboratories, museums, and libraries, until the whole range of physical science is represented by national institutions established by the Government for the purpose of prosecuting researches embracing astronomy, meteorology, geography of land and sea, geology, chemistry, statistics, mechanical inventions, etc. If the various commissions, bureaus, and divisions of the Executive Departments at Washington, which have for their object the prosecution of scientific research, could be combined as integral parts of one scientific institution, such institution would be of greater proportions and more comprehensive than any in the world, and should a university be erected thereon, with a superstructure commensurate with the foundation, it would be without a rival in any country.

"The common-school system, designed to furnish every citizen with an education which ought to be a strict necessity for his daily work of life, constitutes the foundation for our democracy. But that is not enough to satisfy its instincts. In the history of nations democracies have been the cradles of pure thought and art. The same cause which operated in them exists in American society, and whether through a national university or in fragmentary institutions in the several States, sooner or later a higher education, higher than the common school or the academy or the college can furnish, will alone realize and express the higher aspirations of American democracy.

"As final citations of the views of other men upon this important subject, attention is called to the fact that bills similar to the one reported by this committee have been twice before unanimously commended to the National Legislature, once by the Committee on Education, of the House of Representatives, in 1872, and again in 1893 by the Senate's Select Committee to Establish the University of the United States; the first providing for the payment in perpetuity of 5 per cent interest on a registered certificate of twenty millions; the last mentioned for one-half the net proceeds of the sales of the public lands without limit of time.

"The views of the said House committee are concisely summed up in the following concluding passage of their unanimous report:

"If, then, it be true, as the committee have briefly endeavored to show, that our country is at present wanting in the facilities essential to the highest culture in many departments of learning; and if it be true that a central university, besides meeting this demand, would quicken, strengthen, and systematize the schools of the country from the lowest to the highest; that it would increase the amount and the love of pure learning, now too little appreciated by our people, and so improve the intellectual status of the nation; that it would tend to homogeneity of sentiment, and thus strengthen the unity and patriotism of the people; that, by gathering at its seat distinguished savans not only of our own but of other lands, it would eventually make of our national capital the intellectual center of the world, and so help the United States of America to rank first and highest among the enlightened nations of the earth, then it is most manifestly the duty of Congress to establish and amply endow such a university at the earliest possible day.

"The committee, therefore, affirm their approval of the bill and recommend its passage by the House.

"The general conclusion of the Senate committee of the last Congress is set forth in no less positive terms, as we have already shown.

"Should the question arise whether action was had upon these several bills, it remains to be said that each of them was, unfortunately, reported during the last week of the Congress that should have considered it, and that time for action was therefore wholly wanting.

"And so of the possible question whether, with the efforts of princely givers and of powerful religious denominational bodies aiming at universities, the wants of our people are not likely to be met without the help of the nation, the answer is simple. If we should wholly ignore the insufficiency of their endowments, even the richest of them, and that denominational bias which they can not escape if they would— which, indeed, was and is and will remain the mainspring of their great endeavors—the answer must still, and necessarily, be a most emphatic negative.

"No institution, whatever its name or aim, that is local, or that rests on either a private or a denominational foundation; no institution with partial aims, however worthy as viewed from a local or a partisan standpoint; no institution with aims less than national and universal, and, on this account, able to command the confidence, active sympathy, and moral as well as material support of the whole people; no institution not so related to the public-school system of the United States, with its primary, secondary, academic, and university gradations, as to furnish the crown and culmination of the whole series, and so become to them a mighty coordinating and uplifting force; no institution resting on a foundation less broad, ample, and unfailing than that which is furnished by the geographic empire and boundless resources of the American Union; no institution with less of dignity, or less loftiness of purpose than with absolute impartiality to meet all the intellectual and ethical aims of a great people, and to secure for that people an acknowledged leadership among the nations in all things that make for the progress and highest welfare of the human race; no institution less than equal to all these exalted ends can satisfy the needs and demands of such a people as dwell under the flag of the American Republic.

"Progress in higher education has indeed been made in this country since the revival of efforts for the proposed national university; but the growth of science, the needs of the people, and the demands of the age have more than kept pace with the increase of instrumentalities, so that relatively we are no nearer the goal, the realization of the aims so long cherished by the patriots and scholars of the nation, than before.

"Indeed, as compared with the leading nations of Europe, we are at a yet greater disadvantage, for the development thére has been more marked than here. France, Germany, Austria, and Italy appear to have gained of late a new realization of how incalculably great a factor is the higher education in the struggle of a people for supremacy. Thus, Germany, having wisely followed the guidance of her farsighted statesmen, and so become during the last quarter of a century the world's leader in the whole field of higher culture, is now lavishing her resources upon her universities, strengthening them on every side, especially the scientific, and providing new accommodations for them at a cost of millions for a single department.

"Austria, not to be outdone in the university rôle, has in one or two cases not only exceeded Germany, but has placed her central institution before all others in the world, in so far as material provision and ambitious plans are concerned, erecting buildings for its use at a cost exceeding the present available endowment of any university in America, and planning researches in the interest of science which are intended to place her in the van of the world's army of progress.

"So of the Dutch, Scandinavian, and English Governments; all have received a new awakening and are moving with a degree of zeal and liberality hitherto unheard of.

"Nor are the Latin nations content to rest on laurels already won. France, having advanced the educational budget beyond all precedent, is now revolutionizing and developing her École Pratique des Hautes Études with a view to highest possible standards; is making the École Libre des Sciences Politique the foremost institution of its kind in the world; is devoting over $3,000,000 to new buildings for the Sorbonne, and dealing hardly less liberally with the College de France and with some of the great professional institutions of Paris. Italy is building palatial structures for her universities at the great centers, fully resolved not to be left in the rear of this grand new movement. Everywhere concentration of means and forces, to the end of leadership and eventual supremacy in the university field, is the watchword.

"It is for America to say whether she will be content to lag forever in the rear of nations so greatly her inferior in resources, or whether she will at last take the one remaining step requisite to fairly meet the demands of learning and of those free institutions for which she assumes to be the supreme representative.

"It would seem, therefore, that it but remains to mature and adopt such a measure as shall in the best manner meet these high demands."

The bill before the Senate, as amended, provides:

That a university of post-graduate rank, with facilities for scientific and literary research and investigation, shall be established in the District of Columbia; that the government of the institution shall be vested in a board of regents and a university council; that the board of regents shall be composed of the President of the United States, who shall be president of the board; the Chief Justice of the United States, the Commissioner of Education, the Secretary of the Smithsonian Institution, the president of the National Academy of Science, the president of the National Educational Association, and the president of the University, and nine other citizens of the United States, no two of whom shall be citizens of the same State, to be appointed by the President by and with the consent of the Senate; that the university council shall consist of the board of regents and twelve other citizens of the United States, to be appointed by the board of regents from eminent educators connected with institutions of learning in the United States; that the board of regents shall have exclusive control of the financial administration of the university and all its affairs not confided to the university council.

That the university council shall have power to prosecute and direct the work of the university in courses of higher instruction, research, and investigation for the increase of knowledge; that it shall also appoint all officers of instruction; that no chair for instruction sectarian in religion or partisan in politics shall be permitted in any form, and no partisan test shall be required or allowed in the appointment of professors or in the selection of any officer of the university; that the facilities afforded by the university shall be open to all who are competent to use them, on conditions prescribed by the executive committee, with the advice of the faculties directly concerned; that degrees shall be conferred upon such persons only as have previously received the degree of bachelor of arts or some equivalent degree, or who have received certificates of graduation from some State educational institution.

That the university shall have authority to establish with other institutions of education and learning in this or in other countries such cooperative relations as shall be deemed advantageous; that, in the admission and appointment of persons to places or privileges in the university, character and competency shall be the sole test of qualifications; that as a means of partially providing building sites for the several departments of the university "University Square," selected and set apart by President George Washington for the use of a national university and heretofore occupied by the Naval Observatory, shall be set apart for the use and benefit of the University of the United States.

That for the organization, preliminary work, and support of the university an appropriation of $15,000 is made for the fiscal year ending June 30, 1897, and $25,000 for the fiscal year ending June 30, 1898. No permanent endowment is contemplated at this time, leaving to Congress in the future to provide for the institution by direct appropriation or by setting aside a portion of the proceeds of the sale of public lands or otherwise. It is the opinion of your committee that a great university can be founded and equipped by the Government at Washington at less expense than at any other place or by any private institution. By act of, and under rules to be prescribed by, Congress all departments and institutions, such as museums, libraries, scientific bureaus, hospitals, and art collections, laboratories, etc., may be placed at the disposal of faculty and students. These in themselves have cost the Government millions of dollars, and would represent an equipment in many lines at the outset unequaled in any country. In and around Washington there exists to-day a scholarship in scientific lines of the highest degree, all of which could be utilized by a national institution.

Why should we not provide the machinery for an organized university by means of which these splendid equipments may bring rich gifts to the people of our land? Such an institution would complete the grandest educational system in the world and enable Americans to take a most conspicuous part in those researches and investigations which are essential to the world's real progress. Your committee have amended the bill, and recommend its passage by the Senate.

HEARINGS BEFORE THE SELECT COMMITTEE TO ESTABLISH THE UNIVERSITY OF THE UNITED STATES.

LETTER OF EX-SENATOR GEORGE F. EDMUNDS, LL. D.

[Addressed to Hon. Galusha A. Grow, chairman of the House Committee on Education. It includes the chief points made by Senator Edmunds before said committee on January 23, 1896, and reported to Senate committee by request of its chairman.]

1505 LOCUST STREET,
Philadelphia, February 8, 1896.

MY DEAR MR. GROW: I have been informed that your committee would like a condensed statement of the grounds upon which I, with others, believe the university of the United States ought to be established at Washington. I am about to depart for Florida for several weeks, for health and rest, and can, therefore, only state such considerations as presently occur to me.

First. The great extent of the United States, and consequently the great distance of the larger body of colleges, academies, and schools of the various States from each other, makes it extremely difficult, if not impossible, for them to work in common sympathy with and in support of each other. This university will, I believe, overcome this difficulty to a very large degree, and will make what, in commercial phrase, might be called a mutual exchange and clearing house of knowledge, administrative and proper, inasmuch as all the States and colleges will be continually from time to time represented in it, and the governors of it.

Second. Besides colleges, academies, and schools, there will always be scattered over the country a very considerable number of persons who will have developed by their private studies and their genius the capacity for great advances in every line of research and progress, not only in mere literature and physical science, but also in social science. These, as the bill provides, will have the opportunity of meeting others of a similar kind from every part of the country, and probably from abroad, and can, at Washington, compare notes and help each other in the great march of the long-time progress to come.

Third. The Congressional Library and the libraries and the collections of objects in almost every branch of human energy and research, already in Washington, make that city the most available place (besides its being the political capital) for the work of such an institution.

Fourth. The United States, with their infinite resources of every kind, ought to stand in the front rank, if not as the leader, of all advancement for the good of mankind, and with such an institution, which coordinates all local institutions of learning, from the bottom up, and which in the main begins where the others leave off, it will certainly do so.

Fifth. The bill has been framed so as to make the work of the university open to all sects, to all political and social ideas, and to exclude all discriminations resting either upon sectarian or political notions. All persons properly fitted and capable are to have an equal field as seekers after the great truths of moral and social theories and problems, and for the discovery of the secrets yet hidden in the vast storehouse of nature.

I need not, with you, refer to the strong desire of the founders of the Government for such an establishment, or to the fact that special provision for it was not inserted in the Constitution for the reason that such a clause would be entirely unnecessary, and might be simply exclusive of the operations of the Government.

I do most earnestly hope that your committee and Congress will see their way clear at this auspicious time, and as a continual remembrancer of the wise hopes of the founders of the Republic, to make provision for now establishing this institution.

Very sincerely yours,

GEO. F. EDMUNDS.

Hon. GALUSHA A. GROW,
  Chairman Committee on Education,
    House of Representatives, Washington, D. C.

REMARKS OF WILLIAM PEPPER, M. D., LL. D.

[Made before the House Committee on Education, January 23, 1896, and reported, by request, to the Senate Committee to Establish the University of the United States.]

Dr. Pepper said, in effect:

The question might naturally be put why is there not already a national university at Washington, instead of what are the reasons for such a foundation? The leading countries of the world have seen to it with great care and liberality that at the capital of the nation there should be a university, so that the national treasures in the way of art galleries, libraries, scientific collections, and laboratories might be used for the purposes of higher education. The failure to develop such a teaching university in London may be quoted as the exception, whose unfortunate results prove the wisdom of the rule.

My interest in this question is not new. Although I have devoted my life to the service of the University of Pennsylvania to aid so far as my strength permitted in the work of building up that institution, I have long felt the importance of a national university in Washington. Even while I was the provost, and straining every nerve to aid the development of the University of Pennsylvania, I advocated the passage of a bill similar to the one before you. I acted then purely in a personal capacity; and of course what I express now is in no way official or representative, but simply my personal conviction of the need of a great university in this city. So far from interfering with the prosperity and growth of collegiate institutions in other places, it would strengthen them. It is understood that, as provided in this bill, the national university would be exclusively for advanced work of postgraduate grade. It would not compete with other institutions for undergraduate students. So far from interfering with postgraduate studies at other universities, it would secure a fuller recognition of the necessity for more ample provision for such studies at every institution prepared to conduct them.

What is the number of fellowships open to-day to students desiring advanced instruction? A few hundreds at the outside. How many thousands of earnest students, who have in many cases exhausted their resources in securing the ordinary collegiate education, would gladly pursue advanced studies to fit them for higher work as teachers, or writers, or investigators, if such opportunities existed in this country. Each great university, it is presumable, will always offer special advantages for such advanced work in some special lines. The establishment of a national university at Washington to utilize the vast educational resources of the capital would surely stimulate activity in the field of advanced study at each and every institution so situated as to properly conduct such studies. Each university finds itself forced to build up at large expense a great library; it seeks original manuscripts and documents; it must enter upon explorations and develop a museum; laboratories must be equipped and maintained, and great sums are needed for these purposes. After all is done it must remain impossible to compete with the resources of the National Government. Washington has already the material for the greatest university in the land—the richest libraries, the most extensive collections, numerous well-equipped laboratories, departments which are practically organized for original research.

The bill now under consideration would secure the coordination of all these rich facilities and utilize them for the benefit of higher education. It calls for no great expenditure for lands or buildings. Endowment will be needed and buildings will be needed as the work develops, but to no extent commensurate with the great work done—for so large a part of this work will always be accomplished by utilizing the educational facilities which now exist here, and which must inevitably become more and more extensive, whether coordinated in one great national educational work or left to be the coveted prize of a dozen rival denominational colleges. In all religious questions I revere the sincerity of individual belief, and I admire the energy of denominational zeal. But in educational matters I would protest against the admission of the denominational spirit. Either the proposed bill will become law and give to the country a truly federal and national institution, free from political and sectarian influence, or the educational resources and prestige of the capital will become more and more the object of injurious rivalry among many competing denominational institutions.

This bill, it is believed, does secure for the proposed university a high degree of protection from political influence. While its finances are intrusted to a small body of regents, all educational questions—the courses to be established, the conditions of admission, the character of examination, the degrees to be conferred, and above all the appointment of all professors and instructors—are delegated to the university council, a large majority of whose members are to be practical educators, preeminently concerned in maintaining the highest standards and in preserving the greatest purity of educational methods.

It is no question of mere academic interest which is urged on your consideration. It is an affair of the highest practical importance. It concerns vitally the future of education in America. It aims to confer upon Washington, the capital of this people of marvelous destiny, the crowning glory of being the center and the source of highest inspiration of a system of higher education worthy of such a nation.

REMARKS OF PROF. SIMON NEWCOMB, LL. D., SUPERINTENDENT OF THE NAUTICAL ALMANAC.

[Made January 24, 1890.]

MR. CHAIRMAN AND GENTLEMEN OF THE SENATE COMMITTEE: I shall attempt but a brief summary of what seem to me the reasons why a university of the United States should be established in the city of Washington.

* 1. It would be an eminently appropriate keystone to our educational system. Our counties, aided and countenanced by State authorities, provide for that elementary education which is necessary to the prosperity and well-being of the masses. The wisdom of this policy is so universally admitted, and so fully sustained by experience, as to be open to no question.

Next in order, many of the States of our Union, notably the newer ones, provide for a higher grade of education, namely, the collegiate and the professional. Experience has justified the wisdom of this policy. I believe that every State which supports the advanced branches of education is proud of its work in that direction in proportion to the liberality of its allowances and the efficiency of its institutions.

The great advancement of the nineteenth century in the arts of life bring before the people complex problems, requiring for their solution the ablest talent the country can produce and the best education it can afford. To provide for this education is clearly the function of the National Government.

2. A striking feature shown by our country—one which has frequently excited the comment of observers, and which has been discussed by Mr. Brice in his great work on the American Commonwealth—is the wide separation between the politics and the learning of our country. That this separation arises from any want of appreciation of learning on the part of the American public can not for a moment be believed. It obviously arises from the fact that our institutions of learning are too widely scattered over the country, and have too few facilities for close intercourse to make themselves felt in public affairs. While it is true that the Government of the United States has in its employ many able scientific investigators, the work of each of these investigators is necessarily confined to his own rather limited sphere, and the position of all as Government employees prevents their serving as a medium of communication between the learning of the country at large and the work of the Government.

3. It is impossible to specify in detail the different ways in which the increased influence of men of learning at the national capital would be useful. The spirit which animates scientific and historical investigation is precisely that of which we now stand most in need. The legislator and the head of a department is so completely engrossed with matters of detail that he finds it difficult, in many cases, to view things from the standpoint of the man of thought. By communication with the latter he would receive precisely the suggestions of which he stands in need. What greater boon can we offer to the official who is oppressed with details of foreign and domestic complications than the calm suggestions of the lifelong student of the special subject in hand, who, though neither a politician nor an administrator, can supply information and make suggestions which could not be obtained from any other source?

4. In the way of illustrative details, I may mention a few of the subjects with which such an organization as that proposed might be expected to concern itself:

A. *International law, and the history of colonization and of treaties.*—How useful to the United States would be a body of impartial experts on these subjects need not be pointed out.

B. *The climatology of the United States.*—In the observations and records of the Weather Bureau we have an inexhaustible mine bearing on this subject. But the working of this mine, so as to learn from it those general laws governing the change of climate and the course of storms, which would be invaluable to our Western settlers, requires a different kind of organization from that of the ordinary Government bureau. Organized the work of such an investigation must be, but the organizer should be the ablest scientific investigator of the subject that the country can produce, and who should be able to call upon the ablest of his fellows for assistance.

C. In the policy of such scientific organizations as the Coast and Geological Surveys and the National Observatory the advice of disinterested experts would be of the greatest value. They would occupy an intermediate position between the people at large, who contribute the money for the support of such institutions, and the administrators who are engaged in carrying them on.

5. I have heard no proposed objections to the new institution which are not founded either upon a misapprehension of principles or a misunderstanding of the purposes and objects of the university.

It is frequently supposed that the latter is intended to compete with the great universities of the country in the work of the higher education. The real effect of the supposed competition would be to increase the scope and usefulness of the colleges and universities of the country at large by offering to their best graduates yet more advanced courses, and by placing them in closer relations with the government of the country. The University of the United States would be in some sort the representative at Washington of all the colleges of the United States.

It is also said that the turmoil of political life is unfavorable to that calmness of mind necessary to the pursuit of study. This would undoubtedly be the case if the students of the university were obliged to take an active and responsible part in political contests. But I speak from experience in saying that no student of any subject would ever experience anything but a wholesome stimulus from his nearness to the focus of political strife. I find it to be a fallacy to suppose that the quiet of a region far removed from the centers of activity is most favorable to the conduct of scientific investigation.

The great academies of sciences, the work of whose members have, during the past two hundred and fifty years, made the nineteenth century what it is, have had their seats at such centers as London, Paris, Berlin, and St. Petersburg. The greater number of their members have worked most effectively at the very center of such scenes as those of the French revolution and the Napoleonic wars. If any instances can be found of work done or discoveries made by isolated men, they will be hard to find and few in number.

I may be pardoned for mentioning a circumstance bearing on this question which is within my own experience. Fifteen years ago I was desirous of an opportunity to devote several months of uninterrupted thought to a very complex and difficult investigation requiring several months of close attention. I thought no place could be more favorable than a quiet nook in some European town, far removed from contact with daily duties. But a very short residence in such a situation convinced me that such was not the case, and that the best place to pursue the investigation was among the haunts of men.

Altogether, it seems clear to me that there is no way in which our Government can more effectually promote the intellectual and material advancement of the people than by the institution now proposed.

REMARKS OF GEN. JOHN EATON, LL. D., EX-UNITED STATES COMMISSIONER OF EDUCATION.

[Before the Committee, January 24, 1896.]

Mr. CHAIRMAN: I am very glad that Professor Newcomb has directed attention to the bearing of the power of knowledge upon human welfare, upon public affairs, in connection with the establishment of the University of the United States, and that he has so far pointed out how the increase of knowledge, of more thorough and deeper thinking, are needed in our legislation and administration; in our business industries—indeed, in all that concerns man; but I regret that the modesty of the Professor has not allowed him to give us some idea of the many ways in which his solution of complicated mathematical and astronomical problems in making the nautical almanac saves time, health, and money. We can not estimate the value of ideas in dollars. The Professor illustrated his point by referring to the Weather Bureau. The whole story is full of meaning. The late war has brought out the advantage of signaling to the eye and by the use of the telegraph. Professor Abbe, in the study of the heavens, has gained facts of advantage for men to know in the common pursuits of life. The nation now, through the Weather Bureau using the telegraph and signals, gathers the necessary data from all parts of the country and announces its warnings for the benefit of all the people of the land.

At first the whole thing shocked certain common ideas. What had the United States Government to do with the weather business? But patriotic common sense soon saw its wisdom. A little more thinking showed that winds and storms had to do with the floods of rivers, and so now lives and property are saved by foretelling the arrival of floods. The profoundest scientists engaged in that work feel that they are only on the threshold of its opportunities. The many relations of education to sanitation drew my attention to the efforts to preserve public health. When the most important investigations of recent years were begun, the nation had kept itself so completely out of all these subjects that there was no money to gather the facts about yellow fever and cholera that were at the time afflicting portions of our land. A good woman, Mrs. Elizabeth Thompson, came to the relief of our far-sighted doctors and furnished a small amount of money. Sufficient data were gathered and maps were made telling in yellow and black by city squares the destructive prevalence of these plagues, to awaken the public mind to the importance of keeping them from our shores.

Congress, rising to the emergency, provided money, and scientists began the profounder investigations which the conditions suggested; but a spirit of opposition began to ask, "What has the National Government to do with affairs of this kind?" and the greater results possible in preserving public health were not reached. These researches are in abeyance until some future plague wakes us up. [Illustrating the amount of data lying about in Government records full of lessons for the benefit of the people, he mentioned the problems arising out of the relation of race to disease, and referred to the mass of facts gathered in the war, and later in Freedmen's Hospitals, bearing upon these important subjects.] We delight in believing that our Government is by the people and for the people. As has been said, no Government expends more for science; no national capital has more scientists gathered in it than Washington. I believe that a university of the highest grade here will make this money and these men vastly more effective for the Government and more efficient in promoting the welfare of the people at large. The ideas which the fathers sought to plant, that the Government is not solely for the benefit of its officers, but for the people—for all the people—should be cultivated by every means within reach.

Russia is on the alert to bring to the advantage of its departments of administration every forward step in science and art, but it does not exert itself to disseminate these advantages among all its people, high and low, for their benefit. Perhaps Russia has the best pedagogical museum in the world. It is not devoted to universal education, but is maintained to promote education in the army and under the direction of the war department. Just as the French Republic was rising out of the ruins of the Empire, acknowledging to our Bureau of Education the receipt of its report, which he had sought, a great French statesman wrote: "Our reports are made for officials, and imperfections and rottenness are concealed. Your American reports are made for the people as well as officials, and facts are accurately reported." Senator Howe, of Wisconsin, who so often urged the establishment of a national university, was accustomed to point out its advantages in elevating our civil service. It would immeasurably exalt and extend scholarship in all departments of learning. New inspiration would be applied to every field of research. Some assail certain officers of the Army and Navy for not keeping up a scholarly spirit. What would not a national university do in this behalf?

An incident in my early educational experience opened my eyes to the extent to which our national statesmen had come to divorce themselves from the consideration of principles fundamental to the people, and greatly shocked my youthful notion that the more exalted the man, the more wise would he be with regard to the profounder interests of the people. An educational question of the deepest importance engaged my attention, and I tried to gather facts and opinions bearing upon it from every quarter. Governor Seward had entered the United States Senate. I greatly admired him, and had the presumption to address him my inquiry. According to his rule to answer every letter, he replied to mine. How I was shocked. It was in effect that he was engaged in national politics and had no opinions worthy to be expressed upon the subject. We have no national system of education, and we seek none. We want the advantages of diversity. Our national existence depends upon the balancing of great forces and the harmonizing of great influences. The administration of education is wisely left to the several States, and the States are wise in still further localizing it by towns and cities; ultimately it must be an affair of the individual. The fathers disclosed their notion of the relation of the nation to education by making it the patron of learning, beginning even before the formation of the Constitution in the ordinance of 1787, by both indicating the grade of instruction from the lowest to the highest round of learning in giving the sixteenth section of the public domain for the establishment of public schools and the township—always one and sometimes two or more—for the establishment of a university in each new State to complete its system of public instruction.

Washington's idea was that this vast scheme should be crowned by a still higher university at the national capital. There is a natural irrepressible conflict between slavery and education, notwithstanding the teacher in ancient times, and more recently, even, has been a slave. Slavery in our country was especially thought to be imperiled by universal instruction. As a consequence, the common school made little headway where slavery was strongest. Only one feature of Jeffersons's scheme for education in Virginia, the university, could be organized in his day. The nation having assumed the appropriate position of benefactor of education, all questions arising in Congress touching education were closely watched by the slave interest. That interest allowed the policy of national grants to go on, but the establishment of a national university, or any other act which would be likely to tone up and energize the spirit of universal education, could not be encouraged, could not be tolerated. Even the act making grants of land for colleges of agriculture and mechanic arts was vetoed by Mr. Buchanan. The new spirit, represented by Mr. Lincoln, was ready to sign the bill whose stupendous beneficence will go on increasing while the Government stands.

A few years later the organization of an office of education was urged by wise and patriotic men who felt that there was serious lack in our educational forces, that we allowed to go to waste lessons of educational experience which the nation alone could gather and disseminate. Our theory of government staked all on the virtue and intelligence of the people. There had been given for their education a domain larger than some kingdoms. The lessons derived from the administration of these gifts were most valuable. Should they not be recorded and used? The Bureau of Education was established. As Vice-President Henry Wilson observed, "The Government should do for the education of its children what it did for the cultivation of pumpkin seeds." The chief of the office was provided with a salary of $4,000 and a few clerks, and the man of all Americans most eminent in educational literature was made Commissioner. An office so beneficent in its aims, so limited in its functions, and so ably manned, it would seem should have received the Godspeed of every patriot. But there is a theory abroad that would reduce government to a shrievalty. It would allow a government to punish crime but not to prevent it; it would allow a government to make war but not to promote peace.

The original idea of a census was to count the people in order to determine their capacity for war. Our Constitution provides for a decennial census in order to secure the data necessary to fix the ratio of Congressional representation. Items touching the intelligence of the people were not included until 1840. There are those now who believe that the census tells too much about the people for the people—the Government gives too much information. Let those who want it pay for it. Of course, they would leave those who can't pay for it without it. Persons of these opinions were horrified at the little office of education. They saw in it the destruction of local systems and institutions. The nation had no business with education. It was a most dangerous centralization of power, although the proposition did not include the appointment of a teacher or the establishment of a school. The result was that Congress refused to publish the reports which the law required, took $1,000 from the Commissioner's salary, and reduced his clerks to two of the lowest grade. The story is most significant in its bearing on the proposition to establish a national university. The opposition sought to strike the office out of the appropriation bill, but General Grant said: "We have abolished slavery and made the freedmen voters; education must perform an important part in the solution of the questions arising out of the new conditions, and the office ought to be further tried."

The result of its continuance is now known to the country and the world. A simple educational exchange, focusing all educational experience without the authority to touch a single school in a single State, it has come to be declared again and again by most eminent educational authorities to be the most influential educational office in the world. Other offices may issue decrees, but this office, by its vast accumulation of data, is able to point out those averages—those uniformities—which indicate the laws of educational action. My experience of half a generation in that office, with the educational thought and experience of the country passing before me, left me in no doubt in regard to the question of establishing a national university. Its opposition will be much of the same character as that already described, but its location and functions are wholly within the constitutional powers of Congress, as affirmed by the most eminent constitutional authorities. It accords with the traditional ideas of national action in its relation to local interests. It can exercise no authority over them. Its influence must be determined by its merits. By its elevated grade of instruction it is put out of competition with all other schools of learning, but becomes an inspiration to them all. There are those who believe that all education should be under exclusive religious direction, but this is not the American theory coming down from our fathers.

We separate church and state in education as in all other matters. The American theory provides that the state must educate to make sure of that universality and that amount of education which is necessary to guarantee the intelligence of its citizens and the provision of officers capable of wisely directing its affairs. Governor Jenkins, of Georgia, in opening the constitutional convention of that State, made a strong declaration of this doctrine. But the American theory, in affirming this view of the responsibility of the state in education, does not limit itself to what can be done under its own direction; it invites the church to do all it can, and freely provides charters for institutions under religious or other private auspices. Nowhere has the church, as the organization specially intrusted with the care of the divine oracles and the enforcement of their doctrines upon the individual conscience, been more liberally treated or been more successful in establishing and maintaining institutions of learning. Private benefactions find their way in the main to institutions under private corporate direction having a religious aim. Clear it is that no other country approaches ours in the amount of gifts for the purposes of higher education. The Bureau of Education reports that those coming to its knowledge in the last two dozen years have reached the sum of $168,000,000. Religious colleges work in harmony with our State universities. The same will be true of all religious institutions and of the national university. Some have feared the injurious effect of great cities upon institutions of learning, but the benefits of such proximity have been found greatly to counterbalance all disadvantages.

There has also been great fear in many minds of the injurious effect upon seats of learning from their proximity to political capitals. This fear was especially manifested in connection with the establishment of the University of Berlin. But the benefits to the university arising from its location there have already been pointed out, as well as the advantages to the Government of the location of the university in its capital. Indeed, there is much data from other countries illustrating these advantages, leaving little ground to doubt the satisfactory results. In the establishment of great denominational universities in and about Washington the opinion of our most astute religious thinkers is made manifest. The leaders of these great interests see how they can utilize the great scientific opportunities of our national capital. I believe they will see also in due time how a great national university over and above them all will aid rather than hinder the realization of their purposes. Anyone who will carefully consult the bill before you will see how it is guarded alike against local, personal, or partisan control of every kind. The corporation is to be made up of men selected for their eminence from different States.

The administration of the Peabody Southern Educational Fund is an illustration of the wisdom with which such a board is likely to act; and in the matter of internal administration, the selection of professors, the establishment of courses of study and research, and the regulation of discipline, the university council, made up in part of regents and in part of eminent educators representing educational institutions in different States, manifestly constitutes a body under the corporation to which these responsibilities can be most safely intrusted, and that will surely guard them against any untoward interference. That the time for this action has come is clearly indicated by the increase of the number of post-graduate students in the country, running up from a few hundred in 1870 to over 4,000 at the present day, while there are some 3,000 American students, it is believed, pursuing similar courses in European institutions. If ours is to be a leader among the nations, should we not have a university worthy not only to retain our own students of the highest aspirations, but to bring here those from other lands seeking the rarest opportunities for instruction and research? The existence of such an institution for a very limited period will, I believe, so manifest its advantages that there will be left no grounds to doubt the wisdom of its establishment.

REMARKS OF HON. GARDINER G. HUBBARD, LL. D., PRESIDENT OF THE NATIONAL GEOGRAPHIC SOCIETY.

[Before the committee, January 24, 1896.]

MR. CHAIRMAN AND GENTLEMEN: While feeling a profound interest in the subject of a national university, so ably discussed from various standpoints this morning, owing to the limited time allotted, I shall confine my own remarks to a single phase of it, to wit, the great importance of the proposed post-graduate university as an essential part of what we are accustomed to call the American system of public education—as, indeed, the necessary climax which it has always lacked, and without which it has suffered beyond the power of calculation.

In colonial times educational opportunities were provided almost entirely by religious organizations. Much valuable work was done, and many were the youths who by means of them made themselves most useful and distinguished citizens in the various spheres of life, both public and private, as the history of our country so well illustrates. But, after all, the work done was practically limited to the few, and was marked by many errors and deficiencies. It was only they who were favored in some degree by fortune who could avail themselves of even such opportunities as were offered. The masses were unprovided for.

The dawn of the Republic brought the beginning of that better day when the great body of the people, in their organized capacity, should regard the needs of each member of society, and so devise measures for increasing the popular intelligence.

It was Daniel Webster who said, "I doubt whether any one single law of any single lawgiver, ancient or modern, has produced results of more distinct, marked, and lasting character than the ordinance of 1787, wherein it set forth and declared it to be a high and binding duty of the Government to support schools and advance the means of education."

"REVOLUTIONS NEVER GO BACKWARD."

Having slowly, from small beginnings, developed a great system of popular education—one which, whatever its imperfections, has already gained recognition everywhere as a great and indispensable instrumentality for that enlightenment of the whole people, upon which the welfare of the individual and the security of our free institutions must depend—there will be no return to antiquated institutions and agencies.

Vast are the sums which in the States are annually derived from investments of the proceeds of school, college, and university lands and devoted to the maintenance of the whole series of educational agencies, from the district school to the State university, so that it becomes a question of practical importance whether anything is yet wanting to improve the instrumentalities in use and to meet those demands of our aspiring youth for that which lies beyond the ability of even the foremost of our institutions to supply.

That we have a number of universities, so called, which are excellent of their kind, are doing the best of collegiate work, and are reaching out into the vast field beyond by worthy efforts in research and investigation—all this is not enough.

We should have somewhere—and certainly there is no spot more suitable or half so well supplied with facilities for this high work as Washington—we should have in America, the best possible opportunities the whole world can afford, unless we conclude to content ourselves with ranking second among the nations in the means of education, whereas the very nature of our Government demands of us that we offer to the lover of learning and the young man of genius for research the very best facilities the world can afford.

This constitutes a reason which everyone can understand, and which strongly appeals to our national pride, why there should be planted here a great and true university, and that we begin the work of founding it now, in the centennial year since Washington, by authority, set apart grounds for its site, and gave of his own resources what in those days was a very handsome sum toward its pecuniary foundation.

Nor are the reasons which I had in mind when I rose less plain and imperative why this central university should be a *national* university—the University of the United States—with certain organic relations to the colleges and universities of this country, especially the State universities, even as they sustain such relations to high schools, secondary schools, and primary schools in their order below.

Forward impulses and furtherances in education proceed from above downward, not from the bottom upward. Hence a national university of post-graduate rank would not only supply better equipped men for all classes of work in the educational field below, but it would, also, by means of its high and unvarying standard, bring about a greater uniformity in all the institutions of the States, stimulating those below to aim higher, and of necessity to reach higher results. This influence of stimulation and coordination would be of immense value.

But there is another consideration. Such a central university, by holding aloft to the youth of the whole nation opportunities beyond those with which they have been familiar, and such as they do not find at home, would fire yet more their ambition for the highest attainments, and thus lead them in yet greater numbers than now to the local and State institutions as the only road to such superior advantages. In other words, it would touch every university, college, academy, and public school in the land, and inspire anew every youth of high aims and ambitions.

Let the Catholic Church make its university, so well begun, as great and useful as it can; and let the Baptists, Methodists, Episcopalians, and other denominations do all they can to meet the special demands of their people. And so of Harvard and Yale, and all the other of our higher institutions. We offer no hindrance. Nay, we wish them well and bid them Godspeed in all honorable endeavor. But neither these nor the others, nor all together, can meet the growing demand of the American people for a great and true university at the National Capital—one that shall be their own, even as public schools, industrial schools, and State universities are theirs; an institution wholly free from the trammels of either sectarian creed, or party creed; an institution bearing the stamp of the Government of the United States, and hence giving to the higher education a new dignity and value in the estimation of the whole people.

In fine, having the public schools of every grade, the colleges and State universities, let us have, as the next logical step, a grand university of the United States, that shall crown and complete the whole series.

REMARKS OF EX-GOVERNOR JOHN W. HOYT, LL. D., CHAIRMAN OF THE NATIONAL UNIVERSITY COMMITTEE OF ONE HUNDRED.

[Before the Senate committee, January 24, 1896.]

Mr. CHAIRMAN AND GENTLEMEN: The hour accorded for this hearing having already expired, I may not say more on the subject under consideration than a very few words of a general character.

Opposition to the university measure is likely to manifest itself in certain quarters, and for reasons well understood; but the great body of educators, scientists, scholars, and statesmen who have studied the subject quite free from local and other special interest are in hearty accord with the movement, and will warmly support the Senate and House committees should they see fit to favorably report the pending bill.

Faults and deficiencies it may have, which, if found, you will not fail to correct. It is proper to say, however, that the general features of it have been carefully considered by hundreds of persons deemed especially competent to judge, and that it was finally framed by the Executive Council designated for this and other purposes by the National University Committee of One Hundred, engaging the most earnest attention of it members; also that the bill has since been submitted to the scrutiny of members of the National Committee in all sections of the country.

I shall in due time submit the views of a great number of persons upon the general proposition as expressed both before the beginning of this present movement and since. It will appear that there is full concurrence among them on these several points, to wit: (1) That there is great need of an institution for purely post-graduate work; (2) that for many reasons which can not be challenged such institution should be established at Washington, where facilities of so many kinds, already furnished at great cost by the whole people through the Government, are present and but partially utilized; (3) that in addition to the priceless benefits which a post-graduate university of the highest type would confer, not only in the help afforded to college graduates who now seek at foreign institutions what they do not find at home, but also as the means of completing the American system of public education, and of furnishing to it and to all institutions of the country the very coordinating, stimulating, and elevating force so essential to general progress; and (4) that since these great needs can only be met by the Government of the United States, such beginning as is possible should be made without further delay.

VIEWS OF HON. JOHN A. KASSON, LL. D., LATE UNITED STATES MINISTER TO AUSTRIA, AMBASSADOR TO GERMANY, ETC.

[Presented before the House Committee on Education, February 1, and afterwards communicated to the Senate University Committee, by request.]

SIR: As one of the advocates for the establishment of a national university at Washington, I have been requested to forward to your committee the substance of the views which were presented by me before the House Committee on Education.

The reasons for my support of the measure before your committee are undoubtedly largely influenced by my long association with the interests of the Western States, where educational institutions, excellent as they are within their limitations, have neither the endowment nor the facilities to keep pace with modern demands for higher education. Our young men with special genius for certain lines of study and research are balked in their development by the inadequacy of the means of education at their disposal. It is not gratifying to our national pride that even those who have wealth go by hundreds for this instruction to foreign universities, often resulting in the alienation of their patriotic instincts.

Here in Washington are found already the means and facilities for the pursuit of the higher university studies to a degree unequaled by any other town or educational center in America. Here are vast collections for the study of geology, natural history, biology, comparative anatomy, anthropology, and of the history of inventive and other useful arts. Here are great libraries, both general and special, one of the latter admitted to be the best in the world. These collections are the property of the nation, and are continually growing. Original research in agricultural chemistry is continually going on in one Department of the Government. A variety of original investigations are perpetually in progress in the Smithsonian Institution, and in the geological division, and in the Coast Survey, which latter is unsurpassed, if equaled elsewhere in the world, in the authority of its scientific declarations. Here the higher work of astronomy proceeds by day and night, with an admirably equipped observatory and with a master astronomer who has received some of the highest scientific honors which Europe can bestow. Here are active and retired engineers of the Army, masters in road and bridge building, and in tests of economic materials and structures; and engineers of the Navy, masters in machinery and in shipbuilding. Whatever sciences and arts are involved in and for our progress as a nation are here represented.

Why should all these vast resources of education lie unutilized and sterile for the instruction of the youth of America?

Here are an unequaled medical library and an unsurpassed medical museum. Why should the future healers of human diseases not be permitted to utilize them for their higher instruction?

Why should not the youth of our country have the benefit of the masterly teaching of hundreds of scientific specialists now in Government employ at the seat of government, in such manner and under such regulations as the Government shall direct?

The proposed university requires no vast aggregate of buildings for its purposes. It will require ultimately one building for its lecture rooms and laboratories. This will be the nation's memorial tribute to Washington, the first patron and real founder of the university. Its libraries are already built, its museums already constructed and filled. Its dormitory will be the city, its school of oratory and patriotism the Capitol of the nation.

An institution for higher education so founded and conducted will offer its advantages to the intelligent youth of the country of limited means—and they are the great majority, especially in the Western and Southern States, and I think it may be said of the Northern also—at less cost than in Europe, while cultivating in them the spirit of devotion to their own country. From it they will return to their own States prepared to lead their respective communities in the continuous march of civilization, of science, and of material development.

If this education, owing to the facilities already existing, can be furnished at less cost to the student than in other universities of the country, surely the people who have paid by their taxes for the plant already established are entitled to the benefit of the reduction. The great and controlling purposes of its foundation must be to effect the widest possible diffusion among our people of that education which all the foremost nations of the civilized world now recognize as essential to the maintenance of their rank, and to their progress in material welfare. No national investment yields such ample returns as that which enlarges the intelligence and capacity of the citizen. It is the seed which produces "an hundred fold." The vast private contributions of our countrymen to the establishment of institutions of learning proves how well that maxim is understood in this Republic. Such contributions will also flow to this university when once Congress shall have completed its organization and assured its permanence. The "plain people" who go through life under the restraints of a forced economy, but who have laudable ambitions for their sons, will for all time bless the Congress that shall bring the best education within reach of their children.

These views are respectfully submitted.

JOHN A. KASSON.

Hon. JAMES H. KYLE,
    Chairman of Senate Committee to Establish the University of the United States.

REMARKS OF HON. ANDREW D. WHITE, LL.D., EX-PRESIDENT OF CORNELL, LATE AMBASSADOR TO GERMANY, MINISTER TO RUSSIA, ETC.

[Before the committee, February 10, 1890.]

MR. CHAIRMAN AND GENTLEMEN: It seems hardly worth while for me to take up much of your time, either with the opinions of leading men in favor of a national university at Washington, or with the fitness of Washington as the seat of a great university. All this has been very fully and cogently discussed already, and while I may touch upon it later, I prefer now to take up another point which seems to me of great importance, and which, so far as I know, has not yet been developed.

This point is, that the creation of a national university in this city by act of Congress is the logical result of the legislation of Congress upon public education thus far; that it is, indeed, the necessary supplement of what Congress has already done, and most worthily done, with the final approval of all thinking men who have given adequate attention to the subject, not only in this country, but in all other countries.

I need hardly say that the action by the Federal Congress in favor of education in all its grades is no new thing. In laying the foundations of our great new States Congress made at the outset, and most wisely, reservations of public land for public-school systems. This was done in obedience to a deep-seated political instinct. Every citizen who thinks closely upon the history of this and other republics knows that the republican form of government has always been the most difficult of all forms to maintain; that in the great majority of cases in the past, as a simple historical fact, it has not been maintained, and that the main fundamental thing in which this Republic differs from the great number of republics which in times past and in our own times have gone to ruin, is the fact that we have developed, and are developing, a people better fitted by education to exercise self-government than any other, save Switzerland, has ever done.

But Congressional action has not stopped with primary and secondary school systems. At an early day large appropriations were made for universities in the newer States, and with most noble results. It is true that some of the States have not done as well as others, but when we see growing out of these appropriations such great and beneficent institutions of learning as the universities of Michigan, of Indiana, of Illinois, of Iowa, of Wisconsin, of Minnesota, of California, and of other States, we must feel that the country has been far more than repaid for the national outlay upon these foundations.

A still more striking example of the carrying out of this same policy by Congress is seen in the Morrill act of 1862 That act provided for an institution in every State in which instruction should be given in science, pure and applied, in classics, and in military tactics. Proposed at first by the Hon. Justin S. Morrill, when he was in the House of Representatives, it was vetoed by President Buchanan, but, after a change in Administration, having been proposed again by Mr. Morrill, who had come into the Senate of the United States, it became a law by the signature of Abraham Lincoln.

Mr. Chairman, I believe that this act of 1862, known as the Morrill bill, was one of the greatest things in the history of this country, or of any country. That bill, as I have said, created in every State and every Territory of the United States a center for scientific, technical, classical, general, and even military instruction. It was very broad in its scope and liberal in its provisions, and has proved to be a vast benefit to every State and Territory, and therefore to the nation as a whole.

One very noble result of the bill is that, while all these institutions—about fifty in number—endowed by the United States are doing their full work, each is doing it mainly in accordance with the needs of the State in which it is situated, as determined by the legislature of that State and by the trustees and faculty of each institution. In all the management of these institutions there has been no trace of what has been stigmatized as undue centralization or as "paternalism."

You have, no doubt, heard the story of the French minister of public instruction, who, when a gentleman was calling on him one morning, took out his watch, picked up a certain book, and opening it to a certain page, said: "Every college in France is occupied at this moment in giving instruction in a particular way on this particular page of this particular book." Nothing of this centralizing paternalism is to be seen in this great system which Congress has created. Every institution has its own antonomy; it governs itself in accordance with the needs of the State in which it is located, and each bears in mind that great truth enunciated by one of the profoundest men who has ever written on education, John Stuart Mlil, who says that the real danger in public systems of education is that sort of Chinese mandarinism which tends to make men all alike by educating them all in the same way. In the Morrill bill all danger from this source has been obviated. In Senator Walthall's State there is a system suited to the needs of his State, and so in Senator Sherman's State, and so in Senator Kyle's State, as in every other State of the Union.

But this is not all that Congress has done. Having found that these institutions were doing well with the endowments already given them, it, at a later period, increased their endowments and made them still stronger centers in science and literature, in general culture and mental discipline.

But these are not all the evidences of a great educational policy on the part of the United States which Congress has steadily followed out. By the Hatch Act it has created a great number of experiment stations in which scientific investigation, as related to agriculture, is carried on, and these have been, as a rule, attached to the existing institutions created by the Morrill Act, giving them still stronger and wider influence.

The result of all this has been that within the last forty years we have had what may be called a great revolution in education. At the middle of this century there were some 300 so-called colleges and universities, not one of them adequately endowed, and all together producing results which thoughtful men saw to be unsatisfactory.

No one can deny that strong men were graduated at these institutions, but they were in the main developed in spite of the system rather than by means of it. It is a simple fact that, as compared with the rest of the world, our collegiate and unversity system was at the middle of this century utterly inadequate and known so to be by every thinking man who gave attention to it. Here and there, indeed, as at the University of Virginia, at Harvard, at Yale, and a few other institutions, earnest efforts were made to improve the system, yet up to the middle of this century they had produced comparatively little result; but about that time one of these State universities created by the bounty of Congress, the University of Michigan, began to be developed, mainly by the efforts of Chancellor Henry P. Tappan and his compeers. It took on a more decidedly university character than any other university in the country had ever done.

At first this new development was but little known, but it finally attracted the attention of a very eminent professor at Harvard, the Rev. Dr. Hedge, and he called the attention of men interested in higher education throughout New England to it. The result was a new effort in the East; Cornell University came into being as a daughter of the University of Michigan, inheriting some of its best university methods, and the election of President Eliot to Harvard University began a new and most fruitful epoch there. I do not mean to say that there was any servile imitation either at Harvard or at Cornell of what had been done at the University of Michigan, but I do mean to say that the first impulse to higher education in the United States, which brought about this splendid educational revolution, or, as I would prefer to call it, evolution, of the past forty years, proceeded from a State University which owed its origin to an act of Congress.

Of all these creations by Congress I regard that which grew out of the Morrill Act as the most beneficent. As you have seen, it led to the establishment in every State and Territory of the Union of a strong center for scientific and literary education and research, and I think that when we consider the time when this bill was passed we may regard the Morrill bill as one of the glories of this nation.

We have all heard it cited as perhaps the most glorious fact in the history of the old Roman Republic that at the very period when its most terrible enemies—the Carthaginians, under a leader up to that time invincible—were in camp near the city, the land on which this hostile, conquering army was encamped was freely bought and sold in the Roman market. This has always been adduced as a proof of a heroic belief on the part of the Roman people in the perpetuity of their institutions, and this has been counted one of their greatest glories, as showing that they never despaired of the Republic. But to my mind there is something in the passage of the Morrill bill in 1862 far grander than this act of the Romans. For it was at the very darkest period of the civil war; the time when it seemed to many that the union of these States was dissolved; the darkest period indeed, by far, that this Republic has ever known; that Congress thus decreed the creation of a strong educational center in each of the States and Territories, providing for the necessities of future generations; and this not only in the States then fighting for the Union, but also in the States at that time in arms against it. There is no other example of heroic confidence in the perpetuity of a nation equal to that thus offered by the passage of this act of Congress.

It did not, indeed, have the support of many men who were attached to the eastern colleges. Very little, if anything, was done for the Morrill bill by Harvard, or Yale, or the University of Virginia. It was the outcome of the thought and effort of a few men who had not enjoyed the advantages of these older institutions of learning. Fortunately, their thought and effort were recognized by Congress as patriotic and farseeing, and the Morrill bill became a law.

The first result of all these beneficent acts of Congress has been to develop directly a great system of education in literature and science, fitted to the needs of the whole country; but this is only a part of its work. It has done far more than that, for it has indirectly exercised an enormous influence for good upon the whole system of advanced education in the United States. The new and more vigorous growth of Harvard, Yale, Princeton, Dartmouth, Amherst, Brown, and a multitude of other great foundations among the older institutions of learning in the North, and indeed in all parts of the country, dates from the time when the influence of the Congressional acts on education began to be felt.

And now, Mr. Chairman, I come to the relation of the proposed legislation, upon all this great body of institutions for advanced instruction, and, indeed, for all instruction throughout this country. The first result of such a creation which I would name is its effect in meeting what, at this moment, is the greatest and most pressing need of all these institutions; the need of professors and instructors of the highest grade, thoroughly trained in research, and brought completely abreast of the latest and best thought in all those great fields with which universities and colleges have to do. Here it is that a university at Washington could be of vast use. Others have shown fully what enormous opportunities there are here for such research; the libraries, observatories, laboratories, collections of every sort, already vast, are constantly increasing.

Doubtless your attention has also been called to another pertinent fact, so evident to anyone giving attention to the subject, namely, the ease with which the foremost literary and scientific men, not only of this country, but of all countries, could be attracted to this city as professors and lecturers. It is rapidly becoming, in my opinion, the most attractive of modern capitals. No one of the greater capitals of the world is in all respects so well fitted for a winter residence, and few offer so many inducements of every sort to a temporary stay. Such a university as could be here created would seem, then, most likely to meet one of the greatest wants, perhaps the greatest want, at this moment, of all this mass of institutions, now existing, by attracting to itself the foremost men in research and instruction, and by these means, increasing the number of men thoroughly fitted to give the highest instruction in other institutions throughout the land.

And here I trust you will allow me to add another consideration which seems to me of importance. That is, that such an institution as is contemplated, attracting, as it would do, a large number of leaders in scientific, literary, historical, philological, and, indeed, all worthy studies, would exercise a powerful influence for good upon this capital, and upon all who shall come to it, for whatever purpose. The more frequent contact thus brought about between leading scholars of the world and our legislators, could not fail to be of benefit to both. The scholars would be thus brought into practical relations more close than they otherwise could be with the general feeling and modes of thought among the people at large, as shown by their chosen representatives, and these representatives would be brought more fully under the influence of scholars presenting the latest results of thought and study in all the various fields of research and instruction. I can not but believe that this idea was in the mind of such men as Washington, Jefferson, Madison, and many other of the earlier statesmen, when they so strongly favored such an institution at the center of our national political life.

I am aware that certain objections have been made, some of them by gentlemen to whose opinions I usually attribute great importance; and, first of all, President Eliot has been cited. I need hardly say that he has my greatest respect. His work at Harvard has been an honor to the country and to himself. During his presidency it has been developed from a college, or a least a very inferior university, into one of the greatest institutions of learning in the world. But, as regards this question now before us, there seems to be an atmosphere at Harvard University of a very singularly refracting power, which, while very helpful in many ways, seems to influence men at that point unfavorably when they come to take a broad view of other educational institutions throughout the entire country.

One statement attributed to President Eliot, which has been widely reechoed by others, is that Washington is not the place for a great institution of learning, on the ground that a great political capital is not a place fitted for research and study. Now, such a statement flies in the face of the best-known facts in the history of education.

A large number of the greater universities in the world are at national capitals. The greatest university on the continent of Europe to-day—probably the greatest university in the world—is the University of Berlin, and yet it was founded at a time when political excitement in that city had reached a very high point, since the questions then and there discussed related to the very existence of the kingdom of which Berlin was the center; and that institution has been splendidly carried on ever since by a great number of the foremost men of the time in every branch of science and literature in spite of the fact that Berlin has been one of the most active political centers in the world. At the very time when Helmholtz was conducting his famous researches in physics; when Hofmann was carrying on his great work in chemistry; when Du Bois-Reymond and others were carrying on their researches in biology; when Ranke and Sybel and a multitude of others were carrying on their researches in history; and Weber, Hermann Grimm, and other world-renowned scholars, their researches in philology and literature—all at Berlin—the great political effort of which Bismarck was the center was at its height in that same city, and the Austrian and Franco-Prussian wars were going on. It seems, rather, that vigorous political life at the center of a nation stimulates vigorous scientific life. The same is true of Paris and Vienna and Munich. At the period when political action at Paris was most intense and the Franco-Prussian war was drawing on, men like Pasteur and De Ville and a long line of noted men of science were conducting their researches and making their discoveries. I visited Pasteur's laboratory, and I could not see that all the ferment of political thought outside acted unfavorably upon him.

So, too, although we have had a great deal of political ferment in Washington, Professor Henry, Professor Baird, Professor Langley, Major Powell, Professor Gilbert, Professor Newcomb, and a multitude of others, have gone on with their researches in a way which has gained them credit throughout the world. All these gentlemen seem to have been stimulated rather than depressed by political activity at this capital.

But it is said that the creation of a National University here would injure those already created. If I believed for a moment that this were true I should oppose such an institution as that now urged, but it is clear to me that no such danger is to be apprehended. I am deeply devoted to my alma mater, old Yale; I am not less attached to the University of Michigan, where during four or five years I labored as a professor; and certainly if there is one institution in the country to which I am especially devoted, it is to Cornell University, to which I have given the best quarter of a century of my life. If I felt that the institution now proposed would injure any of these institutions, or indeed any of the other leading universities of the country, I would certainly not be here to advocate it; but I firmly believe that such a university as is now proposed would strengthen every one of these institutions, and indeed every institution, large or small, of any importance in the United States; that it would stimulate them, and send new currents of life into them.

But the argument is used that it is not the duty of the Government of the United States to make provision for public instruction; that this should be left to individual munificence.

It is rather late in the day to use this argument, so long after the policy has been fully adopted by Congress, of developing education in all its grades throughout the country, and in face of the fact that this policy has been crowned with admirable results. Certainly I yield to no one in admiration of the munificence of those who have founded, endowed, and made gifts to various institutions of learning in our country. I consider their munificence one of the glories of the nation, but I believe that with this voluntary system there should be united a system fostered by public endowment, and that of the two, the latter is by far the more democratic method of providing for education. I maintain that the plan of leaving the entire advanced public instruction of the country to the ideas, the beliefs, and even the whims of individuals is utterly undemocratic. The advanced education of the country should be largely controlled, at any rate, by the people of the country, as such. I would not interfere with the right of individuals to do for education what seems to them best. But I would interfere with the undue control of education by individuals, no matter how munificent or conscientious. More than once it has been seen in the history of this, as of other countries, that men, who in their day and generation were great benefactors, have become to after generations rather a curse than a blessing; that they have seemed to thrust their arms out of their graves to grasp, and clamp, and hinder the education of times succeeding their own and more enlightened than their own. At this moment there are at some of the Eastern colleges old foundations, endowed by excellent men in bygone days, which are not only useless, but injurious.

It is said that institutions in the immediate neighborhood of Washington, admirable creations like the University of Virginia and Johns Hopkins University, and sundry institutions now existing or likely to exist in Washington might be injured by a powerful institution of learning so near them. On the contrary, I believe that they, being so near the proposed institution, could be brought into such relations with it as would strengthen it and them at the same time.

And finally, it is argued that the creation of such an university here would act as a damper upon private munificence to advanced institutions of learning. I believe that the effect will be just contrary to this; that it will deepen and strengthen the interest already felt by the American people in advanced instruction, and this belief, Mr. Chairman, is not the result of mere theory. It is the result of observations upon facts. Have all these appropriations by Congress for public education since the middle of this century decreased private munificence? Everyone knows that they have not; they have served to stimulate it. Never has there been such a constant flow of splendid gifts to leading institutions of learning as during this period in which Congress has done so much for advanced instruction. Take Cornell University alone, with which I am familiar; it received the proceeds of the land grant made under the Morrill act to the State of New York; the grant has been so carefully managed that it has produced a very large endowment indeed, but has this prevented the flow of private gifts? The facts are notoriously otherwise; gifts amounting to several millions of dollars from individuals have been made to it by a large number of persons whose belief in advanced education has been stimulated by the creation of a grand institution, as it would never have been without such a creation. I believe that if Congress shall make the appropriations which seem to be immediately necessary for the inauguration of a national university at Washington wealthy individuals in various parts of the country will hereafter be proud to aid in the great work by endowing professorships, fellowships, scholarships, and the like.

Then it is said that there are certain subjects of great importance which could not be taught in a university endowed by the nation and maintained at its capital. Among these subjects is especially named that of political economy. It is said that no votaries of protection will aid in supporting an institution which has a professor who believes in free trade, and that no votaries of free trade will aid in supporting an institution which has a professor who believes in protection. This objection seems to me very shallow when considered in the light of what has taken place at our great State universities and other institutions relying upon public funds or even on private munificence. Political economy is not an exact science. It would be, therefore, the duty of those in direct control of any such institution as is here proposed to have various views and phases of the subject presented by the foremost supporters of either side. More than that, even if it be insisted that political economy is an exact science, the question might very properly be discussed, with the approval of both sides, how far even a scientific system of political economy could be put into force in any given country at any given time.

It has also been urged that religious or theological questions might make trouble. In answer to this I may point to the fact that the leading universities of the country have, in the last forty years, become more and more unsectarian, more and more tolerant to men of science of every view in theology and religion; and I may here again cite the example with which I am most familiar. Cornell University, founded mainly by the munificence of the General Government, has been aided to the amount of millions of dollars by individuals of almost every creed. The university charter, as sketched out by myself, and put in shape by Charles J. Folger, afterwards chief justice of the State of New York, and still later Secretary of the Treasury of the United States, expressly declares that men of any religious sect, and of no religious sect, and of all political views, shall be equally eligible to all offices and appointments in the institution. I have sat in the board for thirty years, and never for a moment has the question of the theological, religious, or political views of any professor, instructor, or other person connected with the faculty, or proposed for connection with the institution, been considered for a moment. Never has the question of theology, in any shape, disturbed the deliberations of either the trustees or the faculty. It seems to me that one concrete example of this kind outweighs all theory.

I might take up various other points, but I will conclude by reiterating my belief that such an institution as is now proposed, at the National Capital, would strengthen every one of the institutions now existing in the United States, including any which have been created or are to be created by various religious denominations at this capital. I believe that such a national institution would give strength to every one of these other universities and colleges, by giving them more fully equipped professors and instructors, and by sending new currents of life into them, and I believe it, therefore, to be the logical result and fitting culmination of what has already been done by Congress, and that the same honor which is now done to those who, in days gone by, passed the various acts endowing public-school systems in different States, laying university foundations in various parts of the country, and especially in passing the Morrill act of 1862, will be awarded to those who shall now give to the country a great university here at the national capital.

REMARKS OF EX-GOVERNOR JOHN LEE CARROLL, LL. D., OF MARYLAND, GENERAL PRESIDENT SONS OF THE REVOLUTION.

[Remarks before the House Committee on Education, January 23, and by request reported to the Senate Committee to Establish the University of the United States.]

MR. CHAIRMAN: While the circumstances have been such as to prevent due preparation for the hearing accorded by your committee to friends of the National University measure now before Congress, I am nevertheless glad of the opportunity to briefly express my convictions of its importance.

That a university of the highest rank, for post-graduate work only, would be a fitting supplement to all other educational institutions and agencies of this country is plainly manifest. Nay, that it is urgently demanded as a condition of the best possible work in every grade of schools, as well as of the more rapid advancement of science, is so evident that anything in the way of argument seems superfluous, especially after all that has been said here this morning by the distinguished gentlemen who have spoken.

I am not surprised, therefore, to find that the foremost of educators—I mean those at the head of the most advanced and most progressive of our institutions—are in strong sympathy with the national university movement.

Doubtless such friends of important existing institutions as have not carefully surveyed the whole field will feel more or less anxiety lest their favorites may in some way suffer embarrassment from the establishment of a central institution. As a Marylander, proud of the rapid growth and importance of Johns Hopkins University, I would naturally regard with grave concern any enterprise which should threaten to embarrass that noble young institution. But fears of this sort have not entered my mind, and I am glad to know that the able and distinguished president of Johns Hopkins is in accord with this view. He believes as do I, that, planned as the proposed national university is, not in the interest of the District of Columbia, or in any other interest save those of science and learning, of American education, and of the United States as a leading power among the nations, it would in countless ways prove an incalculable blessing.

That such an institution is demanded by the highest considerations that can be named is to my mind beyond controversy. The objections, if any are made, must arise from misapprehensions or from supposed local and personal interest.

It is no less manifest that Washington, with its vast array of resources in material and men, is the only suitable location for a national university.

Besides all these considerations, it is not to be forgotten that Washington and his most illustrious compatriots saw yet other reasons no less weighty—reasons so related to the peace and harmony of the American people of all geographical divisions and to the security of this new Republic as to render the establishment of such an enlightening, harmonizing, and peace-making institution at the National Capital a political necessity.

I will confess that these historic facts have at once deepened my interest in the present measure and added yet more to the reverence I have been accustomed to pay to the memory of men whose heroism in the contest for freedom and independence was only equaled by the wonderful wisdom and foresight used by them in laying the foundations for a great nation, and in pointing out the means of insuring to it both permanence and future greatness.

Mr. Chairman and gentlemen, both because the proposed National University was planned by the founders of this Republic, the foremost of whom, besides many times urging it upon Congress, made important personal sacrifices that he might the better assure its establishment, and because such an institution is still a real and ever growing necessity, I most sincerely hope that the bill to establish it will have the approval of those who have it under consideration, and that the Fifty-fourth Congress will do itself the high honor to make of it a law of the land within this one hundredth year since the last appeal in this behalf was made by the Father of his Country.

[The Committee listened to Bishop Hurst and others in opposition to the establishment of the university. In reply to these arguments, statements were offered by Hon. Andrew D. White and Gov. John W. Hoyt.]

LETTER OF HON. ANDREW D. WHITE, CORRECTING ERRONEOUS STATEMENTS CONCERNING CORNELL UNIVERSITY.

WASHINGTON, D. C., *March 3, 1896.*

DEAR SIR: On looking over the stenographic report of the remarks made by Bishop Hurst and Dr. Beiler before your committee, I observe that they have fallen into one or two very serious errors regarding Cornell University.

The first is shown in a statement to the effect that the charter of the institution has been changed so as to restrict the choice of professors to certain Christian denominations or "evangelical" denominations. This is completely an error. No such change in the charter has ever been made; none, so far as I know, has ever been thought of. The original charter provides that persons of all political parties and religious sects, or of no party and of no sect, shall be equally eligible to all offices and all appointments, whether in the board of trustees or in the faculty; and this feature in the charter, which was suggested by myself, and put into shape by the late Charles J. Folger, afterwards chief justice of the State, remains to-day, and has remained from the beginning, a part of the fundamental law of the institution.

There is also another statement which may mislead, i. e., the virtual assertion that the professors of the university are confined to these "evangelical" denominations. This also is utterly contrary to fact. From the first there have been and are now Catholics, Episcopalians, Unitarians, and Swedenborgians in the faculty. I may also add that we have had in our faculty, and it is quite likely have now, a representative or representatives of the Jewish community. None of these, of course, are classed among those who call themselves "evangelical denominations." Besides these there are professors who are not connected with any sect whatever. The question has never been raised, in all these thirty years, regarding the political or religious views of any member of the faculty. Indeed, the tendency has been more and more away from everything like sectarian trammels, whether disguised in the name of "evangelical" or not, and among the latest members of the board of trustees there have been elected at least one Roman Catholic and one Hebrew.

I also note another point—the supposed difficulty arising from the teaching of political economy. No such difficulty has ever been experienced at Cornell University, for the reason that political economy, not being an exact science, various controverted questions have been presented by eminent authorities from different points of view. Beside this, there has been presented what is known as the "historical view;" i. e., that even if political economy be an exact science, it is still a question for statesmen to decide as to how far it should be applied under existing conditions in any given country at any given time.

I wish to say distinctly that neither of the questions above referred to have ever been found difficult to deal with by our trustees. The board has included men of both political parties and of every phase of religious thought, yet neither politics nor religion has ever caused, during these thirty years, even a momentary difficulty among them.

I remain, dear sir, very respectfully and truly, yours,

ANDREW D. WHITE.

Hon. JAMES H. KYLE,
    Chairman of the Senate Committee on a
        National University, Washington, D. C.

LETTER OF EX-GOV. HOYT, IN REVIEW OF OBJECTIONS OFFERED BY OFFICERS OF THE "AMERICAN UNIVERSITY."

No. 4 Iowa Circle,
Washington, D. C., February 22, 1896.

Dear Sir: While the friends of a national post-graduate university have met with some surprises during the progress of their labors, the one of yesterday, at the hearing accorded by your committee to representatives of a denominational institution now springing up in the District of Columbia, surpassed them all.

It was perhaps not unnatural that a few of the older and more powerful institutions for higher education, with very considerable endowments, with able faculties and large bodies of students, with beginnings of post-graduate work in some departments, and hence with no little pride of honorable rank in the educational world, should at first see only the promise of a formidable rival instead of the friendly supplementer and co-worker which lies in the plans of those who would promote the establishment of a university of the United States. But that any representative of an enterprise at once strictly sectarian, and entered upon so long since even the more recent beginning of efforts for a national university of the highest rank should have felt justified in making an assault upon the movement is strange indeed. Stranger still when that assault is made in the name of religion, not of learning, and in terms which clearly show that the real motive is not even religious, but denominational at the very best. I say "at the very best" because I refuse to believe that the great religious organization thus seemingly represented is indeed responsible for this attack. It is too practically wise and patriotic a body to approve of what has been done in this matter. Indeed, the leading assailant, when questioned, was forced to admit that he spoke for himself alone, though afterwards claim was made that he represented "the adverse sentiment generally."

What, now, are the points made at the hearing in question? Let us briefly examine them in the order of presentation.

The chief opposer's first argument was to this effect, namely: There can be no university without a school of theology. A national university, which must be impartial, could not teach theology without teaching all the religious faiths, which would be impossible. Therefore, it could never become a university—an institution embracing the whole circle of the sciences, arts, and letters.

It seems not to have occurred to this reverend advocate that so much of theology as is dearest to him is a matter of belief only, and hence not of science at all; or that if some religious belief must be taught in order to constitute a university, the institution which he proposes as a substitute for the National University would find itself about as badly off, since in the estimation of all the other 142 religious denominations in the United States, the educational organization which he represents would be but the one hundred and forty-third part of a university, according to his own theory.

On the other hand, our ecclesiastical opposer does not seem to have had in mind that the greater part of what is taught in a theological course may be as properly taught in the National University as in his own; nor that we are now neither in foreign lands nor in the dark ages, where and when theology led the way, but in the midst of very different conditions, and living under a Government which left the church responsible for its own affairs. Possibly it has not occurred to him that, with the University of the United States at the National Capital, there will still be room for as many purely theological schools as the 143 denominations are likely to find the means to set up; each of them sustaining friendly relations with the great central university and drawing freely from its fountains of pure learning. Nor, last of all, does it seem to have entered the bishop's mind that, with the rapid enlargement of the vast field of human knowledge which the whole world accepts, there has gradually come a new conception of things, and such revision of terms that the mere beliefs of the multitudinous sects are no longer of necessity constituent parts of a true university.

2. This same objector inquires, "How could you teach political economy in a national university?"

What a question! In the first place, what better means of teaching political economy would his own denominational university possess? Would it teach one or both sides of the party questions? If but one side, then he is his own accuser; and if both or all sides, why could not the national university do the same? Does he seriously doubt that the National University would have all the conflicting economies taught, and by representative men of such acknowledged competency as would satisfy all demands? Political economy is taught in the undergraduate courses of all our higher institutions, so that graduates would come to the National University already familiar with the general principles, though ofttimes with a bias, one way or the other, because of the narrowness and unfairness of a professor who could not honorably state the whole argument, pro and con. At the National University they would hear both or all sides, and thus be competent to reach a just conclusion. This objection, like the other, does little credit to the information of the opposer, who ought to know what is already done in this regard at leading institutions, American and foreign.

Touching this whole matter the pending bill distinctly provides that "in all the operations of the university neither sectarian nor partisan preferences shall be allowed." Does our objector's charter guarantee as much? Does he not practically admit that his own proposed institution is to be one-sided in this regard?

The other objections, concerning modern history, etc., are not deserving of confutation.

3. Next it was urged that the non-denominational universities are not extraordinary successes, and in terms which made it very apparent that the reverend objector is not in sympathy with the public-school system of the country, of which so many of said universities constitute a part, and that he would have the American people go back to the good old times when the ambitious lover of learning must choose his creed and pay, or starve.

The assertions as to this matter are not sustained by the facts. Many of the State institutions are so new that it is unfair to compare them with those whose beginnings go back one or two hundred years. But, regardless of this point, it is beyond question that several of these State and other non-denominational universities are at this very hour leading the ancients in most important matters, while yet others are rapidly moving to the front. The statement that the present tendency is rather toward denominational control is not true. Nor is the specific statement concerning Cornell University, to the effect that it had been necessary to change its charter, giving to the evangelical churches a majority control, correct. It is flatly denied in every particular by ex-president Andrew D. White, who drafted the charter and has been familiar with the institution from its very foundation.

As a matter of fact, everything like intensity of denominationalism is on the wane among the greater institutions. Men everywhere are broadened and liberalized by the higher studies. To effect this very thing is one great office of the higher education.

The friends of the coming National University have nothing to say against the denominational institutions. Not a few of them bravely, and with sacrifices to be ever gratefully remembered, met as they could the intellectual cravings of our youth in the times ere there came any just recognition of the obligations resting upon the State and National governments to create and perfect a series of public schools from lowest to the highest possible—a series that should be worthy the high title of American system of public education—and to throw around that system every possible safeguard, as though it were the very cradle of liberty. Let the denominational schools flourish. They meet a demand that will continue. We lay not one straw in their way. Nay, as said before, by the founding of the National University there will be secured to them, as to all our educational institutions, a needed service such as no other instrumentality could offer.

As touching the claims of this denominational opposer, we simply urge that, since only a portion of the 70,000,000 of Americans are of his particular faith, it is illiberal, unpatriotic, and absurd for him, as the self-appointed champion of an incipient sectarian institution, intended, as shown by its charter, for but a new university of the ordinary type, to claim the whole remaining ground, to the total exclusion of such an one as George Washington and other founders of the Government originated and outlined; as eight other presidents of the United States have favored; as so many of our most eminent citizens have at various periods most earnestly advocated; as chiefs of the great body of the higher institutions have strongly recommended and are now recommending; as is warmly urged by State superintendents of public instruction in every State of the Union; as is heartily approved by leading scholars, scientists, and statesmen of the whole country.

We further say to this ecclesiastical objector that the National University is not intended for undergraduate youth at all, but for graduate students who shall have already passed through the courses of moral training supplied by the religious agencies of the country, and are prepared in their manlier years to enter upon those studies which lead into special fields of intellectual activity.

4. Last of all, this distinguished champion of a denominational institution, under an "American" name, made an end to his series of misconceptions and misrepresentations with an attempt to weaken the patriotic sentiment which rightfully attaches to the national university proposition, by saying of Washington, "He spoke only of an institution for instruction in political science. He did not mean such a university as is set forth in this bill; not at all."

To show how strangely this bold declaration before the Senate committee misrepresents the facts in the case, I have but to quote from Washington's letters, as follows:

(1) From his letter of December 15, 1794, to Edmond Randolph, Secretary of State:

"For the reasons mentioned to you the other day, namely, the Virginia assembly being in session, and a plan being on foot for establishing a seminary of learning upon an extensive scale in the Federal city, it would oblige me if you and Mr. Madison would endeavor to mature the measures which will be proper for me to pursue in order to bring my designs into view as soon as you can make it convenient to yourselves."

(2) From his letter of March 15, 1795, to Thomas Jefferson:

"And, lastly, as the seminary is contemplated for the completion of education and study of the sciences, not for boys in their rudiments, it will afford the students an opportunity of attending the debates in Congress, and thereby becoming more liberally and better acquainted with the principles of law and government."

(3) From his letter of March 16, 1795, to Governor Brooke, of Virginia:

"Presuming it to be more agreeable to the general assembly of Virginia that the shares in the James River Company should be assessed for a similar object in some part of that State, I intend to allot them for a seminary to be erected at such place as they shall deem most proper. I am disposed to believe that a seminary of learning upon an enlarged plan, but yet not coming up to the full idea of a university, is an institution to be preferred for the position which is to be chosen. The students who wish to pursue the whole range of science may pass with advantage from the seminary to the university, and the former, by a due relation, may be rendered cooperative with the latter."

(4) From his letter of September 1, 1796, to Alexander Hamilton, Secretary of the Treasury:

"I mean education generally, as one of the surest means of enlightening and giving just views of thinking to our citizens, but particularly the establishment of a university, where the youth of all parts of the United States might receive the polish of erudition in the arts, sciences, and belles-lettres, and where those who were disposed to run a political course might not only be instructed in the theory and principles, but (this seminary being at the seat of the General Government where the Legislature would be in session half the year, and the intersts and politics of the nation would be discussed) would lay the surest foundation for the practical part also."

(5) From his annual message of December 7, 1796:

"The assembly to which I address myself is too enlightened not to be fully sensible how much a flourishing state of the arts and sciences contributes to material prosperity and reputation. True it is that our country, much to its honor, contains many seminaries of learning highly respectable and useful; but the funds upon which they rest are too narrow to command the ablest professors, in the different departments of liberal knowledge, for the institution contemplated, though they would be excellent auxiliaries."

It is everywhere manifest in Washington's correspondence and conversations on this subject that his far-reaching mind and patriotic heart were full of a demand for exactly the kind of an institution which, in honor of his name, for the cause of learning, and for the sacred cause of country, not only we at this distance in time have planned, but which such patriots as Dr. Benjamin Rush, signer of the Declaration of Independence, and a leading scientist of his time, had in mind when, in his appeals to the country in support of the national university proposition, in 1788, he said:

"To effect this great and necessary work let one of the first acts of the new Congress be to establish within the district to be allotted for them a Federal university, into which the youth of the United States shall be received after they have finished their studies and taken degrees in the colleges of their respective States."

5. The vice chancellor of the new denominational university was hardly more fortunate than his predecessor in the discussion.

Passing without comment his reference to the "question of constitutional right," brief notice may be taken of his question of "the moral right to take the money of the many and spend it for the superior educational advantage of the few."

Strange questions these from such a representative! Yes, it is the moral right—and the moral as well as the patriotic duty—of the Government of this Republic to do whatsoever is necessary to the highest possible culture, on American soil and in friendly intercourse from every section, of those to whom in large part are to be committed the destinies of our country; the security of our free institutions; the national development in every field of worthy enterprise; our dignity as a nation, honorably and liberally providing for its own; our proper place in the very front rank of an advancing civilization.

Some 3,000 American graduates are to-day seeking abroad the post-graduate facilities which they can not find at home; and, secretly, some of those who oppose this university movement are pleading for yet other favors of that sort in the universities of France.

Presidents Washington, John Adams, Jefferson, Madison, Monroe, John Quincy Adams, Jackson, Grant, and Hayes were moved by an honorable craving to be free from dependence on foreign powers in all these high regards, and hence officially favored the founding of a national university. The claim by them made is still urged, and with increasing earnestness by a multitude of the foremost of American citizens.

But for reasons not far to seek, this talk of the constitutional and moral right to do a similar thing to that which has been done for the whole series of public schools, from the primary school to the State university, would be incomprehensible. It is only matched by that in which, with the Senate university bill in his hand, this second reverend objector declared that "the institution proposed by this bill will not really supplement the other schools of the country, and does not propose to do anything beyond college work."

6. And then this same vice-chancellor, in the next moment, expresses anxiety about the secular trend of the State and independent institutions, and so is hoping to supply the demand for truth and righteousness by building up an intensely sectarian institution, to the preclusion and everlasting exclusion of a truly national one. Does he assume that a State or national university must of necessity be Godless unless it be under denominational control? Is not this a Christian nation in a broader sense than is represented by any denominationalism? And does not a spirit of reverence, that fundamental element of religion, almost of necessity prevail wherever there is an earnest seeking after truth?

7. Finally, the vice-chancellor, in his sympathy for other institutions, including especially those which his chief had disparaged, was moved to urge that a strong national university would embarrass the universities in the States.

Why, then, do the managers of such institutions want it? Because they clearly see that by establishing such a post-graduate institution at the capital the Government will give a new dignity and value to the higher learning everywhere, and thus insure to the other institutions of the country a larger patronage and a more enthusiastic support—that it will help, and not hinder, as said before; and not alone by the increased interest in higher learning which it will surely awaken everywhere, but also by its new and unfailing supply of men of highest attainments for instruction in their several departments.

8. The rather presumptuous and elaborate attempt of the zealous trustee, put forward by the opposing denominational party to weaken the confidence of the Senate committee in the constitutional powers of the Government as to this matter, might well remain unnoticed (since the arguments offered have been passed upon so many times by the ablest of jurists) but for his statement of certain facts in the records of the Federal Convention in a form and manner quite evidently intended to make it appear that the omission to adopt the proposition of Messrs. Charles Pinckney and James Madison to include in the Constitution the power to establish and provide for a National University was on account of opposition to the thing itself sought to be made secure. On the contrary, it is clearly manifest, from the only accounts we have, that said omission was solely because of the prevailing opinion, (1) that nothing not absolutely necessary should be put into the Constitution, and (2) that an express provision therein for the proposed university was unnecessary, since "the exclusive power at the seat of Government would reach that object."

The record goes further and shows that, notwithstanding this prevailing opinion, five of the twelve delegates who had part in deciding the question voted to include the provision as a means of making the university more sure. It nowhere appears that a solitary word was uttered against the desirability of the proposed university.

9. The novel features of the trustee's discussion were the anti-Catholic argument and his plea for sympathy in behalf of the yet infant denominational institution in the other quarter of the District.

To the first it is sufficient to say that it is not the business of the Government of the United States to have anything to do with the antagonisms or ambitions of religious organizations. It was divorced from the church when it was founded, and must leave this whole matter to those directly concerned.

In answer to the second, I merely call attention to the facts that the effort for a national university began more than one hundred years before his own institution was thought of; also, that the recent renewal of such efforts by the introduction of Senator Edmund's bill and the formation of the Senate's Select Committee to Establish the University of the United States, on May 14, 1890, considerably antedated the charter, from the District Commissioners, of his institution, on May 28, 1891. If these objectors really wanted an American university, why did they not join hands with Senator Edmunds and other able friends of such an institution? There was not difference enough between "American," "National," and "United States" to constitute a bar to any high purpose in so important a matter.

Perhaps I should not disturb the happy dreams wherein a great sectarian school was so easily forming itself with the help of a taking misnomer, or embarrass well-devised schemes for a raising of funds on the strength of rosy views of an "American" institution that would more than realize the aspirations of Washington while under a two-thirds majority control of a single religious sect; nor is it pleasant to interfere with any man's schemes for large fortunes out of lands on the other side of the Potomac. But I will confess to no little surprise at such a showing as these men have made, as if it were argument and a fit illustration of superior ethics in education!

Since the great Catholic Church wants a high university of its own, is frank enough to christen it "The Catholic University of America," and is strong enough in both means and purpose to build it, let it do so; its right can not be challenged. And, in like manner, if any denomination with a contrary faith is ambitious to match this undertaking by building up a great institution of its own, it is equally its right; and they who plan and name it will do well to be as frank and courageous as the vigorous supporters of a more ancient faith. But for the *Nation* there is demanded a National University, wholly free from either sectarian or partisan bias, and for faithful service in the interest of science and learning, of the nation itself, of freedom, and of the highest good of mankind.

JOHN W HOYT.

Hon. JAMES H. KYLE,
*Chairman of Senate Committee to Establish
the University of the United States.*

OFFICIAL COMMUNICATION OF HON. JOHN W. HOYT IN BEHALF OF THE NATIONAL UNIVERSITY COMMITTEE OF ONE HUNDRED.

No. 4 IOWA CIRCLE,
Washington, D. C., March —, 1896.

SIR: Complying with your request for copies of important communications received by me in support of the national university proposition since the recent beginning of systematic effort in its behalf, and for information as to the character of the objections offered by any who may have dissented, I have pleasure in forwarding the accompanying files of letters from eminent statesmen, from a great number of the presidents of colleges and universities in all parts of the country, from State superintendents of public instruction in all the States, from the heads of various national organizations, from chiefs of scientific bureaus of the Government, and from other distinguished citizens who have manifested a deep interest in the university enterprise.

I also take the liberty of forwarding a list of members of the national committee of one hundred to promote the establishment of the university of the United States, with the names of those who form its executive council, and a brief outline of the arguments made by the few who have offered objections to the university measure, together with what are deemed sufficient answers thereto.

Very respectfully, yours,

JOHN W. HOYT,
Chairman of the National University Committee of One Hundred.

Hon. JAMES H. KYLE,
Chairman of Senate Committee to Establish the University of the United States.

EXECUTIVE COUNCIL OF THE NATIONAL UNIVERSITY COMMITTEE OF ONE HUNDRED.

[A council formed of its own members by the national committee for the framing of a bill to be offered to Congress and for the more immediate direction of the national-university enterprise.]

The Honorable Melville W. Fuller, LL. D., Chief Justice of the United States.

Ex-United States Senator George F. Edmunds, LL. D., of Vermont.

Ex-President William Pepper, M. D., LL. D., Philadelphia.

Hon. Andrew D. White, LL. D., ex-president of Cornell University, ex-United States minister to Germany and Russia, member of Venezuelan Commission, etc., New York.

Ex-Governor John Lee Carroll, LL. D., general president Society of Sons of the Revolution, Maryland.

Gen. Horace Porter, LL. D., president-general Society of Sons of the American Revolution, New York.

Ex-United States Senator Eppa Hunton, LL. D., Virginia.

Ex-United States Senator A. H. Garland, late Attorney-General of the United States, Arkansas.

Ex-United States Senator J. B. Henderson, Missouri and District of Columbia.

Col. Wilbur R. Smith, Kentucky University.

Gen. John Eaton, LL. D., ex-United States Commissioner of Education, etc., New Hampshire.

Hon. Gardiner G. Hubbard, LL. D., president National Geographic Society, Regent of Smithsonian Institution, etc., District of Columbia.

Simon Newcomb, LL. D., Director of the Nautical Almanac, District of Columbia.

Hon. John A. Kasson, ex-United States minister to Austria and ambassador to Germany, Iowa.

Hon. Oscar S. Strauss, ex-United States minister to Turkey, New York.

G. Brown Goode, LL. D., assistant secretary of Smithsonian Institution, in charge of the National Museum.

Ex-Govenor John W. Hoyt, M. D., LL. D., chairman of National University Committees, Washington, D. C.

MEMBERS OF THE NATIONAL UNIVERSITY COMMITTEE OF ONE HUNDRED.

GENERAL COMMITTEE.

The Honorable Melville W. Fuller, LL. D., Chief Justice of the United States.

Lieut. Gen. J. M. Schofield, late Commander in Chief of the Army.
Maj. Gen. Nelson A. Miles, Commander in Chief of the Army.
George M. Sternberg, M. D., LL. D., Surgeon-General, U. S. A.

Ex-United States Senator George F. Edmunds, of Vermont.
Ex-United States Senator Eppa Hunton, of Virginia.
Ex-United States Senator A. H. Garland, of Arkansas.
Ex-United States Senator James R. Doolittle, of Wisconsin.
Ex-United States Senator Carl Schurz, of New York.
Ex-United States Senator John J. Ingalls, of Kansas.
Ex-United States Senator Patrick Walsh, of Georgia.
Ex-United States Senator W. D. Washburn, of Minnesota.
Ex-United States Senator Joseph M. Carey, of Wyoming.
Ex-United States Senator Joseph N. Dolph, of Oregon.
Ex-United States Senator J. B. Henderson, of Missouri and District of Columbia.

Hon. Andrew D. White, LL. D., of New York, president of Cornell University, former ambassador to Germany, late United States minister to Russia, etc.
Hon. John A. Kasson, LL. D., of Iowa, late United States minister to Austria and ambassador to Germany.
Hon. Oscar S. Strauss, of New York, late United States minister to Turkey.
Hon. Wayne MacVeagh, LL. D., United States ambassador to Italy.

President B. L. Whitman, D. D., Columbian University, District of Columbia.
President Daniel C. Gilman, LL. D., Johns Hopkins University, Maryland.
William Pepper, M. D., LL. D., former provost, University of Pennsylvania.
President George W. Atherton, Ph. D., LL. D., Pennsylvania State College.
President Henry Coppée, A. M., D. D., Lehigh University, Pennsylvania.
President Charles De Garmo, Ph. D., Swarthmore College, Pennsylvania.
Ex-President Edwin H. Magill, LL. D., Swarthmore College, Pennsylvania.
President A. H. Fetterhoff, LL. D., Girard College, Pennsylvania.
President H. W. MacKnight, D. D. LL. D., Pennsylvania College.
President W. P. Johnston, D. D., Geneva College, Pennsylvania.
President Isaac Sharpless, Sc. D., LL. D., Haverford College, Pennsylvania.
President Theophilus B. Roth, D. D., Thiel College, Pennsylvania.
President Thomas L. Seip, D. D., Muhlenburg College, Pennsylvania.
President Ethelbert D. Warfield, LL. D., Lafayette College, Pennsylvania.
Chancellor W. J. Holland, Ph. D., LL. D., Western University of Pennsylvania.
President F. L. Patton, D. D., LL. D., Princeton University, New Jersey.

UNIVERSITY OF THE UNITED STATES.

Chancellor H. M. McCracken, D. D., LL. D., University of the City of New York.
President George William Smith, D. D., Trinity College, Connecticut.
President T. C. Mendenhall, LL. D., Worcester Polytechnic Institute, Massachusetts.
President Edwin Hewitt Capen, D. D., Tufts College, Massachusetts.
President E. Benjamin Andrews, LL. D., Brown University, Rhode Island.
President A. W. Harris, Sc. D., Maine State College.
President Nathaniel Butler, D. D., Colby University, Maine.
President Ezra Brainerd, LL. D., Middlebury College, Vermont.
President J. G. Schurman, Sc. D., LL. D., Cornell University, New York.
Director R. H. Thurston, Sibley College, Cornell University, New York.
President David D. Cochran, Polytechnic Institute, New York.
President John Hudson Peck, LL. D., Rensselaer Polytechnic Institute, New York.
President Harrison E. Webster, LL. D., Union College, New York.
President David J. Hill, LL. D., University of Rochester, New York.
President Arthur E. Main, A. M., D. D., Alfred University, New York.
President P. B. Reynolds, LL. D., West Virginia University.
President D. Powell, A. M., Ph. D., West Virginia College.
President J. C. Rankin, D. D., LL. D., Howard University, District of Columbia.
President Lyon G. Tyler, Ph. D., William and Mary College, Virginia.
President H. B. Frissell, D. D., Hampton Institute, Virginia.
President J. M. McBryde, Ph. D., Virginia Agricultural and Mechanical College.
President George T. Winston, LL. D., University of North Carolina.
President Charles F. Meserve, Ph. D., Shaw University, North Carolina.
President J. Woodrow, Ph. D., LL. D., South Carolina College.
President Richard C. Jones, LL. D., University of Alabama.
President A. S. Andrews, D. D., LL. D., Southern University, Alabama.
President William Le Roy Brown, Ph. D., Alabama Polytechnic Institute.
President J. W. Nicholson, LL. D., Louisiana State University.
Ex-President D. F. Boyd, LL. D., Louisiana State University.
President Oscar Alewort, LL. D., Straight University, Louisiana.
President Edward C. Mitchell, LL. D., Leland University, Louisiana.
Chancellor R. B. Fulton, LL. D., University of Mississippi.
General Stephen D. Lee, LL. D., president Mississippi State Agricultural College.
President Charles W. Dabney, Ph. D., LL. D., University of Tennessee.
Chancellor W. H. Payne, LL. D., University of Nashville, Tennessee.
President Erastus M. Cravath, D. D., Fisk University, Tennessee.
President J. Braden, D. D., Central Tennessee College.
Chancellor Nathan Green, LL. D., Cumberland University, Tennessee.
Chancellor George W. Sweeney, D. D., etc., S. W. Presbyterian University, Tennessee.
President B. Lawton Wiggins, M. A., etc., University of the South, Tennessee.
President Charles L. Loos, A. M., LL. D., Kentucky University.
Col. Wilbur R. Smith, Kentucky University.
President S. Ryland, D. D., Bethel College, Kentucky.
Chancellor L. H. Blanton, D. D., Central University, Kentucky.
President William A. Oberchaine, Ph. D., Ogden College, Kentucky.
President J. H. Canfield, A. M., LL. D., Ohio State University.
Ex-President William H. Scott, M. A., LL. D., Ohio State University.
President Charles V. Thwing, D. D., Western Reserve College, Ohio.
President W. O. Thompson, D. D., etc., Miami University, Ohio.
President L. Bookwalter, LL. D., Western College, Ohio.
President S. A. Ort, D. D., Wittenberg College, Ohio.
President Cady Staley, Ph. D., Case School of Applied Science, Ohio.
President Jesse Johnson, Ph. D., Muskingum College, Ohio.
President J. A. Peters, A. M., D. D., Heidelberg University, Ohio.

UNIVERSITY OF THE UNITED STATES. 53

President John W. Simpson, LL. D., Marietta College, Ohio.
President E. V. Zollars, LL. D., Hiram College, Ohio.
President Charles W. Super, LL. D., Ohio University.
President F. Scovel, LL. D., University of Wooster, Ohio.
President D. T. McClurg, LL. D., Muskingum College, Ohio.
President W. G. Ballentine, D. D., LL. D., Oberlin College, Ohio.
President Theodore Sterling, M. D., LL. D., Kenyon College, Ohio.
President Faye Walker, D. D., Oxford College, Ohio.
President Daniel Albright Long, D. D., LL. D., Antioch College, Ohio.
President W. A. Sproull, LL. D., University of Cincinnati, Ohio.
President James B. Angell, LL. D., University of Michigan.
President George W. Cairnes, Ph. D., Battle Creek College, Michigan.
President George F. Mosher, D. D., LL. D., Hillsdale College, Michigan.
President Joseph Swain, LL. D., Indiana State University.
President George S. Burroughs, Ph. D., D. D., Wabash College, Indiana.
President J. H. Smart, LL. D., Purdue University, Indiana.
President J. J. Mills, A. M., LL. D., Earlham College, Indiana.
President William R. Harper, LL. D., University of Chicago, Illinois.
Acting Regent T. J. Burrill, Ph. D., LL. D., University of Illinois.
President J. H. N. Standish, Ph. D., Lombard University, Illinois.
President J. B. McMichael, D. D., Monmouth College, Illinois.
President A. E. Turner, Ph. D., Lincoln College, Illinois.
President Holmes Dysinger, D. D., Carthage College, Illinois.
President J. H. Breese, A. M., Ph. D., Northern Illinois College.
President John M. Coulter, Ph. D., LL. D., Lake Forest University, Illinois.
President C. K. Adams, LL. D., University of Wisconsin.
Ex-President T. C. Chamberlin, late of University of Wisconsin.
President Arthur Piper, S. T. D., Racine College, Wisconsin.
President A. T. Ernst, Ph. D., Northwestern University, Wisconsin.
President Cyrus Northrup, LL. D., University of Minnesota.
President James W. Strong, LL. D., Carleton College, Minnesota.
President Charles A. Schaeffer, LL. D., University of Iowa.
Chancellor J. C. Gilchrist, D. D., University of the Northwest, Iowa.
President William M. Beardspear, LL. D., State College, Iowa.
President W. S. Perry, D. D., Griswold College, Iowa.
President Ambrose C. Smith, D. D., Parsons College, Iowa.
President George A. Gates, D. D., Iowa College, Grinnell, Iowa.
President R. H. Jesse, LL. D., University of Missouri.
President J. P. Green, LL. D., William and Jewell College, Missouri.
President F. H. Snow, Ph. D., LL. D., University of Kansas.
President F. W. Colgrove, LL. D., Ottawa University, Kansas.
President George E. MacLean, LL. D., University of Nebraska.
President J. M. Mauck, Ph. D., University of South Dakota.
President William M. Blackburn, D. D., LL. D., Pierre University, South Dakota.
President Webster Merrifield, Ph. D., University of North Dakota.
President James H. Baker, LL. D., University of Colorado.
Ex-President Horace M. Hale, LL. D., University of Colorado.
President William F. Slocum, LL. D., Colorado College.
President William F. McDowell, LL. D., University of Denver, Colo.
President J. T. Kingsbury, Ph. D., University of Utah.
President C. H. Chapman, Ph. D., University of Oregon.
President Thomas McClelland, D. D., Pacific University, Oregon.
President C. C. Stratton, LL. D., Portland University, Oregon.
President Mark W. Harrington, LL. D., University of Washington.
President Martin Kellogg, LL. D., University of California.
President David Starr Jordan, LL. D., Leland Stanford University, California.

UNIVERSITY OF THE UNITED STATES.

Hon. Frank A. Hill, secretary of State board of education, Massachusetts.
Hon. J. W. Dickinson, ex-secretary of Massachusetts State board of education, Massachusetts.
Hon. Charles R. Skinner, State superintendent of public instruction, New York.
Hon. Ed. Porter Thompson, State superintendent of public instruction, Kentucky.
Hon. John R. Kirk, State superintendent of schools, Missouri.
Hon. L. E. Wolfe, ex-State superintendent of schools, Missouri.
Hon. Nathan C. Schaeffer, State superintendent of public instruction, Pennsylvania.
Hon. Charles D. Hine, State superintendent of education, Connecticut.
Hon. Thomas P. Stockwell, State commissioner of schools, Rhode Island.
Hon. E. B. Prettyman, State superintendent of public instruction, Maryland.
Hon. Virgil A. Lewis, State superintendent of free schools, West Virginia.
Hon. John E. Massey, State superintendent of public instruction, Virginia.
Hon. E. T. Bates, State superintendent of public instruction, North Dakota.
Hon. L. J. Eisenhuth, ex-State superintendent, North Dakota.
Hon. C. W. Bean, State superintendent of public instruction, Washington.
Hon. John C. Scarborough, State superintendent of public instruction, North Carolina.
Hon. S. M. Finger, ex-superintendent of public instruction for North Carolina.
Hon. Frederick Gowing, State superintendent of public instruction, New Hampshire.
Hon. Mason S. Stone, State superintendent of education, Vermont.
Hon. Edwin F. Palmer, ex-State superintendent for Vermont.
Hon. J. R. Preston, State superintendent of public education, Mississippi.
Hon. Cortez Salmon, State superintendent of public instruction, South Dakota.
Hon. Henry Sabin, State superintendent of public instruction, Iowa.
Hon. W. W. Pendergast, State superintendent of public instruction, Minnesota.
Hon. C. C. Tindal, secretary State board of education, Delaware.
Hon. A. B. Poland, State superintendent of public instruction, New Jersey.
Hon. Josiah Shinn, ex-State superintendent of public instruction, Arkansas.
Hon. Samuel T. Black, State superintendent of public instruction, California.
Hon. J. W. Anderson, ex-State superintendent of public instruction, California.
Hon. J. M. Carlisle, State superintendent of public education, Texas.
Hon. Henry R. Pattengill, State superintendent of public instruction, Michigan.
Hon. Henry Raab, State superintendent of public instruction, Illinois.
Hon. E. Stanley, State superintendent of public instruction, Kansas.
Hon. H. N. Gaines, ex-State superintendent of public instruction, Kansas.
Hon. A. K. Goudy, State superintendent of public instruction, Nebraska.
Hon. David M. Geeting, State superintendent of public instruction, Indiana.
Hon. Hervey D. Vories, ex-superintendent for Indiana.
Hon. W. W. Stetson, State superintendent of schools, Maine.
Hon. W. D. Mayfield, State superintendent of education, South Carolina.
Hon. F. J. Netherton, State superintendent of public instruction, Arizona.
Hon. S. G. Gilbreath, State superintendent of public instruction, Tennessee.
Hon. John O. Turner. State superintendent of education, Alabama.
Hon. T. B. Lewis, Territorial commissioner of schools, Utah.
Hon. C. A. Foresman, State superintendent of public instruction, Idaho.
Hon. H. C. Cutting, superintendent of public instruction for Nevada.
Hon. Amado Chavez, superintendent of public instruction for New Mexico.
Hon. A. J. Peavey, State superintendent of public instruction, Colorado.
Hon. E. Reed, State superintendent of public instruction, Wyoming.
Hon. G. R. Glenn, State school commissioner for Georgia.
Hon. Albert J. Russel, State superintendent of public instruction, Florida.
Hon. Zalmon Richards, late school superintendent, District of Columbia.

Benjamin Apthorp Gould, LL. D., astronomer, Cambridge, Mass.
Gen. John Eaton, LL. D., for many years United States Commissioner of Education.
Hon. Arthur MacArthur, LL. D., ex-justice of the supreme court of D. C.
Gen. George R. Davis, director-general World's Columbian Exposition.
Right Rev. William Paret, D. D., LL. D., Protestant Episcopal bishop of Maryland.
Hon. Frederick T. Greenhalge, governor of Massachusetts.
Hon. Cephas Brainerd, of New York, chairman American Branch of Committee on an International Court of Arbitration.
Hon. William Wirt Henry, of Virginia.
Gen. James Grant Wilson, New York City.
William D. Cabell, Ph. D., president Alumni Association University of Virginia.
Right Rev. Thomas M. Clark, D. D., LL. D., Protestant Episcopal bishop of Rhode Island.
Andrew J. Rickoff, Ph. D., formerly superintendent of education, New York.
Marshall Field, esq., Chicago.
Col. William O. McDowell, chairman Pan-Republic Committee, etc., New Jersey.
Mr. Justice C. Strawbridge, Philadelphia.
John Henry Barrows, D. D., LL. D., president of late World's Congress of Religions, Chicago.
Edward Everett Hale, D. D., LL. D., Massachusetts.
Right Rev. Ethelbert Talbot, D. D., LL. D., Episcopal bishop of Wyoming and Idaho.
Henry Villard, esq., New York City.
O. Vincent Coffin, governor of Connecticut.
President Samuel R. Shipley, Philadelphia.
Thomas Dolans, esq., Philadelphia.
N. H. Winchell, Ph. D., State geologist for Minnesota.
George Dana Boardman, D. D., LL. D., Philadelphia.
Elmer Gates, Ph. D., Philadelphia.
Lester F. Ward, LL. D., Washington, D. C.
Charles Sprague Smith, Ph. D., Columbia College, New York.
Hon. H. McGraw, governor of Washington.
Hon. Newton Bateman, LL. D., former State superintendent of public instruction for Illinois; also ex-president of Knox College.
J. M. Gregory, LL. D., former president State University of Illinois.
Hon. Richard Edwards, LL. D., formerly State superintendent of public instruction for Illinois.
Hon. John E. Jones, governor of Nevada.
Herbert B. Adams, Ph. D., of Johns Hopkins, secretary of American Historical Association.
Henry Baldwin, LL. D., custodian of American history.
William A. Mowry, Ph. D., ex-superintendent of public instruction, late editor of Education, etc.
M. Schele de Vere, LL. D., late of University of Virginia.
Hon. Ezra S. Carr, M. D., LL. D., former State superintendent of public instruction for California, etc.
Hon. Eugene A. Smith, Ph. D., State geologist for Alabama.
Dr. E. P. Powell, Clinton, N. Y.
Dr. H. von Holst, Chicago.
Hon. E. C. Shortridge, governor of South Dakota.
James Hall, LL. D., State geologist for New York.
Hon. Z. Richards, Ph. D., late superintendent of schools, District of Columbia.
Ulysses S. Grant, Ph. D., Geological survey of Minnesota.
Persifer Frazer, LL. D., late State geologist for Pennsylvania, etc.
Hon. Louis C. Hughes, governor of Arizona.

Hon. Frederick W. Smyth, ex-governor of New Hampshire, railroad president, etc.
Hon. J. E. Richards, governor of Montana.
Hon. Roger Allin, governor of North Dakota.

Ex-Governor John Lee Carroll, LL. D., Maryland, general president of the Society of the Sons of the Revolution.
Gen. Horace Porter, LL. D., president-general of the Society of the Sons of the American Revolution.
Hon. Asa Bird Gardiner, LL. D., secretary-general, Society of the Cincinnati.
Hon. Gardiner G. Hubbard, LL. D., president National Geographic Society, etc.
D. G. Brinton, LL. D., ex-president of the American Association for the Advancement of Science.
Edmund J. James, LL. D., president of the American Academy of Political and Social Science.
H. Randall Waite, Ph. D., president of the American Institute of Civics.
George F. Barker, LL. D., University of Pennsylvania.
F. E. Nipher, LL. D., president Academy of Science of St. Louis.
David L. James, president Cincinnati Society of Natural History.
Maj. Henry E. Alvord, president American Association of Agricultural Colleges and Experiment Stations.

S. P. Langley, LL. D., secretary of the Smithsonian Institution.
G. Brown Goode, LL. D., assistant secretary, in charge of National Museum.
Commodore R. L. Phythian, U. S. N., Superintendent of the Naval Observatory.
Simon Newcomb, LL. D., Director of the Nautical Almanac.
Gen. W. W. Duffield, LL. D., Superintendent of Coast and Geodetic Survey.
Charles D. Walcott, LL. D., Director of the United States Geological Survey.
Maj. J. W. Powell, LL. D., Director United States Bureau of Ethnology.
J. S. Billings, M. D., LL. D., late Superintendent of Army Medical Museum.
Hon. Carroll D. Wright, LL. D., United States Commissioner of Labor.
Wheelock G. Veazey, LL. D., Interstate Commerce Commissioner.

Ex-Governor John W. Hoyt, LL. D., *chairman of the committee, 4 Iowa circle, Washington, D. C., to whom communications may be addressed.*

LETTERS FROM JURISTS, ARMY OFFICERS, AND STATESMEN.

WASHINGTON, D. C., *March 14, 1896.*

MY DEAR SIR: I trust I need not assure you of the deep interest I feel in the success of the movement for the establishment of a national university. No one can overrate the vital importance of the higher education to the perpetuity of the Republic and the happiness and prosperity of its people, or fail to recognize the ever-widening circle of its demands.

The wonderful prescience of Washington anticipated what we are beginning to realize. It seems to me that the reasons in favor of the foundation of the university, substantially in accordance with the plan proposed, are too obvious and weighty to to be disregarded.

Very truly, yours,
MELVILLE W. FULLER
(*Chief Justice of the United States*).

[From an address of Chief Justice Fuller, on occasion of the one hundredth anniversary of the incorporation of Bowdoin College, 1894.]

"It was said of Turgot, that he 'was filled with an astonished, awful, oppressive sense of the immoral thoughtlessness of men; of the heedless, hazardous way in which they dealt with things of the greatest moment to them; of the immense, incalculable misery which is due to this cause;' and although the hundred years may have somewhat modified this conclusion, that thoughtlessness still keeps alive the seeds of peril. To overcome it is the beneficent mission of that training and education which, apart from the acquisition of knowledge, develop character and perfect the man.

It does not follow that the successful actor in affairs need necessarily be the graduate of a college or university. Washington and Franklin and Lincoln were not college men (though each a student according to his opportunities), but Samuel Adams and John Adams and Otis and Hamilton and Jay and Jefferson and Madison and a host of others—the majority of the framers of the Constitution, and the hundreds who, through the pulpit and the press, prepared the way for the Revolution—were; and at this juncture nothing is clearer than that in the coming years the higher education will play the most efficient part in the preservation of institutions and in the leadership essential to avert or to control whatever crisis may be threatened or arise."

NEW YORK, *December 17, 1895.*

DEAR SIR: In reply to your note of the 14th instant, I take pleasure in authorizing the use of my name as one of the national university committee.

Yours, very truly,
J. M. SCHOFIELD
(*Lieutenant-General U. S. A.*).

HEADQUARTERS OF THE ARMY,
Washington, D. C., January 27, 1896.

MY DEAR SIR: I have the honor to acknowledge the receipt of your letter of the 14th instant, and to express my appreciation of your desire that my name shall be included in the list of "members of the national committee," organized for the purpose of establishing a national university.

I consider it a high privilege to be a member of this committee, and am very willing that my name should be added to the list.

Very truly, yours, NELSON A. MILES
(Major-General, U. S. A.).

WAR DEPARTMENT, SURGEON-GENERAL'S OFFICE,
Washington, D. C., 1896.

MY DEAR SIR: I shall be glad to have you add my name to the list of members of the national university committee and to do anything in my power to advance the interests of the project, which has my full sympathy and approval. Such a university as is proposed could not fail to exercise a powerful influence upon the development and diffusion of knowledge in this country; and the special advantages to be derived from locating it in this city are apparent. All this is so well stated in your "Memorial," published in 1892, that it seems unnecessary to advance any further arguments in favor of the project.

Very truly, yours, GEO. M. STERNBERG
(Surgeon-General U. S. A.).

1507 SPRUCE STREET, *Philadelphia, Pa., April 20, 1895.*

DEAR SIR: Yours of the 10th was duly received, but absence has delayed the answer.

You can use my name as a strong friend of the university scheme, which I hope will at some early day be realized.

Yours, very truly, GEO. F. EDMUNDS
(Ex-United States Senator, etc.).

It is but just to say that this assurance from ex-Senator Edmunds was hardly necessary in view of—

(1) His introduction of a bill to establish the university of the United States and his causing the creation of a "Select Committee to Establish the University of the United States," in 1890.

(2) His letter of 1892, in these emphatic and impressive words:

"AIX-LES-BAINS, FRANCE, *September 27, 1892.*

"DEAR SIR: I am glad that you are still interested in the national university. I think it of vast and far-reaching importance, and that it should be established and maintained in line with the fundamental principles of our Government."

(3) Assurances so well confirmed by his letter of November 13, 1895:

"1505 LOCUST STREET, *Philadelphia, November 13, 1895.*

"MY DEAR SIR: I have yours of the 11th instant. I am as deeply interested as ever in the university scheme, and much regret that I am able to do so little in furtherance of it."

(4) By his cooperation in the forming of a national university committee of one hundred and of an executive council of the same; his chairmanship of the committee of revision which drafted the Hawley bill now pending in the Senate; his argument before the House Committee on Education in support of same bill, and his forwarding a copy of these for the consideration of the Senate committee having the bill in charge.

HOMINY HILL, ARK., *September 9, 1895.*
DEAR GOVERNOR: I am glad that you feel the university cause is progressing. To my mind it is the most important of all projects or schemes now before our country, and I fervently hope it will go on to completion. For one I am ready to contribute my best efforts toward it.

Very truly, yours,
A. H. GARLAND
(*Ex-United States Senator and Ex-Attorney-General.*).

In substitution for the several communications from Ex-Senator Eppa Hunton, it seems proper to quote from his speech as chairman of the Senate Select Committee to Establish the University of the United States, delivered in the Senate on December 13, 1894, in support of bill S. No. 1708, Fifty-third Congress, last session:

"It is a fact, not willingly admitted, that European countries, are a long way ahead of us in the facilities they furnish for the highest intellectual training. France, Italy, Spain, Germany, and England have each spent many millions in money to carry to the highest plane their educational institutions. This is an example well worthy of imitation. It can not be right that this country, by neglect to provide the very best facilities, should compel her sons to seek them in foreign lands.

* * * * * * *

"How important to have at least one institution where better equipped teachers and professors may be prepared for our colleges and local universities, thus preparing them to render a better service to their students, and so on to all the lower rounds. In this way the facilities for this higher education will be multiplied and the standard be continuously raised.

"But above all other considerations how important it is to have at least one institution with students from every State where the science of government is taught, and by whom the knowledge thus acquired may be diffused among the people. The questions of tariff and other questions of finance have divided the people of this country from the beginning. The people select their Representatives by whom these questions are to be decided. In theory, at least, the people settle them. How important, then, is it that the people should be helped to understand these great questions; and how much light would be shed upon them by sending forth every year men of talent, who have devoted their time to the study of these questions, not as partisans but as students, anxious to arrive at the very right of the case and to determine, without regard to party, what policy should be adopted by our Government.

"How important to settle these and other great questions in such a manner that a radical change may not take place with every change in the administration of our Government. We know that when great changes in the governmental policy of the country are agitated a stagnation of business ensues; factories are idle, the monetary system of the country is deranged, failures multiply, and general distress prevails.

"It may be that this country will always be divided into parties taking views radically different on these great questions. It may be that it is best for the country that there shall ever be two great parties, but it is certainly to the public interest that these questions shall be finally settled. Who can estimate the value of such a settlement if it had been made long ago?

"I do not maintain that a great national university, with a department devoted especially to the study and teaching of finance, would have secured this. But I do maintain that such an institution, where partisan politics are carefully excluded, and the exact truth carefully sought without prejudice, would tend more than anything else to enlighten the people and bring them to a harmonious conclusion, which would be reflected by their Representatives in both branches of the National Legislature.

"These are some of the reasons that have brought me to the conclusion that a national university in this city is one of the necessities of the age.

* * * * *

"All these distinguished representatives of the best scholarship, scientific culture, and statesmanship of the country, in common with the multitude of illustrious men of the past who have championed the same great cause, plainly see that, while we have already gained a certain acknowledged superiority among the nations by reason of the vastness of our material resources and by the general intelligence and inventive genius of a people living under free institutions, we have not yet reached that higher eminence which pertains to the profoundest culture in letters, science, and philosophy. And they also see that in order to attain such eminence the Government itself should plant and foster, at this national capital, a great and true university, so endowed as to enable it to become not only a supreme leader in the work of the highest instruction for our own people, but also foremost among the universities of the world in the yet grander work of advancing the boundaries of human knowledge.

"Why, then, should Congress hesitate to adopt a measure so earnestly advocated by the foremost of our citizens from the very foundation of the Government? Can any reason be given why Congress should not at once enter upon the great work?

"Will the proposed University of the United States interfere with the colleges and so-called universities? On the contrary, it will tend to increase their prosperity by newly kindling a love of learning throughout the land and by adding to the number of their students, since only through study in these can they become candidates for the honors to be conferred by the coming national university. That such would be the result is conclusively demonstrated by the support the proposition has received from the eminent heads and professors of so many of our principal colleges and State universities.

"Can not the country spare the money to establish it? Our best men in the beginning of the Government wanted it established. If it was possible to do this out of the poor resources of an infant country, just emerged from the throes of a revolutionary struggle, what must be said of our ability to do it now that we have grown from three to sixty-five millions of people, and from 13 original States along the Atlantic coast to nearly fifty States, extending from the Atlantic to the Pacific Ocean?

"Can it be said that there are more pressing demands for our expenditures? Surely none are so pressing as this. The best men in all periods of our Government have urged this expenditure. The Government has given its aid to all classes of education except this by donation of millions of acres of land. It has with a lavish hand extended its aid to schools and colleges, and these very schools and colleges are now crying aloud for this university in order to complete the circle of education and to carry to the highest point the work so well begun by them.

"Is the location at the National Capital objectionable? Surely not, for the many reasons given by eminent men in quotations already made. This of all others is the spot, and in my opinion the only spot, where a national university can be constitutionally established by the Federal Government. Anywhere else in the States the constitutional power of Congress would be wanting. Here Congress has the same relation to the District of Columbia as the several legislatures have to their respective States. It will not be contended that legislatures have no power to establish and endow universities in their several States.

* * * * * * *

"Section 16 gives to the members of this university well-regulated access to the numerous institutions and collections now held by the Government here in Washington City, and brings the Bureau heads, whose work is of a sort to justify it, into proper advisory and cooperative relations with the heads of corresponding departments of the university.

"What a field of scientific study is here laid before the young man ambitious of attainments of the highest order. See what is thus laid before him that he may choose in what particular branch of science he may pursue and perfect his studies. They embrace almost every branch of scientific work, and are presided over by men already familiar with their respective departments, and who, it may be added, most fully realize how great is the loss that results from allowing the opportunities here offered to run waste.

"Examine for yourselves, Senators, the inventory of them:
In the Treasury Department of the United States—
    The Office of the Coast and Geodetic Survey.
    The Office of the Life-Saving Service.
    The Marine-Hospital Service.
    The Bureau of Statistics.
    The Bureau of Engraving and Printing.
In the War Department—
    The several military bureaus.
In the Navy Department—
    The Naval Observatory.
    The Office of the Nautical Almanac.
    The Hydrographic Office.
    The Bureau of Navigation.
    The Bureau of Yards and Docks.
    The Bureau of Ordnance.
    The Bureau of Construction and Repair.
    The Bureau of Steam Engineering.
    The Museum of Hygiene.
    The Bureau of Medicine and Surgery.
    The Dispensary.
In the Department of the Interior—
    The Patent Office.
    The Bureau of Education.
    The Office of the Geological Survey.
    The Census Office.
In the Department of Agriculture—
    The Botanical Division, with the gardens and grounds.
    The Division of Vegetable Pathology.
    The Pomological Division.
    The Microscopical Division.
    The Chemical Division.
    The Ornithological Division.
    The Forestry Division.
    The Entomological Division.
    The Silk Section.
    The Experimental Stations.
    The Office of Statistics.
    The Bureau of Animal Industry.
    The Weather Bureau.
    The Agricultural Museum.
Of establishments not under departmental control—
    The Smithsonian Institution.
    The National Museum, with its twenty-two departments.
    The Medical Museum.
    The Medical Library.
    The Bureau of Ethnology.
    The Light-House Board.
    The Commission of Fish and Fisheries.
    The Arsenal.
    The Congressional Library.
    The United States Botanic Garden.

The Zoological Garden (in preparation).
The Government Printing Office.
The Soldiers' Home.
Office of the National Board of Health.
Government Hospital for the Insane.
The National Deaf-Mute College.
Courts, district, circuit, and Supreme.

"What opportunities for the earnest student of science, and how eagerly would they be accepted!

* * * * * *

"It is in the power of no man to properly estimate the benefits bestowed upon our country by the multitude of college graduates heretofore distributed to all parts of it by the institutions already established—young men who, with the helps thus afforded, have become our leading mechanicians, architects, engineers, experts in every field of science, teachers, physicians, lawyers, and lawmakers, who have infused into the minds of the people a thrist for knowledge, a love of country, and a patriotic desire to preserve this Government as the fathers made it. Neither is it in the power of any man to estimate the possibilities of such an institution as is now proposed—an institution that shall crown and complete the now incomplete system of American education; that shall become a mighty uplifting force in its influence upon all classes of institutions below it; that shall furnish the facilities for which our aspiring young men now visit the Old World by thousands; that shall draw to us men of genius from all other lands, and that shall early become the leading university of the world."

CHICAGO, *December 9, 1891.*

MY DEAR SIR: My professional duties will hardly give me time to devote to the duties of the committee. To the matter of being named in company with such distinguished persons as you have named, I am willing to consent.

Very sincerely, yours,

J. R. DOOLITTLE
(*Ex-United States Senator from Wisconsin*).

BOLTON, LAKE GEORGE, N. Y., *September 15, 1892.*

DEAR GOVERNOR: I have received your kind letter of the 12th instant, and am extremely sorry I can not be with you at the meeting in Washington. I wish you all success at the university making, and am,

Sincerely yours,

C. SCHURZ
(*Ex-United States Senator from Wisconsin*).

NEW YORK, *January 6, 1892.*

MY DEAR GOVERNOR: Your kind note of the 3d instant is in my hands. I am very glad to hear that the prospects for a strong association are promising. Have you any copies of the old bills that you might send me? I should be much obliged to you.

Very truly, yours,

C. SCHURZ
(*Ex-United States Senator, etc.*).

NEW YORK, *December 24, 1894.*

MY DEAR GOVERNOR: I have read your letter and the accompanying printed paper with great interest, and am perfectly willing to join a national university association upon the principles indicated on the leaflet, and composed of such men as you mention in your letter. Whether the present moment is a very propitious one, I do not know, but it is probably as good as any other.

Sincerely, yours,

C. SCHURZ
(*Ex-United States Senator, etc.*).

ATCHISON, KANS., 1895.

DEAR GOVERNOR: Thanks for yours with accompanying documents. My interest in the great work is unabated, and I shall be glad to do anything I can at all times to help it forward. * * * It is of supreme importance that the university should be established now.

Yours, faithfully,
JOHN J. INGALLS
(*Ex-United States Senator, etc*).

AUGUSTA, GA., *April 27, 1895.*

DEAR SIR: I take pleasure in sending you an order on the superintendent of the Senate for documents as requested in yours of the 3d.

I am in favor of the proposition to establish a national university at Washington, and you can refer to me as one of the friends of the movement.

Yours, very respectfully,
PATRICK WALSH
(*Ex-United States Senator, etc*).

UNITED STATES SENATE,
Washington, D. C., January 21, 1895.

MY DEAR SIR: I have yours of the 14th instant in regard to the bill to establish a national university, and I assure you it will give me pleasure to cooperate with the friends of the measure in every way I can.

Yours, truly,
(The late) JAMES F. WILSON
(*As Ex-United States Senator from Iowa*).

WASHINGTON, D. C., *March 17, 1896.*

DEAR SIR: You will please be assured of my deep and abiding interest in the proposition to found a national post-graduate university at Washington, wherein so large a degree the material and forces are already present, as if waiting to be organized.

Such an institution would not only meet the demand so forcibly urged by eminent scholars and statesmen, past and present, as a means of meeting our present deficiencies and of securing to our country its proper rank among the most cultivated of all the great nations, it would also fulfill those high offices of which Washington and a long line of his illustrious successors thought so much, in the way of harmonizing our national life, and of essentially adding to the security of our free institutions.

It would seem that the founding of the proposed University of the United States should not be longer delayed, and that this one-hundredth year since Washington's last appeal to Congress in this same behalf, and of his designation of lands for its use, may be deemed a most fitting time for a beginning of this great work.

I remain, my dear sir, very respectfully, yours,
J. B. HENDERSON
(*Ex-United States Senator from Missouri, etc.*).

CHEYENNE, WYO., *November 16, 1895.*

MY DEAR SIR: I am heartily in favor of the establishment of the great national university in the city of Washington, if it can be kept free from politics and political control. I have no doubt that a plan will be formulated that will avoid these difficulties.

The United States is directly interested in many of the educational establishments in the United States; especially is this the case in the institutions devoted to agricultural branches and scientific investigations.

I wish those who have the matter directly in hand every success in their endeavors to bring about at an early day a great national institution that will be in its scope of work a credit to the people of the United States.

Yours, very truly,

JOSEPH M. CAREY
(*Ex-United States Senator, etc.*).

THE UNION LEAGUE CLUB,
New York, December 24, 1894.

MY DEAR GOVERNOR: Pardon delay in answering your two letters, caused by especial pressure of business.

You have set forth the claims and advantages of a university at Washington admirably, and in so doing have rendered a great public service. What I lately said in the Forum, I say again:

"Our country has already not far short of 400 colleges and universities, more or less worthy of those names, besides a vast number of high schools and academies quite as worthy to be called colleges and universities as many which bear those titles. But the system embracing all these has by no means reached its final form. Probably in its more complete development the stronger institutions, to the number of 20 or 30, will, within a generation or two, become universities in the true sense of the word, restricting themselves to university work, beginning, perhaps, at the studies now usually undertaken in the junior year of our colleges, and carrying them on through the senior year, with two or three years of special or professional work afterwards.

"The best of the others will probably accept their mission as colleges in the true sense of the word, beginning the course two years earlier than at present and continuing it to what is now the junior year. Thus they will do a work intermediate between the general school system of the country and the universities, a work which can be properly called collegiate, a work the need of which is now sorely felt, and which is most useful and honorable. Such an organization will give us as good a system as the world has ever seen, probably the best system.

"Every man who has thought to much purpose upon this mass of institutions devoted to advanced instruction must feel that it is just now far more important to strengthen those we have than to make any immediate additions to their number. How can this best be done? My answer is that this and a multitude of other needs of the country can be best met by the foundation of a university in the city of Washington."

The great thing is to get the institution established in whatever way will secure the approval of the country.

With renewed thanks, I remain,

Very truly, yours,

ANDREW D. WHITE.
(*Ex-United States Minister to Germany and to Russia,*
Member of the Venezuelan Commission, etc.).

WASHINGTON, *October 2, 1895.*

DEAR SIR: Your communication of August 31 and accompanying papers were received on my recent return from Europe, and have been read with great interest.

The establishment of a national university in this District, for the purpose indicated by President Washington, and for the further objects required by the wonderful progress of science and art in our own times, has long been most earnestly desired by me.

It is hardly necessary, therefore, for me to assure you further that I may be counted among the friends of the proposition, leaving the defined plan for further consideration.

I am, sir, very respectfully, yours,

JOHN A. KASSON
(*Ex-Member of Congress from Iowa,*
Ex-United States Minister to Austria and to Germany, etc.).

NEW YORK CITY, *January 15, 1896.*

DEAR SIR: Your letter of 14th instant received. I note with pleasure the progress making with the national university bill. Without promising positively to attend in Washington on the 23d instant between 10 and 12 o'clock a. m., I will endeavor to come if I can manage to leave my affairs here, which require attention during these uncertain times.

Very truly, yours,
OSCAR S. STRAUSS
(*Late United States Minister to Turkey*).

DOUGHOREGAN, MD., *August 19, 1895.*

MY DEAR SIR: I duly received some days ago the papers you were good enough to send me relating to the establishment of a national university in Washington. I also received your letter asking me, as an official of the Society of the Sons of the Revolution, to sanction the use of my name as one of the committee of one hundred who indorse the "national university measure," etc. I have not given much thought to the subject, but am one of those who believe that we can never do too much in the way of universities and colleges for the education and accomplishment of our people. I am therefore frank to say to you that you are entirely welcome to the use of my name if it can be of any service to your cause.

I am, respectfully, etc.,
JOHN LEE CARROLL
(*General President Sons of the Revolution*).

NEW YORK, *October 24, 1895.*

DEAR SIR: I received your letter and have read with very much interest what you say in regard to the national university enterprise. I think the plan that you outline is a very good one.

Wishing you every success in the work to which you have given so much of your time and energy, I am,

Yours, truly,
HORACE PORTER
(*President-General Sons of American Revolution*).

NEW YORK, *November 26, 1895.*

DEAR SIR: I have just returned home to find your letters, and note what you say in regard to the meeting on Saturday, the 30th instant. I should be very glad to attend if I could, and would not allow anything but an imperative previous engagement to prevent my being with you. * * * Wishing you every success, and assuring you that I regret more than I can express having to absent myself from your meeting, I am,

Yours, truly,
HORACE PORTER
(*President-General Sons of American Revolution*).

EMBASSY OF THE UNITED STATES,
Rome, October 5, 1895.

MY DEAR SIR: I beg to acknowledge your favor of August 31, with its accompanying documents, and to say that I warmly sympathize with the efforts to establish a post-graduate university of the highest possible standard at Washington.

It is a noble work in which you are engaged, and I wish you every success in it.

When my mission here is ended, and I find I can in any way lend a helping hand, I will be glad to do so.

Sincerely, yours,
WAYNE MACVEAGH
(*Ambassador to Italy*).

LETTERS FROM COLLEGE AND UNIVERSITY PRESIDENTS.

[Alphabetically arranged by States.]

PRESIDENT'S OFFICE, UNIVERSITY OF ALABAMA,
University, Ala., November 5, 1895.

DEAR SIR: Your communication of recent date in reference to the establishment at Washington of a national post-graduate university is received. No greater stimulus could be given to the cause of higher education in the United States than the establishment of such an institution. I am heartily in favor of it.

Yours, truly,

RICHARD C. JONES,
President University of Alabama.

ALABAMA POLYTECHNIC INSTITUTE, A. & M. COLLEGE,
Auburn, Ala., October 26, 1894.

DEAR SIR: The subject is one in which for years I have been interested and strongly approved, provided it could be made free from political influences. I would be glad to receive the Memorial, etc., now, and will with pleasure write you my views.

Yours, respectfully, WM. LE ROY BROUN (*President*).

ALABAMA POLYTECHNIC INSTITUTE, A. & M. COLLEGE,
Auburn, Ala., December 29, 1894.

DEAR SIR: My interest, which has existed for years, in the proposed University of the United States, designed for graduate students and for those prepared to enter upon post-graduate courses of study, has been recently increased by a careful reading of the speeches of Senators Hunton and Vilas, and my hopes are now renewed that the university, so liberal in its conception and so far reaching in its possibilities, will in the near future be established.

In fact, the material the most valuable for the university already exists in the numerous institutions and collections, embracing varied branches of scientific work, now held by the Government at Washington City, as in the Congressional Library, the Naval Observatory, the Smithsonian Institution, the National Museum, the Office of the Coast and Geodetic Survey, and in many others. With such facilities for investigation and research made accessible to qualified students, under proper restrictions and under proper guidance, the university, organized as proposed in the bill, would prove of inestimable benefit, not only to America, but to the world at large, in the advancement of human knowledge that its existence would promote.

The subject has been fully presented and the argument made in the memorial and addresses referred to, and for the sake of science, of higher education, and expanded human learning it is hoped the result will be favorable and the university be established.

Very truly, yours, WM. LE ROY BROUN (*President*).

ALABAMA POLYTECHNIC INSTITUTE, A. & M. COLLEGE,
Auburn, Ala., April 15, 1895.

DEAR SIR: I beg to acknowledge the receipt of yours of April 10, relating to the University of the United States, in which you say the plan is to found a national committee of one hundred or more, in order more effectually to promote the interests of the university by securing influence for the proposed bill to be introduced next session, and asking consent to use my name as a member of said committee. This consent is cheerfully given, as I heartily approve of the organization of the university out of the abundant and splendid material already existing at the national capital, and will be glad to cooperate in any way in my power.

Yours, respectfully,

WM. LE ROY BROUN (*President*).

ALABAMA POLYTECHNIC INSTITUTE, A. & M. COLLEGE,
Auburn, Ala., October 24, 1895.

DEAR SIR: I concur with you in the plan you propose of having an "executive council" to take charge of all matters appertaining to the proposed national university, and heartily approve the appointment of the gentlemen named in your letter of October 16, or of others accessible to Washington whom you may see proper to appoint.

Wishing you success in this very important movement in behalf of higher education, I am, very respectfully, yours, etc.,

W. LE ROY BROUN (*President*)

SOUTHERN UNIVERSITY,
Greensboro, Ala., February 6, 1894.

DEAR SIR: I am heartily in favor of such an institution. It would, I believe, be a blessing to our country and to humanity. It would greatly stimulate higher education in all departments of life. It would tend to widen every species of intelligence and to infuse life and vigor into scientific and professional enterprises. Our own country and all the interests of our common humanity would be promoted and fostered by such a university.

Yours, truly,

A. S. ANDREWS (*President*).

OFFICE OF THE PRESIDENT,
LELAND STANFORD JUNIOR UNIVERSITY,
Palo Alto, Cal., October 31, 1894.

DEAR SIR: I am most heartily in favor of the establishment of a genuine national university in the city of Washington. Such an institution should not be a school for ordinary collegiate instruction, but a place for advanced research in all departments of science and liberal learning. The development of research is the essential work of the university. To this end the national capital, with its wealth of libraries and museums, offers advantages never to be found elsewhere in our country. These great advantages have never been in any high degree utilized. They can not be utilized except by placing them at the disposal of a body of investigators of various grades such as should compose the faculty and student body of a true university.

Of the multitude of schools called colleges and universities in America only a few are properly equipped for even the elementary work of the grade called collegiate. Not one is prepared to carry on advanced investigations of the character contemplated in the proposed national university. All schools which are capable of really good work are now carrying all that the limits of their endowments permit. The establishment of a national university would mean the setting of higher standards and more worthy ideals in all branches of higher education. It could enter into no rivalry with existing schools. Even should it do so, no harm would be done, for every improvement in aim or methods in one institution helps raise the plane of all others. A genuine university tends to make higher education respectable. Only the narrowest view of education would wish to hold students in existing institutions by preventing the existence of a better one.

The most valuable advance which the American people could take to mark the beginning of the new century would be the establishment of a national university.

Very truly, yours,

DAVID S. JORDAN (*President*).

OFFICE OF THE PRESIDENT,
LELAND STANFORD JUNIOR UNIVERSITY,
Stanford University, Cal., May 2, 1895.

DEAR SIR: By all means use my name where it will help the cause. Pardon the oversight in my former letter.

Very truly, yours,

DAVID T. JORDAN, *President.*

OFFICE OF THE PRESIDENT,
LELAND STANFORD JUNIOR UNIVERSITY,
Stanford University, Cal., November 22, 1895.

DEAR SIR: I have read over the statement of the bill for the national university as reported by the committee.

Senator Sherman's proposed amendment providing for an income for the present of $1,000,000 a year, for ten years, is better than to devote to the university the proceeds of the sale of land. In other words, it would seem better for the university to know exactly what its resources are.

The details in general seem to me to be wise, and the matters I have mentioned are not criticisms of any great importance. I may say that I wish you all success in this enterprise, for the passage of this bill would be the most important and momentous event in the history of this country since the war.

Very truly, yours,

DAVID T. JORDAN, *President.*

OFFICE OF THE PRESIDENT,
LELAND STANFORD JUNIOR UNIVERSITY,
Stanford University, Cal., December 10, 1895.

DEAR SIR: I am very much pleased with the wording of the bill for the national university, and I sincerely hope that it may pass just as it stands. At present no amendment occurs to me as desirable.

Very truly, yours,

DAVID T. JORDAN, *President.*

UNIVERSITY OF CALIFORNIA,
Berkeley, November 12, 1894.

DEAR SIR: I have not time at present to argue the matter of the national university which, of course, has its very attractive aspects. * * * If there is to be a national university, it should (as you intimate) bear to the existing universities and collegiate institutions a relation such as a university bears to the secondary schools. That is, it must be above them and far superior to them. * * *

Yours, truly,

MARTIN KELLOGG (*President*)

UNIVERSITY OF COLORADO,
Boulder, Col., December 31, 1894.

DEAR SIR: I believe a national university under the control of the United States Government is sure to be founded in a few years. Such an institution for the highest research would be the logical outcome of our free institutions and our public-school system. The elementary school for the district, the high school for the town or city, the university for the State, the national university for the country—the desirability of this plan of organization is almost too apparent to need argument.

The safe organization of society depends upon public control of our higher institutions of learning. In the coming time true progress must mean progress of the people as such—not of an exclusive class.

The national university should offer vast facilities for the profoundest research and should not interfere with the present functions of our State universities.

Very truly, yours,

JAMES H. BAKER *(President)*.

UNIVERSITY OF DENVER, CHANCELLOR'S ROOMS,
University Park, Colo., January 1, 1895.

MY DEAR FRIEND: I have only a moment in which to say, God bless you in your great work. I trust the measure may have abundant support and success.

Yours, cordially,

WM. F. MCDOWELL *(Chancellor)*.

COLORADO COLLEGE, PRESIDENT'S OFFICE,
Colorado Springs, Colo., December 26, 1894.

MY DEAR SIR: I will gladly cooperate in any way I can to help on the movement for establishing the University of the United States.

Sincerely, yours,

WILLIAM F. SLOCUM, JR. *(President)*.

TRINITY COLLEGE,
Hartford, Conn., January 10, 1895.

DEAR SIR: I thank you for the speeches of Senators Hunton and Vilas on the establishment of a national university, and, in common with those engaged in educational work, I feel much indebted to you for your persistent labors in the cause.

It seems strange that a Government which has been so lavish of funds in behalf of education should have been so long indifferent to providing for the proper completion of our educational system. We have prepared for such an institution, and we need its corps of professors and students in every branch of public service and in every industrial interest; and it seems hardly to comport with the dignity of so powerful and rich a nation to depend so largely upon private benefactions to provide those exceptional facilities for the highest grade of educational work which have been elsewhere recognized as the proper expression of national interest in the cause.

I trust that you will continue your efforts and be successful.

Faithfully, yours,

GEO. WILLIAMSON SMITH *(President)*.

TRINITY COLLEGE,
Hartford, Conn., April 15, 1895.

DEAR SIR: I regret that the bill for the establishment of the University of the United States failed to pass at the last session of Congress. I hope that the matter will be pushed in the next Congress to a successful issue.

Respectfully,

GEO. WILLIAMSON SMITH, **President.**

THE UNIVERSITY OF CHICAGO,
Chicago, September 6, 1892.

MY DEAR SIR: In reply to your favor of the 2d instant, I assure you that you may count me as one of the friends of the movement in behalf of the national university. I have always believed in such an institution, and will continue to believe in it. There is everything to be gained and nothing to be lost. I have read with much interest the summary and contents of your proposed report. I shall read the same with great interest.

I remain, yours, very truly,   WILLIAM R. HARPER (*President*).

THE UNIVERSITY OF CHICAGO,
Chicago, September 4, 1894.

MY DEAR SIR: Yours of August 24 has been received. I appreciate your kindness in sending me a copy of the Senate committee's report. The question is one of such importance and involves so much that one can not write with reference to it. I should be glad, however, some time while in the East, to talk the matter all over with you.

Wishing you great success, for I believe firmly in the enterprise, I remain, yours, very truly,
     WILLIAM R. HARPER (*President*).

THE UNIVERSITY OF CHICAGO,
Chicago, January 4, 1895.

MY DEAR SIR: Please accept my thanks for your favor of December 20. I rejoice with you in the onward movement of the proposition to establish the university of the United States. I sincerely hope that an early action of Congress on this bill may be secured. Whatever I can do to forward the movement will most gladly be done.

I remain yours, very truly,   WILLIAM R. HARPER (*President*).

THE UNIVERSITY OF CHICAGO,
Chicago, December 5, 1895.

MY DEAR SIR: Your letter of December 2 has been received. I am very much interested in its contents. I have read with much care the bill for the establishment of the University of the United States. I feel that there ought to be some organic connection between this university and other American institutions which deserve the name "university" and that the bill should contain a section which would make it possible for professors in other institutions to be detached to give instruction in Washington, that the list of universities thus connected in accordance with the above suggestion should be worked out very carefully and new universities admitted to the list only by the vote of those already in.

I question the wisdom of having the regents appointed by the concurrent resolution of the two Houses of Congress. I can not but believe that this would mean more or less political influence. Do you not think so?

I wish very much that I could spend a little time with you and talk these things over, but I do not see how it can be arranged.

Yours, very truly,   WILLIAM R. HARPER (*President*).

THE UNIVERSITY OF CHICAGO,
Chicago, December 14, 1895.

MY DEAR SIR: I have read with interest your letter of December 9, and am sure that it is moving along in the right direction. I wish I could be with you in Washington for a little while, but it seems to be out of the question.

Thanking you very heartily for you kindness in keeping me posted, and assuring you that I shall be glad to help you in any way, I remain, yours, truly,
     WILLIAM R. HARPER (*President*).

THE UNIVERSITY OF CHICAGO,
Chicago, December 19, 1895.

MY DEAR SIR: I am very glad to know that the change has been made in the plans for the national university of the United States. I hope that the matter may be pushed, and assure you that we shall be glad to do all that we can.

Yours, very truly,

WILLIAM R. HARPER (*President*).

UNIVERSITY OF ILLINOIS,
Champaign, February 12, 1892.

DEAR SIR: I shall be glad to do anything I can toward the founding by the Government of a great national university at Washington. You certainly may quote me as favorable to the enterprise.

Very truly, yours,

THOMAS J. BURRILL
(*Late Acting Regent*).

LOMBARD UNIVERSITY,
Galesburg, Ill., April 16, 1895.

DEAR SIR: I have only time to say that I am much interested in the project of establishing that university. I will do all for its success possible.

You are at liberty to use my name as you suggest.

Yours, truly,

J. V. N. STANDISH (*President*).

CARTHAGE COLLEGE,
Carthage, Ill., April 18, 1895.

DEAR SIR: In reply to your circular letter of 10th instant, concerning the use of my name in connection with the proposed bill for the establishment of the University of the United States, will say you herewith have permission to use my name in any legitimate way for the furtherance of the project. May success crown your efforts. Should I change my address I will notify you.

Very truly and fraternally, yours,

HOLMES DYSINGER (*President*).

LAKE FOREST UNIVERSITY,
Lake Forest, Ill., November 11, 1895.

MY DEAR SIR: I have your letter of October 31, in reference to the movement for the establishment of a national post-graduate university. If Congress can be induced to appropriate sufficient money for such a purpose it will meet the hearty approval of all interested in higher education. I imagine that the only reason that could be advanced against the movement is the doubt whether Congress would appropriate sufficient money to make such a university as would be commensurate with its name. Of course such a scheme in general meets my hearty approval, and from the list of names you have sent the matter seems to be in the hands of men who will not permit small ideas to prevail.

Yours, sincerely,

JOHN M. COULTER (*President*).

KNOX COLLEGE,
Galesburg, Ill., December 26, 1891.

DEAR GOVERNOR: I shall be greatly pleased to receive a copy of the forthcoming paper on a national university. It is a matter in which I have taken a lively interest for many years, and in furtherance of which I shall be glad to cooperate in every available manner.

I have the honor to remain, very truly, yours,

NEWTON BATEMAN,
President Knox College.

KNOX COLLEGE,
Galesburg, Ill., January 4, 1896

MY DEAR SIR: I shall be very glad and much honored to have my name added to the list recently received. I am in hearty sympathy with the movement. The delay in answering has been due to my absence from town.

Very truly, yours,

JOHN H. FINLEY (*President*).

LOMBARD UNIVERSITY,
Galesburg, Ill., January 21, 1895.

DEAR SIR: The report of which you speak has been received.

I am earnestly in favor of the national university. In my judgment it would be the crowning glory of our system of education. I have seen many of the educational institutions of the Old World, and I verily believe that our national university can be made the equal if not the superior of any one of them. Our present educational advantages, our wealth, and the spirit of our people demand such an institution. Let the youth of the Old World take a few lessons here upon our soil, and let our youth know that the best place to complete their education is at home. Give us, then, the national university.

Yours, truly,
J. V. N. STANDISH (*President*).

CARTHAGE COLLEGE,
Carthage, Ill., December 31, 1894.

MY DEAR SIR: In reply to your favor of December 20, would say that I am heartily in favor of the establishment of a national university at Washington to do postgraduate work solely. As to details of operation I have not had time enough to examine them in order to pronounce judgment.

Trusting, however, that the object you have in view will be realized, I am truly, yours,

HOLMES DYSINGER (*President*).

LINCOLN UNIVERSITY,
Lincoln, Ill., December 24, 1894.

DEAR SIR: The plan for the founding of a great national university has my unqualified indorsement and approval. I should esteem myself happy if by voice or pen I could contribute to the ultimate success of such a magnificent undertaking. Our young people would be glad to forego foreign study for the privilege of studying in such an institution as the University of the United States.

It goes without saying that the institution must be in every way worthy of our country and her scholarship.

Very cordially, yours,
A. E. TURNER (*President*).

THE UNIVERSITY OF INDIANA,
Bloomington, November 12, 1895.

DEAR SIR: I should very much like to see a national university of the very highest grade in Washington. It would be a fitting climax to our public-school system.

Very truly, yours,

JOSEPH SWAIN (*President*).

EARLHAM COLLEGE,
Richmond, Ind., January 6, 1896.

MY DEAR SIR: I have your valued letter of 4th instant. You are at liberty to use my name on the list of members of the national university committee.

Wishing you great and early success in your most worthy enterprise, I am, yours, cordially,

J. J. MILLS, *President.*

STATE UNIVERSITY OF IOWA,
Iowa City, Iowa, December 24, 1894.

MY DEAR SIR: I owe you an apology for not writing you long since on the subject of a national university, concerning which you did me the honor to ask my opinion. As to the main question, I am perfectly willing to admit that I was formerly opposed to the establishment of such an institution, but I am now firmly of the opinion that if we are to take the high stand in education to which we are justly entitled, the United States as a nation must establish such an institution. I believe it would have a most stimulating influence upon all of the machinery of education, and can only hope that the day will quickly come when the national university may be established. The matter has been so thoroughly discussed by others that it does not seem worth while for me to go into details, since there is very little that can be added to what has already been said. I can, however, assure you of my hearty sympathy with the movement, and trust that if I can in any way aid the cause you will call upon me for such assistance as I am able to give.

Very cordially and sincerely, yours,

CHARLES A. SCHAEFFER (*President*).

STATE UNIVERSITY OF IOWA,
Iowa City, Iowa, April 16, 1895.

DEAR SIR: I beg to acknowledge the receipt of your communication of April 10, and shall be very glad to serve as a member of the committee of one hundred in the interest of the national university. I shall be very happy to do all I can to assist the movement.

Very respectfully, yours, CHARLES A. SCHAEFFER (*President*).

STATE UNIVERSITY OF IOWA,
Iowa City, Iowa, November 8, 1895.

DEAR SIR: I have the honor to acknowledge the receipt of your communication of October 16, and beg to thank you for informing me of the present situation of the project for establishing a national university.

So far as I am concerned, I shall be very glad to do anything in my power to help the cause along, and beg that you will consider me at your service if it is possible to use me in any way.

Your plan of establishing a council seems to be a very good one, and I sincerely trust that the council will be able to advance the interests of the university during the coming session of Congress.

Very sincerely, yours, CHARLES A. SCHAEFFER (*President*).

PARSONS COLLEGE,
Fairfield, Iowa, February 23, 1895.

DEAR SIR: I am heartily in favor of a national university at Washington for original investigation and post-graduate work, provided it be so organized as to aid and not to hamper other institutions for the higher education devoted to undergraduate work.

Yours, very truly, AMBROSE C. SMITH (*President*).

WESTERN COLLEGE,
Toledo, Iowa, April 19, 1895.

DEAR SIR: In reply to yours of recent date, will say that I heartily approve of the founding of a University of the United States, and am willing that my name and influence be used in such ways as you may see best for the furtherance of this important project.

Very truly, yours, L. BOOKWALTER (*President*).

WESTERN COLLEGE,
Toledo, Iowa, October 29, 1895.

DEAR SIR: Yours of the 26th is at hand, and in reply will say that I heartily approve of the plan you have outlined, favoring the council and approving of the men named to constitute it.

I shall be glad to aid this movement, and will write to our Representative in relation to this important matter.

Yours, truly,

L. BOOKWALTER (*President*).

UNIVERSITY OF THE NORTHWEST,
Sioux City, Iowa, January 30, 1895.

DEAR SIR: I have received the summary of contents of your paper, "A national university." I desire to say that I have been friendly to the enterprise of a national university, and my sentiment on that question is stronger than it has ever been. A national university would be a crown of glory to this great and enlightened nation—a nation distinguished for its educational advancement. The termination of all the institutions, from the smallest public school to the university, ought to be a national university commensurate with our enterprise, our civilization, and our wealth.

I remain, very truly, yours,

J. C. GILCHRIST (*President*).

IOWA COLLEGE,
Grinnell, Iowa, January 2, 1895.

MY DEAR SIR: I have examined the printed matter you kindly sent me concerning the establishment of the University of the United States. Please count me an unmodified believer in that institution. After reading the large number of strong indorsements which are printed in connection with the speeches of Messrs. Hunton and Vilas, I deem it unnecessary for me to add anything by way of argument or reason for my own views.

Sincerely, yours,

GEORGE A. GATES (*President*).

IOWA COLLEGE,
Grinnell, Iowa, April 17, 1895.

MY DEAR SIR: I shall consider it an honor to be counted among the friends of the proposed national-university scheme, to the extent of accepting appointment on the committee you name in your letter of April 10.

Very truly, yours,

GEORGE A. GATES (*President*).

THE UNIVERSITY OF KANSAS,
Lawrence, November 7, 1895.

MY DEAR SIR: Yours of the 28th ultimo is at hand. Please accept my most hearty indorsement of the plan for a great national university at Washington. I trust that the National Congress will soon make this university an actuality and place it upon a basis which will receive the respect of the educational world.

Yours, sincerely,

F. H. SNOW, *Chancellor.*

OTTAWA UNIVERSITY,
Ottawa, Kans., December 13, 1895.

MY DEAR SIR: I am in entire sympathy with the effort to establish a national university at Washington, and shall be glad to aid in any way possible the establishment of such an institution.

Yours, very truly,

F. W. COLEGROVE (*President*)

WASHBURN COLLEGE,
Topeka, Kans., January 1, 1894.

DEAR SIR: Your favor of the 20th ultimo is received. The effort to found and build up a national university at the capital of the nation meets my heartiest approval. Educationally, it is the great thing to do. The foundations of large scientific facilities are already laid. Why not unify these constantly enlarging endowments in name and superstructure?

Yours, truly, PETER MCVICAR, *President.*

WASHBURN COLLEGE,
Topeka, Kans., April 25, 1895.

DEAR SIR: Your favor of the 10th was duly received. I regret that I can not now accept your kind invitation to become a member of the committee. I believe thoroughly in the feasibility and demand in the founding by the Government of a national university.

Have you data showing what the nation has already at Washington as constituent departments to form a university? A statement as to the foundations already laid and the resources already secured for such a university, if founded, would throw light far and wide and stimulate Congress to action. Have you printed showings of such statistics? If so, I would be glad to get them and use them, perhaps, through the press in the furtherance of the object. I take it that we have already the elements of a great university.

Yours, very truly, PETER MCVICAR (*President*).

KENTUCKY UNIVERSITY,
Lexington, Ky., April 20, 1893.

DEAR SIR: I have received your letter of the 17th instant, and have read it with much interest.

A good while ago I received your memorial and then read it carefully with more than ordinary attention. It is a document of unusual force; its arguments and conclusions struck me with deep conviction. I do not see how any just objection can be urged against the noble aim you so earnestly advocate.

Were it necessary, as it is not, I could go into the particular reasons that support so necessary and so grand an enterprise; your memorial makes all this unnecessary.

Such an institution as your memorial contemplates we need, and we have not. I am fully aware of the doubts and distrusts its establishment by the nation can excite; there is no great enterprise like this that is free from such misgivings and real difficulties. These will have to be looked for and met. Nothing is without its weak points.

The people of this great nation will always need, and want, a host of higher institutions of learning—denominational, State, local—and will always create and sustain them. A national university will not stand in the way of their existence or prosperity; it will not satisfy the want these supply.

Very respectfully, your friend,

CHAS. LOUIS LOOS (*President*).

KENTUCKY UNIVERSITY,
Lexington, Ky., October 31, 1894.

DEAR SIR: The documents you sent me some weeks ago, I think, in the main, so far as I can judge, set forth the right conception of the object in view.

You are advocating a good cause, which I hope will ere long succeed. I trust in the midst of so many other interests just now or at any time engaging the attention of Congress, this noble enterprise will not fail of sufficient friends in and out of that body to give it the support necessary to carry it to victory.

As ever, your friend,

CHAS. LOUIS LOOS (*President*).

KENTUCKY UNIVERSITY,
Lexington, Ky., April 15, 1895.

DEAR SIR: Your letter, of much interest to me, just been received. You have permission to use my name as you desire. I hope you will be successful in the next Congress in pushing this most laudable enterprise through to success.

As ever, very respectfully, your friend,

CHAS. LOUIS LOOS (*President*).

KENTUCKY UNIVERSITY,
Lexington, Ky., November 1, 1895.

DEAR SIR: Yours of October 21 came duly to hand in my absence. I have looked carefully over your plan and can not but approve it.

The nation ought to have such an institution, unbound and unembarrassed by denominational limits and control, and the presence of the two denominational universities is not in the way of the university proposed.

As ever, your friend and well-wisher,

CHAS. LOUIS LOOS (*President*).

KENTUCKY UNIVERSITY,
Lexington, Ky., October 17, 1895.

MY DEAR SIR: The more I contemplate the grandeur of the national-university project, and the great benefit resulting therefrom to our people by its establishment, I become the more enthusiastic in the advocacy of it.

Sincerely, WILBUR R. SMITH.

KENTUCKY UNIVERSITY,
Lexington, Ky., December 13, 1895.

MY FRIEND: Your kind letter was received a few days since. Secretary Goode sent me a copy of the bill as agreed upon by the revisory board, which I think good. I would have been glad to see an appropriation of a few million dollars inserted in section 12.

I am quite anxious to hear of Wednesday's meeting. Hope the bill will be intrusted to a committee in the Senate and House that will be its enthusiastic friends and that it may soon be brought to a successful issue.

Sincerely, yours, WILBUR R. SMITH.

OGDEN COLLEGE,
Bowling Green, Ky., January 5, 1895.

DEAR SIR: I have the honor to acknowledge the receipt of yours of December 20, and also of a copy of the speeches of Senators Hunton and Vilas, in regard to the establishment by the Government of a national university for post-graduate students.

In answer I beg leave to say that I have long advocated this project, and that I am heartily in favor of the bill now pending in the United States Senate.

An experience of twenty-three years as an educator enables me to realize fully the need in our country of an institution of learning with such equipment and facilities that students may pursue in it the same lines of original research and obtain the same high order of intellectual training as in the best universities of the Old World.

With its extensive libraries, its scientific bureaus, observatories, museums, and laboratories, and with all the executive departments of the Government, it seems to me that the city of Washington is preeminently the best location we have for a great national university.

Our Government maintains at West Point and Annapolis academies in which young men intended for the Army and the Navy are thoroughly trained in all that pertains to the science of war. Why should it not establish and maintain also a great university where may be thoroughly studied all that pertains to peace?

Grave social and political problems are now confronting us. To deal with them successfully we need the ripest scholarship, the deepest investigation, and the purest statesmanship. The principles of our Government are, I dare say, the best the world has ever known. But their character is such that the safety of the Government, the preservation of our liberties, and the working out of the great destiny before us depend upon the intelligence of the people.

As a means of increasing this intelligence, I believe the establishment and maintenance by the Government of a national university at Washington would yield larger and more valuable returns in proportion to the annual amounts expended, and conduce more to the general welfare of the people, than anything else the Government could undertake for a like expenditure. As a matter of fact, the resulting benefits would transcend the power of measurement by any money standard.

A great national university like the one proposed would be able to send thoroughly trained professors and lecturers to our higher institutions of learning, and these in turn would prepare better trained teachers for lower schools, and so on to the lowest, until our whole system of education would be vastly improved from the top downward.

Wishing the bill a speedy success, I have the honor to be,

Very truly, yours,

WM. A. OBENCHAIN,
President Ogden College.

OGDEN COLLEGE,
Bowling Green, Ky., April 15, 1895.

DEAR SIR: In answer to yours of the 10th instant, I am, as you well know, a strong advocate of the establishment by the Government of a national university, as set forth in Senate bill 1708 of the Fifty-third Congress. Not only, therefore, are you at liberty to use my name as requested in your letter of the 10th instant, but I shall be glad to do all in my power to further the cause.

Very truly, yours,

WM. A. OBENCHAIN.

BETHEL COLLEGE,
Russellville, Ky., January 1, 1894.

DEAR SIR: I am in receipt of your favor of December 20, 1894, as well as of the copy of speeches by Senators Hunton, of Virginia, and Vilas, of Wisconsin. Please accept thanks for them. I shall place them in the college library along with other valuable papers on education.

I am heartily in favor of the movement for establishing a national university, whatever may be its name.

(1) Because we shall be most likely in this way to have at least one real university more complete than we have now. I have entertained serious doubts if the spirit of denominational conservatism in education is compatible with the true university. I do not mean the sectarian spirit, which, of course, must be eliminated from any denominational university, so called; but that the function of the denominational school is simply that of mental training and moral discipline under positive religious influences, themselves not necessarily sectarian. The university idea must be entirely independent of all strictly denominational bias, as much so as the professions or trades, which are the special beneficiaries of the university plan.

(2) The tendency to a uniform standard of scholarship, as preparatory to university work, will be greatly strengthened. It may be, also, that the standard will be elevated, the requirements becoming more severe as the character and necessity of the university work become more clearly defined. But both these are very desirable results.

(3) The hope of a distinctively American scholarship, reputable, solid, influential, may very reasonably be found in the establishing of such an institution, and this certainly is a hope worthy of any patriot. So much the better if it shall be specifically national and not inferior to that of England, Scotland, or the Continent. It seems strange that one has to go to Germany to study English in a really scientific way. It would seem, at least, that our students might find the best of reasons for staying at home to study their mother tongue, as well as the institutions and sciences in which, as citizens of the United States, we find ourselves most interested.

(4) I must be allowed to add that I find also a hope that in this difference, yet to be made clear, between colleges and universities, there will be a manifest destiny for colleges, a specific demand for their specific work, as well as for the more thorough elementary work in all grades leading to the university.

Wishing you the greatest success with your bill, I have the honor to be,

Yours, respectfully,

W. S. RYLAND, *President.*

LOUISIANA STATE UNIVERSITY AND
AGRICULTURAL AND MECHANICAL COLLEGE,
Baton Rouge, La., April 21, 1893.

MY DEAR SIR: I am in receipt of your favor of the 17th instant, with inclosures of memorial in regard to a national university and Senate bill.

Without entering into details, suffice it to say that in my humble judgment the scheme of a national university, as outlined in your memorial, is eminently a move in the right direction, and has my unqualified indorsement. I will be pleased to serve as a member of the association which has this laudable object in view.

Very respectfully,

J. W. NICHOLSON, *President.*

LELAND UNIVERSITY,
New Orleans, January 7, 1896.

MY DEAR SIR: Your note of the 4th instant came duly, asking permission to place my name on the list of those who favor the establishment of a national university at Washington. Although I do not see how my name can add anything to the illustrious array already presented, yet as I do accord with them in opinion I see no reason why I should not very cheerfully consent; and I remain, with esteem,

Yours, very truly,

EDWD. C. MITCHELL.

STRAIGHT UNIVERSITY,
New Orleans, La., November 13, 1895.

DEAR SIR: In reply to your letter of recent date I take pleasure in saying that I am most heartily in favor of a post-graduate university in Washington.

Yours, sincerely,

OSCAR ATWOOD,
President Straight University.

THE MAINE STATE COLLEGE,
Orono, Me., January 20, 1896.

DEAR SIR: Your letter of January 4 has awaited my return to Orono. I shall be pleased to have my name added to your committee. What are the chances of success? I shall be pleased to render such assistance as I can.

Yours, very truly,

A. W. HARRIS (*President*).

COLBY UNIVERSITY, *Waterville, Me., December 27, 1894.*
DEAR SIR: Your favor of the 20th is received. I am strongly in favor of a national university for graduate work. It seems as if the country owed it to itself to establish such an institution upon a scale in keeping with the greatness of our national life.
Ever truly, yours,
B. L. WHITMAN,
(*Now President of Columbian University, District of Columbia.*)

INDIANAPOLIS, *November 9, 1895.*
DEAR SIR: I regret exceedingly that so long a time has elapsed since the date of your communication to me regarding the establishment of a national post-graduate university at Washington. In explanation of this delay, I beg to say that I have been almost constantly away from home during that time. I hasten now to say that I shall be very glad to have you add my name to the list of those who indorse the national university measure.
With sincere regards, I am, faithfully, yours,
NATHL. BUTLER,
President Colby University, Waterville, Me.

JOHNS HOPKINS UNIVERSITY, OFFICE OF THE PRESIDENT,
Baltimore, January 4, 1893.
DEAR SIR: I thank you for allowing me to see the draft of the bill for a national university, which I return immediately in accordance with your request. * * *
The bill appears to me to be drawn with great care and to avoid most of the difficulties which are inherent in a project of such magnitude. * * * The real province of the university, as it seems to me, should be to provide special facilities for study and work to properly qualified persons, whatever may be their academic standing, especially in connection with the great foundations now gathered and likely to be increased in the national capital.
Yours, very truly,
D. C. GILMAN.

JOHNS HOPKINS UNIVERSITY, *Baltimore, April 16, 1895.*
DEAR SIR: Your note of April 15 reaches me this morning.
I firmly believe that a national university will be established in Washington, and I hope to see it founded upon such principles and with such funds that it will support all other agencies for the advancement of superior education.
Yours, very truly,
D. C. GILMAN, *President.*

TUFTS COLLEGE, MASS., *November 5, 1895.*
MY DEAR SIR: It seems to me that Washington affords unusual advantages for a great national university, and if such an establishment can be properly sustained it will be of incalculable benefit to education, not only in the United States, but throughout the world.
Very truly, yours,
E. H. CAPEN (*President*).

SMITH COLLEGE, NORTHAMPTON, MASS., *October 3, 1895.*
DEAR SIR: The establishment of a national university at Washington, for reasons which have been already stated in the memorial presented to Congress, deserves, in my judgment, the cordial support of all who are interested in popular education and in the advancement of learning.
L. CLARK SEELYE (*President*).

WORCESTER POLYTECHNIC INSTITUTE, *Worcester, Mass., March, 1896.*
DEAR SIR: I wish you to understand that I am thoroughly interested in the success of this movement, and am desirous of being called upon to assist in every way in my power.
I am, yours, faithfully,
T. C. MENDENHALL (*President*).

UNIVERSITY OF MICHIGAN,
Ann Arbor, November 29, 1894.

DEAR SIR: Washington has large facilities to aid in carrying on the work of a genuine university. The libraries, museums, and laboratories, which are in the main under the control of the Government, and the large number of learned men employed in them, could be made of service in such an institution.

The purpose to take up Washington's idea of establishing a great national university at our capital, on a plan comparable to that of the German universities, appeals to our patriotism and our pride, and must commend itself to many if it can be made clear that it will be adequately supported and will be unembarrassed by the interference of political partisans. The plan, before adoption, should be carefully matured and thoughtfully guarded against perils by the conference of able statesmen and men experienced in university administration.

Yours, very truly,   JAMES B. ANGELL
(President University of Michigan).

UNIVERSITY OF MICHIGAN,
Ann Arbor, October 26, 1895.

MY DEAR DOCTOR: Your zeal seems to be unquenchable in spite of all the discouragements and delays to which you are subjected. In reply to your inquiry of October 16, I would say that it seems to me the plan you suggest is the wisest practicable one. The council should be made up of men near enough to Washington to get together. It would be useless to attempt to give it weight by putting on men in remote parts of the country, who could not meet for consultation. I heartily approve of the suggestion.

Yours, truly,   JAMES B. ANGELL.

THE UNIVERSITY OF MINNESOTA,
Minneapolis, November 2, 1894.

DEAR SIR: I take the first opportunity to acknowledge the receipt of yours of October and the memorial in regard to a national university. I need not attempt to formulate the reasons why a national university at Washington, supported by the General Government for the benefit of the whole country, is desirable. These reasons have been clearly stated by others again and again. I can only say that in the interest of the highest education, it seems to me that such an institution ought to be established at the national capital. It ought to take up work where other universities in the country practically leave off. For this work of original investigation and study no place is better than Washington, and no university in the world ought to be better than ours at Washington.

Very truly, yours,   CYRUS NORTHROP *(President).*

THE UNIVERSITY OF MINNESOTA,
Minneapolis, April 17, 1895.

MY DEAR SIR: I have received your letter of April 10, in which you ask for permission to use my name as one of the national committee of one hundred. You are at liberty to use my name in the manner suggested, if it shall seem best to you to do so.

Very truly, yours,   CYRUS NORTHROP *(President).*

THE UNIVERSITY OF MINNESOTA,
Minneapolis, October 22, 1895.

DEAR SIR: Your circular letter of October 15 was received yesterday. I take pleasure in saying that a council constituted as you propose would be exceedingly helpful to the cause, and that the gentlemen named by you as members of the executive council meet my hearty approval.

Very truly, yours,   CYRUS NORTHROP *(President).*

CARLETON COLLEGE,
Northfield, Minn., February 29, 1896.

MY DEAR SIR: There is no danger whatsoever of our doing too much for education, but there is great danger that Congress will adopt a narrow or niggardly policy, under the plea of a necessary economy, and so fail to provide an institution worthy of our opportunities and worthy of our great nation.

Wishing you abundant success, I remain,
Very cordially, yours,   JAS. W. STRONG (*President*).

UNIVERSITY OF MISSISSIPPI,
University, Miss., January 4, 1895.

DEAR SIR: I was away from home last summer and could not then reply to your letter regarding the proposed university of the United States.

The plan proposed seems to be free from most of the objections that would have weight against the general proposition to establish a national university. Undoubtedly such an institution, if so organized and managed as to have its functions entirely outside of those of the State and other universities, could be made the grand capstone in our educational system. Its establishment would be a fitting monument to the wisdom of the founders of our Government who so well recognized the necessity of education to the preservation of our institutions, as well as to the great advances of the closing century. It should be so ordered that its usefulness shall evidently depend upon the quality of the work done in its halls and laboratories, rather than upon the number of its matriculates. Properly regulated, I see no reason why it should not prove a stimulus to all the best colleges in the country. Would it not be well to ingraft the idea of offering a scholarship to every State university and other reputable institutions?

I expect to be in Washington next week on educational business and hope to see you personally.

Yours, very truly,   R. B. FULTON, *Chancellor*.

MISSISSIPPI AGRICULTURAL AND MECHANICAL COLLEGE,
Agricultural College, Miss., November 8, 1895.

DEAR SIR: I heartily approve of all efforts being made for the establishment of a national postgraduate university of the highest character, at the seat of Government in Washington, to furnish facilities for study to students who now have to seek such knowledge in Europe. I deem such an institution necessary to complete the American system of education.

Yours, truly,   S. D. LEE (*President*).

UNIVERSITY OF THE STATE OF MISSOURI,
Columbia, April 18, 1895.

MY DEAR SIR: I have read with interest your letter of April 10, and I should be glad to aid the good cause with the use of my name on the national committee or in any other way.

With kind wishes, I am,
Very truly, yours,   R. H. JESSE (*President*).

UNIVERSITY OF THE STATE OF MISSOURI.
Columbia, October 22, 1895.

DEAR SIR: I have read with interest your letter of October 16. Your views in reference to the formation of an executive council, consisting of such men as you name, seem to me to be wise. If I can help you at any time, I shall be glad to do so.

With kind wishes, I am, very truly, yours,
    R. H. JESSE (*President*).

UNIVERSITY OF THE STATE OF MISSOURI,
Columbia, October 26, 1894.

DEAR SIR: I received some time ago a copy of your memorial concerning a "national university," and I have been intending to write you a letter on the subject, but the coveted opportunity for doing so has not yet appeared.

I am heartily in favor of the establishment of a national university, provided that it be built on the right lines and be adequately supported. It should do nothing but post-graduate work, and much care should be exercised on this point. It should also sustain certain relations to the State universities in the different States. This last point I hold to be of much importance. It carries out in education the general idea of our system of government.

The management of the national university should be separated from politics in every way. Too great care can not be exercised on this point. Another point of less importance, but worth mentioning, is that the management of the university should involve but few persons ex officio. But it is impossible to say more now than that I am very heartily in favor of establishing a national university separate from politics, to be built on proper lines for post-graduate work only, and to be adequately supported by the National Government.

With kind wishes, I am, very truly, yours,

R. H. JESSE (*President*).

WILLIAM JEWELL COLLEGE,
Liberty, Mo., December 26, 1894.

DEAR SIR: Your letter came, and also the report and speeches by Senators Hunton and Vilas. I had heard something of the effort that was being made to establish in Washington the University of the United States. I am greatly in favor of the university. It would offer rare opportunities for post-graduate work. Of course much will depend upon the plan, courses of study, etc.

If the university is not put upon a very high plane of work, it will not meet the approval of our best educators. I think that it should be of such a high grade that graduates of our other universities and of foreign universities would find it to their advantage to pursue a course of study in it.

But I am sure that the university could be properly organized through consultation of our many learned and experienced educators. Let me say again that I favor the bill, and hope that we shall have the university before many years pass away.

Yours, very truly,

J. P. GREENE (*President*).

WILLIAM JEWELL COLLEGE,
Liberty, Mo., April 18, 1895.

DEAR SIR: Yours of the 10th came in due time. Yes; you may use my name if you think that I can be of any service to the "National University." And please take the liberty of omitting my name if you think that someone else will do you better service in my place.

Very truly,

J. P. GREENE (*President*).

NEVADA STATE UNIVERSITY,
Reno, Nev., June 27, 1895.

DEAR SIR: I have in hand your letter of April 10, 1895, with inclosure, setting forth the advisability of establishing a national university at Washington, D. C., and, furthermore, the plans for pressing the matter upon the attention of Congress at its next session.

I concur in the view that a national university, established by the Government, would be a fitting keystone to the educational arch made up of the State universities, which have been largely established and strongly promoted by the General Government.

I shall be pleased to cooperate with you in securing the necessary legislation.

I have the honor to remain, very truly, yours,

J. E. STUBBS, *President.*

UNIVERSITY OF NEBRASKA, EXECUTIVE OFFICE,
Lincoln, October 23, 1894.

DEAR SIR: I recall receiving and reading with interest the printed matter you sent me during the summer, but do not recall any request for an expression of my opinion in this matter.

We are still in the midst of settling the university for the year, and it is a great task because of the enormous and unexpected increase in numbers without a corresponding increase in revenues. It is therefore quite impossible for me to say more than that I heartily favor the general plan of a national university for post-graduate work. It should stand in exactly the same relations to the great and public free-school systems of each State as the State university now occupies with regard to the separate State systems. It would give a great stimulus to higher education in every direction, and would add a desirable uniformity (by which I do not mean absolute identity) to all school work.

I am sorry I can not say more, but I certainly would not be content to say less.

Cordially, yours,

JAMES H. CANFIELD (*Chancellor*).

UNIVERSITY OF NEBRASKA,
Lincoln, November 18, 1895.

DEAR SIR: I am in receipt of your letter of November 4, accompanied by the partial list of distinguished citizens, etc. For years I have been a believer in the desirability of the establishment of the University of the United States at Washington. You may, therefore, add my name to your list. I shall be happy to be kept informed of the progress of the agitation and to contribute, if I may, to its success.

Believe me, very truly, yours,

GEORGE E. MACLEAN (*President*).

PRESIDENT'S ROOMS, CORNELL UNIVERSITY,
Ithaca, N. Y., October 22, 1894.

DEAR SIR: I am heartily in favor of the project of establishing a national university at the Federal capital, to be maintained by the Federal Government and controlled by a board which it shall appoint. Such an institution would not interfere with or rival any existing educational agencies. It would be an institution not for undergraduates, but for graduates; an institution not [primarily] for instruction, but for the conduct of original research and investigation, and for the expansion of the boundaries of human knowledge.

I need not dwell upon the vast and valuable equipment which the Federal Government already possesses for such an institution in the city of Washington. There we have $30,000,000 worth of books, specimens, apparatus, and other appliances either belonging to the Government or under its control, and the Government is spending annually $4,000,000 to maintain and enlarge these collections. The scientific bureaus; the Agricultural Bureau, with its meteorological, zoological, and other divisions; the Navy Department, with its engineering appliances; the Congressional Library, the largest on the continent; the great National Museum; the Smithsonian Institution; the various astronomical appliances and equipments—these all only await organization to supply the equipment which a university devoted to research and investigation absolutely needs.

While it will be admitted that we have the facilities, it will be asked whether it is our national duty to establish such a university. Replying to this question, I take the highest moral ground and assert that it is our duty to minister to our civilization and to increase those intellectual and ideal goods which constitute its imperishable essence. I am unwilling to say that this great free Republic has no other mission than to accumulate wealth and to add to the material comforts and conveniences of the race. The glory of a nation is not its wealth or its territory, but rather its knowledge and its virtue. Virtue the state can not directly undertake to produce or to increase. But knowledge the Republic can increase by organizing facilities which already exist in the city of Washington.

The greatest of our statesmen, from Washington down, have favored the scheme of establishing a national university. The Father of his Country left a portion of his property as a partial endowment of such an institution; Jefferson and Madison and the two Adamses recommended it. This idea has run through our history from the beginning till now; furthermore, the reasons given by Washington remain substantially sound, even to this day. He did not, it is true, insist on the duty of a great nation to enlarge the stock of existing knowledge and contribute its share to the civilization of the race, but he did insist on the importance of the maintenance of higher learning among us; he did feel, with his successors, that if the new Republic was to take a prominent place among the nations of the world it could be only by "exalted intellect," to use the phrase which occurs in a report made by a committee of Congress on this subject. President Washington pointed out that such a university would also tend to allay sectional feeling and promote a sense of harmony and solidarity throughout our great Republic. Though railways and telegraphs have been perhaps a more effectual agency in bringing about this end than even the establishment of a national university would have been, yet all will admit that the presence in a Federal capital of scholars and scientists who are drawn from all parts of the country, and are afterwards to be leaders in their own spheres, would have a most potent influence in developing this sense of harmony and solidarity on which Washington, after the importance of learning, laid the greatest stress.

Think of the effect of such an institution in kindling patriotism and loyalty and awakening public spirit among educated men, and through them among all classes of the community. I recall the glorious description which Thucydides gives of Athens at the time of the Peloponnesian war. He explains why the Athenians have shown such spirit, why they are so proud of their country, and are sacrificing their lives to support her. Foremost of all the incentives to patriotism he places the ideal goods of art and science and literature and philosophy which Greece, and Athens especially, had contributed to the world. I hope this Republic of ours, the largest the world has yet seen, will some day equal the smallest in its service to higher civilization. Animated by this sense of national vocation, I believe most heartily in the establishment at Washington, under the auspices and with the support of the Federal Government, of a national university devoted, not to the teaching of undergraduates, but, first, to the guidance of graduates in research and investigation, and, secondly, to the enlargement of learning and scholarship, the progress of art, science, and philosophy, the elevation of professional and industrial pursuits, and, in a word, the promotion of civilization and the best interests of humanity.

Truly, yours,

J. G. SCHURMAN (*President*).

CORNELL UNIVERSITY,
Ithaca, N. Y., September 4, 1894.

DEAR SIR: I am perfectly in accord with you as regards the character of the proposed University of the United States. It should not come into competition with existing institutions; its aim should be original investigation and the enlargement of human knowledge. It should utilize the vast collections at Washington, and it should have fellowship by which men of genius would be enabled to devote all their time to investigation and research.

I could scarcely come to Washington to attend the conference of educators interested in the project which you suggest, but if it were held at a time when I happened to be there I should certainly desire to attend.

Very truly, yours,

J. G. SCHURMAN (*President*).

CORNELL UNIVERSITY,
Ithaca, N. Y., April 16, 1895.

DEAR SIR: I am in receipt of yours of the 10th instant and am much gratified to learn that the gentlemen who have had charge of the national university bill are enlarging the organization of workers and planning a new campaign for the coming year. I believe very strongly in the project of a national university at Washington. The resources of the people of the United States concentrated at that one point are running shamefully to waste for want of specialists to utilize them in the cause of original research and for the enlargement of human knowledge. It is, therefore, with peculiar satisfaction that I hail the announcement of your new plans and bid you a Godspeed in the work to which you have so loyally devoted yourself.

I shall consider it an honor to have, as you suggest, my name on the roll with those who are working for the national university, and I shall be glad to serve the cause whenever it lies in my power.

Very truly, yours,

J. G. SCHURMAN (*President*).

CORNELL UNIVERSITY,
Ithaca, N. Y., December 9, 1895.

DEAR MR. HOYT: I am in receipt of your letter and inclosed letter to ex-President White, which I have read and forwarded. I have also read the draft of the proposed bill to the United States. I think you are right in not making the regulations too specific and detailed. The discipline of the university should be in the hands of the respective faculties, at the head of which you properly place a dean. When, therefore, it is said in section 5 that the academic council shall be charged with the "planning and direction of instruction and discipline," I take that to mean that the council will prescribe statutes and by-laws, in accordance with which the discipline shall be administered by the faculties. If the phrase means more than that, I should consider the policy a mistaken one. The best judges of the instruction and discipline in any faculty are the members of that faculty; and it seems to me of prime importance that the advantage of their special expertness in this direction should not be lost to the university.

Section 6 throws the university open to all who are competent to profit by its instruction. I think that wise. But I think it ought to be specifically stated that elementary instruction would not be given at the university, and that it was, as defined in section 4, "purely a post-graduate university of the highest type."

With best wishes for the good cause, I remain, very sincerely, yours,

J. G. SCHURMAN (*President*).

ELMIRA COLLEGE,
Elmira, N. Y., November 1, 1894.

DEAR SIR: Replying to your card of recent date, would say that I failed to receive anything from you during the month of August. This was due, possibly, to my absence from home during the summer. I trust your efforts for the establishment of a national university will meet with the success they deserve.

Cordially yours,

RUFUS S. GREEN (*President*).

UNIVERSITY OF THE CITY OF NEW YORK,
University Heights, New York City, November 4, 1895.

DEAR SIR: The third end which you name to be accomplished by a national university, to wit, coordinating and strengthening of the higher schools of our country, is so necessary that I shall favor the establishment of a university at Washington, if it be given means that will enable it to undertake hopefully the achievement of this desirable result.

The other objects proposed for the university are very worthy, but this point which can be attempted from no point so well as from our capital, especially recommends itself to my mind.

Very truly, yours,
H. M. MACCRACKEN
(*Chancellor*).

COLUMBIA COLLEGE, IN THE CITY OF NEW YORK,
November 8, 1894.

MY DEAR SIR: Your letter of November 6 reached me in due course, and later the pamphlet to which you allude. There is undoubtedly very much to be said in favor of a national university at Washington. Something, perhaps, would depend upon its organization and its relation to other institutions of the higher learning.

Yours, faithfully,
SETH LOW (*President*).

UNIVERSITY OF ROCHESTER,
Rochester, N. Y., February 5, 1895.

DEAR SIR: I have carefully examined the documents which you have kindly sent me, relating to the Senate bill to establish a university of the United States. Personally, I am in favor of a national university. I hope if this enterprise is undertaken that it will be so generously provided for, both for the beginning and for the whole future, that there will be no solicitude regarding its development. If confined exclusively to work of the highest character and amply provided for, there is certainly room in our country for such an institution as is proposed, but any attempt merely to duplicate existing institutions is to be deprecated as a further division of patronage and public interest.

Very respectfully, yours,
DAVID J. HILL (*President*).

UNIVERSITY OF ROCHESTER,
Rochester, N. Y., October 29, 1895.

DEAR SIR: I have just received your personal letter of October 26, and the accompanying documents relating to the proposed national university. I thank you for the information as to the progress the enterprise has thus far made. The more I have reflected upon it the more deeply I am convinced that the founding of a national university at Washington in the near future would have an important and salutary influence upon the nation. The merely denominational enterprises can never accomplish the work that is needed, and in my opinion tend rather to interfere with it.

You have my heartiest sympathy in your strenuous efforts to secure the passage of an act establishing a national university. I am personally well acquainted with our Representative in Congress and with many others throughout the State and country, and shall take pleasure in pressing the claims of the enterprise upon them to the extent of my ability. Any service that I can render in this or any other direction for the promotion of the enterprise will be at your command.

Very sincerely, yours,
DAVID J. HILL (*President*).

POLYTECHNIC INSTITUTE,
Brooklyn, N. Y., January 6, 1896.

MY DEAR SIR: If you deem it of any value, you are authorized to use my name upon the committee of one hundred. During the past ten years my absence from all educational meetings during the summer has been enforced by the condition of my health. In fact, I have not attended an educational convention until this last summer since 1882.

Yours, respectfully, DAVID H. COCHRAN (*President*).

SIBLEY COLLEGE, CORNELL UNIVERSITY,
Ithaca, N. Y., December 22, 1894.

SIR: Your report is received. In reply I would say I am glad to see that you are not yet discouraged. I wish that you would consider me as belonging to the list of those who would be glad to promote the movement for a national university at Washington.

Can you not have 25 copies sent me? I can use 100 of your memorial of 1892, and any other documents of interest.

Yours, truly, R. H. THURSTON (*President*).

SIBLEY COLLEGE, CORNELL UNIVERSITY,
Ithaca, N. Y., February 22, 1895.

MY DEAR FRIEND: I wish to thank you very heartily for your kindness in sending me those copies of your admirable report on a national university at Washington. I found the report intensely interesting and full of just those facts that I wished to obtain. I hope that you will lose neither interest nor vigor in your work. It is well worthy of the best effort of every man who can take a hand.

I obtained from our Senators a mail bag full of additional copies, which I distributed among friends and acquaintances who, as I think, are likely to be interested in so grand a scheme. Great works are not accomplished in a day or a year, and yet they do get done. I have not the slightest doubt that, after our legislatures and legislators come finally, as they will, to see clearly that their task is the promotion of the moral and the physical well-being of the nation, they will turn their attention with zeal to this essential element of a nation's education, and then promptly do the work.

I send you a copy of our own paper, containing an abstract of my own presentation of this idea, made many years ago.

Yours, very truly, ROBT. H. THURSTON (*President*).

UNION COLLEGE,
Schenectady, N. Y., January 16, 1896.

DEAR SIR: I am in hearty sympathy with the aims of the national university as outlined, and cheerfully grant you permission to add my name to the committee.

Yours, sincerely, ANDREW W. RAYMOND (*President*).

ALFRED UNIVERSITY,
Alfred, N. Y., December 23, 1894.

MY DEAR SIR: If the proposed national university could be given a rank in all respects and in all departments fitting the many circumstances of the case, it would be of inestimable value to the cause of higher learning and of great honor to our great nation.

Yours, truly, ARTHUR E. MAIN (*President*).

COLLEGE OF NEW JERSEY, PRINCETON UNIVERSITY,
Princeton, N. J., December 30, 1895.

DEAR SIR: I have not hitherto replied to your communication respecting the establishment of a national post-graduate university at Washington, because I was unable when I received your letter to give the matter the consideration which it deserved, and I did not feel so clear with regard to the wisdom of the undertaking as to authorize the use of my name in approval of it. I have, however, paid some attention to the matter lately, and as a result I am entirely favorable to the action contemplated in the bill just now before Congress, and it gives me great pleasure to say that I desire to be counted among those who favor the national university measure.

I am, your obedient servant,

FRANCIS L. PATTON (*President*).

COLLEGE OF NEW JERSEY,
Princeton, N. J., January 2, 1896.

MY DEAR GOVERNOR HOYT: I beg you not to impute to me indifference to the matter respecting the University of the United States because I have failed to write to you upon the subject. I felt from the beginning that the matter was of such vast moment and that it sustained such important relations to our existing scheme of university education that I could not express any opinion without giving the matter very careful consideration. Since my conversation with Senator Edmunds I feel that certain antecedent difficulties which I had felt have been removed, and I accordingly wrote you a few days ago authorizing the use of my name in connection with the proposal. I write this letter in part for the purpose of repeating what I said before and also for the purpose of thanking you for your very kind note of December 30, 1895.

I am, very truly, yours,

FRANCIS L. PATTON (*President*).

UNIVERSITY OF NORTH CAROLINA,
Chapel Hill, N. C., January 19, 1892.

DEAR SIR: I am in hearty sympathy with the proposed university, having thought for many years that our country greatly needs such an institution and that Washington City is the proper place for its location. Indeed, I regret it very much that Mr. Johns Hopkins did not attach his great university to the Smithsonian Institution. The existence of such a university would do more to destroy political corruption and to inform our people upon political abuses than any other or all agencies in existence.

Yours, very respectfully,

GEO. T. WINSTON, LL. D., *President*.

UNIVERSITY OF NORTH CAROLINA,
Chapel Hill, N. C., December 5, 1895.

DEAR SIR: Accept my thanks for a copy of the bill for the national university. I am much pleased with it. I shall write to Senators and Members from North Carolina.

Please send me one dozen copies as soon as introduced and printed.

Very truly,

G. T. WINSTON, *President.*

SHAW UNIVERSITY,
Raleigh, N. C., November 5, 1895.

MY DEAR SIR: In reply to your inquiry of the 31st ultimo, I have to inform you that I am heartily in favor of a national post-graduate university as outlined in your letter.

Faithfully, yours,

CHAS. F. MESERVE, *President.*

SHAW UNIVERSITY,
Raleigh, N. C., December 9, 1895.

MY DEAR SIR: I have your favor of the 5th instant, and after looking it over believe it will be wise to go ahead and try to do something, at least enough to make a start. The times, of course, are against us, but, as you say, it is very important that a beginning be made. I trust that the attempt will be successful, and if it is in my power to be of any service I shall be happy to render that service.
Faithfully, yours,
CHAS. F. MESERVE, *President.*

UNIVERSITY OF NORTH CAROLINA,
Chapel Hill, N. C., November 30, 1895.

DEAR SIR: Accept my thanks for circulars and documents sent, which are duly received. I am in hearty sympathy with the movement to establish a national university, and shall give it such aid as I can.
Very truly, G. T. WINSTON, *President.*

UNIVERSITY OF NORTH DAKOTA,
University, N. Dak., December 21, 1894.

DEAR SIR: I most heartily favor the establishment of a great national university for post-graduate work only, in general accordance with the plan outlined in the bill now before the Senate. Such an institution should be adequately endowed, not depending upon current appropriations for maintenance, and should be securely guarded against political influence.

To secure this latter provision an ample endowment is all-important. The proceeds from the sale of public lands, owing to the practical exhaustion of our public arable domain, will be a rapidly diminishing quantity, and I should seriously question whether one-third of the proceeds from the sale of these lands for the next ten years will afford an adequate foundation for a great national university.

This nation is rich enough to endow the proposed institution on a scale which will make it easily the foremost university in the world. Such a university as the Senate bill proposes, adequately supported, is greatly needed to complete our system of public instruction as already provided for in our public schools and State universities. I quite approve the suggestion of President Jesse that the proposed university should be made to sustain some sort of official relation with the various State universities, so that there may be a completely articulated system of public instruction, from highest to lowest.
Very truly, yours, WEBSTER MERRIFIELD, *President.*

UNIVERSITY OF NORTH DAKOTA,
University, N. Dak., April 20, 1895.

MY DEAR SIR: Your favor of April 10 duly received. You are quite at liberty to name me as a member of your proposed committee of one hundred on national university.
Wishing you abundant success in your commendable enterprise, I am,
Very truly, yours,
WEBSTER MERRIFIELD (*President*).

OHIO STATE UNIVERSITY, OFFICE OF THE PRESIDENT,
Columbus, Ohio, November 8, 1894.

MY DEAR SIR: Your letters and the documents which you kindly sent me have been received. I am interested in the object which you propose, but have not been able as yet to examine the details of the plan. I hope soon to give it some attention, and if it is what I hope, I shall be glad to cooperate to the extent of my ability in securing favorable action by Congress.
Yours, truly, W. H. SCOTT (*President*).

OHIO STATE UNIVERSITY,
Columbus, Ohio, November 26, 1894.

MY DEAR SIR: It will give me pleasure to comply with your request for cooperation in securing the passage of the bill for the establishment of a national university. Will you kindly send me a copy of the bill?

One set of the documents that you have already sent me will be placed in the university library, as you suggested.

Truly, yours, W. H. SCOTT (*President*).

OHIO STATE UNIVERSITY,
Columbus, Ohio, April 16, 1895.

DEAR SIR: I admire the fidelity and energy with which you have devoted yourself to the cause of a national university, and I shall be glad to afford whatever encouragement or assistance may be derived from the use of my name in the way requested in your letter of the 10th instant.

I trust that the next Congress will find time to give careful and, if necessary, protracted attention to the subject.

Very truly, yours, W. H. SCOTT (*President*).

OHIO UNIVERSITY,
Athens, Ohio, January 3, 1894.

MY DEAR SIR: In reply to your second letter, I have to say that I do not suppose it makes much difference what my personal opinion may be in regard to the proposed national university; still, I should be sorry to be found on the wrong side of a question so important in itself. It is an interesting fact to me that it was for this institution (here at Athens) that the name "American University" was first proposed by Dr. Cutler, and that for its maintenance the first Congressional lands were set apart. In the last analysis but two things are necessary to make a great school—plenty of funds and a competent board of regents as little restricted in their action as possible. So far as I see, the proposed bill rests upon this basis. I shall, therefore, be glad to see it pass.

Very truly, yours. CHAS. W. SUPER (*President*).

OHIO UNIVERSITY,
Athens, Ohio, April 15, 1895.

DEAR SIR: I may say in brief, in reply to your letter of the 10th instant, that I have wondered several times whether the national-university bill had passed the Senate. I feared, however, that the brevity of the session was against it. I hope the measure may meet with better success when reintroduced next winter. I shall be glad to aid to the extent of my ability.

Very truly, yours, CHAS. W. SUPER (*President*).

UNIVERSITY OF CINCINNATI,
Cincinnati, Ohio, April 16, 1895.

DEAR SIR: You are at liberty to use my name for the object mentioned—to establish a national university. I believe in it with all my heart.

I remain, yours, truly,

W. O. SPROULL (*Late President, etc.*).

ANTIOCH COLLEGE OF YELLOW SPRINGS,
Greene County, Ohio, December 24, 1894.

SIR: I have carefully examined the report and speeches of the Senators in regard to the proposed national university, which was first so wisely suggested by the Father of the Republic.

I am heartily in favor of the university. As this grand and glorious Republic now looms up the horizon to the admiration of all the earth, and our public-school system is rapidly being improved, and the true spirit of advanced research is being stimulated in hundreds of schools, colleges, and so-called universities, the people will soon demand the leading university in all the world.

I am, dear sir,

DANIEL ALBRIGHT LONG (*President*).

HEIDELBERG UNIVERSITY,
Tiffin, Ohio, January 12, 1895.

DEAR SIR: Your letter of recent date, and certain documents, also by your courtesy, calling my attention to the purpose of founding an institution of learning in the city of Washington, D. C., to be known under the title of "The University of the United States," have been duly received. I take pleasure in expressing to you my gratitude for the privilege thus afforded of examining the report of the select committee on this subject, and of reading the speeches of Senators Hunton and Vilas indorsing the movement. The subject appeals to my judgment as one which should be of momentous interest to all the friends of higher education, and challenges my cordial sympathy. I beg leave to assure you, therefore, of my sincere cooperation, so far as my personal influence shall extend.

The progress of the United States during the past century in civilization, it seems to me, demands, as a complement for the broadest culture of our people, an institution of this character. Hoping that the counsels of the fathers of the Republic may be followed, and that the praiseworthy efforts made by yourself and your colleagues in the movement may receive the sympathy and cooperation of all loyal citizens, I remain, with personal respect,

Very truly, yours,

J. A. PETERS,
President of Literary Department of Heidelberg University.

KENYON COLLEGE,
Gambier, Ohio, December 26, 1894.

DEAR SIR: I most heartily approve of a national university on the plan outlined in the documents you sent me. It is not intended, as I understand, to rival any of the colleges and universities now existing, but mainly to organize for purposes of instruction and research the unrivaled resources at the disposal of the Government.

When this has been accomplished, and well under way, I shall expect to see students coming from Europe to Washington, just as now our young men go to Berlin and Vienna.

Very truly, yours,

THEO. STERLING (*President*).

KENYON COLLEGE,
Gambier, Ohio, April 15, 1895.

DEAR SIR: I very cheerfully give you permission to use my name as one of the national committee to promote the establishment of a national university.

I will gladly do what I can for a university of the right sort.

Very truly, yours,

THEO. STERLING, *President Kenyon College.*

WESTERN RESERVE UNIVERSITY, ADELBERT COLLEGE,
Cleveland, Ohio, December 24, 1894.

MY DEAR SIR: I am heartily in favor of the establishment of such a university as is proposed. The University of the United States should bear such a relation to universities already established as they bear to the colleges. It should have for its greatness, not great buildings, but great men.

I am, sir, with much respect, very truly, yours,

CHARLES F. THWING,
President of Adelbert College and of Western Reserve University.

WESTERN RESERVE UNIVERSITY, ADELBERT COLLEGE,
Cleveland, Ohio, October 30, 1895.

MY DEAR SIR: I think that matters are getting into working shape. Your suggestion, too, for the organization of a council seems to me very wise. I trust that in the next session of the next Congress we may find the proper laws duly passed.

Believe me, with much regard, ever yours,

CHARLES F. THWING (*President*).

WITTENBERG COLLEGE,
Springfield, Ohio, December 11, 1895.

SIR: Replying to your communication concerning a national university, would say that I am in full sympathy with the movement. You may reckon me among its friends.

Respectfully,

S. A. ORT (*President*).

OBERLIN COLLEGE,
Oberlin, Ohio, November 6, 1895.

DEAR SIR: The proposal to establish a national post-graduate university in the city of Washington commends itself strongly to my judgment. I shall esteem it an honor to be counted among those who favor the measure.

Very respectfully, yours,

W. G. BALLANTINE (*President*)

MARIETTA COLLEGE,
Marietta, Ohio, November 7, 1894.

MY DEAR SIR: I am glad to learn of the movement for the establishment of a post-graduate university to be located at Washington. I can see decided advantages in such an institution located in that city. The movement is one in which I am greatly interested and which I should like to see carried out to a successful completion. I hope the committee will be strongly supported, and that the efforts may be crowned with large success.

Very truly, yours,

JOHN W. SIMPSON (*President*).

MARIETTA COLLEGE,
Marietta, Ohio, April 19, 1895.

MY DEAR SIR: I have read with care and interest your letter of April 10, and I hardly need to assure you again of my deep interest in the project which you are seeking to carry successfully through. I have no objection to your using my name as a member of a national committee of one hundred or more, which you wish to form. Will you kindly inform me concerning the progress of the measure, and if any advice or personal influence can be given at any time you can depend upon my cooperation.

With best wishes for the success of the measure, I am, very truly, yours,

JOHN W. SIMPSON (*President*).

HIRAM COLLEGE,
Hiram, Ohio, January 1, 1895.

DEAR SIR: I have read the report of the Senate committee on the University of the United States with great interest. The measure has my most hearty and unqualified approval. I believe the time has come when the interests of higher education demand such action as is proposed by this bill. I can not see how any friend of education could look upon the measure other than with the highest favor.

Very sincerely,

E. V. ZOLLARS (*President*).

MUSKINGUM COLLEGE,
New Concord, Ohio, January 12, 1895.

DEAR SIR: In answer to your circular letter of December 20, 1894, I will say that I am heartily in favor of a national university which shall be strictly post-graduate and which shall not be manned with an intended hostility to the Christian religion. Our country is growing to that period in its life when it naturally should establish such a national institution.

Yours, very truly, JESSE JOHNSON (*President*).

CASE SCHOOL OF APPLIED SCIENCE,
Cleveland, Ohio, December 28, 1894.

DEAR SIR: I believe that Washington is the best place on this continent for a university doing strictly post-graduate work.

The advantages offered by the museums, libraries, laboratories, collections, etc., which are gathered there afford opportunities to the student which can not be had anywhere else.

I should be glad to see the Government establish a national university, and I wish you success in your work.

Very truly, yours, CADY STALEY (*President*).

UNIVERSITY OF CINCINNATI,
Cincinnati, Ohio, December 25, 1894.

MY DEAR SIR: In reply to your letter of December 20, 1894, I write that I am unqualifiedly in favor of establishing a national university at Washington for graduate work. We need in America an institution that can offer at least as thorough an education along all lines as is offered by a German university. In the very nature of things this can be done only by an institution that has back of it Governmental support. Although we have in the United States more than one university that is doing excellent advanced work, yet we must send students abroad who desire the best facilities. We are deceiving ourselves when we say that any university in the United States can be compared with certain of the German universities, either in teaching, force, or equipment.

I do not understand why there should be one dissenting voice.

Trusting that the efforts will be successful, believe me I remain, yours, truly,

W. O. SPROULL (*President*).

MUSKINGUM COLLEGE,
New Concord, Ohio, March 14, 1895.

HONORED SIR: I am more and more interested and see more plainly the need of such an institution. When I first thought of the matter I believed our existing institutions sufficient, but now I can see the need of a great national university to complete this "truncated pyramid." I am sorry no more copies of the report of Senator Proctor and of your memorial are obtainable, but I think I shall write to Senators Sherman and Proctor to know if they can send me a copy of each. All are valuable.

Very respectfully, D. A. McCLUNG (*President*).

THE UNIVERSITY OF OKLAHOMA,
Norman, Okla., October 24, 1894.

DEAR SIR: I was moving about a good deal during the summer and your information regarding the national university escaped my notice. I shall be glad to secure it yet, and from what general information I have in regard to the enterprise I shall be glad to contribute in any way in my power to its success.

Hoping to hear from you again, and assuring you of my interest in the work, I am, yours, most cordially,

D. R. BOYD,
President University of Oklahoma.

PORTLAND UNIVERSITY,
Portland, Oreg., January 2, 1894.

My Dear Sir: In reply to yours of the 20th ultimo permit me to say that I favor a national university, to be located at Washington, D. C., for the following reasons:

1. We need a common head to unify our variant State systems of education and to set the gauge to which all shall look who aspire to a liberal education.

2. In this country, especially, of such ample resources and where popular intelligence is a necessity as well as our common pride, we can not afford to be niggardly, but should forward, by all means in our power, such a vital interest.

3. Without intending to subtract from the credit due the noble institutions of our country which have done so much in the past to promote liberal studies, it seems to me that in the presence of the great universities of the Old World we need a national university of wider plan and larger revenues than private benevolence or State resources could be expected to maintain.

4. The presence in Washington of our great national collections—the Congressional Library, the Patent Office, the Smithsonian Institution, the National Museum, the Capitol with its Congressional assemblies, and the representatives of all foreign Governments—all of which would exert an important influence in stimulating, enlightening, and guiding the minds of students during the formative period of life and character, make it peculiarly fitting that the seat of the General Government should be the seat of the national university.

Trusting that your efforts in this direction will meet with the greatest success, I am, very respectfully, yours,

C. C. STRATTON,
President Portland University.

PORTLAND UNIVERSITY,
Portland, Oreg., May 20, 1895.

My Dear Sir: It will give me pleasure to contribute my influence in every practicable way toward the end in view, and you are at liberty, therefore, to use my name wherever it will be of service.

Wishing you success in your great undertaking, I am, respectfully and sincerely, yours,

C. C. STRATTON (*President*).

NEW YORK, *January 27, 1896.*

Dear Sir: I have your favor of January 4, forwarded from Forest Grove, Oreg. I am in full sympathy with the effort to secure a national university, and shall be glad to have my name added to the committee.

Very truly, yours,

THOMAS MCCLELLAND,
President Pacific University, Oregon.

MIAMI UNIVERSITY,
Oxford, Ohio, November 13, 1895.

Dear Sir: I am in receipt of yours of October 30, relating to the proposed national post-graduate university at Washington.

The plan has my most hearty approval. I trust that the efforts may soon be rewarded with a suitable beginning of the work. The country is abundantly able and, in my judgment, owes it to our educational system and to our scholars to make such provision.

Yours very truly,

W. O. THOMPSON (*President*).

NEWPORT, R. I., *September 11, 1894.*

MY DEAR GOVERNOR HOYT: If by the united efforts of all the friends of the movement the present bill can be passed and become law, it will doubtless be an easy matter, in future years, to secure any amendment found desirable. You may depend upon it that I will cordially and loyally cooperate with you and others. The more rigidly the operations of the proposed university are limited to the field of post-graduate instruction the better. I will await at all times whatever suggestions you may desire to send me, and will always be ready to do all in my power.

Yours very truly,

WILLIAM PEPPER
(*Late President University of Pennsylvania*).

PENNSYLVANIA STATE COLLEGE,
Center County, Pa., November 23, 1894.

DEAR SIR: The establishment at Washington of a national university of the broadest scope, and supported by ample income, is in my judgment one of the most important projects now before Congress. It is a measure worthy of the most earnest efforts of the highest statesmanship. Not only could such a university contribute immensely to the growth of a sound and vigorous citizenship, but there is in our present conditions a peculiar reason why it would be of incalculable service to the cause of public education throughout the United States. It is the peculiarity of all institutions in a free country that they spring up and grow spontaneously, and to some extent irregularly, so that they often fail of proper correlation and mutual support.

That has been true of the growth of our systems of public education, higher and lower. We have as many different systems as there are States and Territories. It is only within recent years, and in only a portion of the States, that an effort has been made to bring institutions of primary, secondary, and higher education into such mutual relations as would give to each the strength and support of all. Unless I greatly mistake, however, the tendency in that direction is now one of the most powerful in the educational world and in the public mind generally. But that movement is at present necessarily confined within State or Territorial limits. There is no bond of connection (except that which is supplied by purely voluntary associations) among the systems of the different States.

Now, Congress has already taken two or three steps of immense importance and of rapidly growing influence in this direction. In providing for the establishment of what are known as the land-grant colleges in every State in the Union, and in supplementing the original act by the laws of 1887 and 1890 (known as the Hatch Act and the Morrill Act, respectively), it has helped to create a great group of institutions, which already hold the leadership in many States and are rapidly approaching it in others. These institutions would find their common head in a great national university.

They are naturally bound together already through their common relationship to the Federal Government, and they closely touch the life of their respective States through their relations to the several State governments.

The graduates of these State colleges and State universities would naturally pass on to the national university, and it would seem natural and proper that special inducements to do so should be offered primarily to them. We have, therefore, all the elements of a magnificent system leading up to one institution which should crown and dignify and inspire the whole. The only suitable place for such an institution is the city of Washington, the capital of the nation, and the movement for its establishment has my most earnest and ardent "Godspeed."

Faithfully yours,

GEO. W. ATHERTON (*President*).

THE PENNSYLVANIA STATE COLLEGE,
Center County, Pá., November 6, 1894.

MY DEAR SIR: Your letter of the 5th instant, with documents under separate cover, is just received. You will be interested to know that in one of my last conversations with the late Postmaster.General Howe, he spoke very earnestly on this subject.

Yours, very truly,

GEO. W. ATHERTON.

THE PENNSYLVANIA STATE COLLEGE,
Center County, Pa., November 5, 1895.

DEAR SIR: Your personal letter of the 25th ultimo and your special No. 2 of the 13th were duly received at this office, but at a time when a serious illness kept me from any attention to business. I have now looked the documents through with very great interest, and fully agree with the wisdom of the steps you have taken toward the formation of an "executive council."

Faithfully yours,

GEO. W. ATHERTON.

GIRARD COLLEGE, *October 29, 1894.*

DEAR SIR: I have received the postal card and also the memorial. Unfortunately, I have mislaid the former, and I do not know exactly in what way you wish me to assist in the movement. Am entirely in sympathy, and will cheerfully contribute toward the enterprise in any direction if you will tell me how and when.

Sincerely yours,

A. H. FETTEROLF (*President*).

GIRARD COLLEGE,
Philadelphia, November 13, 1894.

DEAR SIR: I most cheerfully give my indorsement to the scheme for the establishment of a national university in the city of Washington. Our Government and people need such a seat of learning, where the first scholars and the most eminent scientists of the nation or of the world may be gathered, and who, by their learning and attainments, may draw around them the best and brightest young men of the land.

The national university should have its standard so high as not to be the rival of any institution already existing. Its equipment should be thorough and complete and its endowment ample. Such an institution would inspire not only the young men, but also all other colleges and universities to higher aims and greater efforts.

I shall write to our Senators and Representatives, urging their support of the measure.

Yours, very truly,

A. H. FETTEROLF (*President*).

GIRARD COLLEGE,
Philadelphia, May 8, 1895.

DEAR SIR: Your letter of the 10th ultimo was mislaid, and for this reason remained unanswered.

I am perfectly willing that my name shall be on the national committee. If this comes too late I shall be sorry, as it was all my own oversight.

Wishing you abundant success in the good cause, I am, yours truly,

A. H. FETTEROLF.

WESTERN UNIVERSITY OF PENNSYLVANIA,
Pittsburg, November 10, 1894.

DEAR SIR: I owe you an apology for not having replied before this to your esteemed letters of recent date. I have been too busy to give the matter that attention which the magnitude and importance of the undertaking merits until to-day. Having just completed the reading of the documents you have kindly sent me, I desire now to say that it is impossible for me to add by any words of mine to the presentation of the merits of the cause you have espoused and which has already so long and so ably been advocated by those who possess far more influence, knowledge, and eloquence than I can claim.

The plan set forth in the papers before me is most noble, most feasible, most necessary. The best gift of man to man is an education, using that word in its broadest sense, as involving the development alike of the intellect and moral faculties. The American people are awake to the general necessity of providing an elementary education for the children of the Republic. The older institutions of learning and many of those more recently established have received princely gifts, reflecting alike the wisdom and the generosity of those who have made them, but it remains for the people to set a crown upon all the splendid efforts of the past by establishing through those who are the representatives of the people in the highest sense such an institution as that which it is proposed to bring into being at the national capital.

You have my best wishes for entire success in these truly enlightened efforts, and any help which I can give in forwarding the design I shall be most happy to render.

I have the honor to be, very faithfully, yours,

W. J. HOLLAND
(Chancellor of the Western University of Pennsylvania).

WESTERN UNIVERSITY OF PENNSYLVANIA,
Allegheny, Pa., December 6, 1894.

MY DEAR GOVERNOR: The more I reflect upon the proposition embodied in the proposed legislation the more I like it. It is plain to me, as it already is to you, that the establishment of such an institution will prove a mighty stimulus to the other institutions throughout the land, and could not fail to do a vast amount of practical good.

I am yours, very truly, W. J. HOLLAND,
Chancellor of the Western University of Pennsylvania.

WESTERN UNIVERSITY OF PENNSYLVANIA,
Allegheny, Pa., April 13, 1895.

DEAR SIR: Your favor of April 10 has been received by me and given due consideration. It will give me pleasure to serve as a member of the committee of promotion, which you propose to form, and to do whatever is within my power to promote the objects you have in view. I have already expressed myself as in favor of the plan of establishing a national university at the seat of the Federal Government.

I am yours, very truly, W. J. HOLLAND,
Chancellor of the Western University of Pennsylvania.

WESTERN UNIVERSITY OF PENNSYLVANIA,
Allegheny, Pa., December 14, 1895.

MY DEAR SIR: I owe you a hearty apology for not having long ere this replied to your letter of October 16 in relation to the national university.

I wish to say that I greatly appreciate the energy and enthusiasm which you and others are displaying on behalf of this cause, that you may rely upon me to do all in my power to aid you, and that I quite approve of your suggestions in relation to the formation of an executive council. The gentlemen whom you name in your circular are some of them personal friends of mine; all of them are known to me to be men thoroughly qualified to render most efficient service to the cause. If I can in any way aid by bringing my influence to bear upon friends I will cheerfully do so.

I am yours, very truly, W. J. HOLLAND,
Chancellor Western University of Pennsylvania.

THE LEHIGH UNIVERSITY,
South Bethlehem, Pa., December 24, 1894.

DEAR SIR: In answer to your letter of the 20th December, just received, I beg to say that I am entirely in favor of the establishment of a national university.

I was the organizer and first president of this institution, and am now doing duty as acting president. I am also one of the regents of the Smithsonian Institution, in whose service I make periodical visits to Washington. I shall be glad to aid this excellent cause in any way in my power.

Very faithfully yours,
HENRY COPPEE, LL. D.,
Acting President.

GENEVA COLLEGE,
Beaver Falls, Pa., December 26, 1894.

DEAR SIR: Your letter with regard to the establishment of a national university and the speeches of Senators Hunton and Vilas in advocacy of the same have been received. I hope you may succeed in your undertaking. The General Government ought to do at least as much as the State governments in the cause of education. It would be of vast account if students from all the States could meet at a central university and together get instruction under men of world-wide reputation. There would be more uniformity of view on political questions if State lines were crossed in order to get help at a common source. To be allowed to hear the discussions from time to time—discussions on many questions—in either House of Congress would be of vast account to students who would be giving themselves to investigation on many lines. The Methodists and Catholics are making great schools at the Capital. May the nation do as well as the church, when the needs are so great.

Yours truly,
WM. P. JOHNSTON,
President Geneva College.

BRYN MAWR, PA., *December 26, 1894.*

DEAR SIR: As the subject of a national university to be established at Washington has claimed my thought at times for some years, I do not hesitate to state that I believe the founding of such a university would be for the good of our whole country and that it should be done. It ought to be a true university, for the advanced education of graduates of our universities and colleges, for original research, and for the publication of new additions to our stores of knowledge.

It should set the highest practicable standard in scholarship and investigation, so as to elevate the character of education throughout our country and attract to its instruction the ablest of our graduates, both men and women.

Its several faculties should form corps of experts to whom the Government might apply for information upon subjects of national importance.

I am, very respectfully, yours,
JAMES E. RHOADS
(*Late President Bryn Mawr College*).

LAFAYETTE COLLEGE, *Easton, Pa., January 8, 1896.*

MY DEAR SIR: I shall be glad to cooperate with you in your work as a member of the national committee of one hundred.

Wishing abundant success in the good cause, I am, very truly,
ETHELBERT D. WARFIELD, *President.*

SWARTHMORE COLLEGE,
Swarthmore, Pa., December 4, 1894.

FRATERNAL FRIEND: I was glad of our interview at Baltimore. * * * If our country could have a university truly worthy of that great name it would be a blessing indeed to the cause of education from the highest to the lowest grade. * * *

EDWD. H. MAGILL (*Late President*).

SWARTHMORE COLLEGE,
Swarthmore, Pa., December 26, 1894.

DEAR SIR: Our country can never come up to the full measure of its duty and opportunity in education until it establishes on a broad, liberal foundation a national university for graduate study. No power but the nation, in no place but Washington, can do this work on a scale such as the wealth, dignity, extent, and intelligence of the United States naturally warrant.

It is natural as well as fitting that this enterprise should have had the backing of our best men for a century or more. That this idea, whose importance is in some degree measured by the time required for its development, will be realized at last can not be doubted. I trust the great work may be inaugurated soon, and that its accomplishment may be the initial step for a new century of still greater progress.

Very truly yours,

CHARLES DE GARMO,
President Swarthmore College.

HAVERFORD COLLEGE,
Haverford, Pa., December 24, 1894.

DEAR SIR: A national university devoted to advanced graduate work, paying to professors the highest salaries and wisely selecting them, would be a great advantage, and Washington is the place for it.

Very truly,

I. SHARPLESS (*President*).

SWARTHMORE COLLEGE,
Swarthmore, Pa., December 4, 1894.

ESTEEMED FRIEND: If our country could have a university truly professional and worthy of that great name, it would be a blessing indeed to the cause of education—from the highest to the lowest grade.

Colleges should adhere to their own work, with their own methods, and give bachelor's degrees only. Why should colleges continue the absurd practice of giving second degrees for what is really only university work? Is it not well for us to hold up an ideal to work toward, whether we can reach it in five years or in five decades? The idea is truly a worthy one. All must admit that organization is of great value in these days, and that without mutual concessions and forbearance no organization will ever be possible. I would by no means imitate France and Germany in combining preparatory schools and colleges, as in their lycées and gymnasia, our college course of four years—between the preparatory course and the university—being, I conceive, as we manage it, of the utmost value to our people.

Very cordially,

EDW. H. MAGILL (*Late President, etc.*).

SWARTHMORE COLLEGE,
Swarthmore, Pa., June 21, 1895.

MY DEAR SIR: I am sure that at no time in the past was the public mind so well prepared to receive it as now. The completion of an educational edifice demands our attention. When we compare our system (which is a system without system) with the more complete organizations of England, and especially of France and Germany, Americans should feel that they can no longer afford to remain so far in the background. And the many things needed to secure the proper articulation of the various grades of our schools, colleges, and universities can never be so well secured as by establishing one great national head, which shall not only direct by its influence and example the entire system below it, but which shall stand a great beacon light in the educational world for other nations to follow. What our country is to the rest of the world politically it should become educationally at no distant day.

I am, most cordially, your friend,

EDW. H. MAGILL (*Late President, etc.*).

SWARTHMORE COLLEGE,
Swarthmore, Pa., April 13, 1895.

DEAR SIR: Your favor of April 10 is at hand. You have my full permission to use my name in making up the list of your committee. Whenever I can be of any service in promoting the cause of the national university I shall hope to hear from you.

Very truly yours,

CHARLES DE GARMO *(President).*

THIEL COLLEGE,
Greenville, Pa., December 27, 1894.

DEAR SIR: I can add nothing to the argument in behalf of a great national university. I favor it with all my heart.

THEOPHILUS B. ROTH,
President Thiel College.

MUHLENBERG COLLEGE,
Allentown, Pa., December 27, 1894.

MY DEAR SIR: In answer to your letter of the 20th instant, I would say that I heartily favor the establishment at Washington of the university of the United States for post-graduate work. I need not give the many reasons that influence my judgment in this matter. In truth, the more I think over the subject the more I am surprised that this project of the fathers was not long ago carried to a successful issue, so far as this can be accomplished by national legislation. I shall take pleasure in cooperating with you in this work as far as I may be able.

Very truly yours,

THEODORE L. SEIP *(President).*

THIEL COLLEGE,
Greenville, Pa., April 15, 1895.

DEAR SIR: Your favor of the 10th instant is at hand. Regretting the failure to call up the national university bill, but in no wise despairing of the hope that it will be not only called up, but also passed by a large majority.

Yours, respectfully,

THEOPHILUS B. ROTH *(President).*

MUHLENBERG COLLEGE,
Allentown, Pa., April 17, 1895.

DEAR SIR: In answer to yours of recent date, I would say that it will give me pleasure to cooperate, to the best of my ability, with the committee for the promotion of the establishment of the university of the United States. I therefore accede to your request to use my name as a member of the national committee of one hundred.

Very respectfully yours,

THEODORE L. SEIP *(President).*

GENEVA COLLEGE,
Beaver Falls, Pa., April 15, 1895.

DEAR SIR: Yours of the 10th this day received. You are at liberty to use my name, if of any service to you, in the furtherance of project looking to the establishment of a national university at Washington.

I am truly yours,

W. P. JOHNSTON *(President).*

BROWN UNIVERSITY,
Providence, R. I., May 10, 1895.

MY DEAR SIR: I have your esteemed letter of the 8th, and in reply will say that if my name on the committee of one hundred will be of any service in furthering the great cause of a national university I shall be most happy to have it there.

Cordially,

E. BENJ. ANDREWS *(President).*

BROWN UNIVERSITY,
Providence, R. I., October 19, 1895.

My Dear Sir: Your favor of October 16 to hand. Your enterprise impresses me more and more as a worthy one. What you have done so far I judge to be wise, and the thought of such a committee as you propose strikes me as also in the right direction. How, practically, to enlist Congress you must know far better than any of us who are far away. I think I am confident that all Rhode Island Congressmen will be on the right side when a vote is to be taken.

Sincerely yours,

E. BENJ. ANDREWS (*President*).

UNIVERSITY OF SOUTH DAKOTA,
Vermilion, S. Dak., November 7, 1894.

Sir: I heartily thank you for your letter of August 20, the card of October 22, and the two documents referred to. Though amid extraordinary perplexities, I could not, consistently with any sense of gratitude for your persistent and patriotic endeavors, do less than examine in detail what you sent. This I have done to-day with sincere and growing interest.

It would be a piece of the wisest business economy for the Federal Government to found the proposed university as a means to the fullest fruition of enormous grants heretofore made to many independent schools for primary and secondary education. Schools so aided have their own widely differing standards, and are working in the particular interest of the several States by whose appropriations they are in part maintained. Their services are of necessity largely local, and their instruction upon questions of national application is exposed to such local influences as dominant political views, the temper of legislatures as to appropriations, and the like. If they resist tendencies to sectionalism—one of the gravest tendencies in national affairs—it is in spite of our so-called system of education. The greater the number of such schools the greater the need of a national university.

Can the General Government afford to thus spend millions without adding a reasonable amount for a university which shall fix a standard of excellence, which shall carry that standard, through its graduates, down to the lower schools already receiving Government aid; which shall bring our youth from all parts of the land, and correct their sectional bias by contact with associates of different views, with the National Legislature, Administration, and courts? A university so located could do far more than any other agency in the correction of extreme and harmful sectional tendencies and passions, and in imparting that broader view of national questions which can not be gained outside of Washington.

From the educational standpoint it is a shame that so great a people do not have one university. The word "university," as a misnomer, is so common that the majority of graduates of American institutions have no intelligent conception of the proper function and scope of a university. It is not surprising that public men are slow to appreciate the fact so palpable to educators, that we have not a single university proper in this broad land. So far from interfering with existing institutions, the one you propose would be of incalculable benefit to all.

If there were not other and greater reasons, patriotism and national pride should supply this want for the sole purpose of avoiding the humiliating spectacle of thousands going abroad for the higher education, a standing confession of weakness of their own country, imbibing foreign ideas, expending American wealth upon an education which often requires no more time to acquire than is necessary to adjust it to the needs of their native land. A national university of their own would have none of these disadvantages, and would instill a patriotism akin to that which so conspicuously marks the student of West Point or Annapolis.

Partisan plaudits may reward one who supports measures which are repeatedly changed by mutations of partisan control. Those who found the proposed university will enjoy the lasting credit of favoring an enterprise about which, once established, there will be no question in the future aside from extent of support.

Very respectfully yours,
            JOSEPH W. MAUCK (*President*

          UNIVERSITY OF SOUTH DAKOTA,
            Vermilion, S. Dak., April 17, 1895.

DEAR SIR: Your esteemed favor of April 10 is at hand. I heartily appreciate the honor of your invitation to accept an appointment as a member of the proposed committee of promotion in the interests of the national university. The same is gratefully accepted, and it will be a pleasure to me to do all in my power to further the aims of the committee. It is to be sincerely hoped that your untiring labors in this matter will continue to be rewarded by a growing sentiment in favor of the university, and that they will eventually be rewarded by the complete consummation of all plans.

Very respectfully, yours,   J. W. MAUCK (*President*).

            PIERRE UNIVERSITY,
         East Pierre, S. Dak., December 28, 1894.

DEAR SIR: Respecting the proposed national university, my limited knowledge of its intended character and curricula may excuse me from expressing a very decided opinion. But if it shall promote the leading ideas of George Washington in reference to the foundations of our liberties and Government, expressed in his farewell address, I most cordially favor the establishment of so great an institution. I indorse the statements of the Hon. William F. Vilas as to the main purposes of such a university in the fifth, sixth, seventh, and eighth paragraphs of his speech relative to it.

Respectfully yours,   WILLIAM M. BLACKBURN, (*President*).

            PIERRE UNIVERSITY,
          East Pierre, S. Dak., April 16, 1895.

DEAR SIR: Your circular letter sent me came to hand to-day. The honor of an appointment on the large committee proposed, however highly appreciated, is not the important consideration in my mind. My motive in accepting it would be to represent more fully this part of the country and help in what measure I may to promote the interests of the proposed national university and help to give shape to it. My help can not be very great, yet even one voice may have some influence. I can not add to its funds nor bear much expense of committee work for various reasons; nor can I be expected to attend meetings of the committee, unless in some rare instances. Frankly stating all this, I will say that if you think I can be of any good service in the committee, you are at liberty to use my name.

Yours respectfully,   WILLIAM M. BLACKBURN (*President*).

     UNITED STATES DEPARTMENT OF AGRICULTURE,
        OFFICE OF ASSISTANT SECRETARY,
          Washington, D. C., August 25, 1894.

MY DEAR SIR: It gives me pleasure to acknowledge the receipt of your valued favor of the 20th instant, forwarded to me here from the University of Tennessee. I am very glad to hear from you upon such a subject, for I am favorable to the scheme for a national post-graduate university.

I am at present, and have been since the 1st of January, presiding over this office, where I shall be glad to see you at any time.

With warm personal regards, very truly yours,
              CHAS. W. DABNEY, Jr.
           (*President University of Tennessee*).

DEPARTMENT OF AGRICULTURE,
OFFICE OF ASSISTANT SECRETARY,
Washington, D. C., April 12, 1895.

MY DEAR GOVERNOR: Your circular letter of April 10, giving information in regard to the present condition of the bill for the establishment of the University of the United States, was duly received.

I appreciate the honor of being a member of your proposed new national committee of one hundred, and will be very glad to assist you in any way in my power. I am already loaded down with about as much business as I can carry, and you must not expect too much of me. It will be a great pleasure, however, to assist as far as I may be able.

With best wishes and high regard, very truly yours,

CHAS. W. DABNEY, Jr.
(*President University of Tennessee*).

UNIVERSITY OF NASHVILLE,
PEABODY NORMAL COLLEGE,
Nashville, Tenn., February 20, 1895.

DEAR SIR: The pending bill to establish the university of the United States has my hearty indorsement. Such a university would stimulate and perfect not only the higher education of the country, but also, by a process of downward diffusion, our secondary and primary education. The spirit of the nation at large should be represented by a national institution.

Very respectfully,

WILLIAM H. PAYNE, *Chancellor.*

SOUTHWESTERN PRESBYTERIAN UNIVERSITY,
Clarksville, Tenn., December 25, 1894.

DEAR SIR: Your circular letter of the 20th instant has been received, followed by the documents named therein.

Without knowing all the details of the measure which you advocate, a copy of the bill not having come to me, I will say that I heartily indorse the idea of a national university for post-graduate work. Such an institution would make possible certain lines of study which it is not practicable at this time for even the best-endowed institutions to maintain, and its work would not necessarily conflict with that of the universities already established and doing successful work.

Very truly yours,

GEORGE SUMMEY, *Chancellor.*

CENTRAL TENNESSEE COLLEGE,
Nashville, Tenn., November 15, 1895.

DEAR SIR: It seems to me no one can doubt the utility and necessity of a rational university to a complete system of educational institutions, if we would furnish those seeking advanced education in our own country. I hope the Fifty-fourth Congress may do itself the exalted honor of establishing such a university on a most liberal basis.

Yours truly,

J. BRADEN (*President*).

CUMBERLAND UNIVERSITY,
Lebanon, Tenn., November 2, 1895.

DEAR SIR: Your communications of October 13 and 26 have been received.

As I have heretofore written to you, I heartily approve the movement for a great United States university.

I will take pleasure in seeing our Representative, Hon. Benton McMillin, and will ask him to support the measure. Your plan of operation is fine and ought to succeed. I hope it will.

Ever yours truly,

N. GREEN (*President*).

THE UNIVERSITY OF THE SOUTH,
Sewanee, Tenn., November 22, 1894.

MY DEAR SIR: I am very much interested in the establishment of a national university for post-graduate instruction, and I desire to urge upon Congress the importance of taking immediate and favorable action in the matter. It gives me pleasure to indorse the reasons which have been so admirably set forth by prominent educators throughout the Union. The establishment of such a university would do more for the upbuilding of this great nation than anything else.

With assurances of sympathy in your laudable untertaking, I am,
  Yours, very faithfully,
        B. L. WIGGINS (*Vice-Chancellor*).

THE UNIVERSITY OF THE SOUTH,
Sewanee, Tenn., October 24, 1895.

MY DEAR SIR: Your letter of 16th instant is duly received. I am decidedly of the opinion that it would be advisable for the national committee to elect an executive council, as you propose, and in the way that you propose, in order that immediate and definite steps may be taken to secure the end in view.

I shall be glad to cooperate with you in such measure as I may be able.
  With best wishes, I am, yours, very faithfully,
        B. L. WIGGINS, *Vice-Chancellor.*

FISK UNIVERSITY,
Nashville, Tenn., November 8, 1895.

DEAR SIR: Your favors of the 31st ultimo have been received, and I have given the question of the establishment of a national post-graduate university at Washington somewhat careful consideration. The result is, I am ready to indorse the plan and to do what I can to further the passage of a suitable bill by Congress providing for the establishment of such a university.
  Sincerely yours,
        E. M. CRAVATH (*President*).

THE UNIVERSITY OF UTAH,
Salt Lake City, January 2, 1894.

DEAR SIR: There is no doubt in my mind that a national university established at Washington would prove to be of great importance to our country. A university of this character would open up a way by which all legitimate original work could be done, and by men of all shades of thought. I most heartily favor such a university.
  Respectfully,
        J. T. KINGSBURY,
        Vice-President University of Utah.

THE UNIVERSITY OF UTAH,
Salt Lake City, April 24, 1895.

MY DEAR SIR: Your letter of April 10 addressed to Professor Kingsbury, who for the two years preceding July, 1894, was acting president of the University of Utah, has reached my hand. I assure you of my deep interest and desire for general cooperation in the work of establishing a university of the United States. Should you desire the name of the president of the University of Utah to appear on your committee list, I shall regard the appointment as an honor. Kindly advise me of anything I can do to further the cause of your organization.

  With very best regards, I am, most truly, yours,
        J. E. TALMAGE (*President*).

WASHINGTON AND LEE UNIVERSITY,
Lexington, Va., November 7, 1894.

DEAR SIR: The president of this institution (G. W. C. Lee), who is but just recovering from severe illness, desires me to say, in answer to your letter of the 5th instant, that he is hardly yet able to do much, but will carry out your wishes as soon as he can do so.

Respectfully, THOS. E. MARSHALL, Jr. (*Private Secretary*).

COLLEGE OF WILLIAM AND MARY,
Williamsburg, Va., November 4, 1895.

MY DEAR SIR: I am in receipt of your letter and accompanying pamphlets, regarding the project of a national university. As one who is a thorough friend of education and sincerely believes that in this solitary remedy is found the panacea for all public evils, I am cordially in favor of the proposition of a national post-graduate university of the highest possible rank. I can not understand how any sane person could oppose the scheme on the score of utility. With every advantage in the city of Washington, a public library of gigantic size, the Smithsonian Institution, the National Museum, the National Observatory, and the numerous other educational appliances, a national university would prove the most magnificent success. Washington City is not only monumental in name, but monumental in its public institutions. A university would be the capping stone to the monument.

Of the appropriations of money made by Congress and the laws applied to the Union at large, much complaint of partiality has been expressed. In the operation of the tariff and pension laws, the Southern section of the Union has felt, and justly felt, that it has been discriminated against in the most rigorous manner; but no such feeling can exist in reference to the patriotic measure of a national university in Washington. It is the center of the Union, and the beneficiaries of a university there established would be the people of all sections. As one representing a Southern college, I am sure the proposition would receive the indorsement of the whole South. I trust, therefore, that your splendid suggestion will receive from Congress the consideration it deserves.

I am, truly yours, LYON G. TYLER (*President*).

COLLEGE OF WILLIAM AND MARY,
Williamsburg, Va., November 20, 1895.

MY DEAR SIR: From the tenor of your letter received to-day it would seem that you had not received my letter in reply to your circular. But it gives me pleasure to repeat the assurances already given of my hearty indorsement of your splendid design of a national university. I will consider it a high honor to be a member of your committee of one hundred. Of all questions, this is one as to which there should be least difference of opinion. There have grown up at Washington so many institutions and appliances of an educational character that the monument is in fact already erected and needs only the topping out. The establishment of the university makes available at once numerous factors created at the expense of many million dollars. Without the university, many possibilities will remain undeveloped. I hold that education is the highest good, and that money expended for this purpose is subject to the least abuse and is employed in the best cause. The powers of the Federal Government have been often exerted in a manner to excite sectional dissatisfaction. There is a conviction among different States of the Union that their interests are sacrificed to promote the welfare of other communities of people. But a national university is one which is free from the objection of partiality. The power of Congress to legislate for the District of Columbia was admitted by the strictest of our constitutional interpreters, and it is the only place where it would be expedient and constitutionally right to erect the university of the United States.

Assuring you again of my hearty coöperation in the proposed design,

I am, truly yours,

LYON G. TYLER,
President of William and Mary College.

VIRGINIA AGRICULTURAL AND MECHANICAL COLLEGE,
Blacksburg, Va., November 18, 1895.

DEAR SIR: You are at liberty to enroll my name as a friend and supporter of the plan for a national university.

Yours respectfully,

J. M. MCBRYDE (*President*).

HAMBURG, VA., *January 1, 1895.*

DEAR SIR: Please accept my thanks for speeches, etc., on the proposed national university. I have read them with much pleasure. I have no doubt that Rev. L. Bookwalter, D. D., my successor as president of Western College, will heartily approve of the pending measure, as I most certainly do. I trust that you will be successful.

Sincerely yours,

A. P. FUNKHOUSE,
(*Late President Western College, Iowa*).

HAMPTON NORMAL AND AGRICULTURAL INSTITUTE,
Hampton, Va., December 24, 1894.

DEAR SIR: Yours of December 20 is at hand, and I hasten to express my sincere interest in the plan proposed for a national university.

Those of us who are engaged in practical school work, especially in the lower grades, feel very much the need of more systematic work in the matter of research. Take, for instance, the subject of the Indian and negro races; how few statistics there are at hand, and how little of scientific study has been given to this matter. We are very thankful for the work that Johns Hopkins University and other institutions have done, but there certainly is still need of some institution that can make special study of the great questions that have to do with the welfare of our country, in a broad and scientific way.

Wishing to express my entire sympathy with your enterprise, very truly, yours,

H. B. FRISSELL (*President*).

HAMPTON NORMAL AND AGRICULTURAL INSTITUTE,
Hampton, Va., November 2, 1895.

MY DEAR SIR: I was interested to learn from yours of the 16th ultimo of the progress that has been made toward a national university.

The formation of an executive committee seems to me altogether desirable, and certainly the names mentioned are most excellent and have my most cordial approval.

Very truly yours,

H. B. FRISSELL (*President*).

UNIVERSITY OF WASHINGTON,
Seattle, Wash., November 15, 1895.

DEAR SIR: In reply to your letter of November 6, relating to the national university proposed for Washington City, I would say that I have in other ways become acquainted with the plan, and hope it may be carried out to a successful conclusion.

Yours, respectfully,

MARK W. HARRINGTON, *President.*

WEST VIRGINIA UNIVERSITY,
Morgantown, November 13, 1894.

DEAR SIR: I have your letter and "memorial concerning a national university." From such information as I have about the matter, and from such attention as I have been able to give to it, I am decidedly of the opinion that the project to establish such a national university as proposed is entirely feasible, and that the expenditure necessary to create and maintain such an institution could be devoted to no purpose that would bring more benefit to the country or more honor to the authorities founding it. I shall be ready to contribute whatever I can to the success of the enterprise, and sincerely hope the efforts of yourself and others in its behalf may be successful.

Yours, very respectfully, P. B. REYNOLDS
(President West Virginia University).

WEST VIRGINIA UNIVERSITY,
Morgantown, March 12, 1896.

VERY DEAR SIR: If you so desire you can place my name in the National University committee of one hundred.

A national university at Washington in the interests of higher education would be able to utilize the vast stores of education material in the various national institutions.

Such an educational institution would be a fitting tribute to the Father of his Country, and would be the fit crowning glory of our State and national educational system.

I shall be pleased to lend whatever aid I can in this movement.

Yours, very sincerely and cordially,

J. L. GOODKNIGHT,
President of West Virginia University.

WEST VIRGINIA COLLEGE,
Flemington, W. Va., December 24, 1894.

DEAR SIR: A national university, under the patronage of the Government, seems in every way a necessity to give a more thorough and finished education in our country. Whilst we have schools and colleges of high rank, yet many deem it important to spend a year or two in some of the higher universities of Europe. Why not establish a school here that would wholly obviate such university course in Europe or any other foreign country? A national university would evidently lead to the establishment of a higher grade of scholarship in every department of science and knowledge. This, in itself, is desirable, and the Government should make ample provision to secure a more advanced scholarship; and how could this be done more successfully than by the Government establishing such university? I heartily approve the measure.

Very truly yours, D. POWELL.

UNIVERSITY OF WISCONSIN,
Madison, December 15, 1891.

MY DEAR SIR: I have the pleasure of acknowledging your letter of the 28th ultimo relative to the establishment of a national university, and of expressing my interest therein and concurrence in your plan and effort. I am willing to be serviceable in the matter in any way that may seem fit.

Very truly yours, T. C. CHAMBERLIN *(President).*

UNIVERSITY OF WISCONSIN,
Madison, April 22, 1895.

My Dear Mr. Hoyt: Your perseverance is entitled to the largest possible reward. The papers in regard to the national university have not yet arrived, but I have no doubt they will remove what little hesitation I expressed to you in my last letter. You may count me among the friends of the measure.

Hoping for you that immediate success which you so earnestly desire, I am, very truly yours,

C. K. Adams *(President).*

UNIVERSITY OF WISCONSIN,
Madison, October 28, 1895.

Dear Sir: It seems to me on the whole wise that a committee such as you name should be organized and that an executive force selected from that committee should be appointed from the vicinity of Washington to look after the work necessary to be done. Of course, everybody interested in the measure should see that it has the approval of their Members of Congress, so far as such approval can be secured.

I am, very heartily, yours,

C. K. Adams *(President).*

RACINE COLLEGE,
Racine, Wis., December 31, 1894.

Dear Sir: I am heartily in favor of the university.
Yours, very truly,

A. Piper,
President Racine College.

NORTHWESTERN UNIVERSITY,
Watertown, Wis., January 6, 1895.

Dear Sir: I think that the University of the United States, if established, would be of great benefit to the people. Thousands of young men annually go to Germany to study there, and many of them derive only little benefit on account of the different language. As soon as we have a real university most of such men will stay here. Besides, our colleges will be benefited to a great extent, as they can get well-trained teachers.

I heartily indorse the proposition and wish it all the success it so well deserves.

Yours, very truly,

A. F. Ernst,
President Northwestern University.

NORTHWESTERN UNIVERSITY,
Watertown, Wis., April 15, 1895.

Dear Sir: Yours of the 10th received. I am very willing to allow the use of my name as you may see fit, and shall do all in my power to help you on in the noble work you have undertaken.

With me this is a movement that I have longed for since a long time. Though my college bears the proud name of a university it is none and never will be one. But it is a respectable and successful college, and we shall change the name.

After graduation many students have asked me where to go to study further. Some went to Johns Hopkins, some to Cornell, some to Yale, some to the University of Michigan, of Wisconsin, or to Chicago. But most of them, among them my own sons, went to Germany, and there they liked it best.

Now, I am a German myself and I know what I owe to the German universities. But could and should we not have the same opportunities in this vast and glorious country? And would it not make our young men better fitted to work here? Could not a spirit be developed among students and professors as high as the one we appreciate so much among German students? This can not be done among our western State universities. This can only be done in an institution that admits only graduates of colleges of good standing, and no undergraduates whatever.

Then the university work should be divided into two classes. Some professors should devote their time principally to the development of their science by original research. Others should devote themselves to communicating to their hearers the highest and best results of the work in their science as it then stands.

The men who succeed in establishing the national university will do similar work to that of men like Fichte and Schleiermacher and Humboldt when the Univerersity of Berlin was founded, in 1810.

Yours, very truly, A. F. ERNST (*President*).

LETTERS FROM STATE SUPERINTENDENTS OF PUBLIC INSTRUCTION.

[Alphabetically arranged by States.]

STATE OF ARKANSAS, DEPARTMENT OF EDUCATION,
Little Rock, October 10, 1894.

DEAR SIR: I am in full sympathy with the measure to establish in the United States a national university. I have always agreed with the first and greatest of our Presidents upon this question, and have always been proud of the men who, since his day, have given their abilities to the consummation of the idea.

As I see it, such an institution has become a public necessity. We have hundreds of aspiring institutions that would like to be universities. A national institution comprehensively established would level these and contribute to their real power. It would also exercise a disciplinary as well as an elevating power upon the thousands of colleges and preparatory schools that, with varying standards, not only oppose each other, but lower the real value of education.

Besides this the needs of public elementary education press eloquently for such a school. Systems, city, and State, are everywhere. Each of them has a dimly defined end, and this in turn is reached through the slow stages of experience and experiment. These systems need an inspiring central light—such as can come from a great national school.

I join with you cheerfully in the request that the National Congress give to the United States a national university as the great capstone to our educational development. I trust that the bill now before the Senate will pass.

Respectfully,

JOSIAH H. SHINN
(Superintendent Public Instruction).

STATE OF ALABAMA, OFFICE OF EDUCATIONAL DEPARTMENT,
Montgomery, November 6, 1895.

DEAR SIR: I have carefully read your plan to secure the establishment of a national post-graduate university at Washington. I hereby most heartily give my indorsement to the plan, and hope it may be a success.

Yours, truly,

JOHN O. TURNER,
State Superintendent Education for Alabama.

STATE OF ALABAMA, OFFICE OF EDUCATIONAL DEPARTMENT,
Montgomery, December 10, 1895.

DEAR SIR: I have carefully read yours of November 20, and should have replied much earlier. I have not the time to outline any thoughts for your guidance in the matter. Still I must say I feel a great interest in the success of the final establishment of the national university as indicated by you, and I think your plans will ultimately accomplish the work. With best wishes for your success on that line,

I am, very truly,

JOHN O. TURNER,
State Superintendent Education.

OFFICE OF TERRITORIAL SUPERINTENDENT OF PUBLIC INSTRUCTION,
Mesa, Maricopa County, Ariz., November 11, 1895.

MY DEAR SIR: Yours of the 22d instant is at hand and contents noted. I feel the same interest in the success of the national post-graduate university movement that every loyal American, every advocate of our system of public education, and every student ought to feel in the movement.

Such an institution as the one proposed would certainly be a fitting capstone to the grandest public school system in the world, and I will be glad to be counted as one of its friends and promoters if I can be of any assistance in any way.

Of course, our representative in Congress has no vote, but I doubt not that he will be ready to advocate the proposition whenever opportunity offers.

Very truly yours,

F. J. NETHERTON,
Superintendent of Public Instruction.

STATE OF CALIFORNIA, DEPARTMENT OF PUBLIC INSTRUCTION,
Sacramento, October 30, 1894.

DEAR SIR: A copy of your Senate memorial relative to the establishment of a ational university came to hand in due season, but in consequence of the demand upon my time and labor in the discharge of my official duties, I have put off the consideration thereof to "a more convenient season."

Adverting to the matter now, permit me to say that I am in hearty accord with you in your efforts to accomplish an enterprise that should have been begun and carried to completion many years ago. I fully believe that the organization of such an institution will accomplish more for the great cause of public education and for the inculcation of a higher and purer patriotism than any other agency can hope to accomplish. If instituted upon the broad basis proposed, such a university will be of inestimable benefit in the new and powerful impetus which it will give to our different State universities, to our colleges, and to the cause of education throughout the entire land. That such a university is a leading want of our times and of our nation no lover of our noble institution of free American government can gainsay.

I most fully indorse all that has been said in reference to this important matter, and I sincerely wish for you most abundant success in your efforts to accomplish the object for which you have so earnestly and so disinterestedly labored. It will be my pleasure, as it is my duty, to contribute my mite of influence in aid of an enterprise so abundantly fraught with benefit to the people and to the institutions of our country.

Very truly yours,

J. W. ANDERSON,
(Superintendent Public Instruction.)

STATE OF CALIFORNIA, DEPARTMENT OF PUBLIC INSTRUCTION,
Fresno, December 10, 1894.

MY DEAR SIR: Some time ago I sent you a letter expressive of my opinion as to the desirability of establishing a national university, and I subsequently received from you a letter recognizing the receipt of mine.

The enterprise has my most hearty approval, and I sincerely hope that Congress will, at its present session, take action upon the matter. Such a university will immeasurably add to the interest in higher education throughout the land. On my return to Sacramento I will take pleasure in urging upon our Senators and Representatives a hearty support of the measure now pending.

Truly yours,

J. W. ANDERSON,
Superintendent of Public Instruction.

STATE OF CALIFORNIA, DEPARTMENT OF PUBLIC INSTRUCTION,
Sacramento, November 1, 1895.

DEAR SIR: I have your circular letter of October 22, and note what you say on the margin thereof. Let me say in reply that this is the first communication of the kind sent me. While the documents you speak of have not yet come to hand, I am somewhat familiar with the efforts made from time to time in behalf of a great national university. Please enroll my name as one of the most enthusiastic advocates and supporters of the project. Any suggestions you may make regarding work that I might do with the delegation from this State to Congress I shall be glad to follow.

Cordially and fraternally yours,
SAMUEL T. BLACK,
State Superintendent, California.

STATE OF COLORADO, DEPARTMENT OF PUBLIC INSTRUCTION,
Denver, November 30, 1895.

DEAR SIR: The national post-graduate university at Washington meets with my approval.

Yours truly,
A. J. PEAVEY
(Superintendent Public Instruction).

OFFICE OF SUPERINTENDENT OF FREE SCHOOLS,
Dover, Del., January 21, 1896.

MY DEAR SIR: I most cheerfully indorse the plan of establishing at Washington a national university of the character you describe in your circular.

Very truly,
C. C. TINDAL *(Superintendent).*

EDUCATIONAL DEPARTMENT, STATE OF FLORIDA,
Tallahassee, January 12, 1892.

DEAR SIR: Yours of the 6th present came to my office during my absence in attendance upon the State Teachers' Association, at Jacksonville.

Wishing you the utmost success, and the final establishment of a great national university, I am, truly,
ALBERT J. RUSSELL.
(Superintendent, etc).

OFFICE OF STATE SCHOOL COMMISSIONER,
Atlanta, Ga., January 3, 1896.

MY DEAR SIR: Replying to your favor of December 30, I beg to say that I heartily concur in the movement that you are making to establish a national university at Washington. I shall be very glad to do whatever lies in my power to encourage this movement.

Yours, very truly,
G. R. GLENN,
State School Commissioner.

STATE OF IDAHO, DEPARTMENT OF PUBLIC INSTRUCTION,
Boise, Idaho, January 4, 1896.

DEAR SIR: Yours received. You are duly authorized to add my name to the list of those who favor the national university.

Very truly,
C. A. FORESMAN,
Superintendent of Public Instruction.

STATE OF ILLINOIS, PUBLIC INSTRUCTION,
Springfield, August 31, 1894.

DEAR SIR: I have no doubt that a post-graduate university, such as is described in the memorial you kindly sent me, would be the keystone of the educational system of the country. I hope every effort will be put forth to secure the passage of the bill now before Congress, and any assistance I may be able to render will be cheerfully given.

Very truly yours,

HENRY RAAB,
Superintendent of Public Instruction.

---

629 WEST EDWARDS STREET,
Springfield, Ill., April 16, 1895.

DEAR SIR: Your favor of April 10 is to hand.

I am sure there is no reason why I should not support the measure of establishing a national university at Washington and continue as a silent member of the committee, though I am no longer State superintendent of Illinois.

I can continue the agitation, as I have done heretofore, by speaking to influential men on suitable occasions and be of service in other directions.

Very truly yours,

HENRY RAAB,
Ex-Superintendent Public Instruction.

STATE OF ILLINOIS, PUBLIC INSTRUCTION,
Springfield, November 23, 1895.

DEAR SIR: Replying to your favor, I am deeply impressed with your "Memorial in regard to a national university."

You are doing the cause of truth and higher learning the greatest service in pleading and organizing for this university. You must succeed.

A national university not conflicting with the already existing universities, but organized along higher lines of post-graduate work—a university that shall be both a laboratory of scientific investigation and an institution for the highest scientific instruction—ought to be established at our national capital.

Your plea is no philosopher's dream. It was conceived by the founders of our Republic—by Washington, Jefferson, Hamilton, Madison, and Franklin. And down through the years since this early conception it has been advocated by statesman, scholars, scientist, and teachers.

No other city in the world can offer more opportunities for specialists to enlarge the boundaries of human knowledge.

I will be glad to assist in any way that I can. Please send me another copy of your memorial.

Very respectfully,

J. W. HENNINGER,
Assistant Superintendent of Public Instruction.

STATE OF INDIANA, DEPARTMENT OF PUBLIC INSTRUCTION,
Indianapolis, January 15, 1892.

MY DEAR SIR: I heartily indorse the national university proposition.

Yours, very truly,

HERVEY D. VORIES (*Superintendent*).

STATE OF INDIANA, DEPARTMENT OF PUBLIC INSTRUCTION,
Indianapolis, October 26, 1895.

MY DEAR SIR: I have the honor of acknowledging the receipt of your favor of October 22, in reference to the establishment of a national post-graduate university at Washington. I am interested in this movement, and assure you that I will lend you whatever aid I can in this matter. You may count me among its friends.

Yours, most respectfully,

D. M. GEETING (*State Superintendent*).

STATE OF IOWA,
OFFICE OF SUPERINTENDENT PUBLIC INSTRUCTION,
Des Moines, October 24, 1894.

MY DEAR SIR: Upon the very important question concerning which you write, I fully agree with you in the desirability of establishing a strong national university at Washington. If established under national auspices for post-graduate work, having the support of the General Government, it could in a short time be made to exert an immense influence upon the cause of education throughout the nation. It should be a university, however, worthy the name and worthy the nation which founds it. It should be made the leading university in the Union. How this can be done is a matter of great moment, but it can better be discussed by others who are more conversant with the conditions and circumstances than I am.

Yours, very cordially,

HENRY SABIN
(Superintendent Public Instruction).

———

STATE OF IOWA,
OFFICE OF SUPERINTENDENT PUBLIC INSTRUCTION,
Des Moines, April 16, 1895.

MY DEAR SIR: In answer to yours of April 10, I have no objection to the use of my name in the list of members of the committee, if it will do the cause any good. To my advice, whatever it is worth, and all my personal influence you will be very welcome.

Yours, very cordially,

HENRY SABIN,
Superintendent Public Instruction.

———

STATE OF KANSAS, EXECUTIVE DEPARTMENT,
OFFICE OF SUPERINTENDENT OF PUBLIC INSTRUCTION,
Topeka, Kans, December 6, 1894.

DEAR SIR: Your card of recent date is before me, and in reply will say that the 13,000 teachers of Kansas heartily indorse the establishment of a national university. Personally, I have long felt that such an institution should be established. I trust that you will succeed at this session.

Respectfully,

H. N. GAINES
(State Superintendent Public Instruction).

———

STATE OF KANSAS,
OFFICE OF STATE SUPERINTENDENT OF PUBLIC INSTRUCTION,
Topeka, Kans., October 26, 1895.

DEAR SIR: Your communication of 22d instant received. I assure you I am in sympathy with the views expressed in your communication in regard to the establishment of a national university, and am free to use my influence for whatever it may be worth in that direction. The establishment of such an institution would be the crowning act in the organization of the school system of our country, and very soon, no doubt, it would be the means of holding within our own country multitudes of students who go abroad to secure opportunities for more advanced work in educational lines. You have my hearty support in this matter.

Respectfully,

E. STANLEY,
State Superintendent Public Instruction.

———

DEPARTMENT OF PUBLIC INSTRUCTION,
Frankfort, Ky., November 12, 1894.

DEAR SIR: I am so pressed by my official work that I can not command my time, and I have, therefore, been somewhat tardy in expressing myself as to the national university.

At length, however, I have concluded my examination of all the documents submitted to me; and so important did the matter seem to me from the first that my astonishment has grown with every step of the investigation that the recommendation of the fathers of the Republic was not long ago carried out.

There is no tenable ground for a valid argument against the university, while the reasons for its establishment are many and cogent. It would be not only "the crown and culmination of our whole series" of public schools, but the crowning glory of the practical statesmanship of the century now drawing to its close.

Yours truly,
ED PORTER THOMPSON,
Superintendent of Public Instruction.

DEPARTMENT OF PUBLIC INSTRUCTION,
Frankfort, Ky., July 13, 1895.

DEAR SIR: Yours of the 10th instant is received. If named for the place which you suggest, I will contribute whatever is in my power to the success of the movement which you have so much at heart. Having been renominated to my present position, I hope to continue in charge of the public schools of this State until January 1, 1900, in which case I shall be, I trust, of some use in promoting general educational interests. At any rate, the most earnest efforts shall not be wanting.

Yours truly,
ED PORTER THOMPSON,
(Superintendent of Public Instruction).

DEPARTMENT OF PUBLIC INSTRUCTION,
OFFICE OF SUPERINTENDENT,
Frankfort, Ky., October 10, 1895.

DEAR SIR: I am at your service for all that I can reasonably do to insure the success of the noble enterprise which you have so much at heart—the establishing of the university of the United States.

Yours truly,
ED PORTER THOMPSON.
(State Superintendent of Public Instruction).

STATE OF MAINE, EDUCATIONAL DEPARTMENT,
Augusta, October 30, 1895.

DEAR SIR: The plan of having a national post-graduate university meets with my most hearty approval. I believe that it will be the means of doing a great deal of good, and I shall be glad to promote such an enterprise so far as I can do so consistently with my other duties.

Wishing you the largest success in your efforts to carry this matter through, I am,
Very truly,
W. W. STETSON
(State Superintendent, etc.).

STATE OF MAINE, EDUCATIONAL DEPARTMENT,
Augusta, November 21, 1895.

DEAR SIR: It seems to me that the plan outlined in your circular of November 16 is the one which is most likely to meet with success. I hope, with the force which you have been able to secure in this matter, that you may be able to carry it through at the next session of Congress.

Very truly,
W. W. STETSON
(State Superintendent, etc.).

STATE BOARD OF EDUCATION,
State House, Boston, December 31, 1891.

MY DEAR SIR: I am fully in favor of the national university proposition.

Most truly, yours,

J. W. DICKINSON *(Secretary of the Board).*

STATE BOARD OF EDUCATION,
State House, Boston, October 24, 1894.

DEAR SIR: I beg your indulgence for not acknowledging at an earlier date the receipt of your exhaustive and convincing "Memorial concerning a national university."

I assure you of my very deep interest in the plan. I see in particular fine possibilities for the exertion of a potent and beneficent influence upon all our institutions of learning. Why, for instance, may not some of the work that is now done under the auspices of the National Educational Association toward securing the proper coordination of subjects of study be done more thoroughly and with greater authority by the proposed university?

I should like to write at greater length upon this particular point, but can not do so at present. Meanwhile I content myself with expressions of deep interest in the plan and earnest hopes for its ultimate realization.

Very truly yours, FRANK A. HILL *(Secretary).*

MASSACHUSETTS BOARD OF EDUCATION,
Boston, October 10, 1895.

MY DEAR SIR: In reply to your postal card of October 8, I beg leave to say that I see no reason for changing the attitude of sympathy toward the project of establishing the university of the United States which I have heretofore adopted. It has my indorsement, and will continue to have it so long as the movement seems to be on a high plane.

Very respectfully, yours, FRANK A. HILL,
Secretary State Board of Education.

STATE OF MARYLAND, EDUCATION DEPARTMENT,
Baltimore, November 2, 1894.

DEAR SIR: Referring to your postal of October, 1894, I beg to state that it will give me great pleasure to add anything in my power to the efforts to establish a national university in Washington.

Very respectfully, E. B. PRETTYMAN
(State Superintendent of Public Instruction).

STATE OF MARYLAND, EDUCATION DEPARTMENT,
Baltimore, December 11, 1894.

DEAR SIR: I beg to state that I am most heartily in favor of the establishment of a national post-graduate university in Washington City. This is essential to complete the systems of public education already established by the different States, and to give to American youths the opportunity for full development amid the best possible surroundings at the capital of their own country. The free intercourse of our best and brightest young men from all parts of the country at the period of character molding, mental development, and the establishment of fixed opinions, would tend to curb egotism, provincialism, bigotry, and sectionalism. Such university training certainly has for our youth great advantages over that of any foreign universities, and would confirm patriotism and strengthen the union among our people.

Very respectfully, E. B. PRETTYMAN
(State Superintendent, etc.).

STATE OF MARYLAND, EDUCATION DEPARTMENT,
Baltimore, October 9, 1895.

DEAR SIR: Referring to yours of October 8, 1895, concerning the university of the United States:

You can depend on my cooperation in aid of the great undertaking in charge of the committee of which you are chairman, and I feel quite confident that the measure will be supported by the Senators and Representatives from this State. I shall be pleased to hear from you as to how I may best aid the cause.

Very respectfully,

E. B. PRETTYMAN,
State Superintendent Public Instruction.

DEPARTMENT OF PUBLIC INSTRUCTION, MICHIGAN,
OFFICE OF SUPERINTENDENT,
Lansing, November 5, 1894.

DEAR SIR: Absence from home and press of public business have caused the delay in replying to your memorial concerning a national university. The memorial is mislaid, so I do not know exactly what you wish me to do concerning it, but I would state here that I am most heartily in favor of a post-graduate university in Washington. It would certainly be a fitting climax to the great educational systems of our States. I wish you hearty success in your enterprise.

Yours, very truly,

HENRY R. PATTENGILL
(Superintendent Public Instruction).

DEPARTMENT OF PUBLIC INSTRUCTION, MICHIGAN,
OFFICE OF SUPERINTENDENT,
Lansing, April 18, 1895.

DEAR SIR: Your letter of the 10th is at hand, and I will hold myself in readiness to assist you as much as my time will permit concerning work for a national university.

Yours, very truly,   HENRY R. PATTENGILL
(State Superintendent, etc.).

STATE OF MISSOURI, DEPARTMENT OF EDUCATION,
City of Jefferson, December 6, 1894.

MY DEAR SIR: Having read the report of the committee to establish the University of the United States, I hereby heartily indorse this great institution for pushing investigation beyond the present limits of human knowledge. The original investigator needs greater competence and freedom from class drudgery than are afforded in the average State university.

Yours, very truly,   L. E. WOLFE,
(State Superintendent, etc.).

STATE OF MISSOURI, DEPARTMENT OF EDUCATION,
City of Jefferson, December 2, 1895.

DEAR SIR: I have your letter of some time ago in reference to a national post-graduate university at Washington. I desire to state that I shall take pleasure in rendering you assistance when I am able to do so and that I heartily indorse the movement in which you are engaged.

Very truly yours,

JOHN R. KIRK,
State Superintendent Schools.

OFFICE STATE SUPERINTENDENT OF PUBLIC EDUCATION,
Jackson, Miss., January 2, 1892.

MY DEAR SIR: I beg to state that I favor the establishment of a national university at Washington.

Yours, truly, J. R. PRESTON *(State Superintendent).*

OFFICE STATE SUPERINTENDENT OF PUBLIC EDUCATION,
Jackson, Miss., March 21, 1893.

MY DEAR SIR: I regret that the press of business prevented me from replying to your favor of March 4.

I thoroughly believe in the propriety of a national university, and hope to see one established in which anyone can learn anything.

I trust that it may be my pleasure to attend some of the future meetings of the committee.

Yours, truly, J. R. PRESTON *(State Superintendent).*

THE STATE OF MONTANA,
SUPERINTENDENT OF PUBLIC INSTRUCTION,
Helena, January 31, 1896.

DEAR SIR: I am a believer in "America for Americans." Therefore I say, may we have instituted the strongest post-graduate university that is possible and thus give our graduates the best advantages at home.

I remain, most sincerely, E. A. STEERE,
Superintendent of Public Instruction.

OFFICE STATE SUPERINTENDENT OF PUBLIC INSTRUCTION,
St. Paul, Minn., September 12, 1894.

DEAR SIR: Answering yours of the 27th ultimo, I will say that the plan for establishing a post-graduate university at Washington meets my hearty approval. Let it once be admitted that such an institution would serve any useful purpose whatever, that its influence would be felt for good in the slightest degree throughout the country, and the question is settled. No argument worthy of a moment's consideration can be brought against it. The expense, when distributed among the 70,000,000 inhabitants of the United States, would not be of a feather's weight.

Every movement toward a higher culture and a nobler civilization originated at the head of the column gradually extends to the rear. The educational forces are drawn forward by the magnetism of those in advance, not pushed along by pike poles in the hands of the hindmost. Our colleges, by demanding more and better preparation of students applying for admission year by year, are constantly elevating the standards of the high schools, which in their turn require more and better work in the grammar grades, and this can be accomplished only by a similar movement in the primary schools. So an advance is scored along the whole line. A great post-graduate university at Washington would, if rightly managed, stimulate every college in the land to higher achievements, and the circle thus begun would go on broadening till the most sequestered rural schools would feel the new-born impulse, and even Sleepy Hollow might rub its eyes and ask "What time is it?"

This is not all. The graduates of this grand university of the United States would be in the army of progress as leaders, with influence wider than the continent and lasting as humanity.

One Horace Mann in a community is worth more than a thousand easy-going citizens whose sympathies and aims, so far as they have any, run in the same channels with his, but who are satisfied with simply being "right on all the great moral questions of the day."

Then let us have the university; let it be begun at once, and when done let it be a beacon light for the nations.

Very truly, W. W. PENDERGAST
(Superintendent Public Instruction).

STATE OF MINNESOTA, DEPARTMENT OF PUBLIC INSTRUCTION,
St. Paul, Minn., October 21, 1895.

DEAR SIR: It will give me pleasure to urge upon our members of Congress the importance to the country of immediate favorable action on the national university bill.

Yours, very truly, W. W. PENDERGAST.

STATE OF NEBRASKA, DEPARTMENT OF PUBLIC INSTRUCTION,
Lincoln, September 18, 1894.

DEAR SIR: It affords me pleasure to reply to your favor of August 25 in regard to the establishment in the city of Washington of a great national university.

It may be assumed that in the memorial, the receipt of which I have the honor to acknowledge, the term university means university, the culminating and crowning educational institution of the nation.

Such an institution, to subserve its highest purpose, should be, must be, in proximity to the sources of information; its students making original research must be in the fields to be searched.

These conditions are present in the national capital in the form of museums, libraries, laboratories, art collections; in the form of departments and bureaus of the National Government; in the form of local institutions; in the form of learned associations; and these are side by side with the hundreds of experts in many branches of the Government service.

While all this is true it concerns the location only of such an institution.

We should have such an institution, because in this way only can we meet the demands made upon our nation by learning; because it would afford an enormous incentive to research and consequent scholarship; because it would be a powerful factor in crystallizing, or, better, organizing our many educational systems into one system; because it would offer to students at home and abroad an opportunity for the study of our governmental, our economic, and our social systems, and thus open the way for the correction of errors, as well as for the dissemination among the peoples of the earth of the excellencies that exist in a "government of the people, for the people, and by the people."

Yours, truly, A. K. GOUDY
(Superintendent Public Instruction).

TEACHERS' NATIONAL FRATERNAL BENEFIT ASSOCIATION,
Lincoln, Nebr., October 11, 1895.

DEAR SIR: Responding to your card of October 8, 1895, permit me to say that you may, in the future as in the past, depend upon me for the fullest possible cooperation in this magnificent undertaking.

I should be pleased to receive anything that has been published in connection with the university enterprise.

Yours, truly, A. K. GOUDY,
Late State Superintendent of Public Instruction.

TEACHERS' NATIONAL FRATERNAL BENEFIT ASSOCIATION,
Lincoln, Nebr., January 23, 1896.

DEAR SIR: I inclose a copy of resolutions adopted by the unanimous vote of the Nebraska State Teachers' Association at its recent annual meeting. They were passed as almost the last act of the session, in the presence of an audience of 1,500 to 1,800 people, gathered from all parts of the State.

Yours, truly, A. K. GOUDY.

RESOLUTIONS ADOPTED AT NEBRASKA STATE TEACHERS' ASSOCIATION, 1895.

* * * * * * *

Resolved, That this association reaffirm the unanimous declaration of the Senate committee of the last Congress, as follows: That the cause of American learning demands such an institution; that the highest dignity and welfare of the nation require it; that it should be established at the capital of the country; that after a delay of one hundred years since it was first proposed and sought to be established by the founders of this Government, it would be unworthy of so great a people to wait for a more favorable time in which to meet these high demands.

That we adopt as our own declaration of the National Educational Association of 1871, touching the character and scope of such a university, as follows:

1. That it should be broad enough to embrace every department of science, literature, and the arts, and every real profession.
2. That it should be high enough to supplement the highest existing institutions of the country, and to embrace within its fields of instruction the utmost limit of human knowledge.
3. That, in the interest of truth and justice, it should guarantee equal privileges to all duly qualified applicants for admission to the courses of instruction, and equal rights, as well as the largest freedom, to all earnest investigators in that vast domain which lies outside the limits of acknowledged science.
4. That it should be so constituted and established as to command the hearty support of the American people, regardless of section, party, or creed.
5. That its material resources should be vast enough to enable it not only to furnish, and that either freely or at a nominal cost, the best instruction the world can afford, but also to provide the best-known facilities for the work of scientific investigation together with endowed fellowships and honorary fellowships, open respectively to the most meritorious graduates and to such investigators, whether native or foreign, as, being candidates therefor, shall have distinguished themselves most in the advancement of knowledge.
6. That it should be so coordinated in plan with other institutions of the country as not only in no way to conflict with them, but, on the contrary, to become at once a potent agency for their improvement and the means of creating a complete, harmonious, and efficient system of American education.

DEPARTMENT OF PUBLIC INSTRUCTION,
Trenton, N. J., April 17, 1895.

DEAR SIR: I have the honor to acknowledge your favor of the 10th instant relating to legislation for a national university.

The enterprise has my full sympathy, and you are privileged to make any use of my name you may deem proper.

I have the honor to be, very truly yours, A. B. POLAND,
State Superintendent.

DEPARTMENT OF PUBLIC INSTRUCTION,
Trenton, N. J., October 11, 1895.

DEAR SIR: I am glad to know that excellent progress has been made in the effort to establish a national university in the city of Washington. If I can be of any service to you in aiding the splendid cause that you have at heart, please command my services.

I have the honor to be, very truly yours, A. B. POLAND,
State Superintendent.

DEPARTMENT OF PUBLIC INSTRUCTION,
Albany, N. Y., November 4, 1895.

DEAR SIR: I have your circular letter of October 22, explaining the leading objects to be gained by the establishment of a national post-graduate university at Washington. I have also received the Senate documents which deal with the subject, and have given the matter my attention. The matter had not been called to my notice previously.

I am more than willing to be considered a friend of the project, and will do whatever may lie in my power to promote it.

As a loyal citizen, and one deeply interested in educational affairs, I would like to see a national university established at the capital of our country on a scale corresponding to the magnitude of educational work and educational requirements in this country.

Yours, very respectfully, CHARLES R. SKINNER,
State Superintendent.

SUPERINTENDENT OF PUBLIC INSTRUCTION,
Santa Fe, N. Mex., November 9, 1895.

DEAR SIR: I have your favor of recent date relative to the establishment of a national post-graduate university at the national capital. This is the first time I have heard from you on the subject. In reply, I have to say that the movement meets with my approval, and it will afford me pleasure to be of some service to you in carrying the idea into execution. You may count upon me to do all in my power to aid the cause. If there is anything special that I can do, please command me at all times.

Very truly yours, AMADO CHAVES (*Superintendent*).

SUPERINTENDENT OF PUBLIC INSTRUCTION,
Santa Fe, N. Mex., January 30, 1896.

DEAR SIR: I have your favor of recent date relative to the proposed national university, and in reply I have to say that I have already written to you expressing my willingness to aid you all I can with your measure through our Congressional Delegate. That is all I can do. I have called the attention of Mr. Catron to this matter and urged him to aid with all his power to have the bill put through Congress.

Very truly yours,
AMADO CHAVES, *Superintendent.*

SUPERINTENDENT OF PUBLIC INSTRUCTION,
Raleigh, N. C., January 1, 1892.

DEAR SIR: Replying to your question about a national university, I beg to state that I am in favor of such an institution. * * * That some States, at least, are not financially able to educate their people as the times demand is a fact that can not be successfully disputed.

Very truly, S. M. FINGER,
Superintendent Public Instruction.

OFFICE OF SUPERINTENDENT OF PUBLIC INSTRUCTION,
Raleigh, N. C., October 22, 1894.

MY DEAR SIR: Yours, dated October, 1894, is before me. I had received your Senate "Memorial concerning a national university (wholly post-graduate)", with "Senate committee's unanimous report on the pending bill," but have been too busy in the field lifting up my voice to our people in the "by-ways and hedges," in the woods and fields, in the swamps and on the hills, in the valleys and on the mountains for better support of our public free schools and for longer terms of the schools of the people to give much attention to a great post-graduate national university. If the Congress of the United States shall see fit to establish such a university, with proper safeguards thrown around it, "Barkis is willin'."

Very truly yours,

JOHN C. SCARBOROUGH
(*State Superintendent Public Instruction for North Carolina*).

STATE OF NORTH DAKOTA,
DEPARTMENT OF PUBLIC INSTRUCTION,
Bismarck, September 6, 1894.

DEAR SIR: Yours of the 25th ultimo and a copy of your memorial in regard to the national university at hand. I have examined into the subject carefully. I am heartily in sympathy with the movement, and trust that you may be able to secure the passage of some reasonable bill establishing the university in such a manner as will take it wholly out of competition with existing institutions of this country and make it of universal value to the nation.

I believe that the time is fully ripe for the establishment of such an institution. More, I believe that the condition of our country financially and politically demands such an institution. The Northwest is educationally wide awake and ready to aid in raising the standard of our national educational character, and will heartily join hands with the West, South, and East in aiding toward the proposed university.

Wishing you success, fraternally yours,

L. J. EISENHUTH
(State Superintendent).

STATE OF NORTH DAKOTA,
DEPARTMENT OF PUBLIC INSTRUCTION,
Bismarck, October 31, 1895.

DEAR SIR: Your favor of 22d instant was duly received and its contents noted. I am pleased to know of the university plans in detail, and willingly signify approval of the general proposition, and am pleased to be counted among its friends.

Yours, respectfully,

E. F. BATES,
State Superintendent of Public Instruction.

STATE OF NEVADA, DEPARTMENT OF EDUCATION,
Carson City, October 29, 1895.

DEAR SIR: Your letter asking for my support to the proposition of establishing a national university is just received, and I hasten to say that I am heartily in sympathy with the movement, and beg of you to call upon me for any assistance which I may render.

Respectfully yours,

H. C. CUTTING.

TERRITORIAL BOARD OF EDUCATION,
Guthrie, Okla., January 30, 1896.

DEAR SIR: I very much favor the national university, and will be very glad to do anything in my power to aid in the matter. You can use my name on the committee of one hundred.

Sincerely,

E. D. CAMERON,
Superintendent Public Instruction.

TERRITORIAL BOARD OF EDUCATION,
Guthrie, Okla., January 31, 1896.

DEAR SIR: This is to say to the committees of the Congress of the United States, through you, that I very much favor a national university, to be called the University of the United States. I will not attempt to give reasons here for thinking as I do on this great question. I like the plan outlined. It is a necessity if we propose to keep in the front of the procession among the nations of the world.

Respectfully,

E. D. CAMERON,
Superintendent Public Instruction.

DEPARTMENT OF PUBLIC INSTRUCTION,
Salem, Oreg., September 3, 1894.

DEAR SIR: Returning to this office again to-day I find your favor of August 25 on my table. I shall be pleased to assist you in the matter, and on receipt of the Senate documents mentioned by you I shall be pleased to examine the same carefully. In this matter you have my best wishes.

I remain, yours, very sincerely,
E. B. McELROY,
State Superintendent Public Instruction.

COMMONWEALTH OF PENNSYLVANIA,
DEPARTMENT OF PUBLIC INSTRUCTION,
Harrisburg, October 22, 1894.

DEAR SIR: I have not had time to give the subject of a national university the attention which it deserves, and do not feel prepared to say anything for or against the movement. In a general way I am heartily in favor of any forward movement in the cause of higher education.

Yours, truly,
N. C. SCHAEFFER
(State Superintendent Public Instruction).

PHILADELPHIA, PA., *December 15, 1894.*

DEAR SIR: I have during the last month paid some attention to the scheme of a national university, and the more I study the question the more anxious I feel to see it realized. You can count on me for any support which my official position will enable me to give. I shall make it a point to speak to members of Congress from Pennsylvania as I chance to meet them from time to time.

Very respectfully yours,
NATHAN C. SCHAEFFER,
State Superintendent of Public Instruction.

STATE OF RHODE ISLAND,
OFFICE COMMISSIONER OF PUBLIC SCHOOLS,
Providence, October 23, 1894.

MY DEAR SIR: I have read the bill which has been prepared, and so far as I can judge therefrom I am heartily in favor of its passage. I have long felt that the facilities afforded by our Government for the highest education were very defective; that we should never attain to the position in the world of science and letters to which we are really entitled until the National Government made definite and adequate provision for the support of our best scholars while engaged in the highest realms of knowledge and research.

It is impossible for one engaged in work of this highest order to either make it yield him a livelihood or to turn aside therefrom and earn it. These upper walks allow no subordinate subject to divert the mind.

Such a scheme as that proposed would, it seems to me, tend to correlate and unify the work of our institutions of learning throughout the country and offer an incentive to bright, active, vigorous young men in every State to push their studies to the highest attainable point.

I am confident it would raise the general scholarship of the whole country. I shall hope to see the measure carried through during the next session of Congress.

Wishing you the fullest success, I have the honor to be, yours, very sincerely,
THOS. B. STOCKWELL *(Commissioner).*

OFFICE COMMISSIONER PUBLIC SCHOOLS,
Providence, R. I., April 19, 1895.

DEAR SIR: In reply to your request of the 10th instant, for permission to use my name in making up a committee for the furtherance of the interests of the national university, I would say that if in your judgment it will be of any advantage to the cause I have no objection to your so using it. There is unquestionably a field for such a university, and I shall be glad to promote its establishment.

Trusting that your efforts may at no distant day meet with success, I remain, yours, very truly,

THOS. B. STOCKWELL, *Commissioner.*

STATE OF SOUTH CAROLINA, DEPARTMENT OF EDUCATION,
Columbia, S. C., October 25, 1895.

DEAR SIR: I beg to acknowledge receipt of your favor of October 22, with inclosure, and to signify my approval of the general proposition to secure the establishment of a national post-graduate university at Washington, D. C.

Yours, very truly,

W. D. MAYFIELD,
State Superintendent of Education.

STATE OF SOUTH DAKOTA,
DEPARTMENT OF PUBLIC INSTRUCTION,
Pierre, S. Dak., January 9, 1892.

DEAR SIR: I am heartily in sympathy with the movement for a national university, and hope that we may soon begin to see our way to furnishing our young men with a university education in fact as well as in name. Success to your efforts.

Yours, very truly,

C. SALMON (*Superintendent*).

STATE OF SOUTH DAKOTA,
DEPARTMENT OF PUBLIC INSTRUCTION,
Pierre, October 23, 1894.

DEAR SIR: I sincerely hope that Congress may soon be brought to see the importance of a national university—one that will in time compare favorably with the European universities, and one which, like them, will attract and call together the educational leaders of the country.

I am watching the movement with much interest.

Yours, very truly,

CORTEZ SALMON (*Superintendent*).

STATE OF TENNESSEE,
DEPARTMENT OF PUBLIC INSTRUCTIONS,
Nashville, Tenn., November 13, 1895.

DEAR SIR: Your circular letter of October 22 is before me, and has been given careful consideration. I have also received Senate documents dealing with the same subject.

I am in hearty sympathy with the measure to establish in the United States a national university. Such a university, rightly managed, would stimulate every college and higher institution of learning in the land. It would do much for the cause of education, and would have a powerful tendency to inculcate a broader patriotism.

Yours, truly,

S. G. GILBREATH
(*State Superintendent*).

DEPARTMENT OF EDUCATION,
Austin, Tex., November 2, 1894.

DEAR SIR: I certainly wish much success to the efforts for the establishment of a national university. I regret that I have not the time to give the matter a more careful investigation at this time.

Most respectfully,
J. M. CARLISLE
(*State Superintendent*).

DEPARTMENT OF EDUCATION,
Austin, Tex., April 16, 1895.

DEAR SIR: Replying to your letter of the 10th, permit me to express my sincere thanks for the compliment paid me in your letter by asking me to serve on your committee to present the claims of a national university to the next Congress. I shall be pleased to accept such position, with the understanding that I will not be able to contribute much active service to the efforts of this committee on account of the increasing amount of work to be done in this department.

Most respectfully,
J. M. CARLISLE, *State Superintendent.*

OFFICE OF COMMISSIONER OF SCHOOLS,
Ogden, Utah, October 28, 1895.

DEAR SIR: Your communication of the 22d instant is received. While my manifold duties will not permit me to elaborate my reasons, I can assure you that I heartily indorse the movement to establish a national post-graduate university at Washington.

Respectfully,
T. B. LEWIS,
Territorial Commissioner of Schools.

SUPERINTENDENT OF EDUCATION, STATE OF VERMONT,
Montpelier, September, 1894.

DEAR SIR: During my absence in August the "memorial" was misplaced, and was not discovered till last week, or I should have replied earlier. I meanwhile had been waiting for the document, thinking you had not sent it.

It is a magnificent undertaking, and I heartily hope it will go through.

Very sincerely,
MASON S. STONE (*Superintendent*).

SUPERINTENDENT OF EDUCATION, STATE OF VERMONT,
Montpelier, October 6, 1894.

DEAR SIR: Your communication asking my opinion concerning the establishment of a national university at Washington is received, and I take pleasure in giving my unqualified and hearty indorsement of the project.

Such an institution would meet a national want and form a fitting capsheaf to our educational system.

It would be a means for the perpetuation of those ideas distinctly American and furnish an opportunity and stimulation to such as desire to pursue post-graduate work here in America.

A progressive nation like our own can not afford to have it said that its young men must go to Europe to complete their education.

We have resources sufficient to support such a university, the advancement of learning demands such, and our reputation among the nations of the earth can be enhanced in no better way.

Hoping that the present Congress will be wise in the nation's highest educational interests, I remain, very sincerely, yours,
MASON S. STONE
(*Superintendent of Education, State of Vermont*).

SUPERINTENDENT OF EDUCATION, STATE OF VERMONT,
Montpelier, October 12, 1895.

DEAR SIR: Your card of October 8 is at hand, and I hasten to say that you may rely upon me for any aid that I can consistently render. Congratulating you upon the progress made by our cause, I remain, very truly, yours,

MASON S. STONE.

DEPARTMENT OF PUBLIC INSTRUCTION,
SUPERINTENDENT'S OFFICE,
Richmond, Va., November 4, 1895.

DEAR SIR: Pressing official duties have prevented an earlier answer to your favor of 22d ultimo.

I can only say in reply to it, I am heartily in favor of the establishment of a "national post-graduate university at Washington," and will cheerfully do what I can to further the enterprise.

Very respectfully, JOHN E. MASSEY
(Ex-Lieutenant-Governor of Virginia, Superintendent of Public Instruction).

OFFICE OF SUPERINTENDENT OF PUBLIC INSTRUCTION,
STATE OF WASHINGTON,
Olympia, Wash., September 15, 1894.

MY DEAR SIR: I have long felt a deep interest in the proposition to found a national university at our Federal capital, as suggested by Washington and since urged by many of our distinguished statesmen and scholars, and have at times grown almost impatient with the delay in consummating this grand and patriotic conception. Such a university should stand for all that is modern and scholarly throughout the world; but it should especially emphasize what is distinctively American, and should afford foreign students the opportunity of studying American institutions on their native soil.

I should hardly urge it from the standpoint of the economist as a means of keeping our students at home and offering them all the opportunities available at foreign universities, for I believe it is wise for the student to go abroad; but I urge it most earnestly as a competitor of the best foreign universities for the patronage of students from every nation. It should be the common opinion in all foreign countries within the next fifty years that their scholars could lay no claim to an adequate knowledge of American institutions unless they have studied in the "University of the United States." The fostering of such a sentiment at home and abroad is necessary to the greatness of American scholarship and American institutions.

Very truly yours,
C. W. BEAN
(Superintendent Public Instruction).

STATE OF WEST VIRGINIA, DEPARTMENT OF FREE SCHOOLS,
Charleston, January 1, 1896.

DEAR SIR: Replying to your esteemed favor of the 30th ultimo, I have to say that you have authority to enter my name among the list of those desiring to promote the interest of the national university of the United States. I supposed that my name had been placed in this connection.

Yours, most obediently, VIRGIL A. LEWIS,
State Superintendent Free Schools.

OFFICE SUPERINTENDENT OF PUBLIC INSTRUCTION,
Cheyenne, Wyo., January 6, 1896.

DEAR SIR: I have your letter of December 30, and would be very glad to have you add my name to those who are in favor of a national university, as it is something I would very much like to see established.

Very truly yours, E. REEL *(State Superintendent.)*

LETTERS FROM HEADS OF SCIENTIFIC INSTITUTIONS AND BUREAUS OF THE GOVERNMENT.

SMITHSONIAN INSTITUTION,
Washington, D. C., March 25, 1895.

DEAR SIR: I have the honor to acknowledge the receipt of your note of March 21, with reference to the plan for the national university which has been laid before Congress; and while I regret to find that my official engagements will prevent me from giving the subject the attention that I desire, I have asked Dr. Thomas Wilson, of the Smithsonian Institution, who is much interested in the subject, to represent me in discussing the matter when you may find it convenient to call.

With kind regards, very truly yours,

S. P. LANGLEY, *Secretary.*

SMITHSONIAN INSTITUTION,
Washington, D. C., April 12, 1895.

SIR: In response to your request for the use of my name on the committee of one hundred for the furtherance of the establishment of a national university at Washington, I take pleasure in authorizing you to place my name on the committee.

Very respectfully yours,

S. P. LANGLEY.

[The deep interest of Dr. G. Browne Goode, assistant secretary of the Smithsonian Institution, in charge of the National Museum, and his broad views on the subject of the university are manifest in many ways. For example, in his able address on "The nation's debt of honor," before the late Pan-Republic Congress of 1891, wherein, among other things, he said:]

Mr. PRESIDENT: Congress has, however, failed to extend its direct patronage to any educational enterprise of the highest grade. Unlike most of the Governments of the Old World, it supports no faculties of learned men whose duty it is to discover truth and give it to the world. It has not yet provided a national university so excellent that it is not necessary, in the language of Washington, "for the youth of the United States to migrate to foreign countries in order to acquire the higher branches of education." While it has established a great system of schools under the patronage of the several States, it has failed to provide a central institution which shall serve as a model for all the others, train teachers for their faculties, afford their scholars post-graduate instruction, and add character and dignity, intellectual and moral, to the nation's capital. * * *

The sum of $4,401,000 [amount of Washington's bequest with compound interest to the present time], if appropriated for this purpose by Congress, and placed in the Treasury of the United States, there to remain paying interest at 6 per cent, would yield over $264,000 each year, a sum that would provide for many professorships, lectureships and scholarships, and fellowships, as well as for the current expenses of several seminaries or colleges. Private gifts would in time be added in large amounts, and Congress would of course erect such buildings as from time to time were found necessary.

UNITED STATES NAVAL OBSERVATORY, GEORGETOWN HEIGHTS,
Washington, D. C., October 24, 1895.

DEAR SIR: Please accept my thanks for the "Memorial in regard to a national university," referred to in your letter of the 19th instant.

An institution proposed by Washington and indorsed by the most distinguished men of his own and following generations is well worthy of the intelligent efforts now being made to found it upon a secure basis.

The plan of the committee of which you are the chairman will, if adopted, place the institution upon the high plane that it should occupy.

Referring to the last paragraph of your letter, I shall deem it an honor to be enrolled among the supporters of this plan, and shall cheerfully lend my feeble and humble efforts to its success.

Very respectfully,
R. L. PHYTHIAN,
Commodore U. S. N., Superintendent of Naval Observatory.

DEPARTMENT OF THE INTERIOR,
UNITED STATES GEOLOGICAL SURVEY,
Washington, D. C., November 2, 1894.

DEAR SIR: Yours of November 1 relating to the establishment of a national university at Washington received.

I will bring the matter up before the council of the Geological Society of Washington. I feel a strong interest in the higher education, and shall be happy to do anything in my power to advance it.

I shall read the pamphlets you mention when they come to hand.

Yours, very truly,
CHAS. D. WALCOTT
(Director of the Geological Survey).

DEPARTMENT OF THE INTERIOR,
UNITED STATES GEOLOGICAL SURVEY,
Washington, D. C., December 20, 1894.

DEAR SIR: I fully believe in establishing such a university in the interest of higher education, and I cordially indorse the statements made by the late President James C. Welling, printed on pages 95–97 of your memorial, on the subject. The statements and views expressed in the memorial are so exhaustive and comprehensive that I do not know that I could add to them, except to record my personal approval of the movement.

Yours, very truly,
CHAS. D. WALCOTT.

[The views of the late Dr. James C. Welling, for a long time president of the Columbia University, District of Columbia, referred to, are here quoted:]

"Such a university as I here prefigure would come into no rivalry with any existing institution under the control of any denomination. It would aim to be the crown and culmination of our State institutions, borrowing graduates from them and repaying its debt by contributing in turn the inspiration of high educational standards, and helping also in its measure to train the experts, * * * who should elsewhere strive to keep alive the traditions of a progressive scholarship. * * * It is not enough that our colleges should perpetuate and transmit the existing sum of human knowledge. We must have our workers on the boundaries of a progressive knowledge if we are to establish our hold on the directive forces of modern society."

UNITED STATES COAST AND GEODETIC SURVEY,
Washington, D. C., December 24, 1891.

DEAR SIR: I hope you will not grow weary in pushing this matter.

Yours, faithfully,
T. C. MENDENHALL
(As Superintendent of United States Coast and Geodetic Survey).

UNITED STATES COAST AND GEODETIC SURVEY,
Washington, D. C., October 26, 1895.

MY DEAR SIR: I beg to acknowledge the receipt of your letter of the 15th instant, to which I have given careful attention.

You seem to have covered the whole ground, and I do not think your plan can be improved or even modified to advantage.

I shall always be glad to aid you in every possible way in carrying out your plans to a successful result.

Yours, very respectfully,

W. W. DUFFIELD,
Superintendent.

WASHINGTON, D. C., *March 10, 1896.*

MY DEAR SIR: Your plan for organizing a national university meets with my hearty approval. A national school designed primarily for training men in scientific research is now the great need of American education. There are at the seat of Government libraries, museums, and apparatus for research necessary to the use of such an institution. It yet needs an organization of personnel and the halls in which instructors and pupils may meet.

I am, yours, cordially,

J. W. POWELL.
(Director of the Bureau of Ethnology).

DEPARTMENT OF AGRICULTURE, WEATHER BUREAU,
Washington, D. C., December 9, 1891.

MY DEAR SIR: I have looked over the summary with very great interest. Your plan is a broad one, and I do not know that I have any suggestions to make at present. What I said to you the other day, of course, contemplated the possibility of using the university for professional education. This is not properly in applied science, but in theoretical science.

I will be glad to discuss the matter further with you when I see you again.

Very truly yours,

MARK W. HARRINGTON
(As Chief of Weather Bureau).

INTERSTATE COMMERCE COMMISSION,
Washington, November 26, 1892.

DEAR SIR: Please accept my thanks for the copy of your memorial in regard to a national university. Without having given the subject studied investigation or consideration, it has always awakened feelings of pride and patriotism in my heart, and I am very glad that it has the benefit of your vigorous and intelligent support.

Again thanking you, I am, very truly, yours,

W. G. VEAZEY *(Commissioner).*

1620 P STREET,
Washington, D. C., December 6, 1894.

MY DEAR SIR: Whenever there is anything to be done, please let me know the time and place, and I will be on hand if possible. Glad the project is still alive.

Very sincerely yours,

S. NEWCOMB
(Superintendent Nautical Almanac).

DEPARTMENT OF LABOR,
Washington, D. C., November 8, 1895.

DEAR SIR: I am in receipt of your communication of the 7th instant, relative to the establishment of a national post-graduate university at Washington, and in reply to your inquiry I would say that I have always been in favor of the establishment of such a university. You are at liberty, therefore, to count me as one among its friends.

I am, respectfully,

CARROLL D. WRIGHT
(*Commissioner*).

SMITHSONIAN INSTITUTION, DEPARTMENT OF ENTOMOLOGY,
Washington, December 11, 1894.

MY DEAR GOVERNOR: Nothing that I could say would add weight to the arguments which you have already mustered in favor of the project, and I do sincerely hope that your efforts may soon bear fruit, and that Congress may pass the bill now before it, or some similar bill, in order that so worthy a project may at once be started on its useful career. There is already much of the material centered in the national capital necessary to the founding of such a national educational institution, and I can conceive of nothing that would have a more marked and beneficial influence on our future national life than such an institution, providing its foundation be well laid and its future substantially guaranteed.

Believe me, my dear Governor, yours, sincerely,

C. V. RILEY (*Curator, etc.*).

2115 CHESTNUT STREET,
Philadelphia, Pa., November 11, 1895.

MY DEAR SIR: Your letter of November 6, with inclosure, is received. You may certainly count me as one of the friends of the proposed national university, and you are authorized to add my name to your list of indorsers if you think it worth while to do so.

Very truly yours,

J. S. BILLINGS
(*Late Superintendent of Army Medical Museum*).

2115 CHESTNUT STREET,
Philadelphia, November 25, 1895.

DEAR SIR: I have your note of the 22d instant, with inclosures, for which I am much obliged. I have been retired from the Army at my own request, and have accepted the position of professor of hygiene and director of the laboratory of hygiene in the University of Pennsylvania. I am much interested in your plan for a national university, and shall be glad to do what I can to call attention to the need of action by Congress in the matter.

Very sincerely yours,

JOHN S. BILLINGS
(*Late Superintendent of Army Medical Museum*).

LETTERS FROM HEADS OF NATIONAL ORGANIZATIONS, SCIENTIFIC AND PATRIOTIC.

AMERICAN PHILOSOPHICAL SOCIETY,
Philadelphia, February 1, 1895.

SIR: Your esteemed favor of January 8, 1895, addressed to Dr. Frederick Fraley, president of the American Philosophical Society, was duly received by him, and, with the accompanying documents, was laid before the society at its next regular meeting, and by it referred to the secretaries for reply.

We have the honor to assure you that the society heartily sympathizes in all plans looking toward the promotion and dissemination of useful knowledge. The proposed national university, if established on sound and judicious principles, would undoubtedly contribute potently to this end; and such a scheme therefore merits the encouragement and support of all friends of the higher education.

We remain, most respectfully, yours,

GEORGE F. BARKER,
D. G. BRINTON,
GEORGE H. HORN,
Secretaries.

AMERICAN INSTITUTE OF CIVICS,
New York, April 19, 1893.

DEAR SIR: I was glad to receive your courteous favor of March 19, with the accompanying documents. I am much interested in your efforts to promote the establishment of a national university, and trust that they will be successful. The great work in which the institute is engaged ought to be in some way allied with such an institution as you seek to establish. National, educational, and devoted solely to the promotion of the highest interests of government and citizenship, without regard to party, creed, or class, it would seem that it should be under the fostering care of an institution founded under the auspices of government, at the nation's capital, and intended to qualify American youth for the noblest exercise of their abilities and privileges as American citizens. Whether or not the realization of your plans and the realization of mine can be successfully related to each other, I shall be glad to do anything in my power to assist in your noble undertaking.

With highest respect, I am, very truly, yours,

H. R. WAITE, *President.*

AMERICAN INSTITUTE OF CIVICS,
New York, December 20, 1895.

DEAR SIR: Replying to your favor of December 18, permit me to say that if the plans which you seek to realize are such as I understand them to be, it will give me pleasure to serve as a member of the executive council of the provisional committee of the projected university of the United States.

I have only time at this moment to make this brief reply to your letter. A little later, I shall hope to correspond with you more fully as to present plans and the promise of success which attend your efforts.

With regards, very sincerely yours,

H. R. WAITE (*President*).

WHARTON SCHOOL OF FINANCE AND ECONOMY,
UNIVERSITY OF PENNSYLVANIA,
Philadelphia, April 18, 1893.

MY DEAR SIR: In answer to your favor of the 17th instant, I beg to say that I know no one thing in American education which is more important than the establishment of a national university at Washington, and I should be glad to aid this movement in any way possible.

Very truly yours,
EDMUND J. JAMES
(*President*).

AMERICAN ACADEMY OF POLITICAL AND SOCIAL SCIENCE,
Philadelphia, December 3, 1894.

DEAR SIR: I am much interested in the work of the committee on the national university, of which you are chairman. I hope that you will send me whatever information you may have about the great enterprise. Command my services to the fullest extent in this matter.

Very truly yours,
EDMUND J. JAMES
(*President, etc.*).

UNIVERSITY OF PENNSYLVANIA,
Philadelphia, November 13, 1895.

MY DEAR SIR: Your letter was received this morning. I am glad to hear that you are going to take up the urgent prosecution of the national university idea in the new Congress.

Very truly yours,
EDMUND J. JAMES
(*As President American Academy of Political and Social Science*).

PHILADELPHIA, *November 27, 1894.*

DEAR SIR: The project of establishing a national university at Washington has interested me for years, but I never saw any plan proposed that did not have serious objections or manifest shortcomings. I examined, therefore, your memorial, expecting to find that its scheme, too, would be open to like unfavorable criticism; and was agreeably surprised to perceive that you had avoided the objectionable features visible in others and present a practical, beneficent, and truly liberal outline which, if filled in and carried out in the same spirit, will endow our land with an institution which will prove an advantage and a glory to it for indefinite generations. Wishing your effort every success, I remain,

Very truly yours,
D. G. BRINTON
(*President of the American Association for the Advancement of Science, etc.*).

PHILADELPHIA, *April 13, 1895.*

DEAR SIR: Replying to yours of the 10th, I beg to say I am quite willing that my name should be added to the national committee on the university, as proposed.

Yours, very respectfully,
D. G. BRINTON
(*Late President American Association for the Advancement of Science*).

ASSOCIATION OF AMERICAN AGRICULTURAL COLLEGES
AND EXPERIMENT STATIONS,
Lewinsville, Fairfax County, Va., June 25, 1895.

DEAR SIR: Absence in the West temporarily, as per printing above, accounts for my failure to promptly receive and respond to your letter dated April 10, 1895.

Let me now reassure you of my interest in the important movement under your energetic and able leadership. I shall be only too glad to follow and cooperate in any way I can, and feel sure that the institutions, all beneficiaries of the National Government, which constitute the membership of the association above indicated, would willingly authorize me to speak for them collectively. (I have, however, no right to do this as yet.)

If not too late I should be pleased to be included in the membership of your enlarged committee of promotion, as you kindly suggest, and, as I am now to be in or near Washington City nearly all the time, you may freely call upon me for any assistance I can render.

Very respectfully yours,
HENRY E. ALVORD
(*As President of Association*).

ASSOCIATION OF AMERICAN AGRICULTURAL COLLEGES
AND EXPERIMENT STATIONS,
Lewinsville, Fairfax County, Va., January 16, 1895.

DEAR SIR: Please accept my thanks for your letters of December 20 and January 8, and the documents which accompanied them.

The project for the establishment of the university of the United States has always been of interest to me, and since its recent revival I have said and done the little I could in its behalf. I trust that a realization of the long-cherished desires of the friends of this great enterprise is near at hand.

Through the wise policy of the Federal Government in devoting a portion of the proceeds of public lands to education, endowments for research and for higher instruction have been established in every State. Although properly under local control and upon broad and elastic bases, which enable them to be adapted to local needs and conditions, these institutions constitute a national system, which still lacks a finish and head. They are like the States without the Union. The proposed university, its sphere and relations carefully defined, offers a most appropriate and important finish to the provisions for higher education already made by the Government of the United States.

You and your active colaborers deserve the best wishes and the heartiest cooperation on the part of all friends of education throughout the country I am sure you can especially depend for such aid as lies in their power upon those connected with the existing institutions based upon grants of public land and its proceeds. These institutions keenly feel the need of a closer bond of union and central guide, such as would be admirably supplied by the university of the United States.

Very truly yours,
HENRY E. ALVORD (*President*).

---

31 NASSAU STREET, *New York, August 5, 1895.*

MY DEAR SIR: Your esteemed favor of Saturday last is at hand.

You may count on my friendly cooperation in any direction in my power in your noble efforts.

When the general society meets I shall lay the matter, D. V., before them.

I am, dear sir, with sentiments of respect, faithfully yours,
ASA BIRD GARDINER,
General Secretary of the Society of the Cincinnati.

SOCIETY OF THE CINCINNATI,
New York, August 2, 1895.

MR DEAR SIR: Your esteemed favor of yesterday is at hand. You have my most cordial interest in your proposed educational work. Above all things I hope there will be a properly endowed chair of American history - a subject I have given much attention to. When I was professor of law at the United States Military Academy, West Point, I always found that references to incidents of American history were greedily listened to by the cadets.

Very truly yours, ASA BIRD GARDINER,
General Secretary.

GENERAL SOCIETY SONS OF THE REVOLUTION,
Washington, D. C., December 18, 1894.

MY DEAR SIR: Your valued favor of November 9, with pamphlet, is at hand. I have read both with great interest, and heartily approve of your undertaking.

Yours, very faithfully, JAMES MARTEMIS MONTGOMERY,
General Secretary.

[For letters of Ex-Governor John Lee Carroll, LL. D., of Maryland, General President of Sons of the Revolution, and of Gen. Horace Porter, LL. D., President-General of Sons of American Revolution, see page 65.]

LETTERS FROM OTHER EMINENT CITIZENS IN OFFICIAL AND PRIVATE LIFE.

THE CONCORD,
Washington, D. C., December 5, 1894.

MY DEAR SIR: Careful observation of educational thought in this country for a quarter of a century convinces me that its natural outcome is to be found in the realization of the idea of a national university sustained by Government patronage at the capital of the nation, outranking all others in the land, so earnestly urged by Washington and his compeers. Many have feared the injurious effects of a political capital upon a seat of learning located near it. This fear led some to oppose the establishment of the University of Berlin; but experience has proved that the university was not injured, and the capital was benefited.

Intelligence and virtue joined must indeed be the corner stone of our free institutions, and their influence must pervade them from foundation to capstone. The more their influence is concentrated upon the management of public affairs, the greater the safeguards against ignorance and corruption, and the more likely the improvement of the public service. The greatest republic has need of, and should have at command, the conditions favorable to the highest learning.

The selection of Washington as the seat for great universities under private control points to a growing appreciation of the fact that nowhere else are such favorable conditions possible. The Senate bill does not antagonize them, but would crown them with higher opportunities. Besides, the most remote district school needs, and would be benefited by, the university proposed, and the maintenance at Washington of the grandest university of the world would serve to answer the legitimate demand of the aspiring peoples of the earth that our institutions of learning should afford opportunities for research and instruction not excelled under any other form of government.

Very respectfully yours, etc.,

JOHN EATON
(*Former United States Commissioner of Education*).

CHICAGO, *November 3, 1894.*

MY DEAR SIR: I sincerely hope that the effort to secure the establishment by Congress of a national post-graduate university at Washington may be crowned with speedy success. Such a university will be the noble and worthy representative of the nation in the republic of letters and in the growing empire of science. It will give a new luster to our national capital and a new glory to our national name. I believe that it will stimulate investigation and heighten scholarship and quicken educational interest and enthusiasm throughout the country.

With much regard, I remain, yours, cordially,

JOHN H. BARROWS
(*President Late World's Parliament of Religions*).

FIRST PRESBYTERIAN CHURCH,
Chicago, Ill., April 15, 1895.

MY DEAR SIR: Your letters of April 10 and 11 are received. Did you know that Chauncey M. Depew closed an address before the Chicago University recently with an earnest plea for an international university at Washington?

Yours, very truly,

JOHN HENRY BARROWS
(*Lately President World's Congress of Religions*).

[See p. 138.]

[The following is a single passage from the above-mentioned address of Hon. Chauncey M. Depew, LL. D., of New York:]

"It would be a long step forward in popularizing higher education if the Government should establish at Washington a great national university. As at Oxford or at Cambridge there are historic colleges with foundations running for hundreds of years, each having its own traditions, but all part of the university, so in every State there would be colleges, each having its own traditions, and yet all of them belonging to the grand university which will represent the culture of the New World—the university of the United States."

GEOLOGICAL SURVEY OF ALABAMA,
University, Ala., April 15, 1895.

DEAR SIR: I have received your circular of April 10, and send you herewith permission to use my name in connection with the national committee, as described in that circular. I feel much interest in the success of the undertaking.

Yours, very truly,

EUGENE A. SMITH
(State Geologist).

EPISCOPAL RESIDENCE, 1110 MADISON AVENUE,
Baltimore, August 31, 1892.

DEAR SIR: Without pledging myself to all the details, I am warmly in favor of the general proposition of establishing a national university in the city of Washington.

Yours, truly,

WILLIAM PARET, *Bishop of Maryland.*

CINCINNATI SOCIETY OF NATURAL HISTORY,
Cincinnati, January 21, 1895.

DEAR SIR: Your favor of the 8th instant, addressed to my predecessor, has been put in my hands for attention. I am sure that all patriotic citizens, and especially those who are interested in the promotion of science, will look with great satisfaction upon the establishment of a national university in the capital city of the nation.

I trust that the organization will carefully guard against the greatest peril that can menace the success of such an institution—the entrance in its management of partisan politics or any politics whatsoever.

Wishing you the greatest success in your work, I am yours, truly,

DAVIS L. JAMES,
President Cincinnati Society Natural History.

CINCINNATI SOCIETY OF NATURAL HISTORY,
Cincinnati, April 20, 1895.

DEAR SIR: In answer to your favor of the 10th instant, allow me to say that I shall be honored by having my name included in your national committee on the university of the United States, and shall be pleased to do anything in my power to promote the plan of its establishment.

Very truly,

DAVIS L. JAMES,
President Cincinnati Society Natural History.

THE ACADEMY OF SCIENCE OF ST. LOUIS,
St. Louis, January 5, 1892.

DEAR SIR: Responding to your note, I hasten to reply that I favor the idea of establishing a national university at Washington, if it is properly organized.

Very truly yours,

FRANCIS E. NIPHER *(President).*

TWIN OAKS, *May 13, 1895.*

DEAR SIR: I am in receipt of your favor of the 11th instant, and have read your paper with much interest. I believe in the necessity of a national university, as you well know, and am willing to help on the movement by every means in my power.

GARDINER G. HUBBARD
(*President National Geographic Society*).

UNIVERSITY OF STATE OF NEW YORK, NEW YORK STATE MUSEUM,
Albany, January 19, 1892.

DEAR SIR: I have received your favor of the 9th referring to your plan of a great national university. I need only reply that you are quite at liberty to use my name in the publication which you propose.

Very truly yours,

JAMES HALL, *State Geologist.*

GEOLOGICAL SURVEY OF ALABAMA,
University, Ala., November 5, 1895.

DEAR SIR: Your communication of the 26th of October has been received. Your proposition to create an executive council and the manner of creating it meet my hearty approval. I believe such a body of men would be in position to do much toward promoting the success of the measure. Dr. Jones, president of this university, will write to you immediately in regard to the matters referred to in your letters, as he has great interest therein.

Yours, very truly,

EUGENE A. SMITH (*State Geologist*).

LITTLE ROCK, ARK., *January 15, 1894.*

DEAR SIR: Most decidedly you may count me among the friends of the national university proposition.

Very truly yours,

J. C. BRANNER (*State Geologist*).

GEOLOGICAL AND NATURAL HISTORY SURVEY OF MINNESOTA,
Minneapolis, Minn., January 10, 1895.

MY DEAR SIR: I have received the printed copies of the addresses of Senator Hunton, of Virginia, and of Senator Vilas, of Wisconsin, for which please accept my thanks. I have read of the movement before and am glad of the more full information respecting it. I am heartily in sympathy with the project as it appears in these addresses and in the communications printed in connection therewith, and I shall be glad to cooperate in any way that may be in my power to secure the desired end. Without time now to go into the detailed statement of reasons, accept my personal assurance.

Very cordially yours,

N. H. WINCHELL, *State Geologist.*

STATE OF MISSOURI, BUREAU OF GEOLOGY AND MINES,
Jefferson City, January 12, 1894.

MY DEAR SIR: I trust that there will be established at the capital of the nation a national university supported liberally by the Federal Government. The facilities of Washington for post-graduate work and original investigation are so superior that it becomes the duty of the nation to maintain an institution for advanced study. I sincerely hope that the bill will pass and become a law.

Cordially yours,

CHARLES R. KEYES (*State Geologist*).

OFFICE OF CUSTODIAN OF AMERICAN HISTORY,
2302 Spruce Street, Philadelphia, Pa., October 20, 1891.

DEAR DOCTOR: If Washington left in his will the sum of £5,000 to found a national university why is not that institution now established? I have met with some men who are deeply interested in the subject of the erection of a national university at Washington, and the organizing of a distinctly national system of education that would be the natural outcome of such an institution.

If a national university is established one of the most important schools to be erected would be that of "Americana." The study of civics has been largely omitted in our schools and colleges, and where political economy has entered into the curriculum it has been generally considered not from a purely American standpoint, but usually from the rulings and ideas of Europe, which are more monarchical than republican. Then, too, the teaching has been for the aid of the ruler, while it ought to be for the instruction of the voter first, leaving the study of governmental and diplomatic service as secondary. We have a distinctly American political economy, and it is yet to be fully developed. American history is but little known. The schools learn something of English history and the English constitution, but practically American history and American constitutional law are known by few who have made these studies a specialty. We have a vast country and our post-office reaches to every nook and corner, but the boy of 12 is supposed to have learned all the geography there is for him to know. It seems to me that our countrymen ought to be informed respecting all the various parts of our land—its minerals, its productions, its facilities for transportation, and all the other various things that make the United States one of the richest, if not the richest, lands of the earth. We have an interstate commerce, and we will soon have a reciprocal interchange of commodities with the other remaining American States that are not of our Union. The student of "Americana" ought to be instructed in all the matters relating to our own and our neighbors' public affairs, and be thoroughly informed respecting everything that relates in any way to the American continent, its business, its social life, its history, its geography, its productions, and its laws. Our country needs such a school and a class of men that such a school will graduate.

HENRY BALDWIN
(*Custodian of American History*).

Dr. G. BROWN GOODE,
Smithsonian Institution.

OFFICE OF CUSTODIAN OF AMERICAN HISTORY,
New Haven, Conn., December 13, 1894.

DEAR SIR: I am exceedingly anxious that the bill before Congress for the national university shall meet with favor. I believe that it is a necessity for the faithful education of the community, and I see no other way to establish in our country a uniform educational system than by adopting some method in this direction. I am glad to learn from your letter that there is some hope of a vote being reached in the Senate respecting the national university, and I trust that the House will also meet the matter with favor.

Very sincerely yours,

HENRY BALDWIN,
Custodian of American History.

OFFICE OF CUSTODIAN OF AMERICAN HISTORY,
New Haven, Conn., March 11, 1896.

MY DEAR SIR: While there are very many arguments to be adduced in support of the national university proposition, I prefer to view it from the standpoint of freedom.

The United States is to-day the home of liberty. We enjoy freedom as no other people. This freedom was obtained by the Revolutionary war and the war of 1812, and secured by the result of the civil strife of 1861–1865. It cost much. It remains with us to be maintained. It is to us worth all it cost, and should be esteemed of equal value to the many people outside of our boundaries who live upon our continent and the adjacent islands. Having and enjoying it, we should as far as possible secure it to the Latin Republics. They will be glad to accept such help as we are able to offer. We are before the nations as a lighted candle in a candlestick and "should so let our light shine that others seeing our good works may also glorify God."

We have not only liberty but extent of territory and a vast population. What we need is universal intelligence and means of the highest culture. We are just now in a ripe condition for the introduction of a new feature. We ought to have in our own land the most learned and the most practical men of the world. We have some such, but are not yet in a position to lead.

It is not enough that we are foremost in freedom. We can and should also lead in education, in science, in the highest learning as well.

The university of the United States ought to be distinctly and thoroughly American. The very nature of its institution by the Government will make it so. It will teach Americanism from a standpoint that is not partisan, or sectional, or sectarian. It can not be led by any one society, organization, clique, or party, but must be national in its character, practical in its scope, beneficent in its influence—a sun and shield for all that is best and dearest in the Government bequeathed to us by our fathers.

The university of the United States should be:

(1) The most powerful factor in preserving the institutions of liberty.

(2) It should teach the American people the value of liberty.

(3) It should and would become a powerful factor in removing all sectional feeling among our people; make us one people, and forever obliterate the political significance of North, South, East, and West. We are, and it should come to be understood that we are, one people—the American people.

(4) It should aid Congress and the Executive in upholding liberty at home and in protecting it in the hands of the feebler nations of this continent.

(5) It should help to make the American people the most cultivated and most useful of the nations.

It will cost us less to maintain liberty through the peaceful agency of instruction, authoritative and powerful to guide and restrain, than by the clash of armies.

We want patriots fully competent to fight the battles of peace, and we must have a national university as the best means of producing them.

Sincerely yours,
HENRY BALDWIN.

---

39 HIGHLAND STREET, *Roxbury, Mass., January 1, 1892.*

MY DEAR SIR: I certainly am very much interested in the plan for the national university, and I think, if it is wisely pressed, something important may come of it.

Truly yours,
EDWARD EVERETT HALE.

NEW YORK, *December 20, 1895.*

DEAR SIR: Your letter of the 14th came duly to hand, but in some way or other was mislaid.

I am quite willing to help you if I can about the university. You can use my name if you like if this letter does not reach you at too late a date.

Truly yours,
CEPHAS BRAINERD.

NEWPORT, R. I., *August 20, 1891.*

DEAR SIR: In reply to yours of the 12th instant, allow me to ask that my name be appended to the recommendation for the national university.

Very truly yours,
THOMAS M. CLARK (*Bishop of Rhode Island*),

142   UNIVERSITY OF THE UNITED STATES.

THE SPIRIT OF '76, PUBLICATION OFFICE,
New York, August 24, 1895.

DEAR SIR: I was glad to hear from and will be pleased to serve you if possible. Now, as to the university matter, I want to know:

1. What actually became of the bequest of Washington, and who (by name) were the custodians of the bonds?
2. Did the Virginia Society of the Cincinnati turn over $40,000 (or any amount) to this university fund; if so, where is it now? These are important points, and I exceedingly desire to learn something about them, and as soon as possible.

If you can do nothing, can you refer to any other person who is likely to know anything about these things? I will appreciate a reply.

Yours, respectfully,   A. H. BREARLEY.

PAN-REPUBLIC CONGRESS ORGANIZING COMMITTEE,
Newark, N. J., November 29, 1892.

MY DEAR GOVERNOR: It is a great privilege to be permitted to contribute the first dollar to that which, next to the United States of America, will be the grandest monument to the memory of George Washington. As chairman of the organizing committee of the Human Freedom League I desire to contribute the second, which I inclose. It may be possible that the small contributions of the many will go further in accomplishing the success of the great thought to which you have given your life than the fewer larger contributions from the very rich.

Sincerely yours,   WILLIAM O. McDOWELL.

NEWARK, N. J., *March, 21, 1893.*

MY DEAR GOVERNOR HOYT: I am so glad to know that things are moving satisfactorily in the university matter.

Sincerely yours,   W. O. McDOWELL

GEOLOGICAL SURVEY OF ALABAMA,
University, Ala., February 6, 1895.

DEAR SIR: I have received your letter of the 5th January relative to the national university. The proposition to establish a national university for the United States, as set forth in your memorial and the accompanying papers, meets my hearty approval, and I trust that Congress will soon take such action as will insure the success of the undertaking.

Yours, very truly,   EUGENE A. SMITH
(*State Geologist*).

COMMONWEALTH OF MASSACHUSETTS, EXECUTIVE DEPARTMENT,
Boston, September 13, 1895.

DEAR SIR: Governor Greenhalge is in receipt of your letter of the 4th instant in regard to the establishment of a national university at Washington, also public documents accompanying the same, and his excellency directs me to inform you that you are at liberty to count him as one of the friends of the university.

Yours, truly,   H. A. THOMAS, *Private Secretary.*

STATE OF CONNECTICUT, EXECUTIVE DEPARTMENT,
Hartford, October 4, 1895.

DEAR SIR: Referring to your letter of September 4, the governor has just returned from a prolonged absence from the State and directs me to say he heartily approves the general proposition set forth in your letter, and believes that an institution founded on the basis proposed will be of great value in many ways.

Yours, truly,   FRANK D. HAINES, *Executive Secretary.*

409 CHESTNUT STREET, *Philadelphia, April 30, 1895.*

DEAR SIR: I am favored with your letter of April 23, and also with the documents you were kind enough to send me respecting the establishment of a national postgraduate university at Washington.

I agree with you in believing that it is a most beneficent and important enterprise. I see no reason why there should not be entire unanimity in both the House of Representatives and the Senate in carrying out what was evidently a well-defined purpose of the fathers of the Republic. I heartily approve of the object you have in view.

Yours, truly,

SAMUEL R. SHIPLEY.

LAW OFFICE OF WARREN HIGLEY, 120 BROADWAY,
New York, April 3, 1893.

DEAR SIR: I beg to acknowledge receipt of memorial in re national university, and Senator Proctor's report.

May you have success in your noble effort to found a great national university.

Very sincerely yours,

WARREN HIGLEY.

UNIVERSITY OF VIRGINIA,
Charlottesville, Va., December 28, 1891.

DEAR GOVERNOR HOYT: I have the honor to acknowledge the receipt of your most courteous letter of the 23d instant inviting my cooperation in the national university work. I have ever been and now am deeply interested in the work, and shall deem it a great honor to be counted among its friends and supporters. Whenever the scheme of a national university association shall be matured, I hope you will call upon me for any work that can be done toward furthering and developing the plan. In the meantime I beg to thank you most cordially for the honor of your invitation, and with hearty good wishes for eminent success, remain,

Yours, very respectfully,

M. SCHELE DE VERE.

4333 FORRESTVILLE AVENUE, *Chicago, January 10, 1893.*

MY DEAR SIR: Please accept my sincere thanks for the copy of the "Memorial in regard to a national university." I wish I had known of it before writing my address. At my first moment of leisure I shall read it with all the attention and care it deserves.

I shall anxiously look out for your bill, and whether I agree with it or not as to all details, be sure that there will be no heartier well-wisher to it than

Yours, very sincerely,

H. VON HOLST (*University of Chicago*).

NO. 98 BIBLE HOUSE, *New York, January 15, 1802.*

MY DEAR SIR: By all means make use of my name for the purpose indicated, and accept my best wishes for the complete success of the noble national university scheme. The delay in my answering your letter of the 9th instant has been owing to absence from the city.

Believe me, very truly yours,

JAS. GRANT WILSON.

SARATOGA SPRINGS, N. Y., *August 21, 1892.*

DEAR GOVERNOR: You do me great honor in asking me to sign my name to the general proposition. I firmly believe that the ideal university, such as you seek, would lend dignity to the decrees and wisdom to the deliberations of the National Government. So widely has exact science extended that it is difficult to conceive of a question—even be it that of the establishment of a new consulate or a new fourth-class post-office—but can be decided best, or only decided at all, by the application of general principles founded on observation in one of the many departments of science.

With the highest regards, believe me, sincerely,

PERSIFOR FRAZER.

CHICAGO, *May 1, 1895.*

DEAR SIR: Mr. Marshall Field directs me to acknowledge receipt of your favor, 29th ultimo, contents of which have been duly noted, and are entirely satisfactory. You are therefore at liberty to count him among the friends of the enterprise you speak of.

Yours, very truly, ARTHUR B. JONES (*Secretary*).

1750 M STREET NW., *Washington, D. C., March 11, 1895.*

MY DEAR SIR: I sincerely thank you for your kindness in supplying me with such accurate information as to what you have done in behalf of the establishment by our Government of a national university in Washington, an institution that will stimulate and elevate every educational institution in our whole country; an institution that will be every way competent to train and elevate the intellect of our American youth to the highest possible attainments in every art, science, and occupation that can add to the usefulness, the happiness, the power of self-support and the true dignity of human nature.

With earnest hopes that your efforts may be crowned with perfect success, I remain, yours, very truly,

Z. C. ROBBINS.

PHILADELPHIA, *April 22, 1895.*

MY DEAR SIR: In answer to yours of April 10, if you think I can aid you in the promotion of your enterprise I shall be very glad to be counted among its friends.

Very truly yours, THOMAS DOLAN.

STATE OF NORTH DAKOTA, EXECUTIVE OFFICE,
Bismarck, September 12, 1895.

SIR: Your favor of recent date has been referred to the governor, and I am directed to give you his determination in the matter of recommendation.

The governor authorizes me to state that you are at liberty to use his name as giving a personal recommendation; that he deems the plan not only feasible but practical, and will be pleased to see the friends of the measure push it for favorable consideration before the next session of Congress.

I have the honor to sign, by direction of the governor, yours, respectfully,

WILL M. COCHRAN (*Private Secretary*).

CLINTON, N. Y., *January 4, 1895.*

MY DEAR SIR: I send you to-day my articles on a national university and our completed State systems. If you approve, I wish you would so signify in a note, stating your views. * * * I hope to aid you somewhat in this magnificent work.

Very truly yours, E. P. POWELL,

Salem, Mass., December 12, 1894.

DEAR SIR: Your letter in regard to a national university is at hand. It is high time Congress and the nation were moving in the matter.

Anything I can do to help along the good project will be done cheerfully. I shall be happy to be ranked as a member of the national university commissittee.

Sincerely yours,

WILLIAM A. MOWRY (*Former Editor of Education*).

PHILADELPHIA, *April 22, 1895.*

DEAR SIR: I have much pleasure in giving my hearty approval and assent to the proposition for a national university at Washington.

Yours, truly, J. C. STRAWBRIDGE.

TERRITORY OF ARIZONA, EXECUTIVE OFFICE,
Phœnix, Ariz., September 10, 1895.

DEAR SIR: I most heartily indorse the proposition for the establishment of a national university, as suggested in your letter of August 30. The good results which must flow therefrom will be so general and far reaching, and the impress its influence will make upon the country at large so significant, that, if the consideration the importance of such a national institution should command is given it, I believe it will receive the earnest approval of Congress, and such is my hope.

Respectfully,

L. C. HUGHES (*Governor*).

NEW YORK, *March 24, 1893.*

DEAR SIR: * * * I hope, however, before long to be relieved from these responsibilities, and whenever that happy release may come to me, you will find me ready to cooperate heartily with you.

Truly yours, H. VILLARD

STATE OF WASHINGTON, EXECUTIVE DEPARTMENT,
Olympia, September 12, 1895.

DEAR SIR: In reply to yours of the 31st ultimo, I beg to say that I am heartily in favor of establishing a national post-graduate university at the National Capital, and that I desire to be numbered among the friends of that enterprise.

Yours, very truly, J. H. McGRAW (*Governor*).

BOSTON, *December 10, 1891.*

DEAR SIR: With a lively interest in the great undertaking you have at heart, very respectfully, yours,

FRANK H. KASSON
(*Editor and Publisher of Education, Boston, Mass.*).

PHILADELPHIA, PA., *November 29, 1894.*

MY DEAR SIR: Accept my sincere thanks for your thoughtful kindness in sending me your memorial in behalf of a national university at Washington. I read it with the deepest interest, alike for its rich retrospect and for its bright outlook. I regard it as being, in many respects, the most valuable document of its kind in the world

When I come to Washington again I shall be most glad to confer with you on this momentous matter.

Believe me to be, with great respect, faithfully yours,

GEO. DANA BOARDMAN.

CAMBRIDGE, MASS., *March 28, 1896.*

MY DEAR GOVERNOR: Your kind letter received this morning. * * * Many have striven earnestly to this end, and I wish all possible attainment in its success.

Very sincerely yours,
BENJ. APTHORP GOULD.

NEW YORK CITY, *November 25, 1895.*

MY DEAR SIR: I shall be glad to cooperate with you in any way so as to realize the aim you have in view.

Believe me, very cordially yours, CHARLES SPRAGUE SMITH.

WOODMONT, *Washington, D. C., August 13, 1855.*

MY DEAR GOVERNOR: Allow me to express my approbation of the great scheme with which you are connected, and which I trust may be crowned with success.

Truly yours,
JAMES B. SENER
(*Ex-Member Congress, Chief Justice of Wyoming, etc.*).

STATE OF NEVADA, EXECUTIVE OFFICE,
Carson City, September 19, 1895.

DEAR SIR: Your communication of 31st ultimo duly received in relation "to securing the establishment of a national post graduate at Washington, D. C., and documents relative to the subject, and the objects to be attained by the establishment of such an institution."

The object sought is a most worthy one, and meets with my cordial approval.

Very respectfully,
JOHN E. JONES, *Governor of Nevada.*

STATE OF MONTANA, EXECUTIVE OFFICE,
Helena, September 21, 1895.

DEAR SIR: Relative to the national post-graduate university at Washington, I will say that such an enterprise meets my warmest approval. I can conceive of no movement in an educational way better calculated to keep up the high standard of American school life, or that will do more to promote the interests of the student. There can be no question as to the superior facilities afforded the student in Washington City in so far as various fields of investigation are concerned. I trust your efforts may prove successful.

With great respect, I am, very truly yours, J. E. RICKARDS,
Governor of Montana.

EARNEST WORDS OF AN EARLIER DATE.

Alexander Dallas Bache, LL. D., former Superintendent of the Coast Survey:

"A great university, the want of our country in this our time, and the common school and college, fragments of a system requiring to be united into one."

Dr. Benjamin Apthorp Gould, LL. D., astronomer, Cambridge:

"We want a university which, instead of complying with the demands of the age, shall create, develop, and satisfy new and unheard-of requisitions and aspirations, which, so far from adapting itself to the community, shall mold that community unto itself, and which through every change and every progress shall still be far in advance of the body social, guiding it, leading it, drawing it, pulling it, hauling it onward."

The late President James McCosh, LL. D., of Princeton:
"I like the idea of a national university of a character so high that it would not be a competitor of any existing institution."

Dr. Daniel Read, LL. D., while president of the Missouri State University:
"I can not treat as visionary that which Washington recommended and James Madison and John Quincy Adams advocated, and which other great and patriotic men have zealously urged as a means of elevating all our higher institutions of learning, and of giving unity and concentration of effort to literary and scientific men—constituting, indeed, a bond of unity to the nation itself."

Joseph Henry, LL. D., while Secretary of the Smithsonian Institution:
"Yes, the Smithsonian Institution will do a noble work in the interest of science; but the Government of the United States should not content itself with even the wisest use of a foreign benefaction. It must and will devise such measures of its own for the advancement of knowledge as in course of time will become foundation stones for the upbuilding of a great university that will do honor to American intelligence and help to make of this national capital one of the chief intellectual centers of the world."

Hon. Timothy O. Howe, LL. D., of Wisconsin, United States Senator, Postmaster-General, etc.:
"In the convention which framed the Constitution of the United States the subject of a national university was somewhat considered. The proposition had won friends and no enemies there. It was in 1787 that James Madison, not of Massachusetts but of Virginia, not a professional teacher but a practical statesman, moved in convention at Philadelphia to clothe Congress with express powers to establish such a university. * * * Doubtless the bills are imperfect. It is the business of legislation and the work of time to perfect them. * * * If it be conceded that partial education is of some value, it will hardly be denied that thorough education is of more value. * * * It was in this precise way that Washington and Madison (and Jefferson) so incessantly urged the Government to act."

Hon. Charles Sumner, LL. D., of Massachusetts, while United States Senator:
"If we had in this National Capital such a university as that of Berlin, what an influence for the transformation of Washington, for an increase of the interest of the people of our country in the higher learning, for the advancement of knowledge among men, and for giving to this great and growing Republic the rank it should have among the nations of the earth."

Louis Agassiz, LL. D., late of Washington and Cambridge, in 1872:
"Is it not possible to get the Congress of the United States so far interested in this great cause of the national university that it will find pleasure not only in establishing it, but in providing for it an endowment commensurate with the greatness of the country and with the pressing demands of the higher learning?"

Hon. Salmon P. Chase, LL. D., while Chief Justice of the United States:
"The higher education seems to be progressing in a general way, but the many institutions which represent it are without concurrence. If there were a really great university at this national center, with opportunities that would attract graduate students from all sections, and with standards and conditions that would in effect bring all collegiate institutions into relations with itself, this one great deficiency would be met; besides which, the association of its multitude of students would tend to a community of feeling and so increase the security of the Republic. President Washington thought much of this, and made efforts and sacrifices for the founding of a national university, and the wonder is that Congress has not even yet taken a step in that direction."

OBJECTIONS AND ANSWERS.

OBJECTIONS RAISED BY CITIZENS, FEW IN NUMBER, WHO, IN THEIR CORRESPONDENCE WITH THE NATIONAL UNIVERSITY COMMITTEE OF ONE HUNDRED, HAVE MANIFESTED MORE OR LESS OF OPPOSITION TO THE PRESENT EFFORT TO ESTABLISH THE UNIVERSITY OF THE UNITED STATES, WITH ANSWERS BY THE CHAIRMAN OF SAID COMMITTEE.

The objections lately offered to the national university proposition are substantially those heretofore offered, and so thoroughly answered by eminent educators and statesmen as often as presented. They are not really entitled, therefore, to the space and time requisite to yet another refutation, especially since for the most part they are from sources which have shown little disposition to deal with the subject upon that high plane to which it belongs. Nevertheless, in justice to such right-minded objectors as may not yet have considered the question upon all sides, and for the satisfaction of those who, having heard the objections in times past, may wish to carefully consider the question anew under conditions somewhat changed, they are here restated and again answered.

1. First of all, it is said, there is really no need of better facilities for university education than the country now has—no need of the proposed post-graduate university.

And this notwithstanding the emphatic utterances by a long line of our foremost educators, beginning with President Hill, of Harvard, who again and again, and more earnestly than ever of late, have declared "a true university" to be "the leading want of American education;" this notwithstanding the annual exodus of between 2,000 and 3,000 of our college graduates for study and research in the greater and better-equipped universities of the Old World; this notwithstanding our recent appeal to the universities of France; this notwithstanding the present desperate struggle of every one of even our foremost institutions to meet the demand for better opportunities for post-graduate work at home; this notwithstanding the earnest desire of those heads of considerably more than 100 colleges and universities (including such as are foremost in the entire country) which lead in this work that the Government of the United States should come to the rescue by the establishment of a university which in the early future shall be more amply endowed and better circumstanced than any we now have can reasonably hope to become.

"No need of such an institution?" How narrow must be the range of such an objector. Because his own or a neighboring institution seems to him large and prosperous, though meeting simply the collegiate demands of those who are its students, and looking hopefully to the time when it may become in the true sense a university, he excludes that whole series of important functions and relationships that would attach to and characterize the proposed national university at the seat of Government as they could not possibly attach to any other in the United States. I mean not alone those supplementary, coordinating, and stimulating influences upon all the other educational agencies, to which reference has already been made, but rather those offices which it alone could fulfill in its relation to the people and to the Government itself.

Established by the people and for the people, managed by men of first eminence and chosen from all divisions of the country without distinction of party or creed, conducted interiorly by men illustrious for their attainments and achievements in their several departments of learning, and attended by college graduates of superior gifts and aspirations from every portion of the country, the National University would command the attention of the whole people as no other institution could, giving to them new conceptions of the extent of human knowledge, actual and possible, with a consequent increase in their appreciation of the whole series of schools, which, as so many steps, lead up to the highest, and thus arousing in them a new and increasing interest in the great cause of American education.

Again, furnishing to the Government in every department the highest sources of information of every sort for the solution of the many problems which so constantly arise in the course of administration, it would incidentally render an incalculable service, and secure to the country that priceless advantage which in time would the more surely come of an uncompromising demand for the best-qualified statesmanship on the part of those to be entrusted with the management of our national affairs.

The National University would do yet more—vastly more. By this sense of ownership in common thus awakened in the minds of the people, and through this gathering into its halls and laboratories the many representatives of every State in the Union, and sending them forth again not only with increased knowledge and power, but also with broader views, new friendships, and greater community of feeling, it would deepen and strengthen that fraternal regard between the people of all sections so indispensable to the peace and prosperity of the nation, and thus furnish new guaranties for the greatness and perpetuity of the Republic.

2. It is also said that, if better opportunities for the higher culture are indeed necessary they should not be furnished by one institution, but by many—that "not centralization but decentralization is the order of the day;" that the trend of educational thought is against such a proposition as ours; that the French, German, and Austrian governments are multiplying their universities instead of spending their strength upon one.

So much for the want of a little thoughtful discrimination. Such as entertain this opinion may well be referred to the following from an oration once delivered by the distinguished Dr. Benj. Apthorp Gould, astronomer.

"'Centralization' is a word and an idea now far from popular. But this, like most other principles, has its good as well as evil consequences. And while we, under democratic and republican institutions, feel the full force of the objections to that political centralization under which we see so many nations of the Old World tottering and sinking, we are too apt to overlook the incalculable, the unspeakable advantages which flow from the concentrated accumulation of a whole nation's genius and talent. * * * There is no substitute for the 'encounter of the wise.' Like that of flint and steel it strikes out without cessation the glowing sparks of truth; like that of acid and alkali it forms new, unexpected, and priceless combinations; like the multiplication of rods in the fagot, it gives new strength to all while taking it from none. A spiritual stimulus pervades the very atmosphere electrified by the proximity of congregated genius, its unseen but ever active energy—floating in the air, whispering in the breeze, vibrating in the nerves, thrilling in the heart—prompts to new effort and loftier aspiration through every avenue which can give access to the soul of man.

"Such centralization is eminently distinguished from political centralization, and by this peculiarity, among others, that far from being a combination for the sake of arguing and exercising a greater collective power, it acts, on the contrary to augment individual influence. While forming a nucleus for scientific, literary, artistic energy, it is not a gravitation center toward which everything must converge and accumulate, but is an organic center whose highest function is to arouse and animate the circulation of thought and mental effort and profound knowledge. It is a nucleus of vitality rather than a nucleus of aggregation. * * * An intellectual center for a land is a heart, but subject to no induration; it is a brain, but liable to no paralysis; an electric battery which can not be consumed; it is a sun without eclipse, a fountain that will know no drought. To such a university our colleges would look for succor in their need, for counsel in their doubt, for sympathy in their weal or woe. There is no one of them but would develop to new strength and beauty under its genial emanations; none so highly favored or so great that its resources and powers would not expand; none too lowly to imbibe the vitalizing, animating influences which it would diffuse like perfume."

Our objectors would seem to have lost sight of the fact that each of those Governments naturally, if not necessarily, began their special efforts for supremacy with but one institution; making it so great and strong that they are now able to aid in the planting of others and to supply each of them with a whole galaxy of illustrious men for their many departments. Let America have at least one that shall be unsurpassed, and that shall complete our system of American education.

3. One of the objectors has even ventured to assert that, while it may have been well for the Government to do something for elementary education, higher education on the other hand is rather a luxury and may be left to take care of itself—the very thing it can not do, because of the large sums requisite for the costly manning and equipping of great institutions, and which, if wholly left to private benefactions are ever liable to be ruinously mortgaged to some crudity of the endower or to some tenet of religious faith.

For answer to this point, without stopping to show how, in education, the lower depends on the higher, I have been content to quote the words of two of America's foremost educators, namely those of Hon. Andrew D. White, former president and upbuilder of Cornell University, and of that most illustrious apostle of popular education, Horace Mann.

It was President White who, in discussing this very national university proposition, said: "And, finally, I insist that it is a duty of society itself—a duty which it can not throw off—to see that the stock of talent and genius in each generation has a chance for development, that it may be added to the world's stock and aid in the world's work. Now, it is just this talent and genius which, as all history shows, private capacity and the law of supply and demand will not develop."

And it was Horace Mann who boldly declared, "No man in our country and in our times is worthy the name of statesman who does not include the highest practicable education of the people in all his plans of administration."

4. Again, it is urged that if it must be conceded that better and the very best post-graduate facilities are still needed, in such case it would be more rational and economical to concentrate the necessary resources upon one than to distribute them among several, nevertheless that one should not be established by the National Government, for a number of reasons, to wit:

In the first place, says the objector, "It could hardly be kept out of politics;" quite forgetting how entirely our great military and naval academies have escaped this danger; how perfectly free from political interference has been our own noble Smithsonian Institution from first to last; how the great State universities have developed and flourished under the fostering care of legislative bodies far more liable than the Congress of the United States to be influenced in such matters by party considerations; forgetting, too, that educational and scientific work is less interfered with by both legislative bodies and the public in proportion as it passes into the higher fields.

And then "the location would be unfortunate;" the objector seeming to know little of the real facts in the case, and to have lost sight entirely of the small account to be made of distance in these days of easy transit, of the fact that even Washington is not so far off as Berlin, while being at the same time the most beautiful and attractive of all of our larger cities and also affording readier contact than any other with representatives of all sections and countries, with the broadening and liberalizing influences incident thereto. Moreover he seems surprisingly forgetful that the District of Columbia is the only spot where it could be constitutionally established, and that here at Washington as nowhere else in America are found those important and ever-increasing aggregations of material and men which of themselves almost make a university.

5. Still more serious than any of these is said to be the embarrassment that might come to the existing colleges and universities to be overshadowed, minified, stripped of their professors and students, and reduced to nothingness by the competing central institution.

How strangely such objectors ignore about all the elements involved in the relationship to be established. They seem not to understand that, first of all, the University of the United States is to be exclusively post graduate; which fact of itself relieves the more than 300 of our collegiate institutions of every possible ground of anxiety, and should open to their view (as it does with the majority) the incalculable benefits that would come to them in the consequent correlation of all the higher institutions, in the unification of their work, in the elevation of standards, in the better supply of better-fitted men for their many faculties, in the stimulation the national university would give to their thousands of ambitious students by the opportunities, honors, and distinctions held aloft to them in the face of the whole world.

As for the newer institutions established within the recent years, but few of them have so much as a well-founded hope of doing a very large amount of that work of a university in the higher sense, which consists in original investigations by great leaders in many fields of inquiry, and in the induction of gifted minds into the methods of those researches by means of which the boundaries of knowledge are enlarged and mankind is advanced in material and spiritual power. They are mixed institutions, all of them; seeking to do, first of all, the proper work of the college; second, to supplement this as far as limited means and forces will allow by advance work in the lecture room for such as have already received the bachelor's degree, and third, to attempt such work in the laboratory as may seem in a manner to justify the university title.

It is needless to add that, while many such institutions have done and are doing the work of the college very well—unless it be that they attach too much importance to the learning of many things and too little to that discipline which gives added power—the "university work" attempted is for the most part done very scatteringly, at great disadvantage, and, of course, with very partial results.

The talk of ruinous "competition," is groundless, therefore. Most of the existing institutions would be without the shadow of a claim to sympathy on this ground. Such few as have begun post-graduate work are divided on the question; the older and less progressive taking needless alarm, while the newer ones, though doing a much larger proportion of advanced work, with high courage and a better understanding of what the national university would be, are cordial supporters of the new movement, as will appear from the "Godspeed" they have so often wished the national committee of promotion. They know, first of all, that even if some of their post-graduate work should also be undertaken by the central institution, there are many things worse than an honorable competition—that, as "competition in business is the life of trade," so in the higher fields of original scientific work it often leads to individual triumphs and to scientific progress for the world.

These last also know that a central and national institution, interested above all in the welfare of important university agencies would gladly find ways for a practical realization of all that is so wisely provided for in Section 10 of the pending bill, which reads as follows:

"SEC. 10. The university shall have authority to establish with other institutions of education and learning in the United States such cooperative relations as shall be deemed advantageous to the public interest."

A real university, manned and equipped for this higher work only, would not merely supply this growing demand of our country and age by relieving a multitude of our collegiate institutions of the seeming necessity to keep pace with ambitious and better endowed competitors by attempting impossible things; it would enable them to concentrate their means and forces upon their proper work, and thus contribute to that thorough scholarship of which, with all our schools, colleges, and so-called universities, there is too little in this country anywhere.

If anyone of these were vastly better endowed, officered, and furnished it would still be unable to exert that coordinating, correlating, stimulating, and uplifting force so greatly needed and so sure to be exercised by a post-graduate university of the highest type, established at Washington and bearing the stamp of the nation. Denominational ambitions, local jealousies, and State rivalries would prove insurmountable to even the best of them and there would still be a demand for the University of the United States.

The fear of embarrassment to existing institutions is therefore wholly groundless. The planting of the proposed institution would doubtless have the effect to satisfy some of the so-called universities that they are still far from the mark of their high calling. And that would be an excellent service. The majority, seeing the present impossibility of becoming more than merely nominal universities, would wisely limit themselves to the solid and more useful work of the college, as before intimated, thus perfecting the scholarship of those whom they are to qualify for the business of life or for entrance upon the work of the university itself. And such of the institutions as are really able to do something valuable in the way of research and of leading graduates of genius into the highest fields of effort would naturally limit themselves to fewer subjects, thus increasing the probability of an abler handling of them, and drawing into their work such students as for various reasons would find it for their interest to utilize the facilities near home, instead of coming to Washington. Moreover, while this work of readjustment is going on the central institution will be gathering in those ambitious graduates of many colleges and universities who would otherwise have entered directly into their chosen life pursuits; giving to them opportunities for advanced learning in the various departments, training them for those investigations by means of which the knowledge of mankind is increased, and thus fitting for the highest service in the colleges and universities in the several States a score of men of supreme qualifications for every professor drawn to the national center.

6. But I have reserved the most extraordinary of the objections to the last. It has an antiquated look and provokes a query concerning the means of its fostering and survival to this day. It is said, and said as if settling the whole business, that it is no proper function of the Government to care for the interests of education; that education is not essential to the security of the Republic; that if it can not be had without the help of the Government it is better that it should not be had at all; that this helping of the people to the means of education is even dangerous to our institutions, nay, that it "saps the foundations of public liberty;"—as if the Government of the United States were an independent personality having powers absolutely and wholly its own, capable of giving to the people a force and substance they do not in and of themselves possess, and thus invading their independence and weakening their self-reliance; as if the Government were not in fact a body of servants appointed to do the people's work within prescribed limits, the people themselves being the masters, decreeing and doing through and by their servants whatever is done, and hence being in no sense separable, either in fact or in thought, from the Government itself.

Touching this whole subject of a just relationship between Government and the higher education, we can not do better than to quote from an address by Dr. William T. Harris, present United States Commissioner of Education, before the National Educational Association, at Detroit, in 1874:

"But the most obvious and often repeated objection to the proposed national university is drawn from the nature of our national politics. It is contended that we have a certain low standard of politics, and that whatever is directed, managed, and supported by the State suffers inevitably from political influence. A university founded under the management of our National Government would be the prey of demagogues, it is thought. This view is developed and supported chiefly by those who hold the theory that our Government should exclude from its functions an interference with education or with other functions within the range of civil society.

"This theory has been persistently reiterated in political platforms and political treatises during the period since the formation of our Federal Government. At times it has led to legislation tending to purge away certain complications with civil society which have arisen through various exigencies of war or peace. The history of legislation regarding a national bank, regarding the issue of paper money, or a tariff, regarding various internal improvements, and the status of corporations, is one of the most momentous interest to the thinking statesman and economist. Whatever violent legislation has attempted, to purge the state of all complication with civil society, has failed. Again and again in our history we have come upon conditions which necessitated the interference of Government in affairs of civil society. In latter years, and in proportion as the relations of civil society have become more complex with us, such complication has become more and more frequent and inevitable. Internal improvements, foreign and domestic commerce, intercommunication, money, bonds, and corporate rights and privileges—the General Government can not choose but mediate in those things. Its war caused it to create a mercantile commodity in the shape of bonds to the amount of thousands of millions of dollars, and to throw the same on the market of the world within a period of six years. Civil society and the state are only different phases of the same organic human combination; in the former, in civil society, the individual uses the organization for his own sustenance and support, and the furtherance of his private ends through the agency of wealth; in the latter, the state, the organization, exists in its unity, and subordinates all individuals to its end.

"The state must exist as the logical condition of the existence of civil society and the welfare or rational existence of the individual. Unless the individual devotes his life and property to the state and acknowledges the supreme right to use him and his he does not properly recognize his position. But it exists whether consciously recognized or not by the citizen or statesman. Now, from the reciprocal relations of the functions of the state and civil society as related to the individual, it follows that the state as a directive power of the organism as a whole must legislate regarding all such phases as relate to its own self-preservation and perpetuation. No other people ever before started such a theory as the one which asserts or presupposes in some form the denial of an organic relation of state and society. So long as we undertake to realize this theory we shall act a farce between ourselves and the intelligence of mankind. We shall do practically in spite of ourselves what we condemn in theory.

"By a common movement the foremost nations of Europe have advanced to the position that public education is a concern that vitally interests the state. No state can allow its productive industry to fall behind that of other nations. Independence can not be long preserved on such terms. Directly, as necessary to the war material, and indirectly as essential to productive industry, the education of the whole people is indispensable, and the Government can not afford to leave it to arbitrary private benevolence or to the zeal of the church.

"The great desideratum in this country is to kindle still more the zeal of our legislators on behalf of public education. To attempt to cool their zeal is to work a mischief. It behooves our Government to see to it that education is national and not sectional or sectarian, or a matter of caste. On no other nation is this injunction laid so heavily. The foundations of our Government rest on popular education. Other nations have always seen to it that their directive intelligence was educated at the expense of the state. They even go farther in our time and educate their sinews of war and the quality of their productive industry. We, in America, are committed to universal public education implicitly by the Constitution of our Government, which is a Government of the people by the people. Not only must the citizen here be able to read and interpret the laws of the land for himself, but he is expected to possess and exercise the requisite intelligence to make the laws which he is to obey. All the evils which we suffer politically may be traced to the existence in our midst of an immense mass of ignorant, illiterate, or semi-educated people who assist in governing the country, while they possess no insight into the true nature of the issues which they attempt to decide. If in Europe, and even in China, the directive classes are educated at public expense, how essential is it that the republican state shall, before all, insure universal education within its domain."

The accepted doctrine of to-day is certainly this: That the Government is of the nature of an agency established by the people for their convenience, and for their permanent as well as present advantage—that the Constitution is a binding agreement of the people as to the purpose and organization of this agency and the character of the agents to be employed, the manner of their choosing, and the scope of the duties they are to perform. And who will say that the people, acting through this agency, are not both competent and in duty bound, in constitutional ways, to avail themselves of their own means to their own highest good?

Such was the theory of the founders of the Government and framers of the Constitution; such the view of Washington, who repeatedly, and especially in his last annual message to Congress, pointed out several ways in which a national university, established by the Government, would prove a bulwark of free institutions; such the theory on which the Federal Government not only established those noble training schools for the Army and Navy at West Point and Annapolis, but has also made such provision for elementary and secondary education as has resulted in the public-school system peculiar to this country; such the theory on which Government provision was early made for the partial endowment of universities in a number of the great States of more recent organization; such the theory on which, by the act of 1862, provision was made for the establishment of those schools of agriculture and the mechanic arts which have furnished to thousands of needy students scientific opportunities otherwise impossible, and which have so materially advanced the practical arts, while adding to the resources, attractive powers, and general usefulness of the institutions in connection with which the most of them were established; such the theory on which Congress provided for the so-called experimental stations, with a view to the advancement of the art of husbandry—things done, every one of them, by the people through their agents, and in the joint interest of community, State, and Nation.

Is not this also the theory on which the Government has taken part in our international expositions, and has inaugurated surveys and explorations for discovery in the interest of science and for increasing the honor of the American name? Is not this the theory on which, at a cost of so many millions, have been established and are liberally maintained at this national center that grand cluster of half a hundred educational, scientific, and industrial bureaus, museums, observatories, laboratories, libraries, and the like, which are contributing so greatly to the dignity, honor, and general welfare of the nation? Is not this the theory, last of all, on which was but recently created and equipped a new great Department of the Government, the Department of Agriculture?

In view of all these facts and of that vast array of facts and considerations so easily marshalled, how misconceived and groundless seem all the objections that were ever urged against the one final step, greatest of all, which looks to the more effective service of those important agencies, as well as to their larger utilization in the interest of education—in short, to the earlier opening up, better husbanding, wiser direction, and perpetual development of the resources, both material and intellectual, of a great nation, so magnificently planted and so wonderfully endowed! That such final step will be taken, and with a liberality commensurate with the great end to be accomplished, there is no longer room for question. The Government can not now repudiate or reverse its beneficent and far-reaching policy in the interest of science and learning.

The American people, having early realized the vital necessity for a general enlightenment of the masses, were not slow in coming to understand how the vastness and variety of our resources and the rapid progress of other nations were making both great and growing demands upon the industries of the country, which they were powerless to meet without the help of science; nor can it be doubted that they have now also come to a realization of how truly the conspicuous place we hold among the nations, and the nature of our Government, as well as the genius and aspirations of our people, imperatively demand the best possible facilities for that high culture and that work of research which are essential to intellectual supremacy, and hence are reasons deep and urgent for the earliest possible establishment of the crowning University of the United States.

○

54TH CONGRESS, } SENATE. { REPORT 429,
  1st Session.   Part 2.

IN THE SENATE OF THE UNITED STATES.

April 8, 1896.—Ordered to be printed.

Mr. WALTHALL, from the Select Committee to Establish the University of the United States, submitted the following

VIEWS OF THE MINORITY:

[To accompany S. 1202.]

For a century the proposition to establish a national university, to be endowed and controlled by the General Government, has from time to time been before the Congress of the United States in one form or another.

The following extracts from a Circular of Information issued by the Bureau of Education in 1890 briefly refer to the unsuccessful efforts made in that direction up to that time.

"ATTEMPTS TO FOUND A NATIONAL UNIVERSITY.

" The ideas of Washington respecting a national university at the capital lingered long in the minds of statesmen after his plan was finally rejected. Doubtless it was through his influence that in 1796 a proposition was before Congress in the form of a memorial praying for the foundation of a university. No action was taken in favor of the proposed institution.[1]

"Again in 1811 a committee was appointed by Congress to report on the question of the establishment of a seminary of learning by the national legislature. The committee reported unfavorably, deeming it unconstitutional for the Government to found, endow, and control the proposed seminary.[2]

" In 1816 another committee was appointed to consider the same subject, and again the scheme failed.[3] From this time on the subject seemed practically settled, and we hear little more of it in legislative circles until the discussion of the disposal of the Smithsonian bequest. At this time there were many warm advocates of the proposal to devote the Smithsonian fund toward the founding of a national university.

---

[1] Ex. Doc., Fourth Congress, second session.
[2] Ex. Doc., Eleventh Congress, third session.
[3] Ex. Doc., Fourteenth Congress, second session.

The subject at this time received free discussion, and the result ended in the defeat of the university plan. While the plan for a national university has not yet succeeded, Congress has established and supported the National Museum, the Congressional Library, the Naval Observatory, and the Bureau of Education, for the promotion of education and science.

"An attempt to found a national university was made in 1873, soon after the circulation of the reports of the Paris Exposition.

* * * * * * *

"The bill reported[1] at this time provided for a university at the capital, endowed by the Federal Government to the amount of $20,000,000, yielding 5 per cent interest; the income to be used for buildings, furnishings, and for the general support of the university. It is hardly necessary to state that the bill did not pass.

"It is not intended to discuss the question of a national university, but attention should be called to the great changes that have taken place in higher education in the last fifteen years.

"The old colleges have broadened their courses and increased their endowments. State universities have come into power during this period, and the agricultural colleges, many of them then begun, have developed into flourishing institutions of learning. There has arisen a new class of universities, created by heavy private endowments; such are Johns Hopkins, Cornell, Tulane, Clark, Boston, Stanford, and others. With these new additions and the progress of the old schools, many of the evils complained of in the above report have disappeared. Whether these new institutions, working with the old, will fill the national demands for education, and thus render a national university unnecessary remains to be seen. It is evident that it is not an easy task to create a national university."

On May 14, 1890, Senator George F. Edmunds introduced in the Senate "A bill to establish a university of the United States," which was referred to a select committee, of which he was chairman, but no action was taken upon it.

This bill provided for the appropriation of $500,000 for the purchase of grounds and the erection of buildings, and that $5,000,000 should be set apart in the Treasury of the United States as a perpetual fund, bearing interest at 4 per cent per annum, for the support and maintenance of the university.

On March 3, 1893, Senator Proctor, chairman of this committee, reported favorably a bill to establish a national university. The report shows that its location and endowment were provided for as follows:

"As a partial provision for the location of the necessary buildings the bill grants the site selected for this purpose by President Washington in 1796, and now, since the removal of the Naval Observatory, without

---

[1] House Report No. 89, Forty-second Congress, third session, I, 90.

important use; and for the support of the institution sets apart one-half the net proceeds of the public lands, one-half of such half to be used currently in providing for the opening of the institution and for carrying it on, the remainder to accumulate in the Treasury of the United States as an endowment until competent to yield a sufficient revenue, together with the gifts and bequests that may be attracted to it, for the permanent support of the institution."

There was no action on this bill in the Senate.

On March 24, 1894, Senator Hunton, chairman of this committee, reported favorably "A bill to establish a national university," which provided, as set forth in the report—

"That for the practical establishment, support, and maintenance of the university there shall be used one-third of the net proceeds of the sales of the public lands for the period of ten years from the passage of this act; that the regents shall have power to receive and administer all such gifts, devises, and bequests as are made for the benefit of the university," etc.

This bill was discussed in the Senate but no vote was taken upon it, though urged with great earnestness and ability by the friends of the measure.

Of the various bills that have been considered by this committee the present bill is the first one providing for an appropriation of money for the purpose of a national university which has received the sanction of a majority, the others which have been favorably reported having provided that its support should come from the proceeds of the sales of the public lands.

In support of the present measure the majority quote expressions from the earlier Presidents, commencing with Washington, and from some of the later ones, including President Grant.

Attention is invited to the following extract from the report of the majority:

"It is also a matter of history that Presidents John Adams and Thomas Jefferson favored the university proposition throughout their terms of office, repeatedly urging its importance upon Congress.

"For example, in his sixth annual message, President Jefferson, having already predicted favorable action by Congress and discussed the use of the Treasury surplus for a national endowment, said:

"'Education is here placed among the articles of public care; not that it would be proposed to take its ordinary branches out of the hands of private enterprise, which manages so much better all the concerns to which it is equal, but a public institution can alone supply those sciences which, though rarely called for, are necessary to complete the circle, all the parts of which contribute to the improvement of the country, and some to its preservation. * * * The present consideration of a national establishment for education particularly is rendered proper by this circumstance also, that if Congress, approving the proposition, shall yet think it more eligible to found it on a donation of lands, they have it now in their power to endow it with those which will be among the earliest to produce the necessary income."

From this it might be inferred that Mr. Jefferson favored the use of the Treasury surplus for a national endowment under the power invested by the Constitution in Congress, but an examination of the text of his message from which the above extract was taken clearly shows the contrary. The asterisks in the extract indicate that it is incomplete and a reference to the text reveals that the passage omitted is important, and is as follows:

"The subject is now proposed for the consideration of Congress, because, if approved, by the time the State legislatures shall have deliberated on this extension of the Federal trusts, and the laws shall be passed and other arrangements made for their execution, the necessary funds will be on hand and without employment. I suppose an amendment to the Constitution, by consent of the States, necessary, because the objects now recommended are not among those enumerated in the Constitution, and to which it permits public moneys to be applied."

The extract from President Grant's annual message of 1873 quoted by the majority shows that he favored "the establishment in this District of an institution of learning or a university of the highest order *by donations of lands.*"

When it is considered in connection with Mr. Jefferson's position that a proposition to vest in Congress the express power to establish a national university was voted down in the Constitutional Convention, whatever may be claimed to have been the motive which influenced the vote, it may be seen that there is at least room for discussion as to the constitutionality of such a proposition as that embodied in this bill. There may be precedents to support it, and the minority, while suggesting the constitutional question for consideration, base their opposition to the measure chiefly upon some practical grounds which will be briefly stated.

This project has repeatedly failed when the financial affairs of the Government were in more satisfactory condition than at present. Unless there is an actual necessity for such an institution as that proposed, and the majority think there is not, it should not be established, especially now, when the Government is constantly selling bonds to raise money and its receipts are constantly running behind its expenditures.

It is true the present bill makes an inconsiderable appropriation, but there is no effort to conceal the fact that the Government is to provide the necessary funds to secure the establishment and maintenance of the university, involving, it is believed, an outlay of an immense amount of money. This money must come, as matters now stand, from an addition to the burdens of taxation or from the further issue of bonds, and the minority sanction neither for this purpose, or from the devotion to it of a portion of the public lands, which will be discussed later in this report.

If to this there shall be opposed the conjecture that the necessary funds will come in large part from private benefactions, the answer is if the friends of the measure will be content with a mere charter, such as has been granted to both Catholic and Protestant institutions, carrying no implication that the university is to be founded and maintained by the use of public money, no objection, it is believed, will come from any quarter; certainly none from the minority of the committee. But let us consider the question,

IS THERE A NECESSITY FOR A NATIONAL UNIVERSITY?

The case is very different now from what it was in the time of Washington. He began his advocacy of a national university as early as 1789, but it took distinct and public form in 1794. The only institutions in existence in the United States in 1789 that were at all worthy of the name of college were Harvard, founded in 1638; William and Mary, 1693; Yale, 1701; Princeton, 1796; Washington and Lee, as it is now called, 1749, and Columbia, 1754.

These five institutions at the close of the Revolutionary war, though they were considered colleges, were nearer the grade of academies in the present day. They had but little endowment, their libraries were small, they had practically no museums and no laboratories. Even Harvard, the oldest and strongest of these institutions, did not become a full-fledged college until long after Washington's death, and when he was urging a national university all Harvard's appropriated and unappropriated funds did not amount to more than $50,000.

Columbia, which had been called King's College previously, was closed in 1776, and was in a deplorable condition when the Revolution ended—its board of governors dead or missing, its library scattered, and its apparatus destroyed. When it was reorganized as Columbia it had an income of only $6,000 a year, and had but little more for several years afterwards. The condition of the other institutions named above was not much better at the close of the Revolutionary war.

Several other institutions were organized just before and just after the Revolutionary war—Brown University, 1764; Rutgers, 1766; Dartmouth, 1769; Washington, 1782; Dickinson, 1783; Hampden-Sidney, 1783—but on account of the unsettled condition of the country and the poverty of the people they had but little strength and would hardly be recognized as academies to-day. There was no reasonable prospect of any large gifts to these institutions for at least a generation to come, and the people who were able to educate their sons naturally turned to good institutions abroad, and especially to the lands from which they had recently emigrated. This procession of American youth to foreign schools, where they might imbibe monarchical ideas and sentiments, awakened in Washington the fear of future calamity to the young Republic, and in this it is believed may be found the origin of his advocacy of a strong and well-equipped national institution.

The situation now is very different. There are about four hundred colleges and universities distributed through the country. They have about a hundred and fifty millions of productive funds, and quite as much more invested in buildings, lands, libraries, museums, laboratories, etc. They have an annual income of from twenty to twenty-five millions. It would seem there is no longer any necessity for our young men going abroad for college training.

There are at least twenty institutions distributed over the country that are now doing what is called university work, by which is meant post-graduate work, providing facilities for study beyond the bachelor's degree. They have an income of from ten to twelve millions a year, and can accommodate in this line of work more students than they now have.

In the concluding paragraph, quoted above, from the Circular of Information issued by the Bureau of Education in 1890, the great changes that had taken place in the preceding fifteen years are mentioned, and attention is called to what there appears as showing the disappearance of the evils complained of in the report there referred to.

The munificent gifts that have been devoted to university work of late years are but the beginning of what may be expected hereafter as a result of the large fortunes that have been amassed in this country. In this connection the gift of Leland Stanford may be referred to, and also the wonderful growth of the Chicago University and the several millions received by Columbia, Johns Hopkins, the Clark University, and a number of others.

Here in Washington, besides other institutions of high rank, which are supported by private means and endowment, we have a grand university representing the Catholic faith, and the American University, representing the Protestant faith, will soon commence the erection of its buildings. Both these institutions are backed by great wealth and power, and at least one other is in contemplation; and present and future demands at the capital, it is believed, will be met by institutions existing and projected, embracing all branches of research and learning.

IS A NATIONAL UNIVERSITY DESIRABLE?

There are many practical difficulties in the way. Religion is likely to give rise to one. Let such a university be established, and if the great denominations do not contend with reference to the religious implication of the doctrines taught, they will at least find fault if there is not a religious and Christian spirit in the institution.

Even if this could be avoided and all should consent that education might be purely secular, there are subjects to be taught upon which the great political parties of the country would not agree, and the danger is that the university might become a football between these parties as they come and go from power. The great question of constitutional interpretation would necessarily be discussed. Those who contend for a strict construction would be dissatisfied if a broader construction were taught, and vice versa. There would also be the same kind of question in reference to the relation of this Government to foreign governments in the department of international law. It was recently seen that many instructors in universities did not agree with the position taken by the President upon this subject.

There would certainly be the same question with reference to economics—a subject which is sometimes dealt with as post-graduate work.

Should these departments touch either free trade or protection, disagreement and friction would be inevitable, and it is not seen how anything could be taught concerning the economic conditions of the country without involving these disputed points.

Political history must also be taught in a national university, involving the discussion of the past and present attitude of the great parties touching the political questions that divide them.

Mediæval history with its religious wars, and modern history with its religious contentions, could not be taught without offense to many among the great Protestant and Catholic bodies.

If ethics were touched upon at all it must be either from the naturalistic standpoint of the evolutionist, which would be objectionable to the Christian, or from the Christian standpoint, which would be objectionable to the naturalist. These sciences could not be followed to the origin of things without striking the same religious difficulties.

These and kindred objections seem fatal to the successful and harmonious workings of such an educational establishment as that proposed to be founded and maintained at public expense.

PUBLIC LANDS.

If it shall be proposed to resort to the public lands for this purpose an objection which would seem to be decisive is that this can not be done without a reversal of the settled policy of the Government to devote these lands liberally to educational purposes in the States to aid in the support of both common schools and colleges, so that the immediate benefits so far as possible may reach all the people.

This policy seems to find full justification in the consideration that these lands, the property of the people, should, so far as devoted to educational purposes, be applied as much as practicable for the benefit of the people in general, and not to a purpose which, directly at least, would benefit but a limited class. The annexed document, marked A, shows the extent to which this policy of aiding education in the States has been pursued during the long period which has elapsed since a national university was first proposed. That it has been followed so long with the approval of the people of the country and with satisfactory results vindicates its wisdom and beneficence, and the fact that special grants of lands are constantly being made by Congress in aid of education in the States argues that the policy is sustained by the public and that a diversion of those lands to the uses of a national university would not meet public favor and support.

Documents attached hereto marked B, C, D, and E, containing expressions from a number of distinguished educators and other eminent persons, are referred to as showing that in their opposition to this bill the minority are supported by the judgment of many distinguished Americans who are wholly impartial and peculiarly fitted to deal with this subject. The testimony of many others might be added if considered necessary.

DAVID TURPIE.
JAMES K. JONES.
KNUTE NELSON.
E. C. WALTHALL.

A.
STATE GRANTS OF PUBLIC LANDS—TABLES.

GENERAL LAND OFFICE, *March 12, 1896.*

TABLE 1.—*Showing area of lands donated to States for various purposes, under various general and special grants.*

State and Territory.	Support of common schools.*		Academies, seminaries, or universities.	Agricultural and mechanical colleges.		Public buildings.	Penitentiaries.†	Courthouse and jail.
	Sections.	Lands granted.		Lands.	Scrip.			
		Acres.	*Acres.*	*Acres.*	*Acres.*	*Acres.*	*Acres.*	*Acres.*
Alabama	16	901,725	46,080		240,000			
Arkansas	16	928,057	46,080		150,000	9,600		1,000
California	16 and 36	5,610,702	46,080	150,000		6,400		
Colorado	16 and 36	3,715,555	46,080		90,000	32,000	32,000	
Connecticut					180,000			
Delaware					90,000			
Florida	16	1,053,653	92,160		90,000	5,120		
Georgia					270,000			
Idaho	16 and 36	3,063,271	46,080	90,000		32,000		
Illinois	16	985,141	46,080		480,000			
Indiana	16	601,049	46,080		390,000			
Iowa	16	978,578	46,080	240,000		3,200		
Kansas	16 and 36	2,876,124	46,080		90,000	6,400		
Kentucky					330,000			
Louisiana	16	798,085	46,080		210,000			
Maine					210,000			
Maryland					210,000			
Massachusetts					360,000			
Michigan	16	1,003,573	46,080	240,000		3,200		
Minnesota	16 and 36	2,969,991	92,160	120,000		6,400		
Mississippi	16	833,329	69,120		210,000			
Missouri	16	1,162,137	46,080	330,000				
Montana	16 and 36	5,102,107	46,080		90,000	32,000		
Nebraska	16 and 36	2,637,155	46,080		90,000	12,800	12,800	
Nevada	16 and 36	3,985,422	46,080		90,000	12,800	12,800	
New Hampshire					150,000			
New Jersey					210,000			

*The grant for the support of common schools is of certain sections, in place, in each township of the State, or, in case of the loss of the whole or part of the sections, to indemnity for the loss. The area here reported as granted is the result of a calculation based on the whole area of each State, as reported in Land Office Report, 1895, page 222.

By the act of June 16, 1880 (21 Stat. L., 287), the school-land grant of Nevada, exclusive of lands already sold by the State, was converted into a definite grant of 2,000,000 acres.

The area used as a basis of calculation in the States of Idaho, Montana, and Wyoming excludes the lands comprising the Yellowstone Park—89,280 acres in Idaho, 178,707 acres in Montana, and 2,004,480 acres in Wyoming—since the said lands are not subject to the grant.

The area used as a basis of calculation in the case of Oklahoma Territory excludes 1,528 acres, the area of Greer County.

The grants to the Territories are in the nature of reservations, subject to absolute grants on their admission into the Union.

† Penitentiary buildings and appurtenant lands have been granted to Idaho, Montana, North Dakota, South Dakota, Washington, and Wyoming, but the exact area of lands has not been ascertained.

9

TABLE 1.—*Showing area of lands donated to States for various purposes, etc.*—Continued.

State and Territory.	Support of common schools.		Academies, seminaries, or universities.	Agricultural and mechanical colleges.		Public buildings.	Penitentiaries.	Court-house and jail.
	Sections.	Lands granted.		Lands.	Scrip.			
		Acres.	*Acres.*	*Acres.*	*Acres.*	*Acres.*	*Acres.*	*Acres.*
New York..........	....	....	....	....	990,000	....	....	....
North Carolina...	....	....	....	....	270,000	....	....	....
North Dakota....	16 and 36	2,531,200	46,080	90,000	....	32,000	....	....
Ohio..............	16	710,610	69,120	....	630,000	....	....	....
Oregon	16 and 36	3,387,520	46,080	90,000	....	6,400	....	....
Pennsylvania....	....	....	....	....	780,000	....	....	....
Rhode Island....	....	....	....	....	120,000	....	....	....
South Carolina...	....	....	....	....	180,000	....	....	....
South Dakota....	16 and 36	2,813,511	46,080	120,000	....	32,000	....	....
Tennessee	....	....	....	....	300,000	....	....	....
Texas............	....	....	....	....	180,000	....	....	....
Utah	2,16,32,and 36	6,007,182	156,080	200,000	....	64,000	....	....
Vermont.........	....	....	....	....	150,000	....	....	....
Virginia.........	....	....	....	....	300,000	....	....	....
Washington	16 and 36	2,488,675	46,080	90,000	....	....	....	....
West Virginia...	....	....	....	....	150,000	....	....	....
Wisconsin.......	16	958,649	92,160	240,000	....	6,400	....	....
Wyoming	16 and 36	3,368,924	46,080	90,000	....	32,000	....	....
Arizona	16 and 36	4,050,346	46,080	....	....	....	....	....
New Mexico.....	16 and 36	4,309,369	46,080	....	....	....	....	....
Oklahoma	16 and 36	1,276,204	59,520	59,520	....	177,280	....	....
Total	....	71,112,844	1,644,080	2,599,520	7,830,000	512,000	57,600	1,000

B.
A UNIVERSITY OF THE UNITED STATES.
SHOULD IT BE?

The following, from letters of President Eliot, of Harvard; President Dwight, of Yale; President Low, of Columbia; President Larsen, of Luther College, Iowa; President Candler, of Oxford College, Georgia; President Bissel, of Upper Iowa University; President Smith, of Randolph Macon College, Virginia, and Vice-President R. C. Hughes, Tabor College, Iowa, say "No." Dr. McCosh, of Princeton, said a few years ago, "I do not favor any project yet proposed" (for a national university). Many more opinions as positive might be given. Certainly the judgment of such specialists ought to weigh in this matter:

YALE UNIVERSITY,
New Haven, February 20, 1896.

The plan of establishing a national university in Washington by Congress seems to me an undesirable plan. I think such a university unnecessary. It seems to me much better that institutions of this character in our country should be sustained by private gifts and efforts, and I doubt the wisdom or propriety of governmental appropriations of money for such purposes.

Very respectfully, yours, TIMOTHY DWIGHT.

COLUMBIA COLLEGE,
New York, February 20, 1896.

MY DEAR GOVERNOR: What I believe to be meritorious in your enterprise is the proposition to make available for students the great collections of books and other objects that already exist in Washington on so splendid a scale, and that are certain to increase in value and importance decade by decade. I am also sensible of the sentimental attractiveness of a University of the United States. When I have said this I am obliged to say that I see in the project two different but fundamental dangers. On the one hand there is danger that the University of the United States may exist only in name, and, so far from contributing to the scientific prestige and importance of the country, may be a source of shame to all those who are interested in the higher education.

On the other hand, if it should be really a strong and powerful university, animated by the highest ideals and endowed with adequate resources from the Treasury of the nation, I do not see how it can fail seriously to interfere with the work that is being done by the old and large foundations of the eastern part of the country. These institutions are already doing important and invaluable work for graduate students, and are by no means confined, as you seem to suppose, to undergraduate instruction. If they are called upon to compete in the future with a national university supported by taxation, in which there shall be no charge for tuition, it seems to me inevitable that the effect upon these institutions can not be otherwise than harmful. If only the institutions themselves were concerned, it may be said that that ought not to interfere with the establishment of a University of the United States. Certainly not if it can be shown that the people at large have more to hope for from a national university than from these institutions. That, however, is precisely what I think is not likely to be the case. Under existing conditions, all of these institutions, and others like them, are in receipt of large sums of money, constantly, from the gifts of generous and public-spirited citizens. They are wholly unembarrassed by politics in their administration, and they embody, many of them, more or less completely, the aspirations of strong localities for the higher education. A national university, offering tuition without fee, and supported out of the general Treasury, would tend to sap the source of supply of all these institutions, both in students and in gifts. It is not to be expected, I think, that private citizens will continue to contribute for this cause as they have done during the last twenty years, if the United States, as such, enters the field as a real and genuine competitor.

This leads me to consider the probabilities of the outcome of the act immediately under discussion. I think it would be completely disappointing to those who are favoring the bill. Both the board of regents and the university council are to be named in order, after the first selection, from all the States in the Union, and at no time can any State have more than one representative. The political expediency of this provision is apparent. Its inevitable consequence to the university, I think, are no less apparent. It is not possible, in my opinion, to organize a teaching institution upon such lines that shall approach all subjects of inquiry and research in an atmosphere of intellectual freedom. Again, the proposed university council contains the element of a fatal weakness in the twelve ex officio members who are to represent existing institutions. In the first place, all the men so situated who are worthy to occupy such a relation to the national university are already too busy. It is impossible to believe that the national university can be their first interest; and, under these circumstances, it is inevitable that its interests will be neglected. Furthermore, the national university can not be made a real success as a teaching institution without depopulating, to some extent, the very institutions that are likely to be represented on the university council.

All of this seems to me to lead up to the fact that the national university ought not to be, and ought not to aim to be, a teaching organization. The sole useful function that it can perform without great danger to the educational interests of the country at large, as I am at present obliged to think, is in some way to organize the educational advantages offered by the Government Departments at Washington, and to place them, in a systematic way, at the service of all students. I hope very much that the friends of the measure in which you are interested will consent to limit the scope of the proposed university to this function.

I am, my dear Governor, yours, faithfully,

SETH LOW.

LUTHER COLLEGE,
Decorah, Iowa, February 21, 1896.

I make haste to inform you that I, in every essential point, most heartily agree with the "arguments" against a national university, and am not at all in favor of any bill for the establishment of a university controlled and supported by the Government of the United States.

Yours, respectfully,

LAUR. LARSEN,
President Luther College.

EMORY COLLEGE,
Oxford, Ga., February 22, 1896.

MY DEAR SIR: I beg to say I am emphatically opposed to a national university by the General Government. (1) It is an unconstitutional institution. (2) It is an unnecessary institution. (3) It would be a most vicious institution, educationally and politically.

You are at liberty to use this as you please.

I am, yours, sincerely,

W. A. CANDLER.

UPPER IOWA UNIVERSITY,
Fayette, Iowa, February 20, 1896.

* * * I have very decided convictions against the General Government founding a university at Washington. Recent tendencies in the country and political life lead me to believe that such an undertaking would not be a success, and not in the interest of the highest and best scholarship.

Yours, very truly, J. M. BISSELL.

TABOR COLLEGE,
Tabor, Iowa, February 24, 1896.

DEAR SIR: I heartily agree with your position as opposing the foundation of a national university to be supported by the Government.

We do not need such a university, as the State and denominational colleges and universities cover the ground thoroughly.

Sincerely, yours, R. C. HUGHES.

HARVARD UNIVERSITY,
Cambridge, January 1, 1896.

MY DEAR SIR: Your pleasant letter of December 30 came to hand yesterday. I regret to say that I am not able to join you in advocating the establishment of a university of the United States. * * * I perceive that you have endeavored to make your bill more acceptable than preceding bills to existing institutions; but if the proposed university has any function at all, it must prove to be a competitor with the existing universities. Now, we have too many universities in the United States already. If the Government wishes to go into university work it should, in my opinion, strengthen the universities we have, and not build another.

As to the local needs of the city of Washington, they are surely to be well supplied. The Columbian University, the Catholic University, and the new American University will supply the local needs of the District.

Within the last twenty years so much progress has been made in civil service reform that one may be permitted to hope that the university might be partially exempted from the operation of the spoils system, but, in my judgment, that exemption would be by no means complete even then. I can not feel sure that the professors of philosophy, sociology, political economy, history, constitutional law, and international law in a national university at Washington would be free men. For these reasons, among others, I find myself quite unable to support the bill which has just been put before Congress.

Very truly, yours, CHARLES W. ELIOT.

RANDOLPH MACON COLLEGE,
Lynchburg, Va., February 19, 1896.

DEAR SIR: I think the standard argument against enlarging the sphere and functions of the General Government—multiplying officers and undertaking what can safely be left to individual enterprise and philantropy—coupled with the present condition of the national finances, will avail now, as for so many years past when conditions seemed much more favorable, to prevent the proposition for a university of the United States becoming a law. We are against centralization in this section.

Yours, sincerely, WM. W. SMITH.

The following educators are opposed to a national university:

William F. Warren, LL. D., president of Boston University, said: "No nation without a national church has ever evolved a nationally supported university worthy of mention."

F. A. Walker, LL. D., president of Massachusetts Institute of Technology, says he is strongly opposed to the idea of a national university.

Prof. John Bascom, LL. D., says a national university is to be objected to on the ground that there is no demand for it. "An extreme secular temper would be sure to prevail in such an institution. Its moral force would sink to a minimum."

Dr. J. L. M. Curry, secretary of the Slater fund, is quite outspoken in his opposition to the scheme of a national university.

Prof. E. P. Seaver, superintendent of Boston public schools, says such a scheme would be impractical, have no promise of usefulness, and assure no freedom in teaching.

The great churches are practically committed to another policy by having their own institutions, or by action of their legislative bodies.

The Baptists have Chicago University as their center, and Columbian in Washington.

The Presbyterians are committed to Princeton and other institutions.

The Catholic Church is building a great university for itself here at the national capital.

The Methodist Episcopal Church and the Methodist Episcopal Church South are committed by their general conferences to the American University.

The supreme legislative body of the Protestant Episcopal Church in 1871 adopted the following:

"*Resolved*, That except where weighty local or special considerations intervene it is our duty to sustain our own educational institutions by our gifts and our patronage."

Bishop Chas. B. Galloway, of the Methodist Episcopal Church South, says: "I am convinced of the unwisdom of the proposed university of the United States. I favor State education, but not Federal education."

C.

The following action is very significant in view of the fact that Mr. Pepper, ex-provost, argued in favor of a national university at a hearing before the Senate Select Committee to Establish the University of the United States, and was supposed to represent the feeling in the University of Pennsylvania:

UNIVERSITY OF PENNSYLVANIA, OFFICE OF THE PROVOST,
Philadelphia, March 6, 1896.

The attention of the trustees of the University of Pennsylvania has been called to the proposed act to establish a "University of the United States." At the last meeting of the corporation I submitted a copy of the act and requested an expression of opinion upon the proposal. The sentiment was quite unanimous that there were few things which the Government of the United States is so illy fitted to do as to conduct a great university; that this was a matter which unquestionably should be left to local enterprise and local support. If some arrangement could be made by which advanced students throughout the country should have the benefit of the vast collections of the United States Government in Washington for purposes of study, that would be an excellent arrangement; but it does not seem to us that this would require any elaborate machinery, nor the foundation of a "University of the United States."

Very truly, yours, CHAS. C. HARRISON, *Provost.*

D.

NATIONAL EDUCATIONAL ASSOCIATION,
Department of Higher Education, Tuesday, August 5, 1873.

Charles W. Eliot, president of Harvard University, read the following report on a national university:

This report has three parts: First, an account of what this association has done about a national university since 1869; secondly, an examination of two bills on the subject which were brought before Congress in 1872, and lastly, a discussion of the true policy of our Government upon this matter.

* * * * *

I turn next to my third topic, the true policy of our Government as regards university instruction. In almost all the writings about a national university, and of course in the two Senate bills now under discussion, there will be found the implication, if not the express assertion, that it is somehow the duty of our Government to maintain a magnificent university. This assumption is the foundation upon which rest the ambitious projects before us, and many similar schemes. Let me try to demonstrate that the foundation is itself unsound.

The general notion that a beneficent government should provide and control an elaborate organization for teaching just as it maintains an army, a navy, or a post-office, is of European origin, being a legimate corollary to the theory of government by divine right. It is said that the state is a person having a conscience and a moral responsibility; that the government is the visible representative of a people's civilization and the guardian of its honor and its morals, and should be the embodiment of all that is high and good in the people's character and aspirations. This moral person—this corporate representative of a Christian nation—has high duties and functions commensurate with its great powers, and none more imperative than that of diffusing knowledge and advancing science.

I desire to state this argument for the conduct of high educational institutions by government as a matter of abstract duty, with all the force which belongs to it, for, under an endless variety of thin disguises and with all sorts of amplifications and dilutions, it is a staple commodity with writers upon the relation of government to education. The conception of government upon which this argument is based is obsolescent everywhere. In a free community the government does not hold this parental or patriarchal—I should have said Godlike—position. Our Government is a group of servants appointed to do certain difficult and important work. It is not the guardian of the nation's morals; it does not necessarily represent the best virtue of the Republic, and is not responsible for the national character, being itself one of the products of that character.

The doctrine of state personality and conscience, and the whole argument to the dignity and moral elevation of a Christian nation's government as the basis of government duties, are natural enough under grace-of-God governments, but they find no ground of practical application to modern republican confederations; they have no bearing on governments considered as purely human agencies with defined powers and limited responsibilities. Moreover, for most Americans these arguments prove a great deal too much; for if they have the least tendency to persuade us that the Government should direct any part of secular education with how much greater force do they apply to the conduct by government of the religious education of the people? These propositions are indeed the main argument for an established church.

Religion is the supreme human interest; government is the supreme human organization; therefore, government ought to take care of religion, and a Christian government should maintain distinctively Christian religious institutions. This is not theory alone; it is the practice of all Christendom except in America and Switzerland. Now, we do not admit it to be our duty to establish a national church. We believe not only that our people are more religious than many nations which have established churches, but also that they are far more religious under their own voluntary system than they would be under any government establishment of religion. We do not admit for a moment that establishment or no establishment is synonymous with national piety or impiety. Now, if a beneficent Christian government may rightly leave the people to provide themselves with religious institutions, surely it may leave them to provide suitable universities for the education of their youth. And here, again, the question of national university or no national university is by no means synonymous with the question, Shall the country have good university education or not? The only question is, Shall we have a university controlled and supported by other agencies?

There is, then, no foundation whatever for the assumption that it is the duty of our Government to establish a national university. I venture to state one broad reason why our Government should not establish and maintain a university. If the people of the United States have any special destiny, any peculiar functions in the world, it is to try and work out, under extraordinarily favorable circumstances, the problem of free institutions for a heterogeneous, rich, multitudinous population spread over a vast territory. We indeed want to breed scholars, artists, poets, historians, novelists, engineers, physicians, jurists, theologians, and orators; but, first of all, we want to breed a race of independent, self-reliant freemen, capable of helping, guiding, and governing themselves. Now the habit of being helped by the Government, even if it be to things good in themselves—to churches, universities, and railroads—is a most insidious and irresistible enemy of republicanism; for the very essence of republicanism is self-reliance. With the continental nations of Europe it is an axiom that the Government is to do everything, and is responsible for everything. The French have no word for "public spirit" for the reason that the sentiment is unknown to them. This abject dependence on the Government is an accursed inheritance from the days of the divine right of kings. Americans, on the contrary, maintain precisely the opposite theory, namely, that Government is to do nothing not expressly assigned it to do; that it is to perform no function which any private agency can perform as well, and that it is not to do a public good even, unless that good be otherwise unattainable. It is hardly too much to say that this doctrine is the foundation of our public liberty. So long as the people are really free they will maintain it in theory and in practice. During the war of the rebellion we got accustomed to seeing the Government spend vast sums of money and put forth vast efforts; and we asked ourselves, Why should not some of these great resources and powers be applied to works of peace, to creation as well as to destruction? So we subsidized railroads and steamship companies and agricultural colleges, and now it is proposed to subsidize a university.

The fatal objection to this subsidizing process is that it saps the foundations of public liberty. The only adequate securities of public liberty are the national habits, traditions, and character acquired and accumulated in the practice of liberty and self control. Interrupt these traditions, break up these habits, or cultivate the opposite ones, or poison that national character, and public liberty will suddenly be found defenseless. We deceive ourselves dangerously when we think or speak as if education, whether primary or university, could guarantee republican institutions. Education can do no such thing. A republican people should indeed be educated and intelligent, but it by no means follows that an educated and intelligent people will be republican. Do I seem to conjure up imaginary evils to follow from this beneficent establishment of a superb national university? We teachers should be the last people to forget the sound advice—*obsta principiis*. A drop of water will put out a spark which otherwise would have kindled a conflagration that rivers could not quench.

Let us cling to the genuine American method—the old Massachusetts method—in the matter of public instruction. The essential features of that system are local taxes for universal elementary education, voted by the citizens themselves, local elective boards to spend the money raised by taxation and control the schools, and for the higher grades of instruction permanent endowments administered by incorporated bodies of trustees. This is the American voluntary system, in sharp contrast with the military, despotic organization of public instruction which prevails in Prussia and most other States of continental Europe. Both systems have peculiar advantages, the crowning advantage of the American method being that it breeds freemen. Our ancestors well understood the principle that to make a people free and self reliant it is necessary to let them take care of themselves, even if they do not take quite as good care of themselves as some superior power might.

And now, finally, let us ask, What should make a university at the capital of the United States, established and supported by the General Government, more national than any other American university? It might be larger and richer than any other, and it might not be; but certainly it could not have a monopoly of patriotism or of catholicity, or of literary or scientific enthusiasm. There is an attractive comprehensiveness and a suggestion of public spirit and love of country in the term "national;" but, after all, the adjective only narrows and belittles the noble conception contained in the word "university." Letters, science, art, philosophy, medicine, law, and theology are larger and more enduring than nations. There is something childish in this uneasy hankering for a big university in America, as there is also in that impatient longing for a distinctive American literature which we hear so often expressed. As American life grows more various and richer in sentiment, passion, thought, and accumulated experience, American literature will become richer and more abounding, and in that better day let us hope that there will be found several universities in America, though by no means one in each State, as free, liberal, rich, national, and glorious as the warmest advocate of a single, crowning university at the national capital could imagine his desired institution to become.

E.

1701 MASSACHUSETTS AVENUE,
Washington, D. C., April 3, 1890.

MY DEAR SENATOR: I regard the bill for the proposed University of the United States as one which would bring only disappointment and disaster to the interests of higher education in this country. For a good many years a similar bill has been before Congress, but multitudes of people, who are averse to it on most serious grounds, have never considered it as likely to pass, and therefore Congress has heard but little of these objections; but now that a standing committee has been appointed on the subject, from those who see in it only danger to our educational system the expressions of opposition are becoming numerous. In the few past weeks I have received many such opinions and a selection from these has been placed in the hands of the committee. I sincerely hope that the adverse opinions of the presidents of such institutions as Harvard University, Yale, Columbia, and the entire faculty of the University of Pennsylvania, will have their due weight with the Senators of the United States in calling a halt on such a measure.

Had it been our purpose to have ministerial and other associations send on their opinion of the measure, there would have been such a flood of adverse correspondence as would have been an annoyance to our Senators. We have not done this, but rather discouraged it, hoping that both the committees who have the supervision of these matters would see the wisdom of adhering to the course which the examples and traditions of the past have proved to be the only true national system of education in our Republic, namely: (1) Primary education to be conducted at the public expense. (2) The college curriculum to be provided for by the State universities and colleges. (3) The post graduate and professional schools to be left to the voluntary benevolence of the individual citizen.

It is safe to say that within the last thirty years not less than $100,000,000 have been given by the open hands and generous hearts of private citizens for education in the United States. Why, then, should the current of voluntary generosity be arrested by the proposition to make the United States Treasury responsible for the highest education? Why should the State undertake to do what the citizen is ready and glad to do?

I remain yours, sincerely,   JOHN F. HURST.

Hon. EDWARD C. WALTHALL,
   United States Senate, City.

APPENDIX.

LETTER FROM JOHN F. HURST, 1701 MASSACHUSETTS AVENUE, WASHINGTON, D. C.

APRIL 9, 1896.

DEAR SIR: In the Senate document, Calendar No. 484, I find on page 41 a "letter of Hon. Andrew D. White correcting erroneous statements concerning Cornell University." Mr. White says: "On looking over the stenographic report of the remarks made by Bishop Hurst and Dr. Beiler before your committee, I observe that they have fallen into one or two very serious errors regarding Cornell University. The first is shown in the statement to the effect that the charter of the institution has been changed so as to restrict the choice of professors to certain Christian denominations and 'evangelical' denominations." On this alleged statement, he makes quite an argument in order to refute it. He also says that we made "the virtual assertion that the professors of the university are confined to these evangelical denominations."

I deny having made either of these alleged statements. I simply said that I was once informed, while in Ithaca, N. Y., by one of the most honored trustees and liberal benefactors of Cornell University, that during the absence of the president (Mr. White) in Berlin certain complications had arisen in reference to matters of doctrine, and that the trustees had found it necessary to have the charter so changed that the majority of the board of trustees should consist of members of evangelical denominations. Should Mr. White so desire, I can give you the name of my informant. For the stenographic report, and for Mr. White's construction of it, of course, I should not be held responsible. My remarks were not intended in the least to be a disparagement but rather a commendation of the management of the institution in providing safeguards for its ethical and doctrinal influence. Please do me the favor to see that this correction is made.

I remain, yours sincerely,

JOHN F. HURST.

Hon. JAMES H. KYLE,
Chairman of the Committee on the University of the United States.

www.ingramcontent.com/pod-product-compliance
Lightning Source LLC
Chambersburg PA
CBHW020406230426
43664CB00009B/1204